A GRAMMAR OF THE ARABIC LANGUAGE

A GRAMMAR OF THE ARABIC LANGUAGE

VOLUME-I

By

W. Wright

KITAB BHAVAN
NEW DELHI-110002

KITAB BHAVAN
Publishers, Distributors, Exporters & Importers
1784, Kalan Mahal, Darya Ganj,
New Delhi - 1100 02 (India)
Phones : (91-11) 23277392/93, 23274686, 32906494
Fax : (91-11) 23263383
Website : www.kitabbhavan.com
Email : nasri@vsnl.com
: nusrat@bol.net.in

IInd Reprint : 2010

ISBN : 81-7151-337-9 (Set)
ISBN : 81-7151-338-7 (Vol. I)

Printed & Published in India by :
Nusrat Ali Nasri for KITAB BHAVAN
1784, Kalan Mahal, Darya Ganj,
New Delhi - 1100 02 [India]

PREFACE TO THE SECOND EDITION

A SECOND Edition of my revised and enlarged translation of Caspari's Arabic Grammar having been called for, I have thought it my duty not simply to reprint the book, but to subject it again to a thorough revision. In fact, the present is almost a new work; for there is hardly a section which has not undergone alteration, and much additional matter has been given, as the very size of this volume (351 pages instead of 257) shows.

In revising the book I have availed myself of the labours of Arab Grammarians, both ancient and modern. Of the former I may mention in particular the *'Alfīya* (ٱلْأَلْفِيَّةُ) of 'Ibn Mālik, with the Commentary of 'Ibn 'Aḳīl (ed. Dieterici, 1851, and the Beirūt edition of 1872); the *Mufaṣṣal* (ٱلْمُفَصَّلُ) of 'el-Zamaḫśarī (ed. Broch, 1859); and the *Lāmīyatu 'l-'Af'āl* (لَامِيَّةُ ٱلْأَفْعَالِ) of 'Ibn Mālik, with the Commentary of his son Badru 'd-dīn (ed. Volck, 1866). Of recent native works I have diligently used the *Miṣbāḥu l-Ṭālib fī Baḥṯi 'l-Maṭālib* (مِصْبَاحُ ٱلطَّالِبِ فِى بَحْثِ ٱلْمَطَالِبِ), that is, the *Baḥtu 'l-Maṭālib* of the Maronite Gabriel Farḥāt, with the notes of Buṭrus 'el-Bistānī (Beirūt, 1854); 'el-Bistānī's smaller Grammar, founded upon the above, entitled *Miftāḥu 'l-Miṣbāḥ* (مِفْتَاحُ ٱلْمِصْبَاحِ, second edition, Beirūt, 1867); and Nāṣīf 'el-Yāziǵī's *Faṣlu 'l-Ḫiṭāb* (فَصْلُ ٱلْخِطَابِ, second edition, Beirūt, 1866).

Among European Grammarians I have made constant use of the works of S. de Sacy (Grammaire Arabe, 2de éd., 1831), Ewald (Grammatica Critica Linguæ Arabicæ, 1831–33), and Lumsden (A Grammar of the Arabic Language, vol. i., 1813); which last, however, is based on the system of the Arab Grammarians, and therefore but ill-adapted, apart from its bulk and rarity, for the use of beginners. I have also consulted with advantage the grammar of Professor Lagus of Helsingfors (Lärokurs i Arabiska Språket, 1862). But I am indebted above all to the labours of Professor Fleischer of Leipzig, whose notes on the first volume of De Sacy's Grammar (as far as p. 359) have appeared from time to time in the *Berichte der Königl. Sächsischen Gesellschaft der Wissenschaften* (1863–64–66–70), in which periodical the student will also find the treatises of the same scholar *Ueber einige Arten der Nominalapposition im Arabischen* (1862) and *Ueber das Verhältniss und die Construction der Sach- und Stoffwörter im Arabischen* (1856).

In the notes which touch upon the comparative grammar of the Semitic languages, I have not found much to alter, except in matters of detail. I have read, I believe, nearly everything that has been published of late years upon this subject—the fanciful lucubrations of Von Raumer and Raabe, as well as the learned and scholarly treatises of Nöldeke, Philippi, and Tegnér. My standpoint remains, however, nearly the same as it formerly was. The ancient Semitic languages—Arabic and Æthiopic, Assyrian, Canaanitic (Phœnician and Hebrew), and Aramaic (so-called Chaldee and Syriac)—are as closely connected with each other as the Romance languages—Italian, Spanish, Portuguese, Provençal, and French: they are all daughters of a deceased mother, standing to them in the relation of Latin to the other European languages just specified. In some points the north Semitic tongues, particularly the Hebrew, may bear the greatest resemblance to this parent speech; but, on the whole, the south Semitic dialects, Arabic and Æthiopic,—but especially the former, —have, I still think, preserved a higher degree of likeness to the original Semitic language. The Hebrew of the Pentateuch, and the Assyrian*, as it appears in even the oldest inscriptions, seem to me to have already attained nearly the same stage of gram-

* As regards Assyrian, I rely chiefly upon the well-known works of Oppert, Sayce, and Schrader.

matical development (or decay) as the post-classical Arabic, the spoken language of mediæval and modern times.

I have to thank the Home Government of India for contributing the sum of fifty pounds towards defraying the expenses of printing this work; and some of the local Governments for subscribing for a certain number of copies; namely, the Government of Bengal, twenty, and the Home Department (Fort William), twenty-five; the Government of Bombay, ten; of Madras, ten; and of the Punjab, sixty copies. My friend and former schoolfellow, Mr D. Murray (of Adelaide, S. Australia), has also given pecuniary aid to the same extent as the India Office, and thereby laid me, and I hope I may say other Orientalists, under a fresh obligation.

Professor Fleischer of Leipzig will, I trust, look upon the dedication as a mark of respect for the Oriental scholarship of Germany, whereof he is one of the worthiest representatives; and as a slight acknowledgment of much kindness and help, extending over a period of more than twenty years, from the publication of my first work in 1852 down to the present year, in which, amid the congratulations of numerous pupils and friends, he has celebrated the fiftieth anniversary of his doctorate.

W. WRIGHT

CAMBRIDGE
1st *July* 1874

PREFACE TO THE THIRD EDITION

THE Second Edition of Wright's Grammar of the Arabic Language had been out of print long before the death of its author, but he was never able to find the leisure necessary for preparing a New Edition. The demand for it having become more and more pressing, Prof. W. Robertson Smith, who well deserved the honour of succeeding to Wright's chair, resolved to undertake this task. He began it with his usual ardour, but the illness which cut short his invaluable life soon interrupted the work. At his death 56 pages had been printed, whilst the revision had extended over 30 pages more. Robertson Smith had made use of some notes of mine, which he had marked with my initials, and it was for this reason among others that the Syndics of the Cambridge University Press invited me, through Prof. Bevan, to continue the revision. After earnest deliberation I consented, influenced chiefly by my respect for the excellent work of one of my dearest friends and by a desire to complete that which another dear friend had begun. Moreover Prof. Bevan promised his assistance in correcting the English style and in seeing the book through the press.

I have of course adhered to the method followed by Robertson Smith in that part of the Grammar which he revised. Trifling corrections and additions and such suggestions as had already been made by A. Müller, Fleischer and other scholars, are given in square brackets. Only in those cases where it seemed necessary to take all the responsibility upon myself, have I added my initials. Besides the printed list of additions and corrections at the end of the Second Volume, Wright had noted here and there on the margin of his own copy some new examples (chiefly from the *Naḳāiḍ*) which have been inserted, unless they seemed quite superfluous, without any distinctive sign. I have found but very few notes by Robertson Smith on the portion which he had not definitely revised; almost all of these have been marked with his initials. Wright's own text has been altered in a comparatively small number of passages (for instance § 252, § 353), where I felt sure that he would have done it himself. Once or twice Wright has noted on the margin "wants revision."

The notes bearing upon the Comparative Grammar of the Semitic languages have for the most part been replaced by references to Wright's Comparative Grammar, published after his death by Robertson Smith (1890).

I have to acknowledge my obligations to Mr Du Pré Thornton, who drew my attention to several omissions. But my warmest thanks must be given to my dear friend and colleague Prof. Bevan, who has not only taken upon himself all the trouble of seeing this revised edition through the press, but by many judicious remarks has contributed much to the improving of it.

The Second Volume is now in the printers' hands.

M. J. DE GOEJE

LEYDEN
February 1896

[The Syndics of the Press are indebted to the liberality of Mr F. Du Pré Thornton for the copyright of this Grammar, which he purchased after the death of the author and presented to them with a view to the publication of a New Edition.

They desire to take this opportunity of expressing their gratitude to Prof. de Goeje for the courtesy with which he acceded to their request that he would complete the revision and for the great labour which he has expended upon the task in the midst of many important literary engagements.]

The present Re-issue of Wright's *Arabic Grammar* differs very slightly from the third edition, which was published in 1896–8. Only a few changes, mostly corrections of misprints, have been made in the body of the work. The lists of *Addenda* at the beginning of each volume include, among the *Addenda* here reprinted from the third edition, some new matter (equal to about three pages) for which I am responsible.

A. A. BEVAN

December 1932

CONTENTS

PART FIRST

ORTHOGRAPHY AND ORTHOËPY

PART SECOND

ETYMOLOGY OR THE PARTS OF SPEECH

I. THE VERB

A. GENERAL VIEW

II. THE NOUN

A. THE NOUNS SUBSTANTIVE AND ADJECTIVE

B. THE NUMERALS

C. THE NOMINA DEMONSTRATIVA AND CONJUNCTIVA

III. THE PARTICLES

A. THE PREPOSITIONS

B. THE ADVERBS

C. THE CONJUNCTIONS

ADDENDA ET CORRIGENDA.

VOL. I.

PAGE

15 B add: مُدَيْقٌ from مِدَقٌّ, شُوَيْبَةٌ.

20, Rem. *c*, read: as [perhaps] in the article; comp. § 345. See my reply to Dr Howell, in the *Asiat. Quart. Rev.* 1897, Vol. iii. n. 5, p. 126 *seq.* [D.G.]

30 C add: Hence the use of رَمُوَ, *excellent is he in his shooting*, قَضُوَ *excellent*, or *how excellent is he in his judging*, غَزُوَ, طَمُعَ, هَيُؤَ. Comp. § 183, rem. *c*.

33 after (*c*) add: The third form construed with the preposition بَيْنَ has not unfrequently the signification of a causative of the sixth form, as آخَى بَيْنَ *he united by brotherhood*, قَارَبَ بَيْنَ *he made to be near together*, etc. (Nöldeke, *Zur Grammatik*, p. 26).

34, Rem. *b*. Comp. أَقْذَرُهُ.

36 A. أَشْكَى is properly *to listen, to give attention to a complaint*, as أَعْتَبَ, أَطْلَبَ, etc. (Nöldeke, *Z. Gr.* p. 28).

37 C add: تَقَذَّرَ.

41 C after *narrow;* add: اِنْعَجَزَ.

47 D add: تَغَطْمَطَ (غِطَمٌّ).

59, Rem. *a*. Fleischer, *Kl. Schr.* i. 368, considers the root as a concrete noun.

65, § 113. Rem. *b*, add: اِنْأَطَرَ occurs in the *Ḥamāsa*, p. 295, last line, and اِنْآدَ *to become bent* (from the root أود) in Imru'u-l-Ḳais (ed. Ahlwardt), No. 14, v. 14, *Mufaḍḍalīyāt* (ed. Lyall), p. 376, l. 13, 562, l. 16, *Naḳā'iḍ*, p. 23, l. 18, 706, l. 12.

PAGE

67, § 117. Rem. *b*, add: on the form مُطَّلِعٌ for مُضْطَلِعٌ see *Mufaḍ-ḍalīyāt*, p. 193, l. 8 with footnote, and *Naḳā'iḍ*, p. 899, l. 7, where one Ms. has مُضْطَلِع.

67, § 117*. Vollers, *Zeitschr. f. Assyriologie*, xii. 134 footnote, quotes Ḳor'ān, ch. xiii. 12 مُعَقِّبَاتٌ for مُعْتَقِبَاتٌ (Bèiḍ. i. 477, l. 17) as a proof that this form is not restricted to those verbs that have a dental as second radical.

79 A add: وَجَدَ is said to form an Imperf. يَجُدُ as well as the ordinary يَجِدُ (*Lisān* iv. p. 458, l. 4, 459, l. 3).

79, § 144, Rem. *b*, add: the Perf. وَدَعَ occurs in the *Mufaḍḍalīyāt*, p. 404, l. 6.

91 A add: The tribe of Ṭaiyi' said بَقَا for بَقِيَ, رَضَا for رَضِيَ, بُنَتْ for بُنِيَتْ. so *Ḥamāsa* 77 and comp. De Sacy, *Chrest.* ii. 445. Similarly we find مُنَى for مُنِيَ *Ḥamāsa*, p. 433, l. 20, and سُدَّى for سُدِّيَ *Mufaḍḍalīyāt*, p. 627, l. 12.

96, Rem. *a*. Gāḥiẓ, *Bayān* i. 65, 6 and 3 from below has الْإِيْسِيَّةُ opp. to اللَّيْسِيَّةُ.

98 A, Rem. *c*. On such forms as رَمُوَ, غَزُوَ, قَضُوَ, see above, note to p. 30.

98 C add: after a verb expressing surprise the object is sometimes omitted and must be supplied from the context, e.g. مَا أَدَقَّ (for أَدَقَّهُمْ) *how puny they are! Mufaḍḍalīyāt*, p. 112, l. 14, and أَعْزِزْ عَلَيَّ (for أَعْزِزْ بِهِ عَلَيَّ) *how painful it is to me! Naḳā'iḍ*, p. 585, l. 16.

98 D, Rem. *a*, delete the remark in square brackets. [D.G.]

110, § 195. They are called also أَسْمَآءُ ٱلْحَدَثِ opp. to أَسْمَآءُ ٱلْعَيْنِ (*Ḥamāsa* 90).

PAGE

113 B, Rem. add: The form فِعَالٌ is particularly common in verbal nouns denoting *processes* or *operations* performed on men, animals, or plants, e.g. خِتَانٌ *circumcision*, خِصَاءٌ *castration*, فِصَادٌ the *bleeding* of a camel for food, إِبَارٌ the *fertilisation* of palm-trees, etc.

181 A add: وَفْدٌ (Ṭabarī i. 3158, l. 5).

181 D add: بَلَدٌ *country* (*Bibl. Geograph.* v. p. 154, l. 11 *seq.*).

182 C add: العَصْرُ (for صَلٰوةُ العَصْرِ, Buḫārī i. p. 94, l. 4)—and عُقَارٌ *wine* (*Aġānī* vi. p. 104, l. 15, *Mufaḍḍalīyāt*, p. 664, l. 15, *Kāmil*, p. 62, l. 19).

183 A add: مُدَامٌ *wine* (*Kāmil*, p. 26, l. 12), مَرْكَبٌ *a ship* (Seybold).

195 (*d*). The ending ـِيُّونَ is often shortened to ـُونَ, as usually in الْأَشْعَرُونَ for الْأَشْعَرِيُّونَ. Other instances are النُّمَيْرُونَ, الْخَزْرَجُونَ.

210, footnote. The plur. pauc. of fem. words is ordinarily أَفْعُلٌ, of masc. words أَفْعِلَةٌ.

233 C: אִשָּׁה belongs to انث, comp. Aram. אִתְּתָא (Seybold).

234 footnote. The term مُجْرًى is sometimes used as a synonym of مُنْصَرِفٌ (*Lisān* ii. p. 360, l. 8).

264, § 337. When the Arabs say "every *third* day" they mean "every *other* day," when they say "every *fourth* day" they mean "every *third* day," and so on—see *Kāmil*, p. 446, l. 6 *seq.*

268 footnote. The form كَاكَ exactly corresponds to the Hebrew כָּכָה.

271: to the plural forms of الَّذِى add أُلَا (*Ḥamāsa*, p. 678, l. 21), and الْأُلَاءِ (*ibid.* p. 769, l. 21).

271, Rem. *a*. Likewise الَّذَيْنِ instead of اللَّذَيْنِ Ḳor'ān xli. v. 29.

PAGE

288, § 363: add: أَوَّلُ *first* (adverbially, *Ḥamāsa*, p. 501, l. 23, ȇš-Šanfarā, *Lāmīya* v. 45)—these adverbs are called غَايَاتٌ (*Mufaṣṣal*, p. 67, l. 2).

296, Rem. *c*. A poet allows himself to say لِأُمِّ ٱلْأَرْضِ وَيْلٌ (*Ḥamāsa* 457).

PART FIRST.

ORTHOGRAPHY AND ORTHOËPY.

I. THE LETTERS AS CONSONANTS.

1. Arabic, like Hebrew and Syriac, is written and read from right to left. The letters of the alphabet (حُرُوفُ ٱلْهِجَآءِ, حُرُوفُ ٱلتَّهَجِّى, ٱلْحُرُوفُ ٱلْهِجَائِيَّةُ, or حُرُوفُ ٱلْمُعْجَمِ) are twenty-eight in number, and are all consonants, though three of them are also used as vowels (see § 3). They vary in form, according as they are connected with a preceding or following letter, and, for the most part, terminate in a bold stroke, when they stand alone or at the end of a word. The following Table gives the letters in their usual order, along with their names and numerical values. A

B

NAME.	FIGURE.				NUMERICAL VALUE.
	Unconnected.	Connected.			
		With a preceding letter.	With a following letter.	With both.	
أَلِفٌ Elif.	ا	ـا	. . .	. . .	1
بَآءٌ Bâ.	ب	ـب	بـ	ـبـ	2
تَآءٌ Tâ.	ت	ـت	تـ	ـتـ	400
ثَآءٌ T̲â.	ث	ـث	ثـ	ـثـ	500
جِيمٌ Ǵîm.	ج	ـج [ـج]	جـ	ـجـ [ـجـ]	3
حَآءٌ Ḥâ.	ح	ـح [ـح]	حـ	ـحـ [ـحـ]	8
خَآءٌ H̲â.	خ	ـخ [ـخ]	خـ	ـخـ [ـخـ]	600
دَالٌ Dâl.	د	ـد	. . .	. . .	4
ذَالٌ D̲âl.	ذ	ـذ	. . .	. . .	700

C

NAME.	FIGURE.				NUMERICAL VALUE.
	Unconnected.	Connected.			
		With a preceding letter.	With a following letter.	With both.	
رَآءْ Rā.	ر	ـر ـر	. . .	. . .	200
زَایْ (زَآءْ) Zāy.	ز	ـز ـز	. . .	. . .	7
سِينْ Sīn.	س	ـس	سـ	ـسـ	60
شِينْ Śīn.	ش	ـش	شـ	ـشـ	300
صَادْ Ṣād.	ص	ـص	صـ	ـصـ	90
ضَادْ Ḍād.	ض	ـض	ضـ	ـضـ	800
طَآءْ Ṭā.	ط	ـط	طـ	ـطـ	9
ظَآءْ Ẓā.	ظ	ـظ	ظـ	ـظـ	900
عَيْنْ ‘Ain.	ع	ـع	عـ	ـعـ	70
غَيْنْ Ġain.	غ	ـغ	غـ	ـغـ	1000
فَآءْ Fā.	ف	ـف	فـ	ـفـ	80
قَافْ Ḳāf.	ق	ـق	قـ	ـقـ	100
كَافْ Kāf.	ك	ـك	كـ ڪـ	ـكـ ـڪـ	20
لَامْ Lām.	ل	ـل	لـ	ـلـ	30
مِيمْ Mīm.	م	ـم	مـ	ـمـ ـمـ	40
نُونْ Nūn.	ن	ـن	نـ	ـنـ	50
هَآءْ Hā.	ه	ـه	هـ	ـهـ ـﮩـ	5
وَاوْ Wāw.	و	ـو	. . .	. . .	6
يَآءْ Yā.	ى	ـى ـے	يـ	ـيـ	10

REM. *a.* ا in connection with a preceding ل forms the figures A
لا, لا, لا. This combination is called *lām-ĕlif*, and is generally reckoned a twenty-ninth letter of the alphabet, and inserted before ي. The object of it is merely to distinguish ĕlif as the long vowel *ā*, § 3, from ĕlif as the spiritus lenis (ĕlif with hĕmza, أ, § 15).

REM. *b.* The order of the letters ه and و is sometimes inverted. The Arabs of Northern Africa arrange the letters in a different sequence; viz.

ا ب ت ث ج ح خ د ذ ر ز ط ظ ك ل م ن ص ض ع غ

ف ق س ش ه و لا ى B

They distinguish ف from ق by giving the former a single point below, and the latter one above, thus: ڢ ڢـ *f*, but ڧ ڧـ *ḳ**. At the end of a word these points are usually omitted, ٮ, ٯ.

REM. *c.* In manuscripts and elegantly printed books many of the letters are interwoven with one another, and form ligatures, of which the following are examples.

بح *bḥ.*	سح *sḥ.*	في *fy.*	
تح *tḥ.*	ضح *ḍḥ.*	لج *lǵ.*	C
جح *ǵḥ.*	عج *ʻǵ.*	لمح *lmḥ.*	
حجج *ḥǵǵ.*	فخ *fḫ.*	يح *yḥ.*	

[These ligatures, in which one letter stands above another, are very inconvenient to printers, especially when, as in this book, English and Arabic are intermingled; and most founts have some device to bring the letters into line. Thus حجج appears as حاحج, or, in the fount used for this grammar, as حجج. The latter method is a recent innovation, first introduced by Lane in his D Arabic Lexicon, and its extreme simplicity and convenience have caused it to be largely adopted in modern founts, not only in Europe but in the East. But in writing Arabic the student ought to use the old ligatures as they are shewn in Mss. or in the more elegant Eastern founts.]

---

* This is not confined, in the earliest times, to African Mss. In some old Mss., on the other hand, *ḳ* has the point below, ڧ, ڧـ, or even ڨ, ڨـ.

A REM. *d.* Those letters which are identical in form, and distinguished from one another in writing only by the aid of the small dots usually called *diacritical points* (نُقْطَةٌ, plur. نُقَطٌ), are divided by the grammarians into اَلْحُرُوفُ ٱلْمُهْمَلَةُ, *the loose* or *free*, i.e. *unpointed, letters*, and اَلْحُرُوفُ ٱلْمُعْجَمَةُ, *the bolted* or *fastened*, i.e. *pointed, letters*. To the former class belong ح, د, ر, س, ص, ط and ع; to the latter خ, ذ, ز, ش, ض, ظ and غ. The letters ب, ت, ث and ى are generally distinguished as follows:

B ب is called اَلْبَآءُ ٱلْمُوَحَّدَةُ, *the* ٮ *with one point* (ٮِ);

ت „ اَلتَّآءُ ٱلْمُثَنَّاةُ مِنْ فَوْقِهَا, *the* ٮ *with two points above* (ٮٓ);

ى „ اَلْيَآءُ ٱلْمُثَنَّاةُ مِنْ تَحْتِهَا, *the* ٮ *with two points below* (ٮِ)*;

ث „ اَلثَّآءُ ٱلْمُثَلَّثَةُ, *the* ٮ *with three points* (ٮٓ).

The unpointed letters are sometimes still further distinguished from the pointed by various contrivances, such as writing the letter in a smaller size below the line, placing a point below, or an angular mark above, and the like; so that we find in carefully written

C manuscripts ح ح ح; د د; ر ر ر; س س س س; ص ص ص; ط ط; ع ع ع; etc. Also ه or ه by way of distinction from ة. In some old Mss. ش has only one point above, and then س takes a point below.

REM. *e.* The letters are also divided into the following classes, which take their names from the particular part of the vocal organs that is chiefly instrumental in producing their sounds.

اَلْحُرُوفُ ٱلشَّفَوِيَّةُ or اَلشَّفَهِيَّةُ, the labials (شَفَةٌ *a lip*), ب ف م و.

اَلْحُرُوفُ ٱللِّثَوِيَّةُ, the gingivals, ث ذ ظ, in uttering which the

D tongue is pressed against the gum (اَللِّثَةُ).

اَلْحُرُوفُ ٱلْأَسَلِيَّةُ, the sibilants, ز س ص, which are pronounced with the tip of the tongue (اَلْأَسَلَةُ).

---

* [With final ى the use of the two points below is optional. Some modern prints, especially those issued at Bairût, always insert them except when the ى represents *êlif maḳṣûra* (§ 7, rem. *b*): thus كَيْ, لِي, but رَمَى.]

اَلْحُرُوفُ ٱلذَّلْقِيَّةُ or اَلذَّوْلَقِيَّةُ, the liquids ر ل ن, which are pro- A
nounced with the extremity of the tongue (اَلذَّلْق or اَلذَّوْلَق).

اَلْحُرُوفُ ٱلشَّجْرِيَّةُ, the letters ج ش ض, which are uttered through the open orifice of the lips (اَلشَّجْر).

اَلْحُرُوفُ ٱلنِّطْعِيَّةُ or اَلنِّطَعِيَّةُ, the letters ت د ط, which are uttered by pressing the tongue against the rough or corrugated portion of the palate (اَلنِّطْع or اَلنِّطَع).

اَلْحَرْفَانِ ٱللَّهَوِيَّتَانِ, the letters ق and ك, in uttering which the B
uvula (اَللَّهَاةُ) is brought into play.

حُرُوفُ ٱلْحَلْقِ or اَلْحُرُوفُ ٱلْحَلْقِيَّةُ, the gutturals, أ ح خ ع غ ه.

The letters ا و ى are called حُرُوفُ ٱللِّينِ or اَلْحُرُوفُ ٱللَّيِّنَةُ, *the soft letters*, and حُرُوفُ ٱلْعِلَّةِ, *the weak letters*.

2. The correct pronunciation of some of these letters, for example ح and ع, it is scarcely possible for a European to acquire, except by long intercourse with natives. The following hints will, C
however, enable the learner to approximate to their sounds.

ا with *hèmza* (أ, إ, see § 15) is the *spiritus lenis* of the Greeks, the א of the Hebrews (as in אָמַר, זְאֵב, תְּאַלֵּף). It may be compared with the *h* in the French word *homme* or English *hour*.

ب is our *b*.

ت is the Italian dental, softer than our *t*.

ث is pronounced like the Greek *θ*, or *th* in *thing*. The Turks and Persians usually convert it into the surd *s*, as in *sing*. [In Egypt it is commonly confounded with ت, less often with س.] D

ج corresponds to our *g* in *gem*. In Egypt and some parts of Arabia, however, it has the sound of the Heb. גּ, or our *g* in *get*.

ح, the Heb. ח, is a very sharp but smooth guttural aspirate, stronger than ه, but not rough like خ. Europeans, as well as Turks and Persians, rarely attain the correct pronunciation of it.

خ has the sound of *ch* in the Scotch word *loch*, or the German *Rache*.

د is the Italian dental, softer than our *d*.

ذ bears the same relation to د that ث does to ت. It is sounded

A like the δ of the modern Greeks, or *th* in *that, with.* The Turks and Persians usually convert it into *z.* [In Egypt it is sometimes *z* but oftener *d.*]

ر is in all positions a distinctly articulated lingual *r*, as in *run.*

ز is the English *z.*

س is the surd *s* in *sit, mist;* ش, *sh* in *shut.*

ص, the Heb. צ, is a strongly articulated *s*, somewhat like *ss* in *hiss.*

B ض is an aspirated *d*, strongly articulated between the front part of the side of the tongue and the molar teeth (somewhat like *th* in *this*). The Turks and Persians usually pronounce it like *z.* [In Egypt it is an emphatic *d*, without aspiration, more difficult to an English tongue than the true Bedouin ض.]

ط, the Heb. ט, is a strongly articulated palatal *t.*

ظ bears, strictly speaking, the same relation to ط that ث and ذ do to ت and د. It is usually pronounced like a strongly articulated palatal *z*, though many of the Arabs give it the same sound as ض
C [with which it is often confounded in Mss.]. The Turks and Persians change it into a common *z.* To distinguish it from ض, ظ is sometimes spoken of as اَلظَّاءُ ٱلْمُشَالَةُ. The ض is then called اَلضَّادُ ٱلْمَبْطُوحَةُ.

ع, the Heb. ע, is a strong (but to [most] Europeans, as well as Turks and Persians, unpronounceable) guttural, related in its nature to ح, with which it is sometimes confounded. It is described as produced by a smart compression of the upper part of the windpipe and forcible emission of the breath. It is wrong to treat it, in any of the Semitic languages, as a mere vowel-letter, or (worse still) as
D a nasal *n* or *ng.*

غ is a guttural *g*, accompanied by a grating or rattling sound, as in gargling, of which we have no example in English. The γ of the modern Greeks, the Northumbrian *r*, and the French *r grasséyé*, are approximations to it*.

ف is our *f.*

ق, the Heb. ק, is a strongly articulated guttural *k*; but in parts of Arabia, and throughout Northern Africa, it is pronounced as a

* [Hence غ is sometimes replaced by ر as in the Yemenite مُضَّار for مُضَّاغ, Hamdānī ed. Müller 193, 17 etc., and often in Mss.—De G.]

hard *g*; whilst in [Cairo and some parts of] Syria it is vulgarly con- A
founded with èlif hèmzatum, as *'ultu, ya'ūlu*, for *ḳultu, yaḳūlu*.

ك, ل, م, and ن, are exactly our *k, l, m, n*. When immediately followed by the letter ب, without any vowel coming between them, ن takes the sound of *m*: as جَنْبٌ *ǵèmb*, عَنْبَرٌ *'ambar*, شَنْبَاءُ *śèmbā'u*, not *ǵènb, 'anbar, śènbā'u*.

is our *h*. It is distinctly aspirated at the end, as well as at the beginning, of a syllable; e.g. هُمْ *hum*, أَهْلَكَ *'ahlaka*. In the grammatical termination ـَةٌ, the dotted ة [called هَاءُ ٱلتَّأْنِيثِ] is pronounced like ت, *t*)*. B

و and ى are precisely our *w* and *y*. The Turks and Persians usually give و the sound of *v*.

II. THE VOWELS AND DIPHTHONGS.

3. The Arabs had originally no signs for the short vowels. To indicate the long vowels and diphthongs they made use of the three consonants that come nearest to them in sound: viz. ا (without *hèmza*. see § 1, rem. *a*, and § 15) for *ā*, ى for *ī* and *ai*, و for *ū* and *au*. E.g., C
لَا *lā*, فِى *fī*, كَى *kai*, ذُو *ḏū*, لَو *lau*.

4. At a later period the following signs were invented to express the short vowels.

(*a*) ـَ *fètḥ* (فَتْحٌ) or *fètḥa* (فَتْحَةٌ), *a*, *è* (as in *pet*), *e* (nearly the French *e muet*); e.g. خَلَقَ *h̲alaḳa*, شَمْسٌ *śèmsun*, كَرِيمٌ *kerīmun*.

(*b*) ـِ *kèsr* (كَسْرٌ) or *kèsra* (كَسْرَةٌ), *i* (as in *pin*), *ì* (a dull, obscure *i*, resembling the Welsh *y*, or the *i* in *bird*); e.g. بِهِ *bihi*, أُقِطٌ *ùḳiṭun*. D

(*c*) ـُ *ḍamm* (ضَمٌّ) or *ḍamma* (ضَمَّةٌ), *u* (as in *bull*), *o*, *ö* (nearly as the German *ö* in *Mörtel*, or the French *eu* in *jeune*); e.g. لَهُ *lahu*, حُجَّةٌ *ḥöǵǵètun*, عُمْرٌ *'ömrun*.

---

* In point of fact, this figure ة is merely a compromise between the ancient ـَتْ (Heb. ת ָ, ת ַ), the old pausal ـَهْ (*ah*), and the modern ـَه (Heb. ה ָ), in which last the ه is silent.

A REM. *a.* The distinction between the names *fèth*, *kèsr*, *ḍamm*, and *fètḥa*, *kèsra*, *ḍamma*, is that the former denote the *sounds a, i, u*; the latter the *marks* ◌َ, ◌ِ, ◌ُ. Compare the Hebrew פַּתַח, שְׁבָר, and קִבּוּץ. The terms نَصْب and رَفْع, commonly used of the case-endings *a, u*, are sometimes applied to ◌َ, ◌ُ in other positions; e.g. ٱلْحَرُورِيَّةُ بِنَصْبِ ٱلْحَاءِ. [Another name for *ḍamm* is *ḳabw*, قَبْوٌ.—De G.]

REM. *b.* A vowel is called حَرَكَةٌ, *a motion*, plur. حَرَكَاتٌ; its
B mark is termed شَكْلٌ, *form* or *figure*, plur. أَشْكَالٌ or شُكُولٌ.

REM. *c.* In the oldest Mss. of the Ḳor'ān, the vowels are expressed by dots (usually red), one above for fetḥa, one below for kèsra, and one in the middle, or on the line, for ḍamma. As regards the signs ◌َ, ◌ِ, ◌ُ the third is a small و and the other two are probably derived from ا and ى or ـ respectively.

5. Rules for the cases in which these vowel-marks retain their original sounds, *a, i, u*, and for those in which they are modified, through the influence of the stronger or weaker consonants, into *è, e,*
C *ì, o,* or *ö*, can scarcely be laid down with certainty; for the various dialects of the spoken Arabic differ from one another in these points; and besides, owing to the emphasis with which the consonants are uttered, the vowels are in general somewhat indistinctly enunciated. The following rules may, however, be given for the guidance of the learner*.

(*a*) When preceded or followed by the strong gutturals غ ع خ ح, or the emphatic consonants ق ظ ط ض ص, fètḥa is pronounced as *a*, though with the emphatic consonants its sound becomes rather obscure,
D approaching to that of the Swedish *å*; e.g. خَمْرٌ *ḫamrun*, لَعْبٌ *la‘bun*, بَقِيَ *båḳiya*, صَدْرٌ *ṣådrun*. Under the same circumstances kèsra is

* [Learners whose ears and vocal organs are good, and who have an opportunity of hearing and practising the correct pronunciation of the consonants, will find that the proper shades of sound in the three vowels come without effort when the consonants are spoken rightly and naturally. The approximate rules for pronunciation here given are mainly useful as a guide towards the right way of holding the mouth in pronouncing the consonants as well as the vowels.]

pronounced as *ì*, e.g. عِلْمٌ *'ìlmun*, سِحْرٌ *sìḥrun*, قِشْرٌ *ḳìśrun;* whilst A
ḍamma assumes the sound of an obscure *o*, inclining with the gutturals (especially ح and ع) to *ö*; e.g. لَطُفَ *laṭofa*, لُطْفٌ *loṭfun*, حُسْنٌ *ḥosnun* or *ḥösnun*, رُعْبٌ *ro'bun*, عُمْرٌ *'ömrun*.

(*b*) In shut syllables in which there are neither guttural nor emphatic consonants,—and in open syllables which neither commence with, nor immediately precede, one of those letters,—fèt-ḥa either has a weaker, less clear sound, approaching to that of *a* in the English
words *hat*, *cap*, e.g. كَتَبْتَ *katabta*, أَكْبَرُ *'akbaru;* or it becomes a B
simple *è* or *e* (the latter especially in a short open syllable followed by a long one), e.g. بَلْ *bèl*, مَرْكَبٌ *mèrkèbun*, سَمَكٌ *sèmèkun*, سَمِينٌ *semīnun*, مَدِينَةٌ *medīnètun*. It retains, however, its pure sound of *a* before and after *r* (which partakes of the nature of the emphatics), when that letter is doubled or follows a long *ā* or *ū*, e.g. جَرَّةٌ *ǵarratun*, مَرَّةٌ *marratun*, غَارَةٌ *ǵāratun*, صُورَةٌ *ṣūratun;* and also in general at the end of a word.

6. The long vowels *ā*, *ī*, *ū*, are indicated by placing the marks C
of the short vowels before the letters ا, ى, and و, respectively, e.g. قَالَ *ḳāla*, بِيعَ *bī'a*, سُوقٌ *sūḳun;* in which case these letters are called حُرُوفُ ٱلْمَدِّ, *literae productionis*, "letters of prolongation." The combinations ـِى and ـُو must always be pronounced *ī* and *ū*, not *ē* and *ō*; though after the emphatic consonants ـُو inclines to the sound of *ō*, and *ī* to that of the French *u* or German *ü*, e.g. طُورٌ, طِينٌ, nearly *ṭōrun*, *ṭǖnun*.

REM. *a*. *ā* was at first more rarely marked than the other D
long vowels, and hence it happens that, at a later period, after the invention of the vowel-points, it was indicated in some very common words merely by a fèt-ḥa; e.g. اَللّٰهُ, اَلرَّحْمَنُ, إِبْرَهِيمُ, إِسْحَقُ, هَرُونُ, اَلْمَلَئِكَةُ, اَلسَّمَوَاتُ, اَلْقِيَمَةُ, لَكِنْ or لَكِنَّ, ذَلِكَ, هَذَا, هَهُنَا, هَكَذَا. More exactly, however, the fèt-ḥa should be written perpendicularly in this case, so as to resemble a small èlif; e.g. اَللّٰهُ, اَلرَّحْمٰنُ, اَلْمَلٰئِكَةُ, اَلسَّمٰوَاتُ, اَلْقِيٰمَةُ (*the resurrection*, to be carefully distinguished from

A ٱلْقِيمَةُ *el-ḳīmètu, price, value*), هٰهُنَا, ذٰلِكَ. The words ثَلَاثٌ, ثَلَاثَةٌ, and ثَلَاثُونَ, are also frequently written defectively ثَلٰثٌ, ثَلٰثَةٌ, ثَلٰثُونَ; and occasionally some other vocables, such as ثَمٰنِيَةٌ and ثَمٰنُونَ; تَبٰرَكَ and تَعٰلَى; سُلَيْمٰنُ, رَمَضٰنُ, and other proper names ending in ـٰنُ; ٱلشَّيْطٰنُ; مُعٰوِيَةُ; خٰلِدٌ, مٰلِكٌ, ٱلْحٰرِثُ, ٱلْقٰسِمُ, and other proper names of the forms فَاعِلٌ and ٱلْفَاعِلُ; دِينٰرٌ; e.g. This is more common in Maġribī Mss. than in others.—The long vowel ī is in a very few instances written defectively at the end of a word,
B e.g. ٱلْحَافِ, *el-Ḥāfī*, ٱلْعَاصِ, *el-ʻĀṣī*, حُذَيْفَةُ بْنُ ٱلْيَمَانِ, *Ḥoḏeifètu 'bnu 'l-Yèmānī*, for ٱلْحَافِى, ٱلْعَاصِى, ٱلْيَمَانِى; ٱلْمُهْتَدِ for ٱلْمُهْتَدِى*.

REM. *b*. The letter ه, preceded by ḍamma, is used by the Arabs of North Africa and Spain to indicate a final *o* in foreign words; e.g. قَارْلُه, *Carlo*; دُونْ بِطْرُه, *Don Pedro*; وَادِى آرُه, *the river Guadiaro*.

REM. *c*. The sound of ـَا inclines, in later times and in certain localities, from *ā* to *ē*, just as that of fètḥa does from *a* to *è* (see
C § 4, *a*, and § 5, *b*). This change is called ٱلْإِمَالَةُ, *el-'imāla*, the "deflection" of the sound of *a* and *ā* towards that of *i* and *ī*. The Maġribī Arabs actually pronounce *ā* in many cases as *ī*. Hence رِكَابٌ *rikāb*, لٰكِنْ *lākin*, بَابٌ *bāb*, لِسَانٌ *lisān*, are sounded *rikēb*, *lēkin*, *bīb*, *lisīn*; and, conversely, the Spanish names *Beja*, *Jaen*, *Caniles*, *Lebrilla*, are written بَاجَه, جَيَّان, قَنَالَش, لَبْرَالَه.

7. ا corresponds to fètḥa, ى to kèsra, and و to ḍamma; whence
D ا is called أُخْتُ ٱلْفَتْحَةِ, *the sister of fètḥa*, ى, أُخْتُ ٱلْكَسْرَةِ, *the sister of kèsra*, and و, أُخْتُ ٱلضَّمَّةِ, *the sister of ḍamma*. Fètḥa before ى and و forms the diphthongs *ai* and *au*, which retain their original clear sound after the harder gutturals and the emphatics, e.g. صَيْفٌ *ṣaifun*,

* [The omission of final ى in these cases is hardly a mere orthographical irregularity, but expresses a variant pronunciation in which the final ī was shortened or dropped. See Nöldeke, *Gesch. d. Qorâns*, p. 251.]

خَوْفٌ *ḫaufun;* but after the other letters become nearly *ē* (Heb. ־ֵי) A
and *ō* (Heb. וֹ־), e.g. سَيْفٌ *sèⁱfun,* مَوْتٌ *mᵒotun* (almost *sēfun, mōtun*).

Rem. *a.* After و at the end of a word, both when preceded by ḍamma and by fètḥa, ا is often written, particularly in the plural of verbs; e.g. نَصَرُوا, رَمَوْا, يَغْزُوا. This ا, in itself quite superfluous (èlif otiosum), is intended to guard against the possibility of the preceding و being separated from the body of the word to which it belongs, and so being mistaken for the conjunction وَ *and.* It is called أَلِفُ ٱلْوِقَايَةِ, *the guarding èlif,* or ٱلْأَلِفُ ٱلْفَاصِلَةُ, *the separating èlif.*

Rem. *b.* ى at the end of a word after a fètḥa is pronounced B like ا, e.g. فَتًى *fatā,* رَمَى *ramā,* إِلَى *'ilā*,* and is called, like ا itself in the same position (e.g. بَهْنَسَا *Bèhnesā,* غَزَا *ġazā*), ٱلْأَلِفُ ٱلْمَقْصُورَةُ, *the èlif that can be abbreviated,* in contradistinction to *the lengthened èlif,* ٱلْأَلِفُ ٱلْمَمْدُودَةُ (see § 22 and § 23, rem. *a*), which is protected by hèmza. It receives this name because, when it comes in contact with a *hèmza conjunctionis* (see § 19, rem. *f*), it is shortened in pronunciation before the following consonant, as are the و and ى in أَبُو and أَبِى before ٱلْوَزِيرِ (see § 20, *b*)†.

Rem. *c.* If a pronominal suffix be added to a word ending C in ـَى, the ى is sometimes retained according to old custom, as in رَمَيهُ or رَمَيْهُ, but it is commonly changed into ا, as رَمَاهُ.

---

* [But ـَىْ, with the mark *ġèzma* (see § 10), as in كَىْ, يَدَىْ is the diphthong *ai.*] The diphthong *ai,* when final, is often marked in old Mss. by the letters ے suprascript; e.g. يَدَىٰے كُلِّ مُعْطَآءٍ, i.e. يَدَىْ *yèdai,* not *yèdā.*

† [It would seem that the early scribes who fixed the orthographical usage made a distinction of sound between ـَى and ـَا, pronouncing D the former nearly as *ē*; cf. rem. *d.* On the other hand many Mss., even very ancient ones, write ـَا where the received rules require ـَى. According to the grammarians *èlif maḳṣūra* is always written ـَى in words of more than three letters unless the penultimate letter is Yā (as يَحْيَا *he will live,* دُنْيَا *world*). In words of three letters, the origin of the final *ā* must be considered; a "converted *Yā*" gives ـَى, a "converted *Wāw*" gives ـَا. See the details below §§ 167, 169, 213 etc.]

A REM. *d.* In some words ending in ـَاةٌ we often find ـَوةٌ instead of ـَاةٌ, as حَيَوةٌ or حَيٰوةٌ, صَلَوةٌ or صَلٰوةٌ, زَكَوةٌ or زَكٰوةٌ, نَجْوَةٌ, غَدْوَةٌ, مِشْكَوةٌ, مَنْوَةٌ, and so also رِبَوا, الرِّبَوا for رِبًا, الرِّبَا; further ـَيَةٌ for ـَاةٌ in the loan-word تَوْرَيَةٌ or تَوْرٰيَةٌ; according to which older mode of writing we ought to pronounce the ـَا nearly as $\mathring{a}$ or $\bar{e}$ respectively*.

8. The marks of the short vowels when doubled are pronounced with the addition of the sound *n*, ـً *an*, ـٍ *in*, ـٌ or ـٌّ *un*. This is called اَلتَّنْوِينُ, the *tènwīn* or "nunation" (from the name of the letter ن *nūn*),
B and takes place only at the end of a word; e.g. مَدِينَةٌ *medīnètun*, بِنْتٍ *bintin*, مَالٌ *mālun*. See § 308.

REM. *a.* ـً takes an ا after all the consonants except ة; as بَابًا, رِيحًا, but خَلِيفَةً. However, when it precedes a ى, no ا is written, as in هُدًى; nor, according to the older orthography, when it accompanies a hèmza, as in شَيْءً, for which we more usually find شَيْئًا. This èlif in no way affects the quantity of the vowel, which is always short: *bābăn*, *rīḥăn*.

C REM. *b.* To one word و is added, without in any way affecting the sound of the tènwīn, viz. to the proper name عَمْرٌو *'Amr* (not *'Amrū*), genit. عَمْرٍو, accus. عَمْرًا, rarely عَمْرًوا, [or, when the tènwīn falls away (§ 315, *a*, rem. *b*) عَمْرُو in all three cases], so written to distinguish it from another proper name that has the same radical letters, viz. عُمَرُ *'Omar*, genit. and accus. عُمَرَ. The و of عَمْرٌو and عَمْرٍو is, however, often neglected in old manuscripts. [Cf. the use of ו to represent tènwīn in proper names in the
D Nabataean inscriptions.]

REM. *c.* In old Mss. of the Ḳor'ān, the tènwīn is expressed by doubling the dots which represent the vowels; ∸ = ـً, ⨪ = ـٍ, :– = ـٌ.

---

* Ibn 'Abbās said الأَفْعَوْ for الأَفْعَى "the viper," and الحِدَوْ for الحِدَأْ "kites"—see *Mufaḍḍalīyāt*, ed. Lyall, p. 753, l. 2.

III. OTHER ORTHOGRAPHIC SIGNS A

A. *Ǵèzma or Sukūn.*

9. *Ǵèzma*, جَزْمٌ or جَزْمَةٌ (*amputation*), ْ, is written over the final consonant of all shut syllables, and serves, when another syllable follows, to separate the two; e.g. بَلْ *bèl*, هُمْ *hum*, كَتَبْتُمْ *katabtum*, سَفْسَفَ *sèfsèfa*, قُرْآنٌ *ḳor-'ānun* (not *ḳo-rānun*). It corresponds therefore to the *Shĕvā quiescens* of the Hebrew, with which its other name سُكُونٌ, *rest*, coincides.

Rem. *a.* A letter which has no following vowel is called حَرْفٌ سَاكِنٌ, *a quiescent letter*, as opposed to حَرْفٌ مُتَحَرِّكٌ, *a movent letter*. See § 4, rem. *b*. B

Rem. *b.* Letters that are assimilated to a following letter, which receives in consequence the *tèšdīd* or mark of doubling (see § 11 and § 14), are retained in writing, but not marked with a ǵèzma; e.g. اَلرَّحْمٰنُ, مِن رَّبِّهِ, أَرَدتُّ, not اَلْرَّحْمٰنُ, مِنْ رَبِّهِ, أَرَدْتُّ.

Rem. *c.* The same distinction exists between the words *ǵèzm* and *ǵèzma*, as between *fèth* and *fètḥa*, etc. (see § 4, rem. *a*).

Rem. *d.* Older forms of the ǵèzma are ˆ and ˇ, whence the later ˆ, instead of the common ْ or ْ. In some old Mss. of the Ḳor'ān a small horizontal (red) stroke is used, ـ. C

10. ى and و, when they form a diphthong with fètḥa, are marked with a ǵèzma, as لَيْلٌ, يَوْمٌ, كَيْ, يَدَيْ; but when they stand for *èlif productionis* they do not take this sign (see § 7, rem. *b*, *c*, *d*).

Rem. In many manuscripts a ǵèzma is placed even over the letters of prolongation, e.g. قَاْلَ, صَبُوْرٌ, سِيْمَ; and over the èlif maḳṣūra, e.g. عَلَىْ, هُدًىْ for عَلَى, هُدًى.

B. *Tèšdīd or Šèdda.* D

11. A consonant that is to be doubled, or, as the Arabs say, *strengthened* (مُشَدَّدٌ), without the interposition of a vowel (see rem. *a*), is written only once, but marked with the sign ّ, which is called

A اَلتَّشْدِيدُ, the *tèśdīd* (*strengthening*)*; e.g. اَلْكُلَّ *ĕl-kulla*, كُلًّا *kullan*, اَلسَّمِّ *ĕs-sèmmi*, سَمٍّ *sèmmin*, اَلْمُرُّ *ĕl-murru*, مُرٌّ *murrun*. It corresponds therefore to the *Daghesh forte* of the Hebrew.

REM. *a.* The solitary exception to this rule, in the verbal forms قُووِلَ *ḳūwila* and تُقُووِلَ *tuḳūwila*, instead of قُوِّلَ and تُقُوِّلَ, admits of an easy explanation (see § 159).—When a consonant is repeated in such a manner that a vowel is interposed between its first and second occurrence, no doubling, properly so called, takes place, and

B consequently the tèśdīd is not required; e.g. فَرَرْتَ, 2d pers. sing. masc. Perf. of فَرَّ; تَفَتَّتَتْ, 3d pers. sing. fem. Perf. of the fifth form of فَتَّ.

REM. *b.* A consonant can be doubled, and receive tèśdīd, only when a vowel precedes and follows it. The cases treated of in § 14 form no exception to this rule.

REM. *c.* All consonants whatsoever, not even èlif hèmzatum excepted, admit of being doubled and take tèśdīd. Hence we speak and write رَأَّاسٌ *ra''āsun*, سَأَّالٌ *sa''ālun*, نَأَّاجٌ *na''āǵun*.

C REM. *d.* ـّ is an abbreviated ش, the first radical of the name تَشْدِيدٌ, or the first letter of the name شَدَّةٌ, which the African Arabs use instead of the other. Or it may stand for شد (from مُشَدَّدٌ), since in the oldest and most carefully written manuscripts its form is ـّ. Its opposite is حف, i.e. خف (from مُخَفَّفٌ *lightened, single*); e.g. سِرًّا وَعَلَانِيَةً *secretly and openly*.

REM. *e.* Tèśdīd, in combination with ـَ, ـً, ـُ, ـٌ, is placed between the consonants and these vowel-marks, as may be seen from

D the above examples. In combination with ـِ the Egyptians write ـّ instead of ـِّ; but elsewhere, at least in old manuscripts, ـّ may stand for ـَّ as well as ـِّ. The African Arabs constantly write ـَّ, ـًّ, ـِّ, for ـَّ, ـِّ, ـُّ. In the oldest Mss. of the Ḳor'ān, tèśdīd is expressed by ⌒ or ◡, which, when accompanied by kèsra, is sometimes written, as in African Mss., below the line. In African Mss. the vowel is not always written with the śèdda; ـَ alone may be = ـَّ, &c.

* [The *nomen unitatis* is تشديدة.—De G.]

12. Tèšdīd is either *necessary* or *euphonic*. A

13. The *necessary tèšdīd*, which always follows a vowel, whether short (as in عَلَّقَ) or long (as in مَادٌّ), indicates a doubling upon which the signification of the word depends. Thus أَمَرَ (*àmara*) means *he commanded*, but أَمَّرَ (*àmmara*), *he appointed some one commander*; مُرٌّ (*murrun*) is *bitter*, but a word مُرٌ (*murun*) does not exist in the language.

Rem. The Arabs do not readily tolerate a syllable containing a long vowel and terminating in a consonant. Consequently *tèšdīd necessarium* scarcely ever follows the long vowels و and ى, as in تُمُودَّ ٱلثَّوْبُ, though it is sometimes found after ا, as in مَارٌّ, مَادَّةٌ, يَكْتُبَانِّ (see § 25). Nor does it occur after the diphthongs ـَوْ and ـَىْ, save in rare instances, like خُوَيْصَّةٌ and دُوَيْبَّةٌ [see § 277]. B

14. The *euphonic tèšdīd* always follows a vowelless consonant, which, though expressed in writing, is, to avoid harshness of sound, passed over in pronunciation and assimilated to a following consonant. It is used :—

(*a*) With the letters ت, ث, د, ذ, ر, ز, س, ش, ص, ض, ط, ظ, ل, ن, (dentals, sibilants, and liquids,) after the article اَلْ; e.g. اَلتَّمْرُ *èt-tèmru*; اَلرَّحْمٰنُ *'ar-raḥmānu*; اَلشَّمْسُ *èš-šèmsu*; اَلظُّلْمُ *'aẓ-ẓolmu*; اَللَّيْلُ *èl-lèilu*, or, in African and Spanish manuscripts, اَلْلَيْلُ. C

Rem. *a*. These letters are called اَلْحُرُوفُ ٱلشَّمْسِيَّةُ, *the solar letters*, because the word شَمْسٌ, *sun*, happens to begin with one of them; and the other letters of the alphabet اَلْحُرُوفُ ٱلْقَمَرِيَّةُ, *the lunar letters*, because the word قَمَرٌ, *moon*, commences with one of them. D

Rem. *b*. This assimilation is extended by some to the ل of هَلْ and بَلْ, especially before ر, as هَل رَّأَيْتَ.

(*b*) With the letters ر, ل, م, و, ى, after *n* with ğèzm, e.g. مِن رَّبِّهِ *mir rabbihi*, مِن لَّيْلٍ, أَن يَّقْتُلَ; and after the nunation, e.g. كِتَابٌ مُّبِينٌ *kitābum mubīnun*, for *kitābun mubīnun*. The *n* of the

A words مِنْ, عَنْ, أَنْ, is often not written when they are combined with مَا, مَنْ, لَا; e.g. مِمَّنْ for مِنْمَنْ or مِن مَّنْ, عَمَّا for عَن مَّا, أَلَّا for أَن لَّا.

REM. *a.* If to the above letters we add ن itself, as أَن تَّكْتُبَ, the mnemonic word is يَرْمُلُونَ.

REM. *b.* أَن لَّا is equally common with أَلَّا, but مِمَّنْ, عَمَّنْ, مِمَّا, عَمَّا, are hardly ever written separately; مَن لَّا, on the contrary, always. Similarly we find إِلَّا for إِن لَّا (*if not*), إِمَّا for إِن مَّا (*if*, with
B redundant ما) and occasionally أَمَّا for أَن مَّا (*that*, with redundant ما).

(*c*) With the letter ت after ث, د, ذ, ض, ط, ظ (dentals), in certain parts of the verb; e.g. لَبِثُّ *lèbittu* for لَبِثْتُ *lèbiṯtu;* أَرَدتَّ *'aratta* for أَرَدْتَ *'aradta;* أَتَّخَذتُّمْ *'attaḫattum* for أَتَّخَذْتُمْ *'attaḫaḏtum;* بَسَطتُّمْ *basattum* for بَسَطْتُمْ *basaṭtum.* Many grammarians, however, reject this kind of assimilation altogether, and rightly, because the absorption of a strong radical consonant, such as د, ض or ط, by a
C weaker servile letter, like ت, is an unnatural mutilation of an essential part of the word.

REM. *a.* Still more to be condemned are such assimilations as عُدُّ for عُدْتُ, خَبَطُّ for خَبَطْتُ.

REM. *b.* If the verb ends in ت, it naturally unites with the second ت in the above cases, so that only one ت is written, but the union of the two is indicated by the tèšdīd; as ثَبَتُّ for ثَبَتْتُ.

C. *Hèmza or Nèbra.*

D **15.** Elif, when it is not a mere letter of prolongation, but a consonant, pronounced like the *spiritus lenis,* is distinguished by the mark ء *hèmza* (هَمْزٌ or هَمْزَةٌ, *compression,* viz. of the upper part of the windpipe, see § 4, rem. *a*), which is also sometimes called *nèbra* (نَبْرَةٌ, *elevation*); e.g. أَسَدٌ, سَأَلَ, قَرَأَ, رَأْسٌ, اِقْرَأْ, إِقْلِيدٌ, خَطَأٌ, أُمَرُ, خَطَأٌ.

REM. *a.* In cases where an *èlif conjunctionis* (see § 19, *a, b, c,* and rem. *d, e*) at the beginning of a word receives its own vowel, the grammarians omit the hèmza and write merely the vowel; e.g. اَلْحَمْدُ لِلّٰهِ *praise belongs to God,* اِقْرَأْ, اِبْنٌ, اُقْتُلْ.

Rem. *b.* ـٓ is probably a small ع and indicates that the *ĕlif* is to A
be pronounced almost as *'ain*. In African (and certain other) Mss. it is sometimes actually written ع; e.g. اِعْذْ، اَعْخَلَقْ. In the oldest Mss. of the Kor'ân, hèmza is indicated by doubling the vowel-points; e.g., القرآن = اَلْقُرْءَانُ، المومنون = اَلْمُؤْمِنُونَ. It is also marked in such Mss. by a large yellow or green dot, varying in position according to the accompanying vowel (see above, § 4, rem. *c*).

Rem. *c.* Hèmza is written between the ا and the vowel that accompanies it, or the ǵèzma (see the examples given above); but B
we often find خَاسِئِينَ for خَاسِيِينَ, سَئَرَ for سَيَرَ (see § 16), and occasionally خَطَأً or خَطَاً for خَطَأً, أَنَّ or أَنَّ for إِنَّ, سُئِلَ for سُئِلَ or سُئِلَ, and the like.

Rem. *d.* The effect of the hèmza is most sensible to a European ear at the commencement of a syllable in the middle of a word, preceded by a shut syllable; e.g. مَسْأَلَةٌ *mas-'alatun* (not *ma-salatun*) اَلْقُرْآنُ, *ĕl-ḳor-'ānu* (not *ĕl-ko-rānu*).

16. ى and و take hèmza, when they stand in place of an *ĕlif* C
*hèmzatum** (in which case the two points of the letter ى are commonly omitted); e.g. جِئْتُ for جِأْتُ, خَاسِئِينَ for خَاسِإِينَ, بُؤْسٌ for بُأْسٌ, رُؤُوسٌ for رُأُوسٌ.

17. Hèmza alone (ء) is written instead of أ, إ, ئ, ؤ, in the following cases.

(*a*) Always at the end of a word, after a letter of prolongation or a consonant with ǵèzma, e.g. جَاءَ, *ǵā'a*, رِدَاءٌ, رِدَاءٌ; جِيءَ, *ǵī'a*, D
رَدِيءٌ; سُوءٌ, *sū'un*; ضَوْءٌ, قَيْءٌ, ظِمْءٌ, or more commonly ظِمْئًا (see § 8, rem. *a*); and in the middle of a word, after an *ĕlif productionis*, provided the hèmza has the vowel fètḥa, as يَتَسَاءَلُونَ, أَعْدَاءَكُمْ (but for أَعْدَاءُكُمْ and أَعْدَاءِكُمْ the Arabs usually write أَعْدَاؤُكُمْ and أَعْدَائِكُمْ).

Rem. Accusatives like شَيْئًا and ظِمْئًا are often written, though

* [See below, §§ 131 *seq.*]

A contrary to rule, شَيْأً, ظِمْأً ; and in old Mss. we find such instances as رِدَاآً for رِدَآءً.

(*b*) Frequently in the middle of words, after the letters of prolongation و and ى, or after a consonant with ǵèzma, e.g. مَقْرُوءَةٌ for مَقْرُووَةٌ, مُوءِبَاتٌ for مُوئِبَاتٌ, تَوْءَمٌ for تَوْأَمٌ, يَسْءَلُ for يَسْأَلُ ; and also after kèsra and ḍamma before the ى and و of prolongation, e.g.
B خَاطِءِينَ for خَاطِئِينَ, رُءُوسٌ for رُؤُوسٌ. Hèmza between *īă*, *ūă*, *ăī*, *ĭī*, *ăū*, and *ŭū*, is, however, more frequently, though improperly, placed over the letter of prolongation itself; e.g. مَقْرُوؤَةٌ for مَقْرُوءَةٌ, خَطِيئَةٌ for خَطِيءَةٌ or خَطِيئَةٌ, رُؤُوسٌ for رُءُوسٌ or رُؤُوسٌ, which words must always be pronounced *maḳrū'atun*, *ḫaṭī'atun*, *ru'ūsun*.

REM. *a*. After a consonant with ǵèzma, which is connected with a following letter, hèmza and its vowel may be placed above the
C connecting line; as أَسْـَٔلُ, for أَسْأَلُ.

REM. *b*. A hèmza preceded by *u* or *i*, and followed by *a* or *ā*, may be changed into pure و or ى ; as جُوَنٌ for جُؤَنٌ, سُوَالٌ for سُؤَالٌ ; مِيَةٌ for مِئَةٌ, لِيَامٌ for لِئَامٌ.—If preceded by *ū* or *ī*, or the diphthong *ai*, the hèmza may likewise be changed into و or ى, whatever be the following vowel; as مَقْرُوَّةٌ for مَقْرُووَةٌ, from مَقْرُوءَةٌ; نَبِيٌّ for نَبِيِيٌ, from نَبِيءٌ ; بَرِيَّةٌ for بَرِييَةٌ, from بَرِيئَةٌ ; فَيٌّ for فَيْيٌ, from فَيْءٌ,
D شَيٌّ for شَيْيٌ.—If the hèmza has ǵèzma, it may [lose its consonantal power and] be changed into the letter of prolongation that is homogeneous with the preceding vowel, as رَاسٌ for رَأْسٌ, لُومٌ for لُؤْمٌ, بِيرٌ for بِئْرٌ ; necessarily so, if the preceding consonant be an èlif with hèmza, as آمَنَ or أامَنَ, أُومِنُ, إِيمَانٌ, for أَأْمَنَ, أُؤْمِنُ, إِئْمَانٌ. [This is called تَخْفِيفُ ٱلْهَمْزَةِ.]

REM. *c*. The name دَاوُودُ or دَاؤُدُ, *David*, is often written دَاوُدُ, but must always be pronounced *Dā'ūdu*.

D. *Waṣla.*

18. When the vowels with hèmza (أ إ أُ), at the commencement of A
a word, are absorbed by the final vowel of the preceding word, the elision of the spiritus lenis is marked by the sign ٱ, written over the èlif, and called وَصْلٌ, or وَصْلَةٌ, or صِلَةٌ (see § 4, rem. *a*), i.e. *union*; e.g. عَبْدُ ٱلْمَلِكِ *'abdu 'l-mèliki* for عَبْدُ أَلْمَلِكِ *'abdu èl-mèliki*; رَأَيْتُ ٱبْنَكَ *raèitu 'bnaka* for رَأَيْتُ إِبْنَكَ *raèitu 'ibnaka*.

Rem. *a*. ٱ seems to be an abbreviation of ص in وَصْلٌ or صِلَةٌ; or rather, it is the word صلة itself. In the oldest Mss. of the B
Ḳor'ān the waṣl is indicated by a stroke (usually red), which sometimes varies in position, according to the preceding vowel. In ancient Maġribī Mss. the stroke is used, with a point to indicate the original vowel of the elided èlif; e.g., فِي سَبِيلِ ٱللّٰهِ, i.e. ٱللّٰهِ; عَرَضَ ٱلْحَيٰوةَ, i.e. ٱلْحَيٰوةَ. Hence even in modern African Mss. we find ٱ ٱ ٱ ٱ ٱ instead of the usual ٱ.

Rem. *b*. Though we have written in the above examples أَلْمَلِكِ and إِبْنَكَ, yet the student must not forget that the more correct C
orthography is ٱلْمَلِكِ and ٱبْنَكَ. See § 15, rem. *a*, and § 19, rem. *d*.

19. This elision takes place in the following cases.

(*a*) With the أ of the article أَلْ; as أَبُو ٱلْوَزِيرِ for أَبُو أَلْوَزِيرِ, *the father of the wèzīr*.

(*b*) With the إ and أُ of the Imperatives of the first form of the regular verb; as قَالَ ٱسْمَعْ for قَالَ اِسْمَعْ, *he said, listen*; قَالَ ٱقْتُلْ for D
قَالَ اُقْتُلْ, *he said, kill*.

(*c*) With the إ of the Perfect Active, Imperative, and Nomen actionis of the seventh and all the following forms of the verb (see § 35), and the أُ of the Perfect Passive in the same forms; e.g. هُوَ ٱنْهَزَمَ for هُوَ اِنْهَزَمَ, *he was put to flight*; وَٱسْتُعْمِلَ for وَاُسْتُعْمِلَ, *and he was appointed governor*; ٱلْإِقْتِدَارُ *the being able* (to do something); إِلَى ٱلْإِنْقِرَاضِ *till the downfall* or *extinction*.

A (*d*) With the ا of the following eight nouns:

اِبْنٌ, and اِبْنُمٌ or اِبْنَمٌ, *a son.* اِبْنَةٌ, *a daughter.*

اِثْنَانِ, *two* (masc.). اِثْنَتَانِ, *two* (fem.).

اِمْرُؤٌ, or اِمْرَؤٌ, *a man.* اِمْرَأَةٌ, *a woman.*

اِسْتٌ, *the anus.* اِسْمٌ (rarely اُسْمٌ), *a name.*

REM. *a.* With the article اِمْرُؤٌ and اِمْرَأَةٌ take, in classical
B Arabic, the form اَلْمَرْءُ and اَلْمَرْأَةُ.

REM. *b.* The hèmza of أَيْمُنٌ, *oaths,* is also elided after the asseverative particle لَ, and occasionally after the prepositions مَعَ and مِنْ (which then takes fètha instead of ǵèzma); as لَاَيْمُنُ ٱللّٰهِ *by God* (lit. *by the oaths of God*), for which we may also write لَيْمُنُ ٱللّٰهِ, omitting the ا altogether, or, in a contracted form, لَيْمُ ٱللّٰهِ.

C REM. *c.* In the above words and forms, the vowel with hèmza is in part original, but has been weakened through constant use (as in the article, and in أَيْمُنٌ after لَ); in part merely prosthetic, that is to say, prefixed for the sake of euphony to words beginning with a vowelless consonant, and consequently it vanishes as soon as a vowel precedes it, because it is then no longer necessary.

REM. *d.* It is naturally an absurd error to write آ at the beginning of a sentence instead of èlif with hèmza, as آلْحَمْدُ لِلّٰهِ instead of أَلْحَمْدُ لِلّٰهِ. The Arabs themselves never do so, but, to indicate
D that the èlif is an *èlif conjunctionis* (see rem. *f*), they omit the hèmza and express only its accompanying vowel, as اَلْحَمْدُ لِلّٰهِ. See § 15, rem. *a*, and § 18, rem. *b*.

REM. *e.* In more modern Arabic the elision of the *èlif conjunctionis* (see rem. *f*) is neglected, especially after the article, as اَلْإِقْتِدَارُ, إِلَى ٱلْإِنْقِرَاضِ, بِئْسَ ٱلْإِسْمُ, بَعْدَ اِنْقِرَاضِهِمْ; but the grammarians brand this as خُرُوجٌ عَنْ كَلَامِ ٱلْعَرَبِ وَلَحْنٌ فَاحِشٌ.

Rem. *f.* The ĕlif which takes waṣla is called أَلِفُ ٱلْوَصْلِ or هَمْزَةُ ٱلْوَصْلِ, *ĕlif* or *hĕmza conjunctionis*, the connective ĕlif; the opposite being أَلِفُ ٱلْقَطْعِ, *ĕlif sejunctionis* or *separationis*, the disjunctive elif. A

20. The ĕlif conjunctionis may be preceded either by a short vowel, a long vowel, a diphthong, or a consonant with ǵĕzma. To these different cases the following rules apply.

(*a*) A short vowel simply absorbs the ĕlif conjunctionis with its vowel; see § 19, *b* and *c*. B

(*b*) A long vowel is shortened in pronunciation, according to the rule laid down in § 25; e.g. فِى ٱلنَّاسِ *fĭ 'n-nāsi, among men;* أَبُو ٱلْوَزِيرِ *'abŭ 'l-wĕzīri, the father of the wĕzīr*, for *fī* and *'abū*. This abbreviation of the naturally long vowel is retained even when the *lām* of the article no longer closes the syllable containing that vowel, but begins the next syllable, in consequence of the elision of a following ĕlif (either according to § 19 or by poetic license). Hence فِى ٱلَابْتِدَآءِ, *in the beginning*, is pronounced as if written C فِلَبْتِدَآءِ; فِى ٱلَارْضِ (for ٱلْأَرْضِ), *upon the earth*, as فِلَرْضِ; ذُو ٱلَاعْلَالِ (for ٱلْإِعْلَالِ), *subject to change* (*a weak letter*), as ذُلَعْلَالِ. In the first of these examples the ا is an ĕlif conjunctionis; in the other two it is an ĕlif separationis, but has been changed for the sake of the metre into an ĕlif conjunctionis. The suffixes of the 1st pers. sing., ـِى and نِى, may assume before the article the older forms ـِىَ and نِىَ; e.g. نِعْمَتِىَ ٱلَّتِى *my grace which*, اِهْدِنِىَ ٱلصِّرَاطَ *guide me on the* D *way*, instead of نِعْمَتِى ٱلَّتِى and اِهْدِنِى ٱلصِّرَاطَ, which latter forms are equally admissible.

(*c*) A diphthong is resolved into two simple vowels, according to the law stated in § 25, viz. *ai* into *ăĭ*, and *au* into *ăŭ*; as فِى عَيْنَيِ ٱلْمَلِكِ *fĭ 'ainăĭ 'l-mĕliki, in the eyes of the king*, for فِى عَيْنَىْ ٱلْمَلِكِ; اِخْشَيِ ٱلْقَوْمَ *iḫšăĭ 'l-ḳauma, fear the people;* مُصْطَفَوُ ٱللّٰهِ *muṣṭafăŭ 'llāhi, the elect of God*, for مُصْطَفَوْ ٱللّٰهِ. The silent ĕlif (§ 7, rem. *a*) does not prevent the resolution of the diph-

A thong, as رَمَوُا ٱلْحِجَارَةَ *ramăŭ 'l-ḥiǵārata, they threw the stones;* فَلَمَّا رَأَوُا ٱلنَّجْمَ *fa-lammā ra'ăŭ 'n-nèǵma, and after they saw the star.* But أَوْ and لَوْ take *kèsra*, as أَوِ ٱسْمُهُ *or his name;* لَوِ ٱسْتَقْبَلَ *if he went to meet.*

(*d*) A consonant with ǵèzma either takes its original vowel, if it had one; or assumes that which belongs to the èlif conjunctionis; or adopts the lightest of the three vowels, which in its nature approaches nearest to the ǵèzma, viz. kèsra. Hence the pronouns of the
B 2d and 3d pers. plur. masc., أَنْتُمْ *you*, and هُمْ *they*, the pronominal suffixes of the same pronouns, كُمْ *your, you* (accus.), and هُمْ *their, them*, and the verbal termination of the 2d pers. plur. masc. Perf. تُمْ, take *ḍamma* (in which they originally ended); as أَنْتُمُ ٱلْكَاذِبُونَ *ye are the liars;* لَعَنَهُمُ ٱللّٰهُ *may God curse them!* رَأَيْتُمُ ٱلرَّجُلَ *ye have seen the man.* The same is the case with مُذْ, *since, from which time forth*, because it is contracted for مُنْذُ. The preposition مِنْ, *from*, takes
C *fèṭha* before the article, but in other cases *kèsra;* as مِنَ ٱلرَّجُلِ, مِنِ ٱبْنِهِ. All other words ending in a consonant with ǵèzma take *kèsra;* viz. nouns having the tènwīn, as مُحَمَّدٌ ٱلنَّبِيُّ *Moḥammèduni 'n-nèbīyu;* the pronoun مَنْ, as مَنِ ٱلْكَذَّابُ *mani 'l-kaddābu;* verbal forms like قَتَلَتْ, تَكْتُبْ, اِجْلِسْ, as قَتَلَتِ ٱلرُّومُ *ḳatalati 'r-Rūmu;* and particles, such as عَنْ, إِنْ, بَلْ, قَدْ, هَلْ, لٰكِنْ, etc.

D REM. *a.* In certain cases where هُمْ becomes هِمْ (see § 185, rem. *b*) the waṣl may be made either with ḍamma or kèsra, هِمُ or هِمِ.

REM. *b.* If the vowel of a prosthetic èlif be *ḍamma*, the waṣl is sometimes effected by throwing it back upon the preceding vowelless consonant or tènwīn; as قُلُ ٱنْظُرُوا, for قُلْ اُنْظُرُوا, instead of قُلِ ٱنْظُرُوا; وَقَالَتُ ٱخْرُجْ; سَلَامٌ ٱدْخُلُوا *selāmunu 'dḫulū.*

REM. *c.* The final ن of the second Energetic of verbs (see § 97) is rejected, so that the waṣl is effected by the preceding fèṭha; as

لَا تَضْرِبَ ٱبْنَكَ *lā taḍriba 'bnaka*, and not لَا تَضْرِبَنِ ٱبْنَكَ *lā taḍribani* A
'bnaka.

21. ٱ is altogether omitted in the following cases.

(*a*) In the solemn introductory formula بِسْمِ ٱللّٰهِ, for بِٱسْمِ ٱللّٰهِ, *in the name of God*, בשם האלהים. As a compensation for the omission of the ا, the copyists of Mss. are accustomed to prolong the upward stroke of the letter ب, thus: بسم.

(*b*) In the word ٱبْنٌ, *son*, in a genealogical series, that is to say, B
when the name of the son precedes, and that of his father follows in the genitive; provided always that the said series, as a whole, forms part either of the subject or the predicate of a sentence. For example, ضَرَبَ زَيْدُ بْنُ خٰلِدٍ سَعْدَ بْنَ عَوْفِ بْنِ عَبْدِ ٱللّٰهِ *Zèid, the son of Ḫālid, struck Sa'd, the son of 'Auf, the son of 'Abdu 'llāh.* [Cf. § 315, rem. *b*.] But if the second noun be not in apposition to the first, but form part of the predicate, so that the two together make a complete sentence, then the ٱ is retained; as زَيْدٌ ٱبْنُ عَمْرٍو *Zèid* (*is*) *the son of* C
'Amr; عُمَرُ ٱبْنُ ٱلْخَطَّابِ *'Omar* (*is*) *the son of ĕl-Ḫaṭṭāb.*

Rem. *a.* Even in the first case the ٱ of ٱبْنٌ is retained, if that word happens to stand at the beginning of a line.

Rem. *b.* If the name following ٱبْنٌ be that of the mother or grandfather, the ٱ is retained; as عِيسَى ٱبْنُ مَرْيَمَ, *Jesus the son of Mary;* عَمَّارُ ٱبْنُ مَنْصُورٍ, *'Ammār the* (*grand*)*son of Manṣūr.* Like-
wise, if the following name be not the real name of the father, but a D
surname or nickname; as مِقْدَادُ ٱبْنُ ٱلْأَسْوَدِ, *Miḳdād the son of ĕl-'Aswad* (the real name of *ĕl-'Aswad*, "the black," being *'Amr*, عَمْرٌو). Or if the series be interrupted in any way, as by the interposition of an adjective; e.g. يَحْيَى ٱلْكَرِيمُ ٱبْنُ مَيْمُونٍ, *Yaḥyā the noble, the son of Mèimūn;* رِدْبَى كَظِرْبَى ٱبْنُ مُوسَى, *Riḍbā* (pronounced *like* the word *ẓirbā*) *the son of Mūsā.*

(*c*) In the article ٱلْ, when it is preceded:

(*α*) by the preposition لِ *to*, as لِلرَّجُلِ *to the man*, for لِٱلرَّجُلِ.

A If the first letter of the noun be ل, then the ل of the article is also omitted, as لِلَّيْلَةِ *to the night*, for لِلْلَّيْلَةِ, and that for لِٱلْلَّيْلَةِ.

(β) by the affirmative particle لَ *truly, verily*, as لَلْحَقُّ, for لَٱلْحَقُّ*.

(*d*) In nouns, verbs, and the article أَلْ, when preceded by the interrogative particle أَ; as أَبْنُكَ, for أَٱبْنُكَ, *is thy son—?* أَنْكَسَرَتْ, for أَٱنْكَسَرَتْ, *is it* (fem.) *broken?* أَتَّخَذْتُمْ, for أَٱتَّخَذْتُمْ, *have ye received?*

B أَلْمَآءُ, for أَٱلْمَآءُ, *is the water—?* The èlif of the article may however be retained, so that ٱلْمَآءُ with the interrogative أَ is often written أَآلْمَآءُ.

REM. *a.* In this last case, according to some, when the second èlif has fètḥa, the two èlifs may blend into one with mèdda (see below); as آلْحَسَنُ عِنْدَكَ, *is èl-Ḥasan in thy house?* for أَأَلْحَسَنُ; آلْقُرَشِيُّ أَمِ ٱلثَّقَفِيُّ, *he of Ḳorèiš or he of Ṯaḳīf?* آيْمُنُ ٱللّٰهِ يَمِينُكَ, *is thy oath 'by God'?* (see § 19, rem. *b*) for أَأَيْمُنُ ٱللّٰهِ.

C REM. *b.* The prosthetic èlif of the Imperative of سَأَلَ, *to ask*, is frequently omitted, in Mss. of the Ḳor'ān, after the conjunction فَ; as فَسْأَلْ, for فَٱسْأَلْ. [Cf. § 140, rem. *a.*]

E. *Mèdda or Maṭṭa.*

22. When èlif with hèmza and a simple vowel or tènwīn (أً, إٍ, etc.) is preceded by an èlif of prolongation (ـَا), then a mere hèmza is written instead of the former, and the sign of prolongation, ٓ *mèdda* or *maṭṭa*

D (مَدٌّ, مَدَّةٌ or مَطَّةٌ, i.e. *lengthening, extension*), is placed over the latter; e.g. سَمَآءٌ *semā'un*, جَآءَ *ǵā'a*, يَتَسَآءَلُونَ *yatasā'alūna*, for سَمَاأٌ, جَاأَ, يَتَسَاأَلُونَ.

REM. *a.* As mentioned above (§ 17, *a*, rem.), we find in old Mss. such forms as جَاأَ, رِدَاأً, for جَآءَ, رِدَآءً.

REM. *b.* In the oldest and best Mss., the form of the mèdda is مـــد (i.e. مد). Its opposite is قصر (i.e. قَصْرٌ, *shortening*), though

---

* [Note also the cases, in poetry, cited in § 358, rem. *c*; further the contracted tribal names بَلْعَنْبَرِ, بَلْحٰرِثِ for بَنُو ٱلْعَنْبَرِ, بَنُو ٱلْحٰرِثِ.—De G.]

this is but rarely written. In some old Mss. of the Ḳor'ān mèdda A
is expressed by a horizontal yellow line ـٓ.

23. When, at the beginning of a syllable, an èlif with hèmza and fètḥa (أَ) is followed by an èlif of prolongation or an elif with hèmza and ǵèzma (أْ), then the two are commonly represented in writing by a single èlif with mèdda; e.g. إِسَآدٌ for إِسْأَادٌ, آكِلُونَ for أَأْكِلُونَ, آمَنَّا for أَأْمَنَّا (see § 17, rem. *b*). In this case it is not usual to write either the hèmza, or the vowel, along with the mèdda. [But we some- B
times find آءَ, see § 174.]

Rem. *a.* آ is called ٱلْأَلِفُ ٱلْمَمْدُودَةُ, *the lengthened* or *long èlif*, in opposition to ٱلْأَلِفُ ٱلْمَقْصُورَةُ, *the èlif that can be abbreviated* or *shortened* (§ 7, rem. *b*).

Rem. *b.* Occasionally a long èlif at the beginning of a word is written with hèmza and a perpendicular fètḥa, instead of with mèdda (see § 6, rem. *a*); e.g. أٰمَنَّا instead of آمَنَّا or أَأْمَنَّا.

Rem. *c.* Mèdda is sometimes placed over the other letters of C
prolongation, و and ى, when followed by an èlif hèmzatum, only the hèmza being written (§ 17, *a*); as يَسُوٓءُ, يَجِيٓءُ. Also over the final vowels of the pronominal forms أَنْتُمْ, كُمْ, ـهُ or ـهُ, هُمْ or هِمْ, and the verbal termination تُمْ, when they are used as long in poetry; e.g. أَنْتُمُٓ, هُمُٓ.

Rem. *d.* The mark ـٓ, often written over abbreviations of words, has nothing in common with mèdda but the form. So تعٓ for تَعَالَى, *He (God) is exalted above all;* عمٓ for عَلَيْهِ ٱلسَّلَامُ, *peace be* D
upon him! صلعمٓ for صَلَّى ٱللّٰهُ عَلَيْهِ وَسَلَّمَ, *God bless him and grant him peace!* رضهٓ for رَضِيَ ٱللّٰهُ عَنْهُ, *may God be well pleased with,* or *gracious to, him!* رحٓ or رحهٓ for رَحِمَهُ ٱللّٰهُ, *may God have mercy upon him!* الخٓ for إِلَى آخِرِهِ or إِلَى آخِرِهَا, *to the end of it,* i.e. *etc.;* ثنا for حَدَّثَنَا, *he narrated to us;* انا or نَا for أَخْبَرَنَا, *he informed us;* حٓ for حِينَئِذٍ, *then.*—The letters م م are written over words or verses that have been erroneously transposed in a manuscript, for

A مُؤَخَّر, *to be placed last*, and مُقَدَّم, *to be placed first*.—On the margin of Mss. we often find words with the letters خ, ن, and صح over them. The first of these indicates a variant, and stands for نُسْخَة, *a copy, another manuscript;* the second means that a word has been indistinctly written in the text, and is repeated more clearly on the margin, بَيَان, *explanation;* the third implies that the marginal reading, and not that of the text, is, in the writer's opinion, the correct one صَحَّ, *it is correct*, or تَصْحِيح, *correction, emendation.*

B Written over a word in the text, صح stands for صَحَّ, and denotes that the word is correct, though there may be something peculiar in its form or vocalization.—Again معا (i.e. مَعًا, *together*) is written over a word with double vocalization to indicate that both vowels are correct. لعله over a word on the margin implies a conjectural emendation لَعَلَّهُ, *perhaps it is.*

IV. THE SYLLABLE.

C **24.** The vowel of a syllable that terminates in a vowel, which we call an open or simple syllable, may be either long or short; as قَالَ *ḳā-lă.*

25. The vowel of a syllable that terminates in a consonant, which we call a shut or compound syllable, is almost always short; as قُلْ *ḳŭl*, not قُولْ (Heb. קוֹל). Generally speaking, it is only in pause, where the final short vowels are suppressed, that the ancient Arabic admits of such syllables as *īn, ūn, ān*, etc.

D REM. Before a double consonant *ā* is however not infrequent (see § 13, rem.). [Such a long *ā* preceding a consonant with *ǵèzma* sometimes receives a *mèdda*, as ضَآلُّونَ.]

26. A syllable cannot begin with two consonants, the first of which is destitute of a vowel, as *sf* or *fr*. Foreign words, which commence with a syllable of this sort, on passing into the Arabic language, take an additional vowel, usually before the first consonant; as إِسْفَنْجٌ, σπόγγος; أَفْلَاطُونُ, Πλάτων; الْإِفْرَنْجُ, *the Franks* (*Europeans*); إِكْسِيرٌ, *an elixir*, τὸ ξηρόν (medicamentum siccum).

27. A syllable cannot end in two consonants, which are not either separated or followed by a vowel (except in pause).

V. THE ACCENT. A

28. The last syllable of a word consisting of two or more syllables does not take the accent. Exceptions are:

(*a*) The pausal forms of § 29 and § 30, in which the accent remains unaltered; as *ya-ḳúl, ḳā-nún, mu'-mi-nín, kā-ti-bất, fi-rínd, 'a-ḳál, ma-fár, ḳu-béil, bil-láur, bu-néi.*

REM. But words ending in ـِىٌّ, ـُوٌّ, ـَآءٌ or ـَاءٌ, ـُوءٌ, and ـِىءٌ, throw back the accent as far as possible in their pausal forms; قُرَشِىٌّ *Ḳo-ra-ší-yun* becomes *Ḳó-ra-šī*, نَبِىٌّ *nè-bí-yun, né-bī;* عَدُوٌّ *'a-dú-wun, 'á-dū;* اقْتِنَآءٌ *'iḳ-ti-ná-'un, 'íḳ-ti-nā;* حَمْرَآءُ *ḥam-rá-'u, ḥám-rā;* B مَقْرُوءٌ *maḳ-rú-'un, máḳ-rū;* بَطِىءٌ *ba-ṭí-un, bá-ṭī.*

(*b*) Monosyllables in combination with أَ, بِ, كَ, لَ, وَ, and فَ, which retain their original accent; as أَلَا *'a-lá,* أَفَلَا *'a-fa-lá,* بِمَا *bi-má,* بِهِ *bi-hí,* كَذَا *ka-ḏá,* لِمَنْ *li-mán,* لَنَا *la-ná,* وَلَمْ *wa-lám,* فَقَطْ *fa-ḳáṭ,* وَقُلْ *wa-ḳúl.*

REM. The only exception to this rule in old Arabic is the interrogative enclitic مَ; as بِمَ *bí-ma,* لِمَ *lí-ma,* in contrast with C بِمَا *bi-má,* لِمَا *li-má.* See § 351, rem.

29. The penult takes the accent when it is long by nature, i.e. is an open syllable containing a long vowel; as قَالَ *ḳá-la,* يَقُولُ *ya-ḳú-lu,* قَانُونٌ *ḳā-nú-nun,* مُؤْمِنِينَ *mu'-mi-ní-na,* كَاتِبَاتٌ *kā-ti-bá-tun.*

30. The penult has likewise the accent when it is a shut syllable and consequently long by position; as قَلْبٌ *ḳál-bun,* ذِئْبٌ *ḏí'-bun,* بُرْءٌ *búr-'un,* اِجْلِسْ *'íǵ-lis,* فِرِنْدٌ *fi-rín-dun,* أَقَلُّ *'a-ḳál-lu,* مَفَرٌّ *ma-fár-* D *run,* يَقُولَنَّ *ya-ḳū-lán-na,* قُبَيْلَ *ḳu-béi-la,* بِلَّوْرٌ, *bil-láu-run,* بُنَىٌّ *bu-néi-yun.*

31. When the penult is short, the accent falls upon the antepenult, provided that the word has not more than three syllables, or, if it has four or more syllables, that the antepenult is long by nature or position; as كَتَبَ *ká-ta-ba,* كَتَبَتْ *ká-ta-bat,* كَتَبُوا *ká-ta-bū,* كَاتِبٌ *ká-ti-bun,* طَلَبٌ *ṭá-la-bun,* أَيْنَمَا *'éi-na-mā;* تَرَاسَلُوا *ta-rá-*

A *sa-lū*, قَانُونُهُمْ *ḳā-nū-nu-hum*, كَتَبْتُمَا *ka-táb-tu-mā*. In other cases the accent is thrown as far back as possible; as كَتَبَتَا *ká-ta-ba-tā*, مَسْأَلَةٌ *más-'a-la-tun*, مَسْأَلَتُهَا *más-'a-la-tu-hā*, قَصَبَتُهُمَا *ḳá-ṣa-ba-tu-hu-mā*.

REM. On deviations from these principles of accentuation, in Egypt and among the Bèdawīn, see Lane in the Journal of the German Oriental Society, vol. iv., pp. 183–6, and Wallin in the same journal, vol. xii., pp. 670–3, [also Spitta, *Gram. des arab. Vulgärdialectes von Aegypten* (1880), p. 59 *sqq.*]

B

VI. THE NUMBERS.

32. To express numbers the Arabs use sometimes the letters of the alphabet, at other times peculiar signs. In the former case, the numerical value of the letters accords with the more ancient order of the Hebrew and Aramaic alphabets (see § 1). They are written from right to left, and usually distinguished from the surrounding words by a stroke placed over them, as غضعد, 1874. This arrangement of the alphabet is called the *'Abuǵèd* or *'Abǵèd*, and is contained in the barbarous words:

C

أَبُجَدٍ هَوَزٍ حُطِي كَلَمَنَ سَعْفَصْ قُرِشَتْ ثَخَذْ ضَظَغْ

(otherwise pronounced:

أَبْجَدْ هَوَّزْ حُطِّي كَلَمَنْ سَعْفَصْ قَرَشَتْ ثَخَذْ ضَظَغْ)

or, as usual in North Africa:

أَبُجَدٍ هَوَزٍ حُطِي كَلَمَنَ صَعْفَضْ قُرِسَتْ ثَخَذْ ظَغَشْ

The special numerical figures, ten in number, have been adopted

D by the Arabs from the Indians, and are therefore called اَلرَّقْمُ الْهِنْدِيُّ, *the Indian notation*. They are the same that we Europeans make use of, calling them *Arabian*, because we took them from the Arabs. Their form, however, differs considerably from that which our ciphers have gradually assumed, as the following table shows.

Indian:	१	२	३	४	५	६	७	८	९	०
Arabic:	١	٢	٣	٤ ۴ ٤	٥ ۵ ٥	٦	٧	٨	٩	٠
Europ.:	1	2	3	4	5	6	7	8	9	0

They are compounded in exactly the same way as our numerals; e.g. ١٨٧٤, 1874.

PART SECOND.

ETYMOLOGY OR THE PARTS OF SPEECH.

I. THE VERB, اَلْفِعْلُ. A

A. General View.

1. *The Forms of the Triliteral Verb.*

33. The great majority of the Arabic verbs are triliteral (ثُلَاثِيٌّ), that is to say, contain three radical letters, though quadriliteral (رُبَاعِيٌّ) verbs are by no means rare.

34. From the first or ground-form of the triliteral and quadri- B literal verbs are derived in different ways several other forms, which express various modifications of the idea conveyed by the first.

35. The derived forms of the triliteral verb are usually reckoned fifteen in number, but the learner may pass over the last four, because (with the exception of the twelfth) they are of very rare occurrence.

اِفْعَالَّ XI.	تَفَاعَلَ VI.	فَعَلَ I.	
اِفْعَوْعَلَ XII.	اِنْفَعَلَ VII.	فَعَّلَ II.	
اِفْعَوَّلَ XIII.	اِفْتَعَلَ VIII.	فَاعَلَ III.	C
اِفْعَنْلَلَ XIV.	اِفْعَلَّ IX.	أَفْعَلَ IV.	
اِفْعَنْلَى XV.	اِسْتَفْعَلَ X.	تَفَعَّلَ V.	

Rem. *a.* The 3d pers. sing. masc. Perf., being the simplest form of the verb, is commonly used as paradigm, but for shortness' sake we always render it into English by the infinitive; قَتَلَ *to kill*, instead of *he has killed*.

A REM. *b*. The Arab grammarians use the verb فَعَلَ (פָּעַל) as paradigm, whence the first radical of the triliteral verb is called by them اَلْفَآءُ *the fā*, the second اَلْعَيْنُ *the 'ain*, and the third اَللَّامُ *the lām*.

REM. *c*. As the above order and numbering of the conjugations are those adopted in all the European Lexicons, the learner should note them carefully.

36. The *first* or ground-form is generally transitive (مُتَعَدٍّ) or intransitive (غَيْرُ مُتَعَدٍّ or لَازِمٌ) in signification, according to the vowel which accompanies its second radical.

B **37.** The vowel of the second radical is *a* in most of the transitive, and not a few of the intransitive verbs; e.g. ضَرَبَ *to beat*, كَتَبَ *to write*, قَتَلَ *to kill*, وَهَبَ *to give*; ذَهَبَ *to go away*, رَشَدَ *to go the right way*, جَلَسَ *to sit*.

38. The vowel *i* in the same position has generally an intransitive signification, *u* invariably so. The distinction between them is, that *i* indicates a temporary state or condition, or a merely accidental quality in persons or things; whilst *u* indicates a permanent state, or a
C naturally inherent quality. E.g. فَرِحَ or جَذِلَ *to be glad*, حَزِنَ *to be sorry*, أَشِرَ or بَطِرَ *to be proud and insolent*, أَدِمَ *to become whitish*, شَهِبَ *to become gray*, سَلِمَ *to be safe and sound*, مَرِضَ *to be sick*, كَبِرَ *to become old*, عَمِيَ *to be blind*; but حَسُنَ *to be beautiful*, قَبُحَ *to be ugly*, ثَقُلَ *to be heavy*, شَرُفَ *to be high* or *noble**, سَفُلَ *to be low* or *mean*, كَبُرَ *to be large*, صَغُرَ *to be small*.

D REM. *a*. Many verbs of the form فَعِلَ are transitive according to our way of thinking, and therefore govern the accusative, e.g. عَلِمَ *to know* (scire), حَسِبَ *to think*, رَحِمَ *to pity* or *have mercy upon*, سَمِعَ *to hear*.

---

* [Or, *to become noble*, for the form with *u* of the second radical often means *to become what one was not before*, Kāmil, p. 415.—De G.]

Rem. *b.* The same three forms occur in Hebrew and Aramaic, A
though the distinction is in these languages no longer so clearly marked. [See *Comp. Gr.* p. 165 *seq.*]

39. The *second* form (فَعَّلَ) is formed from the first (فَعَلَ) by doubling the second radical.

40. The signification agrees with the form in respect of being intensive (لِلْمُبَالَغَةِ) or extensive (لِلتَّكْثِيرِ). Originally it implies that an act is done with *great violence* (intensive), or during a *long time* (temporally extensive), or to or by a *number* of individuals (numerically extensive), or *repeatedly* (iterative or frequentative). E.g. ضَرَبَ *to* B
beat, ضَرَّبَ *to beat violently*; كَسَرَ *to break*, كَسَّرَ *to break in pieces*; قَطَعَ *to cut*, قَطَّعَ *to cut in pieces*; فَرَقَ *to separate*, فَرَّقَ *to disperse*; قَتَلَ *to kill*, قَتَّلَ *to massacre*; جَالَ or طَافَ *to go round*, جَوَّلَ or طَوَّفَ *to go round much* or *often*; بَكَى *to weep*, بَكَّى *to weep much*; مَوَّتَ ٱلْمَالُ *the cattle died off rapidly* or *in great numbers* (مَاتَ *to die*); بَرَكَ ٱلْجَمَلُ *the camel kneeled down*, بَرَّكَ ٱلنَّعَمُ *the (whole drove of) camels kneeled down.*

41. From this original intensive meaning arises the more usual C
causative or *factitive* signification. Verbs that are *intransitive* in the first form become *transitive* in the second; as فَرِحَ *to be glad*, فَرَّحَ *to gladden*; ضَعُفَ *to be weak*, ضَعَّفَ *to weaken*. Those that are *transitive* in the first become *doubly transitive* or *causative* in the second; as عَلِمَ *to know*, عَلَّمَ *to teach*; كَتَبَ *to write*, كَتَّبَ *to teach to write*; حَمَلَ *to carry*, حَمَّلَ *to make carry.*

Rem. *a.* The causative or factitive signification is common to D
the second and fourth forms, the apparent difference being that it is original in the latter, but derived in the former.

Rem. *b.* The second form is often rather *declarative* or *estimative* than factitive in the strict sense of the term; as كَذَبَ *to lie*, كَذَّبَ *to think* or *call one a liar*; صَدَقَ *to tell the truth*, صَدَّقَ *to think that one tells the truth, to believe him.*

A REM. *c.* The second form is frequently *denominative*, and expresses with various modifications the *making* or *doing of*, or *being occupied with*, the thing expressed by the noun from which it is derived; e.g. خَيَّمَ *to pitch a tent* (خَيْمَةٌ), *to dwell* in a place, جَيَّشَ *to collect an army* (جَيْشٌ), رَخَّمَ *to pave with marble* (رُخَامٌ), قَوَّسَ *to become bent like a bow* (قَوْسٌ), مَرَّضَ *to nurse the sick* (مَرِيضٌ), جَلَّدَ *to skin* an animal, *to bind* a book (جِلْدٌ *the skin*, compare our "to stone fruit" and "to stone a person"), قَرَّدَ *to clean an animal of ticks* (قُرَادٌ), قَذَّى *to take a mote* (قَذًى) *out of the eye*. Compare in

B Hebrew סִקֵּל, יִלֵּד, זִנֵּב, דִּשֵּׁן, etc. Similarly, جَدَّعَهُ *he said to him* جَدْعًا لَكَ (*may thy nose*, or the like, *be cut off*), حَيَّاهُ *he said to him* حَيَّاكَ ٱللّٰهُ (*may God prolong thy life*), سَلَّمَ عَلَيْهِ *he said to him* سَلَامٌ عَلَيْكَ (*peace be upon thee*), كَبَّرَ *he shouted the Moslem war-cry*, (اَللّٰهُ أَكْبَرُ); مَنْ دَخَلَ ظَفَارِ حَمَّرَ *he who enters* (the city of) *Ẓafār*, *must speak Ḥimyaritic* (the language of Ḥimyar, حِمْيَرُ). Sometimes, like the fourth form, it expresses movement towards a place; as وَجَّهَ *to set out in any direction* (وَجْهٌ), شَرَّقَ *to go to the east* (اَلشَّرْقُ), غَرَّبَ *to go to the west* (اَلْغَرْبُ).

C REM. *d.* فَعَّلَ corresponds in form, as well as in signification, to the Heb. קִטֵּל and Aram. קַטֵּל, ܩܰܛܶܠ.—[See *Comp. Gr.* p. 198 *seq.*]

42. The *third* form (فَاعَلَ) is formed from the first (فَعَلَ) by lengthening the vowel-sound *ă* after the first radical, as is indicated by the *ĕlif productionis*.

43. It modifies the signification of the ground-form in the following ways.

D (*a*) When فَعَلَ denotes an act that immediately affects an object (direct object or accusative), فَاعَلَ expresses *the effort* or *attempt to perform that act upon the object*, in which case the idea of *reciprocity* (اَلْمُشَارَكَةُ) is added when the effort is necessarily or accidentally a mutual one. E. g. قَتَلَهُ *he killed him*, قَاتَلَهُ *he* (*tried to kill him* or) *fought with him*; جَلَدَهُ *he beat him*, جَالَدَهُ *he fought with him*; صَرَعَهُ

he threw him down, صَارَعَهُ *he wrestled with him;* غَلَبَهُ *he overcame him,* A
غَالَبَهُ *he tried to overcome him;* سَبَقَهُ *he outran him,* سَابَقَهُ *he ran a race*
with him; شَرَفَهُ *he surpassed him in rank,* شَارَفَهُ *he strove to do so;*
فَخَرَهُ *he surpassed him in glory,* فَاخَرَهُ *he strove to do so, he vied with*
him in rank and glory; شَعَرَهُ *he excelled him in composing poetry,*
شَاعَرَهُ *he competed with him in doing so;* خَصَمَهُ *he got the better of*
him in a lawsuit, خَاصَمَهُ *he went to law with him.*

(*b*) When the first or fourth form denotes an act, the relation B
of which to an object is expressed by means of a preposition (indirect
object), the third form *converts that indirect object into the immediate*
or *direct object of the act* (accusative). The idea of *reciprocity* is here,
as in the former case, more or less distinctly implied. E. g. كَتَبَ إِلَى
ٱلْمَلِكِ *he wrote* (*a letter*) *to the king,* كَاتَبَ ٱلْمَلِكَ *he wrote to the king,*
corresponded with him; قَالَ لَهُ *he said to him* (*something*), قَاوَلَهُ *he*
conversed with him; أَرْسَلَ إِلَى ٱلسُّلْطَانِ *he sent* (*a message*) *to the sultan,* C
رَاسَلَ ٱلسُّلْطَانَ *do.;* جَلَسَ عِنْدَ أَمِيرِ ٱلْمُؤْمِنِينَ *he sat beside the Com-*
mander of the Faithful, جَالَسَ أَمِيرَ ٱلْمُؤْمِنِينَ *do.;* وَقَعَ بِهِ *he fell upon*
him, attacked him, وَاقَعَهُ *do.;* أَشَارَ عَلَيْهِ *he advised him,* شَاوَرَهُ *he con-*
sulted with him.

(*c*) When فَعَلَ denotes a quality or state, فَاعَلَ indicates *that*
one person makes use of that quality towards another and affects him
thereby, or *brings him into that state.* E.g. خَشُنَ *to be rough* or D
harsh, خَاشَنَهُ *he treated him harshly;* حَسُنَ *to be good* or *kind,* حَاسَنَهُ
he treated him kindly; لَانَ *to be soft* or *gentle,* لَايَنَهُ *he treated him*
gently; قَسَا *to be hard,* قَاسَاهُ *he hardened himself against him* or *it;*
نَعَمَ or نَعِمَ *to lead a comfortable life,* نَاعَمَهُ *he procured him the means*
of doing so.

Rem. *a.* The third form is sometimes *denominative*, but the
ideas of effort and reciprocity are always more or less clearly
implied. E.g. ضَاعَفَ *to double,* from ضِعْفٌ *the like* or *equal;* طَارَقَ

A *to double*, fold (طَرَّقَ) on fold; عَافَاكَ ٱللهُ *may God keep thee safe and well*, from عَافِيَةٌ *robust health*; سَافَرَ *to go on a journey* (سَفَرٌ).

REM. *b.* فَاعَلَ corresponds in form and signification to the Heb. קוֹטֵל (Arab. *ā* = Heb. *ō*); see *Comp. Gr.* p. 202 *seq.*

[REM. *c.* In a few verbs the third form is used in the sense of the fourth. Thus داخل, ساقط (*Gl. Geog.* s.v. دخل). Zamahšarī, *Fāik*, i. 197 cites باعده, جاناه, عالاه for أبعده *etc.* Also بالغ = أبلغ,
B *Aghānī* xiii. 52.—De G.]

iv **44.** The *fourth* form (أَفْعَلَ) is formed by prefixing to the root the syllable أَ, in consequence of which the first radical loses its vowel.

45. Its signification is *factitive* or *causative* (لِلتَّعْدِيَةِ). If the verb is intransitive in the first form, it becomes transitive in the fourth; if transitive in the first, it becomes doubly transitive in the fourth. E.g. جَرَى *to run*, أَجْرَى *to make run*; جَلَسَ *to sit down*,
C أَجْلَسَ *to bid one sit down*; أَكَلَ ٱلْخُبْزَ *he ate bread*, آكَلَهُ ٱلْخُبْزَ *he gave him bread to eat*; رَأَى ٱلشَّىْءَ *he saw the thing*, أَرَاهُ ٱلشَّىْءَ *he shewed him the thing.*

REM. *a.* When both the second and fourth forms of a verb are causative (§ 41, rem. *a*), they have in some cases different significations, in others the same. E.g. عَلِمَ *to know*, عَلَّمَ *to teach*, أَعْلَمَ *to inform one of a thing*; نَجَا *to escape*, نَجَّى and أَنْجَى *to set at liberty, to let go*. Comp. خَبَّرَ and أَخْبَرَ.

D REM. *b.* The fourth form is sometimes *declarative* or *estimative*, like the second; as أَبْخَلَهُ *he thought him*, or *found him to be*, *niggardly*; أَجْبَنَهُ *he thought him*, or *found him to be*, *cowardly*; أَحْمَدَهُ *he found him*, or *it*, *to be praiseworthy* or *commendable*; أَحْيَى ٱلْأَرْضَ *he found the district abounding in fresh herbage.*

REM. *c.* The fourth form comprises a great number of *denominatives*, many of which are apparently intransitive, because the Arabs often regard as an *act* what we view as a *state*. Such verbs combine with the idea of the noun, from which they are derived, that of a transitive verb, of which it is the direct object. E.g. أَبْقَلَ

to produce herbage (بَقْلٌ), أَوْرَقَ *to put out leaves* (وَرَقٌ), أَثْمَرَ *to bear* A
fruit (ثَمَرٌ), أَمْطَرَ *to give* or *yield rain* (مَطْرٌ); أَنْجَبَ *to beget a noble son*, أَذْكَرَتْ, آنَثَتْ, *she bore a male* or *a female child*, أَتْأَمَتْ *she bore twins* (compare "to flower," "to seed," "to calve," "to lamb"); أَبْلَغَ *to speak eloquently*, أَفْصَحَ *to speak with purity and correctness*, أَبْلَى *to give a proof* (بَلَآءٌ) *of his prowess in battle*; أَحْسَنَ, أَسَآءَ, *to act well* or *ill*, أَذْنَبَ *to commit a sin*, أَخْطَأَ *to commit a blunder, fault* or *error*, أَصَابَ *to do* or *say what is right*; أَبْطَأَ *to be slow* or B
tardy; أَسْرَعَ *to make haste*; أَعْنَقَ *to run with outstretched neck*; أَسَنَّ *to become fullgrown* (from سِنٌّ *a tooth*); أَقَامَ *to dwell* or *remain in a place*.—Another class of these denominatives indicates movement towards a place (compare "to make for a place"), the entering upon a period of time (being, doing, or suffering something therein), getting into a state or condition, acquiring a quality, obtaining or having something, or becoming something, of a certain kind*.
E.g. أَقْبَلَ *to advance*, أَدْبَرَ *to retire* ("reculer"), أَقْدَمَ *to go on boldly* C
(compare, in Hebrew, הֵימִין, *to go to the right*, and הִשְׂמְאִיל, *to go to the left*); أَشْأَمَ *to go to Syria* (اَلشَّأْمُ), أَيْمَنَ *to go to ĕl-Yèmèn* (اَلْيَمَنُ), أَنْجَدَ *to go to ĕl-Nèǵd* (اَلنَّجْدُ), أَتْهَمَ *to go to Tihāma* (تِهَامَةُ), أَعْرَقَ *to go to ĕl-'Irāḳ* (اَلْعِرَاقُ), أَحْرَمَ *to enter the ḥaram* or *sacred territory*; أَصْبَحَ, أَظْهَرَ, أَمْسَى, *to enter upon the time of morning* (اَلصَّبَاحُ), *mid-day* (اَلظُّهْرُ), or *evening* (اَلْمَسَآءُ); أَصَافَ, أَشْتَى, *to enter upon the summer* (اَلصَّيْفُ) or *winter* (اَلشِّتَآءُ); أَجْمَلَ *to have many* D
camels, أَسْبَعَ *to abound in beasts of prey* or *to have one's flocks devoured by them*, أَضَبَّ *to abound in lizards* (ضَبٌّ) or *to be foggy* (ضَبَابٌ); أَقْفَرَ *to become desert*, أَجْدَبَ *to suffer from drought* (of people) or *to be dry* (of a season), أَفْلَسَ *to become penniless* (*to be*

---

* [Hence in a few cases IV. serves (instead of VII. or VIII.) as the مُطَاوِع of I. Thus كَبَّهُ *he threw him on his face*, أَكَبَّ *he fell on his face*, حَجَمَهُ *he held him back*, أَحْجَمَ *he drew back, he retired*.]

A *reduced to the last farthing,* فَلْسٌ), أَعْدَمَ, أَعْوَزَ, *to be reduced to utter want;* أَغْيَمَ *to become cloudy,* أَخْلَقَ *to become worn out* (of a garment); أَشْكَلَ *to become dubious* or *confused;* أَبَانَ *to become plain* or *clear;* أَمْكَنَ *to become possible.*—Another shade of meaning (اَلسَّلْبُ, deprivation) may be exemplified by such words as أَخْفَرَ, *to break one's compact with a person;* أَشْكَى *to remove one's cause of complaint;* أَعْجَمَ ٱلْكِتَابَ *he pointed* (*the text of*) *the book,* literally,
B *took away its* عُجْمَة, *obscurity* or *want of clearness.*

REM. *d.* أَفْعَلَ corresponds in form and signification to the Heb. הִקְטִיל, Phœn. יקטל (*iḳṭīl*), Aram. אַקְטֵל, ܐܩܛܠ. See *Comp. Gr.* p. 204 *seq.* The Hebrew, it will be observed, has ה as the prefix, instead of the feebler Arabic and Aramaic א. Some traces of the *h* are still discoverable in Arabic; as هَرَاحَ for أَرَاحَ *to give rest to, to let rest;* هَرَادَ for أَرَادَ *to wish;* هَرَاقَ for أَرَاقَ *to pour out*
C (הֵרִיק); هَنَارَ for أَنَارَ *to mark a cloth;* هَاتِ *give,* for آتِ (rad. أَتَى, אָתָה, *to come*); هَيْمَنَ = הֶאֱמִין *to believe.* Forms like هَرَاقَ are treated in Arabic as quadriliterals (see §§ 67, 69, and 118), e.g. imperf. يُهَرِيقُ or يُهْرِيقُ, يُهَيْمِنُ, nom. patient. مُهَرَاقٌ or مُهْرَاقٌ, مُهَيْمَنٌ.

46. The *fifth* form (تَفَعَّلَ) is formed from the second (فَعَّلَ) by prefixing the syllable تَ.

D **47.** This form annexes to the significations of the second the *reflexive* force of the syllable تَ; it is the مُطَاوِعٌ of the second form, that is to say, it expresses the state into which the object of the action denoted by the second form is brought by that action, as its effect or result. In English it must often be rendered by the *passive.* E.g. تَكَسَّرَ *to be broken in pieces,* تَفَرَّقَ *to be dispersed,* تَقَطَّعَ *to be cut in pieces,* تَضَرَّبَ *to be moved* or *agitated;* تَخَوَّفَ *to be afraid* (خَوَّفَ *to terrify*), تَقَلَّدَ سَيْفَهُ *he girt on his sword* (قَلَّدَهُ سَيْفًا *he girt a sword upon him*—another person); تَكَبَّرَ, تَعَظَّمَ, *to be proud;* تَقَيَّسَ, تَنَزَّرَ, *to side*

with Ḳais or *Nizār*, تَزَرَّقَ, تَشَيَّعَ, *to adopt the tenets of the 'Azāriḳa* A
(اَلْأَزَارِقَةُ) or *of the Šī'a* (اَلشِّيعَةُ), تَعَرَّبَ *to call oneself an Arab*, تَهَوَّدَ *to become a Jew* (يَهُودِيٌّ), تَمَجَّسَ *to become a fire-worshipper* (مَجُوسِيٌّ), تَنَصَّرَ *to become a Christian* (نَصْرَانِيٌّ), تَنَبَّأَ *to give oneself out as a prophet* (نَبِيٌّ), تَأَسَّدَ *to become as bold* or *fierce as a lion* (أَسَدٌ), تَنَمَّرَ *to become as savage as a leopard* (نَمِرٌ); تَحَلَّمَ *to try to acquire*, or *to affect, clemency*, تَشَجَّعَ, تَمَرَّأَ, *to affect courage* or *manliness*, B
تَصَبَّرَ *to constrain oneself to endure with patience*; تَأَثَّمَ, تَحَرَّجَ, تَحَوَّبَ, تَحَنَّثَ, *to abstain from*, or *avoid, sin* or *crime*, تَذَمَّمَ *to avoid blame.*

Rem. *a.* The idea of intensiveness may be traced even in cases where it seems, at first sight, to have wholly disappeared, leaving the fifth form apparently identical in meaning with the eighth. Thus تَفَرَّقَ ٱلنَّاسُ and اِفْتَرَقَ ٱلنَّاسُ are both translated *the people dispersed*, but اِفْتَرَقَ expresses the mere separation, تَفَرَّقَ the separation into a great many groups or in various directions. C

Rem. *b.* The idea of reflexiveness is often not very prominent, especially in such verbs as govern an accusative; e.g. تَتَبَّعَ *to pursue step by step* (literally, *to make oneself*, or *turn oneself into*, *a pursuer* of something), تَطَلَّبَ *to seek earnestly*, تَعَرَّفَ *to try to understand*, تَبَيَّنَ *to examine* or *study* a thing *carefully*, so that it may be quite clear, تَيَقَّنَ, تَحَقَّقَ, *to ascertain* a thing *for certain*, تَقَصَّى *to investigate thoroughly*, تَشَمَّمَ *to smell leisurely and carefully*, تَبَصَّرَ *to look at long* or *repeatedly*, *to examine* or *study*, تَسَمَّعَ *to hear* D
or *listen to*, تَكَلَّمَ *to speak*, تَوَلَّى *to have charge of*, *to discharge the duties of*, تَجَرَّعَ *to swallow by mouthfuls*, تَحَسَّى *to sip* or *sup*, تَفَوَّقَ *to milk* or *suck at intervals*, تَعَرَّقَ *to gnaw*, تَأَبَّطَ *to put* or *take under one's arm*, تَوَسَّدَ *to put under one's head as a pillow*, تَدَيَّرَ *to take as an abode*, تَبَنَّى *to adopt as a son**.

---

* [In some cases the difference between II. and V. entirely disappears. Thus for وَجَّهَ, قَوَّسَ (§ 41, rem. *c*) we may substitute تَوَجَّهَ, تَقَوَّسَ without change of sense.]

A REM. *c.* The above examples show that the subject of the fifth form is sometimes the direct object of the act (accusative), sometimes the indirect object (dative).

48. Out of the original reflexive signification arises a second, which is even more common, namely the *effective*. It differs from the passive in this—that the *passive* indicates that a person is the object of, or experiences the effect of, the action of *another;* whereas the *effective* implies that an act is done to a person, or a state produced in him, whether it be caused by *another* or by *himself*. E. g.
B عَلِمَ *to know,* عَلَّمَ *to teach,* تَعَلَّمَ *to become learned, to learn,* quite different from عُلِّمَ (passive of عَلَّمَ) *to be taught.* We can say عُلِّمَ وَلَمْ يَتَعَلَّمْ, *he was taught* (*received instruction*), *but did not learn* (*become learned*)*. Again, بَانَ *to be separate, distinct, clear,* بَيَّنَ *to make clear, explain,* تَبَيَّنَ *to appear clear* or *certain;* تَحَقَّقَ *to become,* or *prove to be, the reality* or *fact.*

REM. *a.* Such of these verbs as govern an accusative admit not
C only of an impersonal, but also of a personal passive; e.g. تَعَلَّمَ ٱلطِّبَّ *he learned the art of medicine,* تُعُلِّمَ ٱلطِّبُّ *the art of medicine was learned.*

REM. *b.* تَفَعَّلَ sometimes assumes the form اِتْفَعَّلَ (§ 111), whence we see its identity with the Heb. הִתְקַטֵּל or הִתְקַטַּל and the Aram. אִתְקְטֵל, ܐܬܩܛܠ (see § 41, rem. *d*).

D **49.** The *sixth* form (تَفَاعَلَ) is formed from the third (فَاعَلَ), likewise by prefixing the syllable تَ.

50. It is the مُطَاوِعٌ (see § 47) of the third form, as بَاعَدْتُهُ فَتَبَاعَدَ, *I kept him aloof and he kept* (or *staid*) *aloof.*—The idea of effort and attempt, which is transitive in the third form, becomes *reflexive* in the sixth; e.g. تَرَامَى *to throw oneself down* at full length, تَغَافَلَ *to be off one's guard, to neglect* a thing, تَبَارَكَ بِٱلشَّيْءِ *to draw a good omen from*

---

* Using a Scoticism, we might say, *he was learned* (= *taught*), *but did not learn.*

the thing, تَمَاوَتَ *to pretend to be dead,* تَعَامَى *to pretend to be blind,* A
تَخَازَرَ *to pretend to squint,* تَبَاكَى *to pretend to cry,* تَمَارَضَ *to feign sickness,* تَجَاهَلَ *to feign ignorance,* تَخَادَعَ *to pretend to be deceived.* Further, the possible reciprocity (اَلْمُشَارَكَةُ) of the third form becomes a *necessary reciprocity,* inasmuch as the sixth form includes the object of the third among the subjects that exercise an influence upon one another; e.g. قَاتَلَهُ *he fought with him,* تَقَاتَلَا *the two fought with one another;* كَالَمَاهُ *the two spoke to him,* تَكَالَمُوا *they* (the three) B
conversed together; جَاذَبَهُ ٱلثَّوْبَ *he tried to pull away the garment from him,* تَجَاذَبَا ٱلثَّوْبَ *the two pulled the garment to and fro between them;* نَازَعَهُمُ ٱلْحَدِيثَ *he conversed* or *argued with them,* تَنَازَعُوا ٱلْحَدِيثَ *they conversed together* or *argued with one another;* نَاسَاهُ ٱلْبَغْضَاءَ *he tried to make him forget the hatred between them,* تَنَاسَيَا ٱلْبَغْضَاءَ *the two forgot their mutual hatred;* whence in the passive, تُجُوذِبَ ٱلثَّوْبُ,
تُنُوزِعَ ٱلْحَدِيثُ, and تُنُوسِيَتِ ٱلْبَغْضَاءُ. C

REM. *a.* When used in speaking of God, the assertory (not optative) perfects تَبَارَكَ and تَعَالَى are examples of the reflexive signification of this form: تَبَارَكَ ٱللّٰهُ *God has made Himself* (*is become of and through Himself*) *blessed,* or *perfect, above all;* تَعَالَى ٱللّٰهُ *God has made Himself uplifted,* or *exalted, above all;* قَالَ ٱللّٰهُ تَبَارَكَ وَتَعَالَى *God* (*blessed and exalted is He above all*) *has said* [cf. vol. ii. § 1 f. rem.]. Somewhat similarly, تَعَاظَمَهُ ٱلْأَمْرُ D
the thing made itself (*became* or *was*) *too great,* or *difficult, for him;* هُوَ أَمْرٌ لَا يَتَعَاظَمُهُ شَيْءٌ *it is a matter than which nothing makes itself greater* (or *more important*), *with which nothing can vie in importance.*

REM. *b.* As the reciprocal signification requires at least two subjects, the singular of the sixth form is in this case always collective; e.g. تَسَامَعَ بِهِ ٱلنَّاسُ *the people heard of it from one another,* تَتَابَعَتِ ٱلْأَمْطَارُ *the rains followed one another closely,* تَدَارَكَتِ ٱلْأَخْبَارُ *the tidings followed one another rapidly,* تَتَامَّتْ إِلَيْهِ

A قُرَيْشٌ *(the tribe of) Koreiš came to him, all of them, following one another.*

REM. *c.* The idea of reciprocity may be confined to the parts of one and the same thing; e.g. تَمَاسَكَ "partes habuit inter se cohærentes," *to be of compact and firm build;* تَعَاوَنَتِ ٱلْمَرْأَةُ *the woman became middle-aged and corpulent* (each part of her body, as it were, supporting, and so strengthening, the others); تَدَاعَى ٱلْبِنَآءُ *the building cracked and threatened to fall* (as if its parts
B *called on one another* to do so; compare تَدَاعَى عَلَيْهِ ٱلْعَدُوُّ *the enemy advanced against him from every side,* تَدَاعَتِ ٱلسَّحَابَةُ بِٱلْبَرْقِ وَٱلرَّعْدِ *the cloud lightened and thundered from every quarter*). [Hence this form is appropriate to actions that take place bit by bit, or by successive (and painful) efforts, as تَسَاقَطَ *to fall piece by piece,* تَحَامَلَ *to carry oneself with difficulty* (فِي ٱلْمَشْيِ, *in walking**).]

C REM. *d.* تَفَاعَلَ sometimes assumes the form اِتْفَاعَلَ (§ 111), and is consequently identical with the Heb. הִתְקוֹטֵל (see § 43, rem. *b*).

51. The *seventh* form (اِنْفَعَلَ) is formed from the first (فَعَلَ) by prefixing a ن, before which is added a prosthetic ا to facilitate the pronunciation (see § 26).

REM. For the cases in which this ا becomes آ, and why, see §§ 18 and 19, *c*, with rem. *c*; and as to the orthography إ instead of اِ, § 19, rem. *d*.

D **52.** The seventh form has also originally, as مُطَاوِعٌ of the first, a *middle* or *reflexive* signification. It must be remarked, however, (*a*) that the reflexive pronoun contained in it is never the indirect object (dative), to which may be added another direct object (accusative), but always the direct object itself; and (*b*) that it never assumes the reciprocal signification. By these two points the seventh form is distinguished from the eighth, and approaches more nearly

* [See *Gl. Geog. s.v.* حمل, *Ḥamāsa* p. 20 first vs. and comm.—De G.]

to a passive. At the same time, the *effective* signification is often A developed in it out of the reflexive. E. g. اِنْشَقَّ *to open* (of a flower), lit. *to split itself;* اِنْكَسَرَ *to break* (intrans.), *to be broken;* اِنْقَطَعَ *to be cut off, to be ended, to end;* اِنْكَشَفَ *to be uncovered, to be made manifest, to appear;* اِنْحَطَمَ *to become broken, to break into pieces;* اِنْقَالَ *to be uttered* or *spoken.*

53. Sometimes the seventh form implies that a person allows B an act to be done in reference to him, or an effect to be produced upon him; e.g. اِنْهَزَمَ *to let oneself be put to flight, to flee;* اِنْقَادَ *to let oneself be led, to be docile* or *submissive;* اِنْخَدَعَ *to let oneself be deceived;* اِنْجَرَّ *to let oneself be drawn* or *dragged.*

Rem. *a.* Hence it is clear that such words as اِنْحَمَقَ, from حَمُقَ, *to be stupid* or *foolish;* اِنْعَدَمَ *to be non-existent* or *missing, not to be found,* from عَدِمَ *not to have;* اِنْهَوَى, from هَوَى *to sink* C *down, to fall;* اِنْعَادَ *to be repeated,* from عَادَ *to return;* اِنْضَاقَ *to be in straits* or *distress,* from ضَاقَ *to be narrow;* are incorrectly formed, though in actual use, especially in more recent times.

Rem. *b.* Sometimes, particularly in modern Arabic, the seventh form serves as the مُطَاوِعٌ of the fourth; e.g. اِنْغَلَقَ *to be bolted,* from أَغْلَقَ *to bolt;* اِنْطَفَأَ *to be extinguished,* from أَطْفَأَ *to extinguish;* اِنْصَلَحَ *to be put to rights,* from أَصْلَحَ *to put to rights.* [Similarly D اِنْزَعَجَ, اِنْطَلَقَ, اِنْضَجَعَ, the last in a tradition, and so ancient, *Fāiḳ* i. 63.—De G.]

Rem. *c.* اِنْفَعَلَ corresponds to the Heb. נִקְטַל; see *Comp. Gr.* p. 215 *seq.*

54. The eighth form (اِفْتَعَلَ) is formed from the first (فَعَلَ) by inserting the syllable تَ between the first and second radicals. The first radical in consequence loses its vowel, and it becomes necessary to prefix the prosthetic ا (§ 51, rem.).

A REM. One would expect تَ to be placed *before* the first radical, as in the fifth and sixth forms, and in the Aramaic reflexive ܐܶܬ݂ܩܛܶܠ. [For a possible explanation of the actual form see *Comp. Gr.* p. 208.]

55. The eighth form is properly the *reflexive* or *middle voice* (مُطَاوِعٌ) of the first. The reflex object is either (*a*) the direct object or accusative, as فَرَقَ *to divide*, اِفْتَرَقَ *to go asunder, to part;* عَرَضَ *to place* (*something*) *before one*, اِعْتَرَضَ *to put oneself in the way, to oppose;*
B ضَرَبَ *to beat*, اِضْطَرَبَ *to move oneself to and fro, to be agitated* (compare the French *battre* and *se débattre*); or (*b*) the indirect object or dative, implying *for oneself, for one's own advantage*, as فَرَسَ *to tear a prey in pieces*, اِفْتَرَسَ *do.;* لَمَسَ *to touch*, اِلْتَمَسَ *to feel about for a thing, to seek for it;* كَسَبَ and اِكْتَسَبَ *to earn one's living;* حَطَبَ and اِحْتَطَبَ *to collect firewood;* كَالَ and اِكْتَالَ *to measure* corn; شَوَى and اِشْتَوَى *to roast* meat.

C **56.** Out of the reflexive arises the *reciprocal* signification, which is common to this form with the sixth; as اِقْتَتَلَ ٱلنَّاسُ *the people fought with one another*, = تَقَاتَلَ ٱلنَّاسُ; اِخْتَصَمَا *the two disputed with one another*, = تَخَاصَمَا; اِسْتَبَقَا *the two tried to outrun one another*, = تَسَابَقَا; اِجْتَوَرُوا *they were neighbours*, = تَجَاوَرُوا; اِلْتَقَوْا *they met one another*, = تَلَاقَوْا.

D **57.** Occasionally the original reflexive meaning passes into the *passive*, especially in verbs which have not got the seventh form (see § 113); as اِيتَفَكَ *to be overturned* (from أَفَكَ), اِرْتَدَعَ *to be turned back*, اِنْتَصَرَ *to be helped* (*by God*), *to be victorious;* اِمْتَلَأَ *to be full.*

REM. In not a few verbs the first and eighth forms agree, like the Greek active and middle voices, so closely in their signification, that they may be translated by the same word; e.g. قَصَّ and اِقْتَصَّ, *to follow one's track, to relate;* قَفَا and اِقْتَفَى, *to follow;* خَطِفَ and اِخْتَطَفَ, *to snatch away, to carry off by force.*

58. The *ninth* form (اِفْعَلَّ) is formed from the first (فَعَلَ) by A
doubling the third radical; the eleventh (اِفْعَالَّ) from the ninth by lengthening the fĕtḥa of the second syllable.

Rem. As the third radical, when doubled, draws the accent upon the penult, the first radical, being more rapidly pronounced, loses its vowel, and therefore requires the prosthetic ا (see § 51, rem.).

59. Neither of these forms is very common, and the eleventh
is the rarer of the two. They serve chiefly to express *colours* and B
defects, these being qualities that cling very firmly to persons and things; and hence the doubling of the third radical, to show that the proper signification of both is *intensiveness* (اَلْمُبَالَغَةُ). E.g. اِصْفَرَّ and اِصْفَارَّ *to be yellow;* اِسْوَدَّ and اِسْوَادَّ *to be black;* اِبْيَضَّ and اِبْيَاضَّ *to be white;* اِيرَاقَّ (from وَرَقَ) *to become purple* (of a grape); اِعْوَجَّ and اِعْوَاجَّ *to be crooked;* اِضْجَمَّ and اِضْجَامَّ *to be wrymouthed* or *wry-necked;* اِحْوَلَّ *to squint,* اِحْوَالَّ *to become verdant;* اِزْوَرَّ and اِزْوَارَّ *to*
turn away or *retire from;* اِرْبَدَّ *to be ash-coloured, to be stern* or *gloomy;* C
اِرْبَثَّ or اِرْبَاثَّ *to be scattered* or *disordered;* اِرْغَادَّ *to become commingled, confused,* or *languid;* اِرْفَضَّ *to be dispersed, to drop* or *flow* (of tears), اِرْقَدَّ *to run quickly, to hasten;* اِشْعَانَّ *to be dishevelled* (of hair); اِبْهَارَّ ٱللَّيْلُ, *the night reached its middle point.*

Rem. *a.* If the third radical of the root is و or ى, the ninth and eleventh forms take the shape اِفْعَلَلَ and اِفْعَالَلَ; as اِجْذَوَى
(for اِجْذَوَوَ, see § 167, 2, *a*) *to stand* or *rest on the tips of the toes,* D
اِحْوَوَى and اِحْوَاوَى *to be blackish brown* or *blackish green,* اِرْعَوَى *to refrain* or *abstain.*

Rem. *b.* According to some grammarians, the distinction between the ninth and eleventh forms is, that the ninth indicates permanent colours or qualities, the eleventh those that are transitory or mutable; as جَعَلَ يَحْمَارُّ تَارَةً وَيَصْفَارُّ أُخْرَى, *it began to become red at one time and yellow at another.* [Others hold that XI. indicates a

A higher degree of the quality than IX.: so most European grammarians, and the former editions of this work; but this view was ultimately abandoned by the author. The better view seems to be that the two forms are indistinguishable in sense: see Ḥafāġī's comm. on the *Durrat al-ġawwāṣ* (Const. A. H. 1299) p. 50 *seq.*]

60. The *tenth* form (اِسْتَفْعَلَ) is formed by prefixing the letters ست to the first (فَعَلَ). The prosthetic ا is necessary, according to § 26 (compare § 51, rem.), and the fètḥa of the first radical is thrown

B back upon the ت of اِسْتَ.

61. The tenth form converts the factitive signification of the *fourth* into the *reflexive* or *middle*. E.g. أَسْلَمَ *to give up, deliver over,* اِسْتَسْلَمَ *to give oneself up;* أَوْحَشَ *to grieve* or *distress,* اِسْتَوْحَشَ *to be grieved* or *sorry;* أَعَدَّ *to make ready, prepare, equip,* اِسْتَعَدَّ *to get oneself ready, to be ready;* أَخْلَصَ *to yield up (something) wholly,* اِسْتَخْلَصَ *to claim (something) for oneself, to take entire possession (of it);* أَحْيَا *to bring to life, to preserve alive,* اِسْتَحْيَا *to preserve alive*

C for one's own advantage; اِسْتَجَابَ دُعَاءَهُ *He* (God) *answered,* or *accepted, his prayer,* اِسْتَجَابَ لَهُ *he complied with his desire,* or *obeyed him,* in doing something.

62. The tenth form often indicates that a person thinks that a certain thing possesses, in reference to himself or for his benefit, the quality expressed by the first form. E.g. حَلَّ *to be lawful,* اِسْتَحَلَّ *he thought that it was lawful* (for himself to do); وَجَبَ *to be necessary,* اِسْتَوْجَبَ *he thought it was necessary* (for him);

D اِسْتَحْسَنَ *to think him,* or *it, good* or *beautiful;* اِسْتَجَادَ *to think it good* or *excellent;* اِسْتَخَفَّ *to think it light, to think lightly of,* or *despise, one;* اِسْتَثْقَلَ *to find it heavy, oppressive* or *troublesome, to think one a bore.*

REM. In this case the factitive is combined with the middle sense; for as the fourth form (like the second) is frequently not

strictly factitive, but estimative or declarative (§ 45, rem. *b*), so A
also the tenth. Hence اِسْتَوْجَبَ literally means *to make something necessary for oneself, to think it so* or *say it is so*; but أَوْجَبَ *to make it necessary for others, to think* or *say that it is so.*

63. The tenth form likewise often expresses the *taking, seeking, asking for*, or *demanding*, what is meant by the *first.* E.g. غَفَرَ *to pardon*, اِسْتَغْفَرَ *to ask pardon*; سَقَى *to give one to drink*, اِسْتَسْقَى *to ask for something to drink, to pray for rain*; أَذِنَ *to permit*,
اِسْتَأْذَنَ *to ask permission*; غَاثَ *to help*, اِسْتَغَاثَ *to call for help*; B
حَضَرَ *to be present*, اِسْتَحْضَرَ *to require one's presence, to desire that he should be fetched.*

Rem. This signification is also a combination of the factitive and middle: *to procure a drink, permission, &c., for oneself.*

64. In many verbs the tenth form has apparently a *neuter* sense, but in such cases a more minute examination shows that it was, at least originally, reflexive. E.g. اِسْتَقَامَ *to stand upright*,
lit. *to hold oneself upright*; اِسْتَكَانَ *to be humble*, lit. *to make oneself* C
humble, to conduct oneself humbly; اِسْتَحَقَّ *to be worthy of, to deserve*, lit. *to cause something to be due to oneself as a right* or *desert* (حَقٌّ); اِسْتَحْيَا *to be ashamed*, lit. *to make oneself ashamed* (حَيِىَ *to be ashamed*).

65. The tenth form is frequently *denominative*, in which case it unites the factitive and reflexive or middle senses. E.g. اِسْتَوْلَى
to make oneself master (وَلِىٌّ) *of a thing, to take possession of it*; D
اِسْتَخْلَفَ *to appoint one as deputy, successor*, or *caliph* (خَلِيفَةٌ); اِسْتَوْزَرَ, اِسْتَعْمَلَ, اِسْتَقْضَى, *to appoint one as wĕzīr* (وَزِيرٌ), *governor* (عَامِلٌ), or *judge* (قَاضٍ).—Further, اِسْتَحْجَرَ *to become like* (lit. *to make itself like*) *stone* (حَجَرٌ); اِسْتَتْيَسَتِ ٱلْعَنْزُ *the she-goat became like a he-goat* (تَيْسٌ); اِسْتَنْوَقَ ٱلْجَمَلُ *the he-camel became like a she-camel* (نَاقَةٌ);

A إِنَّ ٱلْبُغَاثَ بِأَرْضِنَا يَسْتَنْسِرُ *the kite in our country becomes a vulture* (نَسْرٌ, *our geese are all swans*).

REM. The tenth form is probably the reflexive of a form سَفْعَلَ, which is not in use, corresponding to the Aram. שַׁקְטֵל, ܫܰܩܛܶܠ, and its passive אִשְׁתַּקְטַל, ܐܶܫܬܰܩܛܰܠ, which stand in exactly the same relation to one another as the Arabic first and eighth. Perhaps سَلْقَى *to throw down flat on the back,* سَقْلَبَ *to dash to the ground,* and سَلْعَفَ *to swallow,* with one or two more, may be
B regarded as traces of the form سَفْعَلَ, since they are nearly identical in meaning with أَلْقَى, أَقْلَبَ, and أَلْعَفَ (IV. of لَقِيَ, قَلَبَ, and لعف). If so, سَلَقَ, which has the same signification as سَلْقَى, must be a later triliteral formation.

66. Of the remaining forms of the triliteral verb it may be sufficient to give a few examples, so as to exhibit their mode of formation.—XII. اِجْذَوْذَى *to bear oneself erect* (جَذَا *do.*); اِحْدَوْدَبَ *to be arched, curved,* or *humpbacked* (حَدِبَ *do.*); اِحْلَوْلَكَ *to be jet*
C *black* (حَلَكَ *do.*); اِحْلَوْلَى *to be sweet* (حَلُوَ *do.*); اِخْشَوْشَنَ *to become very rough* (خَشُنَ *to be rough*); اِخْضَوْضَرَ *to become blackish brown* or *blackish green* (=اِخْضَرَّ), *to become soft* or *tender* (خَضِرَ *do.*); اِخْضَوْضَلَ *to become moist* (=اِخْضَلَّ); اِعْرَوْرَى *to ride on a horse without a saddle* (عَرِىَ *to be naked*); اِعْشَوْشَبَ *to be covered with luxuriant herbage* (عُشْبٌ); اِعْصَوْصَبَ *to be gathered together* (عَصَبَ
D *to bind*); اِغْدَوْدَنَ *to be green and rank* (of a plant), *to be long and thick* (of the hair).—XIII. اِخْرَوَّطَ *to be long* or *last long, to go quickly* (rad. خرط); اِجْلَوَّذَ *to last long* (rad. جلذ); اِعْلَوَّدَ *to be heavy* (عَلِدَ *to be hard*); اِعْلَوَّطَ *to cling* or *adhere to firmly, to mount a camel* (rad. علط).—XIV. اِجْحَنْشَشَ *to be big* (rad. جحش); اِسْحَنْكَكَ *to be dark, to be obscure* (rad. سحك); اِحْلَنْكَكَ *to be jet black* (حَلِكَ *do.*);

اِعْلَنْكَكَ *to be long and thick* (of the hair, rad. علك); اِعْفَنْجَجَ *to go* A *quickly* (rad. عفج); اِقْعَنْسَسَ *to have a hump in front* (the reverse of اِحْدَوْدَبَ, قَعِسَ *do.*).—XV. اِعْلَنْدَى *to be stout and strong* (عَلِدَ *to be hard*); اِحْبَنْطَى *to be swollen* or *inflated, to be filled with rage* (حَبِطَ *do.*).

Rem. All these forms are habitually intransitive, but there are a few exceptions, as XII. اِعْرَوْرَى ٱلْفَرَسَ *he mounted the horse;* B اِحْلَوْلَاهُ *he found it sweet* (but also اِحْلَوْلَى, *it was sweet*).—XV. عَلَوْتُهُ = اِسْرَنْدَيْتُهُ Ibn Doraid, *Kit. al-Iśtiḳāḳ*, p. 227.

2. *The Quadriliteral Verb and its Forms.*

67. Quadriliteral (رُبَاعِىٌّ) verbs are formed in the following ways.

(*a*) A biliteral root, expressing a sound or movement, is repeated, to indicate the repetition of that sound or movement. E.g. بَأْبَأَ *to* C *say baba* (*papa*), غَرْغَرَ *to gargle*, وَسْوَسَ *to whisper*, زَلْزَلَ *to shake*, حَمْحَمَ *to neigh*, غَمْغَمَ *to bellow, to shout*, خَشْخَشَ *to make rustle* or *rattle.*

(*b*) A fourth letter, generally a liquid or sibilant, is prefixed or affixed to, or inserted in the middle of, a triliteral verbal form. E.g. شَمْخَرَ *to be proud* (شَمَخَ *to be high*); شَمْعَلَ *to be scattered* = شَمَعَ; جَمْهَرَ *to collect* (compare جَمَّ and جَمَعَ); زَحْلَفَ *to roll along* D (زَحَفَ *to advance slowly*), *to drive back* (زَحَلَ *to withdraw, to retire*); سَنْبَسَ *to hasten* (perhaps connected with نَبَسَ); خَلْبَسَ *to deceive with soft words* = خَلَبَ; جَلْمَطَ *to shave* the head = جَلَطَ; زَحْوَلَ *to make retire* (زَحَلَ *to retire*).

(*c*) They are denominatives from nouns of more than three letters, some of them foreign words. E.g. جَوْرَبَ *to put stockings* (جَوْرَبٌ, Pers. كُورَبْ) *on one;* جَلْبَبَ *to put on one the garment called a* جِلْبَابٌ; قَلْسَى and قَلْنَسَ *to put on one the cap called a* قَلَنْسُوَةٌ;

A قَطْرَنَ *to pitch*, from قَطِرَانٌ *pitch;* تَمَنْطَقَ *to put on a girdle* (مِنْطَقَةٌ); تَسَرْوَلَ *to put on trousers* or *drawers* (سَرَاوِيلُ, Pers. شَلْوَارْ); تَمَدْرَعَ *to wear a* مِدْرَعَةٌ or *tunic;* تَمَنْدَلَ *to wipe one's fingers with a napkin* (مَنْدِيلٌ *mantile*); تَمَسْكَنَ *to affect lowliness* or *humility, to abase oneself* (مِسْكِينٌ *lowly, humble, poor*); تَمَذْهَبَ *to follow a sect* (مَذْهَبٌ); تَمَعْدَدَ *to assimilate oneself (in dress,* etc.) *to the tribe of Ma'add*
B (مَعَدٌّ); تَلْمَذَ *to become a pupil* or *disciple* (تِلْمِيذٌ, Heb. תַּלְמִיד); تَفَلْسَفَ *to philosophize* (from فَيْلَسُوفٌ, φιλόσοφος); بَيْطَرَ *to practise the veterinary art* or *farriery* (بَيْطَارٌ *a farrier,* ἱππίατρος).

(*d*) They are combinations of the most prominent syllables or letters in certain very common formulas. E.g. بَسْمَلَ *to say* بِسْمِ ٱللّٰهِ (*in the name of God*); حَمْدَلَ *to say* اَلْحَمْدُ لِلّٰهِ (*praise belongs to God*); حَوْلَقَ and حَوْقَلَ *to say* لَا حَوْلَ وَلَا قُوَّةَ إِلَّا بِٱللّٰهِ (*there is no*
C *power and no strength save in God*); فَذْلَكَ *to cast up an account,* saying فَذْلِكَ كَذَا وَكَذَا *this then is so and so much.*

68. The derived forms of the quadriliteral verb are three in number.

فَعْلَلَ I.

اِفْعَلَلَّ IV. اِفْعَنْلَلَ III. تَفَعْلَلَ II.

69. The *first* form of the quadriliterals corresponds in formation and conjugation to the *second* form of the triliterals, and is both
D transitive and intransitive in signification. E.g. شَمْلَلَ *to gather ripe dates,* also *to be active* or *nimble;* شَمْرَخَ *to pluck unripe dates;* دَحْرَجَ *to roll;* زَهْزَقَ *to laugh much;* هَرْوَلَ *to run quickly.*

70. The *second* form agrees in formation and signification with the *fifth* of the triliteral verb. E.g. تَجَلْبَبَ *to put on* or *wear a* جِلْبَابٌ; تَدَحْرَجَ *to roll along;* تَسَلْطَنَ *to make oneself sultan* (سُلْطَانٌ), *to act as if one were sultan, to lord it over another;* تَشَيْطَنَ *to act like a devil* (شَيْطَانٌ, שָׂטָן), تَعَفْرَتَ *id.* from عِفْرِيتٌ.

71. The *third* form of the quadriliteral verb corresponds to the *seventh* of the triliteral, with this difference, that the characteristic ن is not prefixed, but inserted between the second and third radicals. E.g. اِبْرَنْشَقَ *to open* (of a flower), *to bloom* or *flourish*; اِحْرَنْجَمَ *to be gathered together in a mass* or *crowd*; اِحْوَنْصَلَ *to puff out its crop* (حَوْصَلَةٌ, of a bird); اِسْلَنْطَحَ *to lie on one's face, stretched on the ground*; اِسْلَنْقَى *to lie on one's back*; اِثْعَنْجَرَ *to flow.* A

72. The *fourth* form of the quadriliterals, which answers to the *ninth* of the triliterals, is intransitive, and expresses an extensively or intensively high degree of an intransitive act, state, or quality. E.g. اِدْلَهَمَّ *to be very dark*; اِشْمَخَرَّ *to be very high* or *proud*; اِضْمَحَلَّ *to vanish away*; اِسْبَطَرَّ *to lie stretched out on one's side*; اِشْمَعَلَّ *to make haste, to be scattered* or *dispersed*; اِبْذَعَرَّ *to be scattered* or *dispersed*; اِقْشَعَرَّ and اِشْمَأَزَّ *to shudder with horror*; اِطْمَأَنَّ *to be at rest* (from طَمْأَنَ *to lean back*); اِحْزَأَلَّ *to rise high*; اِشْرَأَبَّ *to raise the head and stretch out the neck*; اِصْمَأَلَّ *to be very hard.* B C

3. *The Voices.*

73. All the verbal forms, both primitive and derivative, have two voices, the *active* and the *passive*; with the exception of intransitive verbs of the form فَعُلَ (§ 38) and of the 9th, 11th, 12th, 13th, 14th, and 15th forms (cf. § 66, rem.) as well as of those verbs of the forms فَعِلَ and فَعَلَ, which designate not an act (transitive or intransitive) but a state or condition (being or becoming), as خَضِرَ *to become green*, nearly = اِخْضَرَّ or اِخْضَوْضَرَ; صَلَحَ *to be good, right, in order*, = صَلُحَ; فَسَدَ *to be bad, wrong, in disorder*, = فَسُدَ. The subject of the active voice is always an agent (person or thing), whose act may affect an object, or not; the subject of the passive voice is either the object of the former (personal passive), or the abstract idea of the act (impersonal passive). D

A **74.** The passive is especially used in four cases; namely (*a*) when God, or some higher being, is indicated as the author of the act; (*b*) when the author is unknown, or at least not known for certain; (*c*) when the speaker or writer does not wish to name him; (*d*) when the attention of the hearer or reader is directed more to the person affected by the act (patiens, the patient), than to the doer of it (agens, the agent).

REM. The active voice is called by the Arab grammarians
B صِيغَةُ ٱلْفَاعِلِ *the mould* or *form of the agent*, بِنَآءُ ٱلْفَاعِلِ *the build of the agent*, بَابُ ٱلْفَاعِلِ *the category of the agent*, فِعْلُ ٱلْفَاعِلِ *the action of the agent*, and ٱلْفِعْلُ ٱلْمَبْنِىُّ (ٱلْمَصُوغُ) لِلْفَاعِلِ, or عَلَى ٱلْفَاعِلِ, *the action* (or *verb*) *put into that form of which the agent is the subject.* The passive voice is in like manner called صِيغَةُ ٱلْمَفْعُولِ *the mould* or *form of the patient*, etc.; also فِعْلُ مَا لَمْ يُسَمَّ
C فَاعِلُهُ *the doing*, or *being done*, *of that, whereof the agent has not been named*, or, more shortly, مَا لَمْ يُسَمَّ فَاعِلُهُ, though this latter is, strictly speaking, equivalent to ٱلْمَفْعُولُ ٱلَّذِى لَمْ يُسَمَّ فَاعِلُهُ, *the patient whereof the agent has not been named*, i.e. the passive subject. The active voice is also shortly called ٱلْمَعْرُوفُ or ٱلْمَعْلُومُ, and the passive ٱلْمَجْهُولُ, elliptical forms of expression for ٱلْفِعْلُ ٱلْمَعْرُوفُ (ٱلْمَعْلُومُ) فَاعِلُهُ, *the action of which the agent is known*,
D and ٱلْفِعْلُ ٱلْمَجْهُولُ فَاعِلُهُ, *the action of which the agent is unknown.* These terms, ٱلْمَعْرُوفُ or ٱلْمَعْلُومُ and ٱلْمَجْهُولُ, are also used to designate the subjects of the active and passive voices.

75. Verbs that express a state or condition, or signify an act which is, by its very nature, confined to the person of the subject, and cannot pass to another individual as its object (as مَرِضَ *to be sick*, نَامَ *to sleep*), are aptly called *neuter* verbs, since they are neither really active nor really passive, but something between the two. The Arab grammarians cannot class them otherwise than among the active verbs,

and they therefore distinguish اَلْأَفْعَالُ ٱلْمُتَعَدِّيَةُ, *transitive verbs*, from A
اَلْأَفْعَالُ غَيْرُ ٱلْمُتَعَدِّيَةِ, *intransitive verbs*, or اَلْأَفْعَالُ ٱللَّازِمَةُ, *verbs that are confined to the subject.*

• **76.** The idea of the passive voice must not be thought to be absolutely identical with that of the fifth, seventh, and eighth forms. These are, strictly speaking, *effective* (see § 48), whilst the other is *purely passive.*

4. *The States (Tenses) of the Verb.*

77. The temporal forms of the Arabic verb are but *two* in B
number, the one expressing a *finished* act, one that is done and completed in relation to other acts (the *Perfect*); the other an *unfinished* act, one that is just commencing or in progress (the *Imperfect*).

Rem. *a.* The names *Preterite* and *Future*, by which these forms were often designated in older grammars do not accurately correspond to the ideas inherent in them. A Semitic Perfect or
Imperfect has, in and of itself, no reference to the temporal C
relations of the speaker (thinker or writer) and of other actions which are brought into juxtaposition with it. It is precisely these relations which determine in what sphere of time (past, present, or future) a Semitic Perfect or Imperfect lies, and by which of our tenses it is to be expressed—whether by our Past, Perfect, Pluperfect, or Future-perfect; by our Present, Imperfect, or Future. The Arabian Grammarians themselves have not, however, succeeded in keeping this important point distinctly in view, but have given an undue importance to the idea of time, in connection with the verbal forms, by their division of it into the past (اَلْمَاضِى), the
present (اَلْحَالُ or اَلْحَاضِرُ), and the future (اَلْمُسْتَقْبَلُ), the first of D
which they assign to the Perfect and the other two to the Imperfect.

Rem. *b.* On the forms of these tenses see § 91 etc. The Syntax will give more precise information as to their meaning and use.

5. *The Moods.*

78. The Arabic verb has *five* moods; namely, the Indicative, Subjunctive, Jussive or Conditional, Imperative, and Energetic.

A **79.** Of these moods the first is common to the perfect and imperfect states; the second and third are restricted to the imperfect; the fourth, or imperative, is expressed by a special form; and the fifth can be derived not only from the imperfect, but also from the imperative.

REM. On the forms of the moods see § 91 etc. The Syntax treats of their significations and use.

80. Instead of the Infinitive, the Arabs use *nouns expressing the*
B *action or quality* (nomina actionis or verbi). In place of participles, they have two *verbal adjectives*, the one denoting the *agent* (nomen agentis, active participle), and the other the *patient* (nomen patientis, passive participle). [Cf. § 192.]

6. *The Numbers, Persons, and Genders.*

81. There are three numbers, the *Singular* (اَلْفَرْدُ, اَلْمُفْرَدُ, or اَلْوَاحِدُ), the *Dual* (اَلتَّثْنِيَةُ or اَلْمُثَنَّى), and the *Plural* (اَلْجَمْعُ, اَلْجِمَاعُ,
C اَلْجَمِيعُ, اَلْمَجْمُوعُ, or اَلْمُكَثَّرُ); and likewise three persons, the *speaker* (first person), اَلْمُتَكَلِّمُ, the individual *spoken to* (second person), اَلْمُخَاطَبُ, and the individual *spoken of* (third person), اَلْغَائِبُ (*the absent*). The genders are two, namely the *masculine* (اَلْمُذَكَّرُ) and the *feminine* (اَلْمُؤَنَّثُ); but they are not distinguished from one another in some of the persons (1st pers. sing., 2d pers. dual, and 1st pers. plur.).

D
B. THE STRONG VERB (VERBUM FIRMUM).

82. Verbs are divided into *strong* (verba firma) and *weak* (verba infirma). We include the verba mediæ radicalis geminatæ (ע״ע) in the former class; the verbs which have أ for one of their radicals, in the second (see § 128).

83. Strong verbs are those of which all the radical letters are *strong*, and consequently neither undergo any change, nor are rejected in any of the inflexions, but are retained throughout.

Rem. A verb which contains one of the two letters و or ى is called فِعْلٌ مُعْتَلٌّ, *a weak verb*, as opposed to فِعْلٌ سَالِمٌ, *a verb that is free from defect, a sound verb*. A verb which has أ for one of its radicals, or which belongs to the class med. rad. gemin. (ע״ע), is designated by the special term فِعْلٌ صَحِيحٌ; but some grammarians treat صَحِيحٌ and سَالِمٌ as synonyms. A

1. *The Active Voice of the First Form in the Strong Verb.—Table I.** B

a. THE INFLEXION BY PERSONS.

84. The numbers, persons, and genders of the verb are expressed by means of personal pronouns, annexed to the various moods and tenses.

85. The personal pronoun [ضَمِيرٌ, مُضْمَرٌ: see § 190, *f.*] is either *separate* [مُنْفَصِلٌ], standing by itself, or *connected* [مُتَّصِلٌ], that is *prefixed* or *suffixed*. The separate pronouns have longer, the connected shorter forms. C

86. The *suffixed* pronouns are partly *verbal*, partly *nominal* suffixes.

87. The *verbal* suffixes express partly the *nominative*, partly the *accusative*. The former are much more closely united with the verb than the latter.

88. The connected pronouns which express the *nominative* to the verb are also in part *prefixes*. D

Rem. On the verbal suffixes which express the *accusative* see § 185; and on the *nominal* suffixes, § 317.

89. The following tables give a general view of the *separate* personal pronouns, and of those pronominal prefixes and suffixes which express the *nominative* to the verb.

---

* The *nomina verbi, agentis*, and *patientis*, are given along with the strictly verbal forms in all the Tables.

A

1. *Separate Pronouns.*

Singular.

	Masc.	Common	Fem.
3 p.	هُوَ *he.*	...	هِيَ *she.*
2 p.	أَنْتَ *thou.*	...	أَنْتِ *thou.*
1 p.	...	أَنَا *I.*	...

B

Dual.

	Masc.	Common	Fem.
3 p.	...	هُمَا *they two.*	...
2 p.	...	أَنْتُمَا *ye two.*	...
1 p.	...	...	...

Plural.

	Masc.	Common	Fem.
3 p.	هُمْ *they.*	...	هُنَّ *they.*
2 p.	أَنْتُمْ *ye.*	...	أَنْتُنَّ *ye.*
C 1 p.	...	نَحْنُ *we.*	...

REM. *a.* When هُوَ and هِيَ are preceded by the conjunctions وَ and فَ, *and*, the affirmative لَ, *certainly, surely*, or the interrogative أَ, the vowel of the ه may either be dropped or retained; as وَهُوَ or وَهْوَ, فَهِيَ or فَهْيَ, لَهُوَ or لَهْوَ, أَهِيَ or أَهْيَ.

REM. *b.* The second syllable of أَنَا is regarded as short by the
D old poets (⏑⏑), except in pause, where we find both أَنَا (⏑–) and أَنَهْ*. Compare the Æthiopic *ănă*, which, in combination with the enclitic particle *să*, becomes *ănsă*. أَنَا is, therefore, an example of *scriptio plena*, to distinguish the pronoun from the particles أَنْ, أَنَّ, إِنْ, إِنَّ. The *scriptio defectiva* is found, for example, in the interjectional هَأَنَذَا or هَاأَنَذَا *here I am* (הִנְנִי, *eccome*), for هَا أَنَا ذَا. The form أَنْ is said also to occur.

---

* But أَنَا, out of pause, is occasionally scanned as an iambus even in old poetry. See Nöldeke in *ZDMG.* xxxviii. 418, note 3.

Rem. *c.* Older forms of هُمْ and أَنْتُمْ are هُمُ and أَنْتُمُ, used in poetry, and also in the *waṣl* (§ 20, *d*, and § 23, rem. *c*). [Though written defectively this terminal *u* is commonly scanned as a long vowel.] A

Rem. *d.* For a comparison of the pronominal forms of the Arabic with those of the other Semitic languages see *Comp. Gr.* p. 95 *seq.*

2. *Suffixed Pronouns, expressing the Nominative.* B

Singular.

	Masc.	Common	Fem.
3 p.	. . .	. . .	ـَتْ *she.*
2 p.	تَ *thou.*	. . .	تِ (ـِى, ـِينَ) *thou.*
1 p.	. . .	تُ *I.*	. . .

Dual.

	Masc.	Common	Fem.
3 p.	ـَا (ـَانِ, ـَا) *they two.*	. . .	ـَتَا (ـَانِ, ـَا) *they two.*
2 p.	. . .	تُمَا (ـَانِ, ـَا) *ye two.*	. . .	C
1 p.	. . .	. . .	. . .

Plural.

	Masc.	Common	Fem.
3 p.	ـُوا (ـُونَ, ـُوا) *they.*	. . .	نَ *they.*
2 p.	تُمْ (ـُونَ, ـُوا) *ye.*	. . .	تُنَّ (نَ) *ye.*
1 p.	. . .	نَا *we.*	. . .

Rem. *a.* The forms within brackets are those of the Imperfect and Imperative; the others those of the Perfect.

Rem. *b.* The suffix of the 1st pers. plur. is sometimes shortened in poetry (*nă*) and written defectively, نَ. D

3. *Prefixed Pronouns, expressing the Nominative.*

Singular

	Masc.	Common.	Fem.
3 p.	يَ *he.*	. . .	تَ *she.*
2 p.	. . .	تَ *thou.*	. . .
1 p.	. . .	أَ *I.*	. . .

A *Dual.*

	Masc.	Common.	Fem.
3 p.	ى *they two.*	. . .	ت *they two.*
2 p.	. . .	ت *ye two.*	. . .
1 p.	. . .	. . .	. . .

Plural.

3 p.	. . .	ى *they.*	. . .
2 p.	. . .	ت *ye.*	. . .
1 p.	. . .	ن *we.*	. . .

B REM. *a.* These forms are restricted to the Imperfect. They are called by the grammarians حُرُوفُ ٱلْمُضَارَعَةِ, and are comprised in the mnemonic word أَنَيْتُ or نَأْتِى.

REM. *b.* The prefix of the third person plural of the Imperfect is ى for both genders. But the grammarians cite some rare cases where, in the fem., ى is replaced by ت, so that the distinction between 3 pl. fem. and 2 pl. fem. is lost. Thus in the Ḳor'ān, Sūra xlii. 3, a reading تَتَفَطَّرْنَ for يَتَفَطَّرْنَ is recorded. This must be
C explained as due to false analogy from the sing. In the Heb. תִּקְטֹלְנָה the false form has become the rule.

90. Of the two fĕtḥas with which the first and third radicals of a verb are always pronounced (قَتَلَ, فَرِحَ, حَسُنَ), the former is rejected after prefixed pronouns, as يَقْتُلُ, تَقْتُلُ; the latter before suffixed pronouns beginning with a consonant, as قَتَلْتُ, قَتَلْنَا. When the suffix begins with a vowel, that vowel takes the place of the fĕtḥa,
D as قَتَلَتْ, قَتَلُوا.

REM. *a.* When the third radical is ت, it unites in pronunciation with the ت in some of the suffixes. In such cases only one ت is written, and the union of the two is denoted by the tĕšdīd. Thus from ثَبَتَ, *to stand firm,* we get ثَبَتَّ, ثَبَتِّ, ثَبَتُّمْ, for ثَبَتْتَ, ثَبَتْتِ, ثَبَتْتُمْ. See § 14, *c*, rem. *b*.

REM. *b.* When the third radical is one of the letters ث, د, ذ, ض, ط, ظ, it may unite in pronunciation with the ت of the suffixes, so as to form a double ت, but it is nevertheless retained in writing.

To indicate the assimilation, the ت takes tèšdīd, and the ǵèzma, A
with which the third radical ought properly to be marked, is omitted. Thus, عَبَدتُّ for عَبَدْتُ, *I have served;* رَبَطتَّ for رَبَطْتَ, *thou hast bound;* أَخَذتُّمْ for أَخَذْتُمْ, *ye have taken.* On this assimilation see § 14, *c*.

Rem. *c*. When the third radical is ن, it unites with the ن of the suffixes into a single ن with tèšdīd; as آمَنَّ *they* (women) *believed*, آمَنَّا *we believed*, for آمَنْنَ and آمَنْنَا.

Rem. *d*. For a view of the Inflexion of the Perfect and Imperfect Indicative in Hebrew and Aramaic as compared with Arabic see *Comp. Gr.* p. 165 *seq.*

b. FORMS OF THE TENSES AND MOODS. B

91. When the second radical of the Perfect has *fètḥa*, it may take either *ḍamma* or *kèsra* in the Imperfect; as قَتَلَ *to kill*, يَقْتُلُ; كَتَبَ *to write*, يَكْتُبُ; ضَرَبَ *to strike*, يَضْرِبُ; جَلَسَ *to sit down*, يَجْلِسُ. Many verbs admit of both forms; as عَطَسَ *to sneeze*, يَعْطُسُ and يَعْطِسُ; سَمَطَ *to remove the hair by scalding*, يَسْمُطُ or يَسْمِطُ;
رَكَزَ *to stick upright into the ground*, يَرْكُزُ. C

Rem. *a*. Verbs, of which the second or third radical is a guttural letter, are an exception to the rule, for they commonly retain in the Imperfect the *fètḥa* of the Perfect; as فَعَلَ *to do*, يَفْعَلُ; قَطَعَ *to cut*, يَقْطَعُ; مَنَعَ *to hinder*, يَمْنَعُ; بَرَأَ *to create*, يَبْرَأُ; سَأَلَ *to ask*, يَسْأَلُ; ذَهَبَ *to go away*, يَذْهَبُ; لَحَظَ *to look at*, يَلْحَظُ; طَرَحَ *to throw*, يَطْرَحُ. Not a few, however, conform to the rule, particularly when the second radical is خ or غ; as شَعَرَ
to perceive, know, يَشْعُرُ; قَعَدَ *to sit*, يَقْعُدُ; طَعَنَ *to transpierce*, D
يَطْعُنُ; زَعَمَ *to say*, يَزْعُمُ; طَلَعَ *to ascend*, يَطْلُعُ; صَلَحَ *to be sound, right, good*, يَصْلُحُ; بَلَغَ *to attain to, reach*, يَبْلُغُ; نَفَخَ *to blow*, يَنْفُخُ; شَخَبَ *to flow*, يَشْخُبُ; رَجَعَ *to return*, يَرْجِعُ; نَزَعَ *to draw or pull away*, يَنْزِعُ; شَخَرَ *to bray*, يَشْخِرُ. Some verbs have two

A forms; as نَعَقَ *to croak,* يَنْعِقُ; مَنَحَ *to give as a present,* يَمْنِحُ; نَكَحَ *to marry,* يَنْكِحُ; نَطَحَ *to butt,* يَنْطِحُ; سَلَخَ *to flay,* يَسْلُخُ; دَبَغَ *to tan,* يَدْبَغُ; صَبَغَ *to dye,* يَصْبُغُ; فَرَغَ *to be at leisure, to have done with,* يَفْرُغُ; and even three, as نَحَتَ *to cut* or *hew,* يَنْحِتُ; رَجَحَ *to incline* (of a scale of a balance), يَرْجُحُ; نَبَعَ *to gush out,* يَنْبُعُ.

B REM. *b.* Verbs of the form فَعَلَ denoting superiority, فَعَلَ ٱلدَّالُّ عَلَى ٱلْغَلَبَةِ (see § 43, *a*), always have *ḍamma* (the grammarian ĕl-Kisāʼī alone admitting *fètḥa* with a guttural), as شَعَرَهُ *he excelled him in composing poetry,* يَشْعُرُهُ; فَخَرَهُ *he surpassed him in glory,* يَفْخُرُهُ; unless they be primæ rad. و, med. rad. ى, or tert. rad. ى, when they take *kèsra*, as وَعَدَهُ *he outbid him in promising,* يَعِدُهُ; خَارَهُ *he excelled him in goodness,* يَخِيرُهُ; رَمَاهُ *he surpassed him in shooting with arrows,* يَرْمِيهِ.

C REM. *c.* Excessively rare are cases like رَكَنَ *to incline to, lean upon,* يَرْكُنُ, which is probably a combination of the two forms رَكَنَ, يَرْكُنُ, and رَكِنَ, يَرْكَنُ. See § 175, rem. *b.*

92. When the second radical of the Perf. has *kèsra*, the Imperf. takes *fètḥa*; as عَلِمَ *to know,* يَعْلَمُ; شَرِبَ *to drink,* يَشْرَبُ; حَزِنَ *to be sorrowful,* يَحْزَنُ; مَرِضَ *to be sick,* يَمْرَضُ; سَلِمَ *to be safe,* يَسْلَمُ.

REM. *a.* A few verbs may retain in the Imperf. the *kèsra* of the Perf., as حَسِبَ *to think* or *suppose,* يَحْسِبُ or يَحْسَبُ; نَعِمَ
D *to be green and flourishing,* يَنْعِمُ; بَئِسَ *to be in distress* or *poverty,* يَبْئِسُ or يَبْأَسُ. See also §§ 142 and 146.

REM. *b.* Very rare are cases like حَضِرَ *to be present,* يَحْضُرُ; رَكِنَ *to incline to, lean upon,* يَرْكُنُ; فَضِلَ *to be in excess, abound,* يَفْضُلُ; نَعِمَ *to be affluent, comfortable,* يَنْعُمُ; بَرِئَ *to be clear, quit,*

or *innocent of,* يَبْرُؤُ or يَبْرَأُ. The most common example of this kind A
is a verb med. و, viz. مَاتَ, *to die* (for مَوِتَ, 1st p. sing. Perf. مِتُّ),
يَمُوتُ.—Similar cases in Syriac and Hebrew, *Comp. Gr.* p. 180*.*

93. When the second radical of the Perf. has *ḍamma*, that vowel is retained in the Imperf.; as حَسُنَ *to be beautiful,* يَحْسُنُ; شَرُفَ *to be high, noble,* يَشْرُفُ; بَلُدَ *to be dull* or *stupid,* يَبْلُدُ.

Rem. With the above forms compare the Heb. יִשְׁלַח, יִכְתֹּב, B
יִכְבַּד. In Heb., however, verbs in *o* usually take *a* in the Imperf., as יִקְטַן, יִשְׁכַּל, whereas in Arabic instances like لَبُبْتُ *I became wise,* دَمُمْتُ *I became ugly,* شَرُرْتُ *I became bad,* أَلُبُّ, أَدُمُّ, أَشُرُّ, are very rare. Some authorities admit the forms أَلُبُّ, أَدُمُّ, أَشُرُّ.

94. The difference between the Perf. and Imperf. in regard to their inflexion is, that the marks of the numbers, genders, and persons, are only *suffixed* to the Perf.; whereas they are both *suffixed* and *prefixed* to the Imperf., more generally the latter. C

Rem. *a*. In the Perf. the *act* is placed conspicuously in the foreground, because completed; in the Imperf. the *agent*, because still occupied in the act (see § 77, rem. *a*). If we look upon the root قتل as primarily conveying the abstract idea of "killing," we may regard قَتَلْتُ as meaning "killing-of-me" (i.e. done by me), "my killing," = "I have killed;" and أَقْتُلُ as meaning "I-killing," = "I am killing."

Rem. *b*. In the Imperf. the pronominal *prefixes* mark the state D
or tense, and to some extent the gender; whilst the *suffixes* serve solely to indicate the gender. Thus, the 2d pers. sing. masc. تَكْتُبُ is sufficiently distinguished from the 3d pers. sing. masc. يَكْتُبُ by the form of the temporal prefix; but to distinguish the 2d pers. sing. masc. from its fem. a suffix is necessary, and accordingly we get masc. تَكْتُبُ, fem. تَكْتُبِينَ.

---

* [Anbārī, *Nozhat el-alibbā* p. 459 states from personal observation in Yèmèn and Ḥigāz that in some dialects every verb فَعِلَ makes يَفْعِلُ and يَفْعُلُ.—De G.]

A REM. *c*. In the active voice of the first form, the prefixes of the Imperfect are pronounced with *fètḥ*. But a pronunciation with *kèsr* instead of *fètḥ* is regarded as admissible and was used by some of the old Arabs with any of the preformatives except ى, save in the case where the next consonant has *ḍamma* (verbs med. و). That is, one must not say إِقُومُ, تِقُومُ, إِقْمُ for أَقُومُ *etc.* nor يِعْلَمُ for يَعْلَمُ; but on the other hand the pronunciation نِعْبُدُ and نِسْتَعِينُ in Sūra i. 4, and إِعْهَدْ in Sūra xxxvi. 60 are recognized as
B legitimate dialectic variations of the usual نَعْبُدُ *etc.* In one case, إِخَالُ for أَخَالُ, *I suppose*, the pronunciation with *kèsr* is generally preferred. The tribe of Kèlb used *kèsr* even with the prefix ى (يِعْلَمُ). Dialectically, too, the vowel of the prefix might be assimilated to a following *ḍamm*, as in نُعْبُدُ for نَعْبُدُ.

95. The *Indicative* of the Imperf. is distinguished by the third radical having *ḍamma*, the *Subjunctive* by its having *fètḥa*; as Indic.
C يَكْتُبُ, Subj. يَكْتُبَ. The *Jussive* is denoted by the *absence* of any vowel with the third radical, as يَكْتُبْ; whence it is sometimes called the apocopated Imperfect.

REM. *a*. The ḍamma and fètḥa of the Indicat. and Subjunct. Imperf. in the verb, correspond to the ḍamma and fètḥa of the Nom. and Accus. in the noun (see § 308); for the Imperf. is closely akin to the noun, and its government in the Subjunct. falls under the same category with the government of the noun in the Accus. Hence the technical name of the Imperf., اَلْمُضَارِعُ, because it
D *resembles* the noun. [The Indicative is called اَلْمَرْفُوعُ, the Subjunctive اَلْمَنْصُوبُ, and the Jussive اَلْمَجْزُومُ.]

REM. *b*. The peculiar meaning of the Jussive has brought along with it the rejection of the final vowel, which seems originally to have been *i*. At least the poets make use of the form يَقْتُلِ in rhyme. [Cf. vol. ii. § 247.]

96. The forms of the Indicat. which end in نِ and نَ reject these syllables in the Subjunct. and Jussive, because the genders, numbers, and persons are distinctly indicated even after their omission. The

2d and 3d pers. plur. fem. are exceptions, for in them نَ is retained, A
because it is absolutely necessary in order to mark the gender. Compare يَكْتُبُونَ , يَكْتُبُوا, with كَتَبُوا ; يَكْتُبَانِ , يَكْتُبَا, with كَتَبَا ; and تَكْتُبِينَ, تَكْتُبِي, with كَتَبْتِ.

97. The *Energetic* is formed by adding the termination ـَنَّ or ـَنْ (called by the grammarians اَلنُّونُ ٱلْمُؤَكِّدَةُ, or *the corroborative n*) to the Jussive. If the Jussive ends in *ī* or *ū*, the fèthạ of ـَنَّ or ـَنْ is elided, and the long vowel of the verbal form shortened, because it is in a shut syllable: تَكْتُبِنَّ, تَكْتُبِنْ, from تَكْتُبِي; يَكْتُبُنَّ, يَكْتُبُنْ, from يَكْتُبُوا; etc. In the dual, the first fèthạ of ـَنَّ is absorbed by the ـَا B
of the termination, and the second weakened into a kèsra through the influence of the same long vowel: يَكْتُبَانِّ, تَكْتُبَانِّ, from يَكْتُبَا, تَكْتُبَا. In the 2d and 3d pers. plur. fem. the fèthạ of the verb unites with the initial fèthạ of ـَنَّ into a long *ā*, and in consequence the second fèthạ of ـَنَّ becomes kèsra: يَكْتُبْنَانِّ (تَ) from يَكْتُبْنَ (تَ).

Rem. *a.* The syllable ـَنْ of the second Energetic is appended only to those persons which have, in the first Energetic, a short vowel before نَّ; and not to the dual, because its forms would then C
coincide with those of the singular, nor to the fem. plur., apparently because the sound of the syllable نَنْ (يَكْتُبْنَنْ) was disagreeable to the ear.

Rem. *b.* Before an *èlifu 'l-waṣl* (§ 19) the *n* of the termination ـَنْ is rejected (§ 20, rem. *c*), as لَا تُهِينَ ٱلْفَقِيرَ, *despise not the poor*, for تُهِينَنْ, from أَهَانَ, IV. of هَانَ.

Rem. *c.* The syllable ـَنْ is often written ـًا, and pronounced D
in pause ـَا. Compare the Hebrew Energetic or Cohortative in ָה, *Comp. Gr.* p. 194.

98. The *Imperative* (اَلْأَمْرُ *the order* or *command*) may be described as formed from the Jussive by rejecting the prefix of the 2d pers. sing. Hence it has always the same characteristic vowel as the Jussive; but, since it begins with two consonants, it takes, according to § 26, a short

A prosthetic vowel. When the second radical is pronounced with *fèthа* or *kèsra*, this vowel is *kèsra*; when with *ḍamma*, it is *ḍamma*. E.g. اُكْتُبْ, اِضْرِبْ, اِفْعَلْ.

REM. *a*. Regarding the elision of the prosthetic vowel (اَ), see § 19, *b*; and on the orthography ا and اِ, in cases where that elision does not take place, § 19, rem. *d*.

REM. *b*. Fètḥa is never employed as a prosthetic vowel.

B REM. *c*. As an Imperative the Arabs also use the indeclinable form قَتَالِ; as حَضَارِ *be present!* حَذَارِ *beware!* نَزَالِ *alight!* سَمَاعِ *listen!* تَرَاكِ *let alone!* دَبَابِ *creep along!* نَعَاءِ *announce the death of—!* from نَعَى. This corresponds to the Hebrew *Infinitive absolute* קָטוֹל (*ō* for *ā*, and the final short vowel dropped), which is also used in the same way; as זָכוֹר *remember!** In quadriliterals this form is very rare, the only examples mentioned being

C قَرْقَارِ = قَرْقِرْ بِٱلرَّعْدِ, *let thy thunder crash*, and عَرْعَارِ, *come and play the game called ʻarʻara*. Occasionally it seems to take its meaning from one of the derived conjugations, as خَرَاجِ *bring out!* دَرَاكِ *overtake!* = أَخْرِجُوا, أَدْرِكُوا, Imper. IV.

99. The same remarks apply to the energetic forms of the Imperative as to those of the Imperf. (§ 97).

D [REM. The common phrase اِضْرِبًا عُنُقَهُ, *strike off his head*, is sometimes pointed without tènwīn (اِضْرِبَا) and is then explained by the grammarians as a dual used in an intensive sense (تَثْنِيَة عَلَى ٱلتَّوْكِيدِ, cf. vol. ii. § 35, *a*, rem. *b*) in addressing a single person. Similarly Ḳor'ān l. 23, أَلْقِيَا with a various reading أَلْقِيَنْ.—De G.]

---

* [And again the phrase عقّقت عَقاق Ṭab. i. 1842, l. 15 is parallel to the Hebrew use of the Inf. Abs. with the finite verb.—De G.]

2. *The Passive Voice of the First Form in the Strong Verb.—Table II.* A

100. The Perf. and Imperf. Passive are distinguished from the corresponding tenses of the Active by a change of vowels. In the Perf. Pass. the *first* radical has *ḍamma*, and the *second* radical *kèsra*. In the Imperf. Pass. the *prefixes* take *ḍamma*, and the *second* radical *fètḥa*.

Rem. The vocalisation of the Passive remains always the same, whatever be the vowel of the second radical in the Perf. and Imperf. Active.

101. There is no special form to express the Imperative Passive, B the Jussive being used instead.

3. *The Derived Forms of the Strong Verb.—Table III.*

102. The second radical of the Perf. Act. is pronounced with *fètḥa* in *all* the derived forms.

103. The second radical of the Imperf. Act. is pronounced with *fètḥa* in the *fifth* and *sixth* forms, with *kèsra* in the rest. C

Rem. The Imperfects of the ninth and eleventh forms, يَقْتَلُّ and يَقْتَالُّ, are contractions for يَقْتَلِلُ and يَقْتَالِلُ. This may be seen from the Jussives يَقْتَلِلْ and يَقْتَالِلْ, and the Imperatives اِقْتَلِلْ and اِقْتَالِلْ. See §§ 106 and 120.

104. In the *second, third,* and *fourth* forms, the *prefixes* of the Imperf. Act. are pronounced with *ḍamma,* in the rest with *fètḥa.*

105. The characteristic èlif of the fourth form disappears when D another letter is prefixed; as يُقْتِلُ, not يُأَقْتِلُ, from أَقْتَلَ.

[Rem. But we find قِدْرٌ مُؤْثَفَاةٌ, *a pot set on the fire,* and also يُؤَثْفَيْنَ, Sībawèih, i. 9, l. 21, where the أ is treated like the ه of يُهَرِيقُ, § 118, rem. *b.*—De G.]

106. The ninth and eleventh forms were originally اِفْعَلَلَ and اِفْعَالَلَ. But, by a rule of the language (see § 120), if the last radical

A in such words has a vowel, the preceding radical loses its vowel, and the two are combined into one letter with tèšdīd; e.g. اِصْفَرَّ for اِصْفَرَرَ, يَصْفَرُّ for يَصْفَرِرُ. If the last radical has no vowel, the word remains uncontracted; as اِصْفَرَرْتُ, يَصْفَرِرْ, اِصْفَرِرْ (see § 120).

107. The formation of the Perf. and Imperf. Passive in the derived forms is exactly analogous to that in the ground-form.

Rem. *a.* The Imperfects Pass. of the first and fourth forms are identical.

B Rem. *b.* The Imperfects Pass. of the fifth and sixth forms are distinguished from their Imperfects Act. only by the vowel of the prefixes, which is *ḍamma* instead of *fètḥa*.

108. Since the idea of the Perf. Pass. is expressed by pronouncing the first radical with ḍamma, and the idea of the third form by lengthening the vowel of the first radical, there results in the Passive of the third form (in which both ideas are united) the form قُوتِلَ; and hence in the Pass. of the sixth, تُقُوتِلَ.

C **109.** In the Perf. Pass. of the fifth and sixth forms, not only is the fètḥa of the first radical changed into ḍamma, but also the fètḥa of the characteristic تَ (which expresses the reflexive idea of these forms); e.g. تُقُتِّلَ, تُقُوتِلَ. In like manner, in the Perf. Pass. of the seventh, eighth, and tenth forms, not only is the first radical, or the characteristic ت, pronounced with ḍamma, but also the prosthetic èlif; e.g. اُنْقُتِلَ, اُقْتُتِلَ, اُسْتُقْتِلَ. Compare § 98 and rem. *a*.

D **110.** The ninth and eleventh [to fifteenth] forms, being neutral in their signification, have of course no passive (see § 73).

111. When the verbal root begins with ت, ث, ج, د, ذ, ز, س, ش, ص, ض, ط, or ظ, the characteristic ت of the fifth and sixth forms occasionally (in the Ḳor'ān frequently) loses its vowel, and unites with the first radical to form a double letter. The forms thus originated take a prosthetic èlif, when they happen to commence with two consonants (compare § 54). E.g. اِتَّابَعَ, اِثَّاقَلَ, اِدَّثَّرَ, اِدَّارَأَ, اِزَّيَّنَ,

اِسَّاقَطَ, اِسَّمَّعَ, اِشَّمَّرَ, اِطَّيَّرَ, for تَتَابَعَ, تَثَاقَلَ, تَدَثَّرَ, تَدَارَأَ, تَزَيَّنَ, تَسَاقَطَ, A
تَسَمَّعَ, تَشَمَّرَ, تَطَيَّرَ : يَذَّكَّرُ, يَزَّكَّى, يَصَّدَّقُ, يَطَّهَّرُ, for يَتَذَكَّرُ, يَتَزَكَّى, يَتَصَدَّقُ, يَتَطَهَّرُ. The language in its later stages admits this in all verbs of the fifth and sixth forms, merely rejecting the vowel of the preformative تَ; as اِتْنَفَّسَ for تَنَفَّسَ, *to take breath.*

Rem. See § 48, rem. *b*, and compare such Hebrew forms as הִדַּבֵּר, הִזַּכָּה, הִטַּהֵר; *Comp. Gr.* p. 110 *seq.*

112. The تَ of the fifth and sixth forms is sometimes omitted B in those persons of the Imperf. Act. to which تَ is prefixed (2d pers. sing. du. and plur. masc. and fem., 3d pers. sing. and du. fem.); e.g. تَكَسَّرُ, تَحَمَّلُ, تَبَاعَدُ, تَقَدَّمُونَ, for تَتَكَسَّرُ, تَتَحَمَّلُ, تَتَبَاعَدُ, تَتَقَدَّمُونَ [and necessarily تَتَابَعُ for تَتَتَابَعُ (*Fāik* i. 130)—De G.]. These shortened forms are sufficiently distinguished by the fèthas of the prefixed تَ and of the second radical from the same persons in the active voice of the second and third forms (تُكَسِّرُ, تُبَاعِدُ); and by the fètha of the prefixed تَ from the same persons in the passive of C the second and third forms (تُكَسَّرُ, تُبَاعَدُ).

113. Verbs of which the first radical is أ, و, ى, ر, ل, or ن, have no seventh form in classical Arabic, but use the fifth or eighth, or the passive of the first, instead. In the (so far as we know) solitary example of the seventh form from a verb beginning with ن,—namely اِنَّمَسَ, *to lie concealed,*—the characteristic ن is united by tèšdīd to the first radical.

Rem. *a.* Some grammarians regard اِنَّمَسَ as being of the eighth D form, by assimilation for اِنْتَمَسَ.

Rem. *b.* In modern Arabic such forms as اِنْأَخَذَ, اِنْأَطَرَ (*Kāmil,* p. 569, note i.), اِنْرَضَّ, اِنَّصَرَ, اِنْوَجَدَ, اِنْوَلَدَ, are of common occurrence.

114. If the first radical is م, the characteristic ن of the seventh form often unites with it into مّ; as اِنْمَحَقَ or اِمَّحَقَ from مَحَقَ,

A اِنْمَحَى or اِمَّحَى from مَحَا, اِنْمَعَطَ or اِمَّعَطَ from مَعَطَ, اِنْمَلَسَ or اِمَّلَسَ from مَلَسَ, اِنْمَلَصَ or اِمَّلَصَ from مَلَصَ.

REM. These forms are sometimes assigned to the eighth form; اِمَّحَقَ for اِمْتَحَقَ, اِمَّحَى for اِمْتَحَى, اِمَّرَطَ for اِمْتَرَطَ, etc.

115. If the first radical be ت or ث, the characteristic ت of the eighth form unites with the initial ت into تّ, with the initial ث into ثّ or تّ. E.g. اِتَّبَعَ, for اِتْتَبَعَ, from تَبِعَ; اِثَّأَرَ or اِتَّأَرَ, for اِثْتَأَرَ, from ثَأَرَ; اِثَّرَدَ or اِتَّرَدَ from ثَرَدَ; اِثَّغَرَ or اِتَّغَرَ from ثَغَرَ.

B REM. The same assimilation is sometimes extended to the letter س, as اِسَّمَعَ, for اِسْتَمَعَ, from سَمِعَ.

116. If the first radical be د, ذ, or ز, the characteristic ت of the eighth form is changed into د, which unites with an initial د into دّ, and with an initial ذ into دّ or ذّ. E.g. اِزْدَجَرَ, for اِزْتَجَرَ, from زَجَرَ; اِزْدَادَ, for اِزْتَادَ, from زَادَ; اِدَّرَكَ, for اِدْتَرَكَ, from دَرَكَ; اِدَّرَى, for اِدْتَرَى,
C from دَرَى; اِدَّعَى, for اِدْتَعَى, from دَعَا; اِدَّخَرَ or اِذَّخَرَ, for اِذْتَخَرَ, from ذَخَرَ; اِدَّكَرَ or اِذَّكَرَ, for اِذْتَكَرَ, from ذَكَرَ; اِدَّرَعَ or اِذَّرَعَ, for اِذْتَرَعَ, from ذَرَعَ.

REM. *a.* Whether the form with دّ or ذّ is to be preferred, depends upon usage; for instance, اِدَّخَرَ and اِدَّكَرَ are preferable to اِذَّخَرَ and اِذَّكَرَ, but Lane gives in his Lexicon only اِذَّبَحَ, اِذَّرَقَ, and اِذَّرَى. The unassimilated اِذْدَكَرَ is also said to occur, as well as
D اِذْدَرَى.

REM. *b.* Some grammarians extend this assimilation to the letter ز, as اِزَّانَ, for اِزْدَانَ, from زَانَ.

REM. *c.* The letter ت is sometimes changed into د after an initial ج; e.g. اِجْدَرَّ, اِجْدَزَّ, اِجْدَمَعَ, instead of the usual اِجْتَرَّ, اِجْتَزَّ, اِجْتَمَعَ, from جَرَّ, جَزَّ, جَمَعَ.

117. If the first radical be ص, ض, ط, or ظ, the characteristic A
ت is changed into ط, which unites with initial ط into طّ, with initial ظ into ظّ or طّ, and occasionally with initial ض into ضّ. E.g. اِصْطَبَغَ, اِصْطَفَى, اِصْطَلَى, اِصْطَلَحَ, from صَبَغَ, صَفَا, صَلَى, صَلَحَ ; اِطَّبَخَ, اِطَّرَدَ, اِطَّعَنَ, اِطَّلَبَ, from طَبَخَ, طَرَدَ, طَعَنَ, طَلَبَ ; اِظَّلَمَ, اِطَّلَمَ, or اِظْطَلَمَ, from ظَلَمَ ; اِظَّأَرَ, or اِظْطَأَرَ, from ظَأَرَ ; اِظَّعَنَ, اِظَّفَرَ, اِظَّهَرَ, from ظَعَنَ, ظَفِرَ, ظَهَرَ ; اِضْطَرَبَ, or اِضَّرَبَ, from ضَرَبَ ; اِضْطَجَعَ, or اِضَّجَعَ, from ضَجَعَ ; اِضْطَرَّ, اِضْطَلَعَ, from ضَرَّ, ضَلَعَ.

Rem. *a.* The letter ص sometimes assimilates the following ط ; B
as اِصَّبَرَ, اِصَّفَى, اِصَّلَى, اِصَّلَحَ, اِصَّادَ, for اِصْطَبَرَ, etc.

Rem. *b.* From ضَجَعَ the form اِطَّجَعَ also occurs.

[**117*.** If the second radical be ت the characteristic ت of the eighth form may lose its vowel and unite with it. The first radical then necessarily assumes a vowel, either *a* or *i*, and the helping vowel ا is unnecessary and disappears. Thus for اِسْتَتَرَ we may have سَتَّرَ or سِتَّرَ ; Imperf. يَسَتِّرُ, يَسِتِّرُ or يِسِتِّرُ or even يَسْتِّرُ (with a furtive *kesra* to the first radical) ; Part. act. مُسَتِّرٌ (مُسِتِّرٌ) ; Inf. سِتَّارٌ (see § 202, C
rem. *a*). Similar forms from verbs whose second radical is د, ذ, ص or ط occur (or are recorded as variants) in the Ḳor'ān. (*Sūr.* x. 36, ix. 91, ii. 19, xxxvi. 49).]

4. *The Quadriliteral Verb.—Table IV.*

118. The four forms of the quadriliteral verb follow throughout D
their inflexion the second, fifth, seventh and ninth forms of the triliteral (see §§ 69—72).

Rem. *a.* The تَ, which is prefixed to certain persons in the Imperf. Act., is omitted in the second form of the quadriliteral verb, just as in the fifth form of the triliteral (see § 112).

Rem. *b.* As mentioned in § 45, rem. *d*, words like هَرَاقَ (for أَرَاقَ), *to pour out*, and هَيْمَنَ, *to believe*, are treated as quadriliterals:

A The latter is inflected exactly like قَمْطَرَ, but the former is irregular: Imperf. يُهَرِيقُ, Imperat. هَرِقْ, Nom. act. هِرَاقَةٌ, Perf. Pass. هُرِيقَ. The form أَهْرَاقَ, Imperf. يُهْرِيقُ, is also used.—The tenth form of طَاعَ, viz. اِسْتَطَاعَ, *to obey*, is sometimes shortened into اِسْطَاعَ or اِسْتَاعَ, Imperf. يَسْطِيعُ or يَسْتِيعُ, and then converted into أَسْطَاعَ, Imperf. يُسْطِيعُ. [Also, in verse, we find مُسْطَارٌ for مُسْتَطَارٌ.]

B 5. *Verbs of which the Second and Third Radicals are Identical.—Table V.*

119. These verbs are usually called *verba mediæ* or *secundæ radicalis geminatæ* (ע"ע). The Arab grammarians name them اَلْفِعْلُ ٱلْأَصَمُّ, *the solid verb*, or اَلْفِعْلُ ٱلْمُضَاعَفُ, *the doubled verb.*

120. They differ from other strong verbs in two points.

(*a*) When both the first and third radicals have vowels, the
C second radical rejects its vowel, and unites with the third, so as to form a double letter, which is marked with tèšdîd. E.g. فَرَّ *to flee*, for فَرَرَ ; شَقَّ *to split* or *cleave*, for شَقَقَ ; مَسَّ *to touch*, for مَسِسَ ; شَمَّ *to smell*, for شَمِمَ ; حَبَّ *to become dear* (*to one*), for حَبُبَ ; لَبَّ *to become wise* or *intelligent*, for لَبُبَ.

(*b*) If the third radical has a vowel, but the first is without one, the second radical throws back its vowel upon the first, and then
D combines with the third, so as to form a double letter. E.g. يَجِلُّ for يَجْلِلُ, يَمُدُّ for يَمْدُدُ, يَمَلُّ for يَمْلَلُ. But if the third radical has no vowel, the second retains its vowel, and no contraction takes place; as فَرَرْتُ, مَلِلْتُ, لَبُبْتُ, يَفْرِرْ, يَمْدُدْ.

REM. *a.* Transitive verbs of this class, of the form فَعَلَ, have ḍamma in the Imperfect, with the exception of six, which also admit kèsra; viz. بَتَّ *to sever* or *separate entirely, make decisive* or *absolute*, رَمَّ *to repair*, شَدَّ *to make hard* or *firm, tie firmly*, عَلَّ *to*

water (camels) *a second time*, نَمَّ *to spread abroad* or *divulge secretly*, A
هَرَّ *to abhor, detest*, Imperf. يَبُتُّ or يَبِتُّ, etc. One verb has only kèsra, viz. حَبَّ *to love* (instead of the common IV. أَحَبَّ), Imperf. يَحِبُّ.

Rem. *b*. Uncontracted verbs of the forms فَعِلَ and فَعُلَ sometimes occur; as صَكِكَ *to be knock-kneed* or *weak in the hocks*, مَشِشَ *to have a swelling* [splint] *on the pastern* (of a horse), أَلِلَ *to smell badly*, ضَبِبَ *to abound in lizards* (ضَبٌّ), لَحِحَ *to be sore* (of the eye), B
قَطِطَ *to be curly*, حَكِكَ *to have its hoof worn at the edges* (of a horse, etc.); لَبُبَ *to be wise* or *intelligent*, دَمُمَ *to be ugly*, شَرُرَ *to be bad*, فَكُكَ *to be silly, in one's dotage*, عَزُزَ *to have narrow orifices of the teats* (of a she-camel, ewe, etc.).

Rem. *c*. Forms like فَرِرْتَ, مَدَدْتَ, ظَلِلْتَ, are, however, sometimes contracted in different ways.—1. The second radical is dropped, along with its vowel, or else its vowel is transferred to C
the first radical; as, رَدْتَ, رَدْنَ, for رَدَدْتَ, رَدَدْنَ, أَحَسْتَ for أَحْسَسْتَ, ظَلْتَ or ظِلْتَ for ظَلِلْتَ, مَسْتَ for مَسِسْتَ (compare the Aramaic form בַּזְתְּ for בְּזַזְתְּ) [also يَقِرْنَ for يَقْرِرْنَ, يُزِفْنَ for يُزْفِفْنَ *etc.**].
2. The third radical is united with the second, and a vowel-sound inserted before the pronominal suffix. This may be either (*a*) the diphthong ـَيْ, as قَصَّيْتَ for قَصَصْتَ, اِسْتَسَرَّيْتَ for اِسْتَسْرَرْتَ, a form which is not uncommon in the fifth conjugation, as تَسَرَّيْتَ, تَظَنَّيْتَ, تَقَضَّيْتَ, تَلَعَّيْتَ, for تَسَرَّرْتَ, تَظَنَّنْتَ, تَقَضَّضْتَ, تَلَعَّعْتَ D
(compare in the Hebrew Imperf. תְּסֻבֶּינָה for תְּסֻבֶּבְנָה); or (*b*) the long vowel ـَا, as مَدَّاتَ for مَدَدْتَ (compare in Hebrew סַבּוֹת, where ō = ā). The form described under 2 *a* is the usual one in modern Arabic, but in N. Africa *ai* becomes ī, as *reddīt* for رَدَّيْتُ. Such forms as أَحْسَيْتُ for أَحْسَسْتُ also occur.—*Comp. Gr.* p. 227 *seq.*

---

* [See De Goeje, *Gloss.* to Ibn al-Faḳīh s.v. زَقَّ.]

A **121.** In the Jussive, however, the second radical not unfrequently throws back its vowel upon the first, and combines with the third, in which case the doubled letter necessarily takes a supplemental vowel (§ 27). In verbs that have *a* or *i* in the Imperf., this vowel may be either *fètḥa* or *kèsra;* in those that have *u*, it may be any one of the three vowels. E.g. يَعَضَّ or يَعَضِّ, يَمَلَّ or يَمَلِّ, for يَعْضَضْ, يَمْلَلْ; يَفِرَّ or يَفِرِّ, يَحِبَّ or يَحِبِّ, for يَفْرِرْ, يَحْبِبْ ; يَمُدَّ, يَمُدِّ, or يَمُدُّ, يَرُدَّ, يَرُدِّ, or يَرُدُّ, for يَمْدُدْ, يَرْدُدْ*.

B **122.** Those persons of the Imperative in which the third radical has a vowel (sing. fem., dual, and plur. masc.), sometimes do not follow the rule given in § 120, *b*, but keep the second radical apart from the third; as اِفْرِرِى, اِفْرِرَا, اِفْرِرُوا. When the usual contraction takes place, the prosthetic èlif is obviously no longer necessary, and therefore the Arabs say فِرِّى, فِرَّا, فِرُّوا—not اِفِرِّى, اِفِرَّا, اِفِرُّوا,—instead of اِفْرِرِى, etc. The masc. sing. undergoes exactly the same contraction as the Jussive (§ 121), rejecting at the same time the prosthetic ا; e.g. عَضِّ for اِعْضَضْ, فِرِّ for اِفْرِرْ, مُدِّ for اُمْدُدْ.

C REM. If the verb has a suffix, the choice of the supplemental vowel depends to some extent upon that of the suffix; say رُدُّهُ (رُدَّهُ), عَضُّهُ (عَضِّهِ), but رُدَّهَا, عَضَّهَا, not رُدُّهَا, عَضِّهَا. In the *waṣl* (§ 20) say رُدِّ ٱلْقَوْمَ or رُدَّ ٱلْقَوْمَ.

123. The same rules that apply to the Active of the first form, apply also to its Passive, and to the third, fourth, sixth, seventh,
D eighth, and tenth forms. But in the second, fifth, ninth, and eleventh, the second or third radical cannot be united with the other, because it is already doubled. Consequently فَرَّرَ, تَفَرَّرَ, اِفْرَرَّ, and اِفْرَارَّ, undergo no contraction. [But cf. § 120, rem. *c*, for Conj. V.]

---

* [The uncontracted forms are said to belong to the dialect of Ḥiǵāz, the contracted to that of Tamīm, *Fāiḳ* ii. 566.—De G. Cf. Sībawèih ii. 443.]

REM. In the Passive some of the Arabs substituted kèsra for damma, as حِلَّ for حُلَّ (contracted from حُلِلَ), whilst others gave the vowel of the first radical a sound between those of kèsra and damma (technically called الْإِشْمَامُ, *giving* the one vowel *a scent* or *flavour* of the other), as رُدَّ, شُدَّ, *rüdda*, *śüdda* (with the German *ü* or French *u*), instead of *rudda*, *śudda*. A

124. In the third, sixth, and eleventh forms, a long vowel, namely *ā*, precedes the double consonant, which is allowed in the case of *fèṯha* alone (§ 25, rem.). However, the uncontracted forms, B
such as سَارَرَ, قَاصَصَ, حَاجَجَ, شَاقَقَ, شَاحَحَ, يُسَابِبُ, يُمَادِدُ, مُصَافَفَةٌ, مُحَاجَجَةٌ, not unfrequently occur. Forms like فُورِرَ, تُفُورِرَ, and اِفْرِيرَارٌ, are not contracted.

125. The Jussive of the derived forms may undergo exactly the same contraction as the Jussive of the ground-form, by throwing back the vowel of the second radical upon the first, combining the second radical with the third, and giving the double letter an auxiliary vowel. E.g. أُذِلَّ for أُذْلِلْ, أُقِلَّ for أُقْلِلْ, the 1st pers. sing. Juss. of the fourth C
form of ذَلَّ and قَلَّ.

C. THE WEAK VERB.

126. Weak Verbs (*verba infirma*) are those in which one of the radicals is subject, on account of its weakness, to transformation or rejection; and which consequently differ more or less, in some parts of their inflexiön, from strong verbs (see §§ 82 and 83). D

127. The weak letters are أ, و, and ى.

128. There are two sorts of weak verbs.

(*a*) Those that have among their radicals a moveable èlif or hèmza, the weakest of the gutturals. These are called *verba hèmzata*.

(*b*) Those that have among their radicals one of the weak consonants و and ى, which approach very nearly in their nature to the vowel-sounds *u* and *i*. These are more particularly called *weak verbs*.

A REM. The Arab grammarians do not reckon the *verba hèmzata* among the *weak verbs*, restricting this appellation to those that contain a و or ى (§ 83, rem.).

129. In a root there may be two, or even three weak letters; as رَأَى, وَقَى, أَوَى. Verbs that have two weak radicals are said to be *doubly weak*; those that have three, to be *trebly weak*. These may be reckoned as forming a third class of weak verbs.

1. *Verbs that have a Hèmza among their Radicals (Verba Hèmzata).—Tables VI., VII., VIII.*

B **130.** These are divided into three classes, according as the hèmza is the first, second, or third radical (verba primæ, mediæ, ultimæ radicalis hèmzatæ). The following sections point out wherein they differ from the strong verbs.

131. If the èlif with hèmza and ǵèzma, at the end of a syllable (أْ), be preceded by one of the heterogeneous vowels ḍamma and kèsra, it is converted, after the ḍamma, into و with hèmza (ؤْ); after the kèsra, into ى with hèmza (ئْ). Hence بُرِئْتُ for بُرِأْتُ, 1st pers. sing. Perf.
C Pass. of بَرَأَ; يُوثَرُ for يُأْثَرُ, 3d pers. sing. masc. Imperf. Pass. I. or IV. of أَثَرَ; دَنُوتَ and شَنِئْتَ for دَنُأْتَ and شَنِأْتَ, 2d pers. sing. masc. Perf. Act. of دَنُؤَ and شَنِئَ, for دَنُأَ and شَنِأَ (see § 133).

132. The و and ى represent in these cases the sound to which the hèmza inclines through the influence of the preceding vowel*.

---

* [This is a convenient formula, and cannot well be improved upon without reference to the history of the Arabic language and writing, a
D consideration that lay quite beyond the scope of the native systematic grammarians, to whose method of exposition this work, for good practical reasons, is closely conformed. But from an historical point of view, when we consider the cases when *hèmza* is expressed by ؤ, ئ or by ء alone without a *kursī*, or supporting letter, we must distinguish between two pronunciations—that indicated by the consonants alone, which in the oldest times were written without any supplementary signs, and that indicated by the later points, such as ء. It is known

The hèmza is retained, not only to show their origin from أ, but also to A
remind us that the syllables ـُؤْ and ـِئْ are not to be confounded in pronunciation with ـُو, *ū*, and ـِي, *ī*. The ḍamma and kèsra remain *short*, whilst ؤ and ئ are pronounced like أ itself; that is to say, at the commencement of a syllable, with the spiritus lenis between the preceding syllable and the vowel that accompanies the hèmza (as دَنُؤَ, *danu-'a*, not *danu-wa*); at the end of a syllable, with a slight emphasis and resting of the voice upon the soft breathing (as شَنِئْتَ, *śani'-ta*, not *śanī-ta*).

Rem. *a.* In modern Arabic, hèmza in the middle and at the B
end of words has so completely disappeared, that ؤ and ئ, when preceded and followed by vowels, become و and ي; except when the former has ḍamma (ؤُ) and the latter kèsra (ئِ), as explained in §§ 133–4. The modern Arab also pronounces ـُؤْ and ـِئْ like the long vowels ـُو *ū* and ـِي *ī*. Even in the ancient language, especially among the poets, we find traces of a softer pronunciation, or total rejection, of the hèmza [تَخْفِيفُ الهَمْزَةِ § 17, *b*, rem. *b*];
and hence the custom, at the present day, of resolving the verba C
tert. rad. hèmzatæ into verba *tertiæ yā*, as قَرَى for قَرَأَ, *to read*, قَرَيْتُ for قَرَأْتُ, يَقْرِى for يَقْرَأُ. This change has already begun in Hebrew, and is almost universal in Aramaic.

---

that the people of the Ḥiǵāz in the time of Mohammed gave up the original guttural sound of *hèmza* in very many cases where the other Arabs still preserved it. Now the rules of Arabic orthography were
mainly fixed by the Ḳor'ān, which was originally written down in the D
Ḥiǵāz in accordance with the local pronunciation. This pronunciation did not ultimately prevail over the Arabic area, but the old orthography could not lightly be tampered with, having the character of a sacred tradition. The first scribes wrote بوس, جيت, جاك because they said *bawusa*, *ǵīta*, *ǵāka* (or nearly so). The pronunciation that prevailed, however, was *ba'usa*, *ǵi'ta*, *ǵā'aka* and this was expressed, without touching the old consonants, by writing بُؤُسَ, جِئْتَ, جَاءَكَ. Rules for writing hèmza as ؤ, ئ or ء are therefore really rules for preserving the old guttural ', in cases where it was already lost or transformed by the first scribes of the Ḳor'ān.]

A REM. *b*. The hèmza ǵèzmatum over و and ى falls away after an èlif hèmzatum, because of the impossibility of pronouncing it (§ 17, *b*, rem. *b*). Hence ايسِرْ, not ائْسِرْ, Imperat. of أَسَرَ; ايذَنْ, not ائْذَنْ, Imperat. of أَذِنَ; اومُلْ, not اؤْمُلْ, Imperat. of أَمَلَ; ايتَمَرَ, not ائْتَمَرَ, 3d pers. sing. Perf. Act. VIII. of أَمَرَ; اُوتُمِنَ, not اُؤْتُمِنَ, 3d pers. sing. Perf. Pass. VIII. of أَمِنَ, all with èlif
B conjunctionis (هَمْزَةُ ٱلْوَصْلِ); أُومِنَ, not أُؤْمِنَ, 3d pers. sing. Perf. Pass. IV. of أَمِنَ; إِيمَانٌ, not إِئْمَانٌ, Infin. IV. of أَمِنَ; أُوثِرُ, not أُؤْثِرُ, 1st pers. sing. Imperf. Act. IV. of أَثَرَ, all with èlif separationis (هَمْزَةُ ٱلْقَطْعِ).—When a word of this sort, beginning with the èlif conjunctionis, comes into the waṣl, the èlif conjunctionis falls away in pronunciation, though it may be retained in writing. In Imperatives, when preceded by وَ or فَ, *and*, it is usually rejected; as
C وَأْسِرْ, فَأْذَنْ, فَأْمُلْ, فَأْتِ (from ايتِ, Imper. of أَتَى *to come*), وَأْتَمِرُوا, فَأْتَمِنْ. In other cases it is retained, and the radical hèmza is left in its altered form (ؤ, ئ); as فَٱئْتَزَرَتْ *fa'tazarat*, بَعْدَ ٱئْتِلَافٍ *ba'dă'tilāfin*, ٱلْهُدَى ٱئْتِنَا *èlhudă'tinā*, يَقُولُ ٱئْذَنْ *yaḳūlŭ'ḏan*, ٱلَّذِى ٱؤْتُمِنَ (also written ٱلَّذِى ٱئْتُمِنَ) *èllaḏī'tumina*. In later times the pronunciation was softened in some of these cases by rejecting the hèmza and lengthening the preceding vowel; e. g. *èlhudātinā*, *yaḳūlūḏan*, *èllaḏītumina* (as if written ٱلْهُدَاتِنَا, يَقُولُوذَنْ, ٱلَّذِيتُمِنَ).

D REM. *c*. أْ is always retained after fètḥa in the ancient language, as يَأْسِرُ; but in modern Arabic it passes into the èlif of prolongation, as يَامُرُ, يَاكُلُ, for يَأْمُرُ, يَأْكُلُ. [And so even of old in Mecca, Nöldeke *Gesch. d. Qorâns*, p. 250, 257, whence with *scriptio defectiva* (§ 6, rem. *a*) such variations as يَلِتْكُمْ for يَأْلِتْكُمْ Sūra xlix. 14.] Those who used the form تِعْلَمُ (see § 94, rem. *c*) also said تِيثَمُ for تِئْثَمُ, from أَثِمَ.

133. In the same way, أ passes into ؤ or ئ, when it is pronounced A
with ḍamma or kèsra and preceded by fèṭḥa, or with fèṭḥa and preceded by ḍamma or kèsra; and into ئ, when it is pronounced with kèsra and preceded by ḍamma (see § 17, *b*). E.g. بُؤُسَ, for بَأُسَ, *to be brave;* يُلَائِمُ, for يُلَاءِمُ or يُلَاإِمُ, *it agrees with*, Imperf. III. of لَأَمَ; اِلْتَئِمْ, for اِلْتَإِمْ, *agree with, be reconciled to*, Imperat. VIII. of لَأَمَ; دَنُؤَ, for دَنُأَ, *to be mean, worthless;* يُؤَثَّرُ, for يُأَثَّرُ, *an impression is made*, Imperf. Pass. II. of أَثَّرَ; اِلْتِئَامٌ, for اِلْتِإَامٌ, Infin. VIII. of لَأَمَ; سُئِلَ *he* B
was asked, for سُإِلَ, Perf. Pass. of سَأَلَ; لُوئِمَ *peace is made (between them)*, for لُوإِمَ, Perf. Pass. III. of لَأَمَ.

Rem. At the end of a word, أ, pronounced with ḍamma and preceded by fèṭḥa, is usually left unchanged; as يَقْرَأُ from قَرَأَ, يَهْنَأُ from هَنِئَ, يُبَرَّأُ Imperf. Pass. II. of بَرِئَ, instead of يَقْرَؤُ, يَهْنَؤُ, يُبَرَّؤُ. But the latter form is commonly used before the accusative suffixes, as يَقْرَؤُهُ.

134. Finally, أ pronounced with ḍamma or kèsra (أُ or إِ), be- C
comes ؤ or ئ at the beginning of a syllable which is preceded by a syllable ending in a consonant. E.g. يَبْؤُسُ, for يَبْأُسُ, Imperf. of بَؤُسَ; مَسْؤُولٌ, for مَسْأُولٌ, Pass. Particip. of سَأَلَ; يَنْئِمُ, for يَنْإِمُ, Imperf. of نَأَمَ, *to groan, to twang;* يُلْئِمُ, for يُلْإِمُ, *he acts stingily and meanly*, Imperf. IV. of لَؤُمَ; اِسْتَلْئِمْ, *put on armour*, Imperat. X. of لَأَمَ.

Rem. أ at the beginning of a word remains unchanged, except in the cases stated in § 135. E.g. أُثِرَ, إِثَارٌ. D

135. At the beginning of a word, if an èlif productionis follows the radical أ, the two èlifs are combined into one, which is written either with mèdda alone, or with mèdda accompanied by a hèmza to the right of the èlif, or sometimes with hèmza and a perpendicular fèṭḥa (see § 6, rem. *a*); as آمَرَ, ءآمَرَ, or أٰمَرَ, for أَامَرَ, *to consult*, III. of

A أَمَرَ *to order.* The same thing takes place when a radical أ with gèzma (أْ) is preceded by an èlif hèmzatum with fètḥa (compare § 132, rem. *b*); as آثَرَ, آاْثَرَ, or أَوْثَرَ for أَأْثَرَ, *to prefer*, IV. of أَثَرَ. In old Mss. we often find أَامَرَ, أَاثَرَ.

136. In a more modern stage of the language, èlif hèmzatum with fètḥa passes into و, when preceded by fètḥa and followed by an
B èlif of prolongation (compare § 17, *b*, rem. *b*); as تَوَامَرُوا, for تَأَامَرُوا or تَآمَرُوا, *they deliberated together*, 3d pers. plur. Perf. Act. VI. of أَمَرَ; تَوَاخَيَا, for تَأَاخَيَا or تَآخَيَا, *the two became intimate friends*, from أَخَا (for أَخَوَ).

REM. The same change sometimes takes place even with the initial èlif of the third form; as وَاخَى *to be intimate with*, وَازَى *to be opposite* or *parallel to*, وَاسَى *to console*, وَاكَلَ *to eat along with*,
C for أَاخَى, etc. It commenced, of course, in the Imperf. and the Nomina agentis and actionis, where, according to § 17, *b*, rem. *b*, و took the place of ؤ; as يُوَاسِي, مُوَاسٍ, and مُوَاسَاةٌ.

137. The verbs أَخَذَ *to take*, أَمَرَ *to order*, and أَكَلَ *to eat*, reject the first radical in the Imperat., making خُذْ, مُرْ, and كُلْ.

138. When preceded by وَ or فَ, *and*, the Imperative مُرْ generally recovers its radical èlif, وَأْمُرْ or وَمُرْ; but not so خُذْ and كُلْ,
D which make only وَخُذْ, فَكُلْ. For the rule as regards other verba prim. rad. hèmz., see § 132, rem. *b*; and on the Imperative of أَتَى, *to come*, see also § 175, rem. *a*.

139. The first radical of أَخَذَ is assimilated in the eighth form to the characteristic ت of that form; اِتَّخَذَ, for اِيتَخَذَ (§ 132, rem. *b*), *to take for oneself.*

REM. *a.* The same assimilation sometimes takes place in أَزَرَ, *to put on one the article of dress called* إِزَارٌ, and أَجَرَ, *to give wages*, which makes اِيتَزَرَ or اِتَّزَرَ, *to put on an 'izār*, and اِيتَجَرَ or اِتَّجَرَ *to*

give alms, to receive wages; still more rarely in أَمِنَ, *to be safe,* A
اِتَّمَنَ, for اِيتَمَنَ, *to trust* or *confide in,* and أَهَلَ, *to marry,* اِتَّهَلَ, for اِيتَهَلَ, *do.*—The tenth form of أَخَذَ may also lose its élif and be written اِسْتَخَذَ.

Rem. *b.* From the above assimilated forms are derived the secondary radicals تَخِذَ, *to take,* and تَجَرَ, *to trade* (see § 148, rem. *b*). Compare in Syriac ܐܶܬܬܰܚܶܕ, ܐܶܬܬܰܓܰܪ, ܬܰܓܳܪܳܐ; and with B
اِسْتَخَذَ, ܐܶܫܬܰܟܰܚ, if from the rad. ܐܟܚ.

140. Verba med. hèmzatæ are occasionally inflected like verba med. rad. و et ى (§ 149, etc.), and take an élif of prolongation instead of the radical hèmza with fètḥa. This is particularly the case with the verb سَأَلَ *to ask,* which has سَالَ for سَأَلَ, 2d pers. sing. m. سِلْتَ [not سَلْتَ], يَسَالُ for يَسْأَلُ, يَسَلُ for يَسْأَلُ, سَلْ for اِسْأَلْ (Imperat.), Perf. Pass. سِيلَ.—Sometimes the élif hèmzatum is elided, its vowel being transferred to the preceding (previously vowelless) consonant. E.g. يَسَلُ C
for يَسْأَلُ, from سَأَلَ; يَرَى for يَرْأَى, from رَأَى *to see;* أَلَكَ *to send,* for أَلْأَكَ, whence مَلَكٌ, for مَلْأَكٌ, *an angel* (מַלְאָךְ).

Rem. *a.* The Imperative سَلْ makes in the fem. سَلِى, du سَلَا, plur. سَلُوا, not سَالِى, etc. When preceded by وَ and فَ, we may say وَٱسْأَلْ or وَسَلْ, فَٱسْأَلُوا, فَسْأَلُوا (§ 21, *d,* rem. *b*), or فَسَلُوا.

Rem. *b.* The elision of the élif occasionally happens in Hebrew, and in Syriac it is the rule; see *Comp. Gr.* p. 46, p. 282. D

2. *Verbs which are more especially called Weak Verbs* (§ 128, *b*).

141. These likewise fall into three classes, according as the letter و or ى is the first, second, or third radical (verba primæ, secundæ, tertiæ rad. و et ى).

A A. *Verbs of which the First Radical is* و or ى (*verba primæ rad.* و *et* ى).—*Table IX.*

142. Those verbs primæ rad. و, which have *kèsra* as the characteristic vowel of the Imperf. and Imperat., reject the و in these forms. E.g. وَلَدَ *to bear children,* Imperf. يَلِدُ for يَوْلِدُ, Imper. لِدْ for اِيلِدْ (اِوْلِدْ); وَعَدَ *to promise,* Imperf. يَعِدُ for يَوْعِدُ, Imper. عِدْ for اِيعِدْ (اِوْعِدْ).

REM. *a.* Eight verbs primæ rad. و, of the form فَعِلَ, have in
B the Imperf. يَفْعِلُ instead of يَفْعَلُ (contrary to the rule laid down in § 92), and hence elide their first radical; وَثِقَ *to trust* or *confide in,* يَثِقُ; وَرِثَ *to inherit,* يَرِثُ; وَرِعَ *to abstain from* (*what is unlawful*), يَرِعُ; وَرِمَ *to swell,* يَرِمُ; وَرِىَ *to be firm and hard* (of fat), يَرِى; وَفِقَ *to be in good condition and handsome,* يَفِقُ; وَلِىَ *to be near, to be in charge of,* يَلِى; وَمِقَ *to love,* يَمِقُ. Of these وَرِعَ has also dialectically the form يَوْرَعُ, and a few more admit both forms;
C e.g. وَحِرَ *to be angry with, full of hatred of,* يَحِرُ, يَوْحَرُ; وَعِرَ *to be rough and broken* (of ground), يَعِرُ, يَوْعَرُ; وَغِرَ *to be hot, angry,* يَغِرُ, يَوْغَرُ; وَلِهَ *to be stupefied with grief, to be melancholy,* يَلِهُ, يَوْلَهُ; وَهِلَ *to be cowardly, to forget,* يَهِلُ, يَوْهَلُ.

REM. *b.* The Imperat. عِمْ in the phrases عِمْ صَبَاحًا *good morning!* عِمْ مَسَآءً *good evening!* seems to come from وَعَمَ, but is in reality from نَعَمَ, Imperf. يَنْعِمُ, *to be happy, comfortable.* This is
D the solitary instance in Arabic of the loss of the initial *n* in the Imperat. of verbs פ״ן, which is so common in Heb. and Aram.

143. But those verbs primæ rad. و, which have fètḥa or ḍamma as the characteristic vowel of the Imperf. and Imperat., retain the و in these forms. E.g. وَجِرَ or وَجِلَ *to be afraid,* يَوْجَرُ or يَوْجَلُ, اِيجَرْ or اِيجَلْ (for اِوْجَرْ or اِوْجَلْ); وَجِعَ *to be in pain,* يَوْجَعُ; وَحِلَ *to stick*

in the mud, يَوْحَلُ ; وَبِقَ *to perish,* يَوْبَقُ ; وَبُؤَ *to be visited by the mur-* A
rain, يَوْبُؤُ ; وَبُلَ *to be unwholesome* or *insalubrious,* يَوْبُلُ ; وَضُؤَ *to be clean and fair,* يَوْضُؤُ. The same is the case with those verbs which are at once primæ rad. و and mediæ rad. geminatæ ; as وَدَّ (for وَدِدَ) *to love,* يَوَدُّ for يَوْدَدُ, إِيدَدْ for اِوْدَدْ.

Rem. In verbs primæ rad. و, of which the second and third radicals are strong, and in which the Imperf. has fètḥa, some Arabic dialects change the و into ا or ى. E.g. يَاجَلُ and يِيْجَلُ, for يَوْجَلُ, B
from وَجِلَ, *to be afraid ;* يَاجَعُ and يَيْجَعُ or يِيْجَعُ, for يَوْجَعُ, from وَجِعَ, *to be in pain ;* يَاهَمُ and يَيْهَمُ, for يَوْهَمُ, from وَهِمَ, *to make a mistake.* Others even use the forms يِيجَلُ, يِيجَعُ, and يِيهَمُ.

144. In a few verbs, of which the eight following are those that most commonly occur, the initial و is dropped in the Imperf. and Imperat., notwithstanding that the characteristic vowel of these forms C
is fètḥa.

وَدَعَ	*to let alone,*	يَدَعُ,	دَعْ.
وَذَرَ	*to let alone,*	يَذَرُ,	ذَرْ.
وَزَعَ	*to restrain,*	يَزَعُ,	زَعْ.
وَسِعَ	*to be wide* or *spacious,*	يَسَعُ,	سَعْ.
وَضَعَ	*to put down* or *place,*	يَضَعُ,	ضَعْ. D
وَطِئَ	*to trample upon,*	يَطَأُ,	طَأْ.
وَقَعَ	*to fall,*	يَقَعُ,	قَعْ.
وَهَبَ	*to give,*	يَهَبُ,	هَبْ.

Rem. *a.* The reason why the و is elided in these verbs probably is, that the fètḥa of the Imperf. and Imperat. owes its existence only to the fact of the second or third radical being in each case a guttural or semiguttural (ر).

Rem. *b.* وَدَعَ and وَذَرَ are not used in the Perf.

A **145.** In those forms in which a kèsra or ḍamma precedes a vowelless و, the و is changed into ى or و productionis, according to the preceding vowel. Hence إِيجَلْ, إِيدَدْ, for إِوْجَلْ, إِوْدَدْ, Imperat. I.; اِيرَاقَّ for اِوْرَاقَّ, Perf. XI.; إِيدَاعٌ, اِسْتِيدَاعٌ, for إِوْدَاعٌ, اِسْتِوْدَاعٌ, Infin. IV. and X.; يُوجِبُ for يُوْجِبُ, Imperf. Act. IV.; أُوجِبَ, أُسْتُودِعَ, for أُوْجِبَ, أُسْتُوْدِعَ, Perf. Pass. IV. and X.

REM. In the Passive of verbs primæ rad. و, the و is sometimes changed into أ, on account of a certain repugnance of the Arabs to
B the sound of the syllable وُ; e.g. أُقِّتَتْ, for وُقِّتَتْ, *it is fixed* or *determined* (of time); أُحِيَ, for وُحِيَ, *it is revealed.*

146. Verbs primæ rad. ى are inflected in almost all their forms like the strong verbs; e.g. يَسَرَ *to play at hazard*, or *to be gentle, easy,* يَيْسِرُ; يَفَعَ *to ascend* (a hill), *to be grown up,* يَيْفَعُ; يَقِظَ *to be awake,* يَيْقَظُ; يَقُظَ *do.*, يَيْقُظُ; يَنَعَ *to become ripe,* يَيْنَعُ or يَيْنِعُ.

C REM. يَبِسَ, *to be dry*, has يَيْبَسُ or يَيْبِسُ, and يَئِسَ, *to despair,* يَيْأَسُ or يَيْئِسُ. See § 92, rem. *a.* Dialectic varieties are يَابَسُ, for يَيْبَسُ, and يِيأَسُ or يَاءَسُ, for يَيْأَسُ. See § 143, rem.

147. In those forms in which a kèsra or ḍamma precedes a vowelless ى, the ى is changed into ى or و productionis, according to the preceding vowel. Hence إِيسِرْ for إِيْسِرْ, Imperat. I.; إِيسَارٌ and اِسْتِيسَارٌ, for إِيْسَارٌ and اِسْتِيْسَارٌ, Infin. IV. and X.; يُوسِرُ, يُوقِظُ, for يُيْسِرُ,
D يُيْقِظُ, Imperf. Act. IV. of يَسَرَ and يَقِظَ.

148. In the eighth form, و and ى are assimilated to the characteristic ت, producing تّ for وْت and يْت; as اِتَّعَدَ, for اِيتَعَدَ, (اِوْتَعَدَ), *to receive a promise*; اِتَّسَرَ, for اِيتَسَرَ (اِيْتَسَرَ), *to play at hazard.*

REM. *a.* Sometimes, however, although many grammarians disapprove of it, و and ى are not assimilated to the ت, but pass after fètḥa, ḍamma, and kèsra, into the homogeneous letters of prolonga-

tion, ا, و, ى. E.g. اِيتَصَلَ for اِوْتَصَلَ, اِيتَعَدَ for اِوْتَعَدَ (§ 145), A
اِيتَسَرَ for اِيْتَسَرَ, اُوتُسِرَ for اُيْتُسِرَ (§ 147), in the Perf.; يَاتَصِلُ for
يُوتَصِلُ, يَاتَعِدُ for يَوْتَعِدُ, يَاتَسِرُ for يَيْتَسِرُ, in the Imperf. Compare § 139, and rem. *a*.

Rem. *b*. From these assimilated forms are derived secondary radicals; such as تَجِهَ *to turn oneself towards, to face*; تَخِمَ *to suffer from indigestion*; تَسِعَ *to be wide* or *spacious*; تَقَى *to fear* (God); تَلَدَ *to be born in one's house* (of a slave), *to be hereditary, inherited,* B
or *long possessed*; تَكَلَ *to rely upon*; تَلِهَ *to be stupefied by grief, to be melancholy*; تَلَا, or تَلَى, *to follow*; and in the fourth form, أَتْكَأَ *to make one lean, to prop him up*; أَتْلَجَ *to insert*; أَتْهَمَ *to suspect* a person. Compare § 139, rem. *b*.

Rem. *c*. For the inflection of verbs of this class in the cognate languages, see *Comp. Gr.* p. 234 *seq.*

B. *Verbs of which the Second Radical is* و *or* ى (*verba* C
mediæ radicalis و *et* ى).—*Tables X.—XIII.*

149. Verba mediæ rad. و et ى (called by the Arab grammarians اَلْفِعْلُ ٱلْأَجْوَفُ, *the hollow verb*) differ from strong verbs only in the first, fourth, seventh, eighth, and tenth forms. The following sections indicate the principal points of difference.

150. If the first radical is without a vowel, and the third has one, the vowel of the second radical is thrown back upon the first, and the و or ى is changed into that letter of prolongation which is homogeneous to the vowel that the first radical has now assumed. E.g. D

يَقْوُلُ, *he says,*	becomes	يَقُولُ,	Imperf. Act. I.
يَسْيِرُ, *he goes,*	,,	يَسِيرُ,	do.
يَخْوَفُ, *he is afraid,*	,,	يَخَافُ,	do.
يَهْيَبُ, *he is afraid,*	,,	يَهَابُ,	do.
يُقْوَلُ, *it is said,*	,,	يُقَالُ,	Imperf. Pass. I.
يُقْيَلُ, *pardon is granted,*	,,	يُقَالُ,	Imperf. Pass. IV.

A	يَقْوُمُ,	*he remains,*	becomes	يُقِيمُ,	Imperf. Act. IV.
	يُلْيِنُ,	*he softens,*	,,	يُلِينُ,	do.
	أَقْوِمُوا,	*remain,*	,,	أَقِيمُوا,	Imperat. Plur. IV.
	أَلْيِنُوا,	*soften,*	,,	أَلِينُوا,	do.
	أَقْوَمَ,	*he remained,*	,,	أَقَامَ,	Perf. Act. IV.
	أَلْيَنَ,	*he softened,*	,,	أَلَانَ,	do.
B	يَسْتَقْوِمُ,	*he stands upright,*	,,	يَسْتَقِيمُ,	Imperf. Act. X.
	أُسْتُلْيِنَ,	*he was thought gentle,*	,,	أُسْتُلِينَ,	Perf. Pass. X.
	يُسْتَقْيَلُ,	*pardon is asked,*	,,	يُسْتَقَالُ,	Imperf. Pass. X.

151. But if the third radical loses its vowel, the long vowels ـَا, ـِى, ـُو, are changed into the corresponding short ones, because a shut syllable does not admit of a long vowel (§ 25). E.g.

C	يَقُلْ,	for	يَقُولْ	(يَقْوُلْ),	Jussive Act. I.
	يَسِرْ,	,,	يَسِيرْ	(يَسْيِرْ),	do.
	يَخَفْ,	,,	يَخَافْ	(يَخْوَفْ),	do.
	يُقَلْ,	,,	يُقَالْ	(يُقْوَلْ),	Jussive Pass. I.
	يُقِمْ,	,,	يُقِيمْ	(يُقْوِمْ),	Jussive Act. IV.
	أَقِلْ,	,,	أَقِيلْ	(أَقْيِلْ),	Imperat. IV.
	أَقِمْ,	,,	أَقِيمْ	(أَقْوِمْ),	do.
D	أَقَمْتَ,	,,	أَقَامْتَ	(أَقْوَمْتَ),	2d p. sing. m. Perf. Act. IV.
	أُقِدْتَ,	,,	أُقِيدْتَ	(أُقْوِدْتَ),	do. Pass. IV.
	أُسْتُلِنْتَ,	,,	أُسْتُلِينْتَ	(أُسْتُلْيِنْتَ),	do. Pass. X.
	أَقَمْنَ,	,,	أَقَامْنَ	(أَقْوَمْنَ),	3d p. plur. f. Perf. Act. IV.
	أَقِمْنَ,	,,	أَقِيمْنَ	(أَقْوِمْنَ),	2d p. plur. f. Imperat. IV.

REM. يَكُنْ, for يَكُونْ, Jussive of كَانَ, *to be*, is sometimes still farther abbreviated, especially by the poets, into يَكُ.

152. In consequence of the changes produced by the operation A
of the two preceding rules, the Imperative of the first form loses its
prosthetic ا (see §§ 98 and 122). E.g.

اُقْوُلْ becomes successively اُقُولْ, اُقُلْ, قُلْ.
اِسْيِرْ „ „ اِسِيرْ, اِسِرْ, سِرْ.
اِخْوَفْ „ „ اِخَافْ, اِخَفْ, خَفْ.
اِهْيَبْ „ „ اِهَابْ, اِهَبْ, هَبْ.
اُقْوُلُوا „ „ اُقُولُوا, . . . قُولُوا. B
اِسْيِرُوا „ „ اِسِيرُوا, . . . سِيرُوا.
اِخْوَفُوا „ „ اِخَافُوا, . . . خَافُوا.
اِهْيَبُوا „ „ اِهَابُوا, . . . هَابُوا.

153. If three open syllables follow one another in immediate
succession, the first of which has fètḥa and the last any vowel, then
the و or ى of the middle syllable is changed into ĕlif productionis,
without any regard to the nature of the vowel that accompanies it. C
E.g.

قَوَمَ becomes قَامَ, Perf. Act. I.
خَوِفَ „ خَافَ, do.
طَوُلَ „ طَالَ, do.
سَيَرَ „ سَارَ, do.
هَيِبَ „ هَابَ, do.
اِنْقَوَدَ „ اِنْقَادَ, Perf. Act. VII.
يَنْقَوِدُ „ يَنْقَادُ, Imperf. do. D
اِقْتَوَدَ „ اِقْتَادَ, Perf. Act. VIII.
اِزْدَيَدَ „ اِزْدَادَ, do.
يَزْدَيِدُ „ يَزْدَادُ Imperf. do.

Rem. The forms زِيلَ and كِيدَ are mentioned as being dialectically used instead of زَالَ (for زَيِلَ), *to cease*, and كَادَ (for كَوِدَ), *to be near* or *on the point of*.

A **154.** But if the vowel of the first syllable be ḍamma, and the و or ى is accompanied by kèsra, the ḍamma is elided and the kèsra substituted in its place, in consequence of which the و or ى becomes ى productionis. E.g.

قُوِلَ becomes (قُوْلَ) قِيلَ, Perf. Pass. I.
سُيِرَ „ (سُيْرَ) سِيرَ, do.
أُسْتُوِقَ „ (أُسْتُوْقَ) أُسْتِيقَ, Perf. Pass. VIII.
B أُخْتُيِرَ „ (أُخْتُيْرَ) أُخْتِيرَ, do.

REM. *a.* Instead of قِيلَ (قول), حِيلَ (حول), سِيقَ (سوق), غِيضَ (غيض), and the like, some Readers of the Ḳor'ān give the vowel ī an إِشْمَامُ ٱلضَّمِّ, *a scent* or *flavour of the u-sound* (حَرَكَةٌ بَيْنَ ٱلضَّمِّ وَٱلْكَسْرِ), that is to say, they pronounce it with the sound of the German *ü* in *hüten* or the French *u* in *lune* (compare § 123, rem.), *ḳüla, ḥüla, süḳa, ġüḍa.*

C REM. *b.* Some of the Arabs take another method of forming the Passive, namely by rejecting the vowel of the و or ى, and changing those letters into و productionis; as قُولَ (for قُوِلَ, قُوْلَ), حُوكَ (for حُوِكَ, حُوْكَ), بُوعَ (for بُيِعَ, بُيْعَ), أُخْتُورَ (for أُخْتُيِرَ, أُخْتُيْرَ). The verb سَالَ, for سَأَلَ (see § 140), is said to admit of the forms سُئِلَ, سِيلَ, *sūla*, and سُولَ.

REM. *c.* In forms like أُخْتِيرَ, أُسْتِيقَ, some assimilate the vowel
D of the prosthetic èlif to the following ī, اِخْتِيرَ, اِسْتِيقَ, pronouncing *i* or *ü*.

155. If the first radical has fètḥa and the third is without a vowel, three cases arise.

(*a*) The second radical is و or ى with fètḥa. In this case the second radical is elided along with its vowel, but its influence is strong enough to change the fètḥa of the first radical into ḍamma, if it was و, and into kèsra, if it was ى. E.g.

قُمْتَ for قَوَمْتَ, 2d pers. sing. m. Perf. Act. I.
سِرْتَ „ سَيَرْتَ, do.

(*b*) The second radical is و with ḍamma or ى with kèsra. In this A
case the second radical is elided along with its vowel, as in *a*, but its influence is sufficient to change the fètḥa of the first radical into the homogeneous vowel. E.g.

طُلْتَ for طَوُلْتَ, 2d pers. sing. m. Perf. Act. I.

هِبْتَ ,, هَيِبْتَ, do.

(*c*) The second radical is و with kèsra. In this case the same elision takes place, but the influence of the characteristic vowel *i*
suffices to change the fètḥa of the first radical into kèsra. E.g. B

خِفْتَ for خَوِفْتَ, 2d pers. sing. m. Perf. Act. I.

مِتَّ ,, مَوِتَّ (مَوِتْتَ), do.

156. In the Perfect Passive of the first, seventh, and eighth forms, if the third radical loses its vowel, the ى productionis (§ 154) is shortened into kèsra, according to § 25. E.g.

بِعْتَ for بِيعْتَ (بُيِعْتَ), 2d pers. sing. m. Perf. Pass. I.

لِمْتَ ,, لِيمْتَ (لُوِمْتَ), do. C

اُسْتِقْتَ ,, اُسْتِيقْتَ (اُسْتُوِقْتَ), do. VIII.

Rem. *a*. In verbs mediæ rad. ى, and in those mediæ rad. و of the form فَعِلَ, the 1st and 2d pers. m. and fem. sing. dual and plural Perf. Act. and Pass. are identical in form; e.g. بِعْتُ for بَيَعْتُ (§ 155, *a*) and بُيِعْتُ ; خِفْتَ for خَوِفْتَ (§ 155, *c*).

Rem. *b*. Those who pronounce in the 3d pers. *ḳūla*, *bū'a*, etc., D
say in the 1st and 2d persons *ḳültu*, *bü'tu*, etc.; whilst those who prefer قُولَ, بُوعَ, say قُلْتُ, بُعْتُ. [The prophet himself in the *ḥadīth al-waḥy* says فَهُلْتُ.—De G.]

157. Most verba mediæ rad. و take ḍamma, and most verba mediæ rad. ى kèsra, as the characteristic vowel of the Imperf.; e.g. from زَالَ (زَوَلَ), *to move away*, comes يَزُولُ (يَزْوُلُ); from نَالَ (نَوَلَ), *to give in a present*, يَنُولُ (يَنْوُلُ); from طَالَ (طَوُلَ), *to be long*, يَطُولُ (يَطْوُلُ, § 93); from زَانَ (زَيَنَ), *to adorn*, يَزِينُ (يَزْيِنُ); from سَارَ (سَيَرَ),

A *to go,* يَسِيرُ (يَسْيِرُ). But in some, which are of the form فَعِلَ, the Imperf. takes fèthạ (§ 92); e.g. from زَالَ (زَيِلَ), *to cease,* comes يَزَالُ (يَزْيَلُ); from نَالَ (نَيِلَ), *to get, obtain,* يَنَالُ (يَنْيَلُ); from شَآءَ (شَيِئَ), *to wish,* يَشَآءُ (يَشْيَأُ); from خَافَ (خَوِفَ), *to fear,* يَخَافُ (يَخْوَفُ); from نَامَ (نَوِمَ), *to sleep,* يَنَامُ (يَنْوَمُ). مَاتَ, *to die,* has usually the form مِتُّ (for مَوِتُّ, مَوِتْتُ, Heb. מֵת, Syr. ܡܺܝܬ) in the Perfect, and أَمُوتُ (Heb. יָמוּת, Syr. ܢܡܽܘܬ) in the Imperfect, though مُتُّ, يَمَاتُ, and
B also يَمِيتُ, are mentioned by the lexicographers.

158. In verba mediæ rad. و et ى, of which the third radical is ت or ن, these letters combine with an initial ت or ن in the pronominal suffixes so as to form تّ and نّ. E.g. مُتُّ, مُتُّمْ, for مُتْتُ, مُتْتُمْ, from مَاتَ (موت) *to die;* بِتَّ, for بِتْتَ, from بَاتَ (بيت) *to pass the night;* صُنَّ, for صُنْنَ, and يَصُنَّ, for يَصُنْنَ, from صَانَ (صون) *to*
C *guard;* بِنَّا, for بِنْنَا, and يَبِنَّ, for يَبِنْنَ, from بَانَ (بين) *to be separate.* See § 90, rem. *a, b, c.*

159. In the Passive of the third and sixth forms of verba med. rad. و, the و productionis (§ 108) does not coalesce with the second radical into وّ, for, if it did, the peculiar feature of these forms would be effaced, and they would become identical in appearance with the second and fifth (قُوِّلَ and تُقُوِّلَ). Hence we write قُووِلَ, تُقُووِلَ, not
D قُوِّلَ, تُقُوِّلَ. For the same reason, no coalition takes place in the same forms of verba mediæ rad. ى, which are always written, for example, بُويِعَ and تُبُويِعَ. See § 11, rem. *a*.

160. Some verba mediæ rad. و, and a few mediæ rad. ى, of the form فَعِلَ, are inflected throughout like strong verbs; as أَوِدَ *to be curved* or *bent,* Imperf. يَأْوَدُ; سَوِدَ *to be black,* Imperf. يَسْوَدُ, IV. أَسْوَدَ; عَوِرَ *to be one-eyed,* Imperf. يَعْوَرُ, IV. أَعْوَرَ; صَوِفَ *to be woolly,* Imperf.

يَصُوفُ ; حَوِلَ *to squint*, Imperf. يَحْوَلُ, IV. أَحْوَلَ ; عَوِزَ *to be wanting*, A
Imperf. يَعْوَزُ, IV. أَعْوَزَ ; صَيِدَ *to have a particular disease* (صَيَدٌ, *the glanders*), said of a camel, Imperf. يَصْيَدُ ; جَيِدَ *to have a long, slender neck*, Imperf. يَجْيَدُ ; غَيِدَ *to be tender and flexible*, Imperf. يَغْيَدُ ; هَيِفَ *to have a slender waist*, Imperf. يَهْيَفُ.

161. Some verba mediæ rad. و et ى follow in the fourth form either the strong or the weak inflection. E.g. أَثَابَ or أَثْوَبَ, *to reward*, from ثَابَ *to return*; أَرَاحَ or أَرْوَحَ, *to perceive the smell* or *odour* of a B
thing, from رَاحَ *do.*; أَغَامَ or أَغْيَمَ, *to be cloudy*, from غَامَ *do.*; أَخَالَ or أَخْيَلَ, *to watch a rain-cloud*, from خَالَ.

162. A few verba mediæ rad. و have only the strong inflection in the eighth form, used to denote reciprocity; as اِجْتَوَرَ *to be neighbours*, from the rad. جَارَ ; اِزْدَوَجَ *to pair, to marry* or *intermarry*, from the rad. زَاجَ ; اِعْتَوَرَ *to borrow*, from the rad. عَارَ ; اِعْتَوَنَ *to help one another*, C
from the rad. عَانَ.

163. Many verba mediæ rad. و admit in the tenth form of either inflection, but they generally prefer the weak, with the exception of a few, [chiefly denominatives], which almost always adopt the strong. E.g. اِسْتَجَابَ or اِسْتَجْوَبَ, *to give an answer, grant a prayer*, from the rad. جَابَ ; اِسْتَصْوَبَ or اِسْتَصَابَ, *to consider right*, from the rad. صَابَ ;
اِسْتَقْوَسَ *to be bent with age*, from قَوْسٌ *a bow*; اِسْتَنْوَقَ *to become like a* D
she-camel (نَاقَةٌ). Similarly, from verba med. rad. ى, اِسْتَتْيَسَ *to become like a he-goat* (تَيْسٌ); اِسْتَفْيَلَ *to become like an elephant* (فِيلٌ).

Rem. *a.* On اِسْطَاعَ or اِسْتَاعَ, shortened from اِسْتَطَاعَ, *to obey, to be able* to do, X. of طَاعَ, and on the secondary أَسْطَاعَ, see § 118, rem. *b*.

Rem. *b.* On the formation of the nomina agentis et patientis of the first form from verba med. rad. و et ى, see §§ 240–1.

Rem. *c.* For the inflection of verbs ע״ו and ע״י in Hebrew and Aramaic see *Comp. Gr.* p. 242 *seq.*

A C. *Verbs of which the Third Radical is* و *or* ى (*verba tertiæ radicalis* و *et* ى ; اَلْفِعْلُ ٱلنَّاقِصُ *the defective verb*).—*Tables XIV.—XVIII.*

164. These verbs are of five kinds ; namely :—

(*a*) Verba tertiæ rad. و of the form فَعَلَ ; as غَزَا *to make a foray* or *raid*, for غَزَوَ (§ 167, *a*, *β*, a).

(*b*) Verba tertiæ rad. ى of the form فَعَلَ ; as رَمَى *to throw*, for رَمَىَ (§ 167, *a*, *β*, a).

B (*c*) Verba tertiæ rad. و of the form فَعِلَ ; as رَضِىَ *to be pleased with*, for رَضِوَ (§ 166, *a*).

(*d*) Verba tertiæ rad. ى of the form فَعِلَ ; as خَزِىَ *to be ashamed.*

(*e*) Verba tertiæ rad. و of the form فَعُلَ ; as سَرُوَ *to be noble.*

165. There are three things to be noticed regarding the third radical of these verbs; namely, that it retains its power as a consonant,
C or it resolves itself into a vowel, or it is elided.

166. At the commencement of a syllable, one of two things takes place. Namely :—

(*a*) The third radical maintains its power as a consonant between the vowels *ă—ā* (ـَوَا, ـَيَا), *ŭ—ă* (ـُوَ), *ŭ—ā* (ـُوَا), *ĭ—ă* (ـِىَ), *ĭ—ā* (ـِيَا); as also when the preceding syllable ends with a consonant. E.g. غَزْوٌ ; تَرْمِيَانِ, تَرْمِىَ, رَضِيَا, رَضِىَ ; يَغْزُوَانِ, يَغْزُوَ, سَرُوَا, سَرُوَتْ ; رَمَيَا, غَزَوَا,
D رَمْىٌ, رِضْوَانٌ. The letter و between the vowels *ĭ—ă* (ـِوَ) and *ĭ—ā* (ـِوَا) always passes into ى ; as رَضِىَ, غُزِىَ, for رَضِوَ, غُزِوَ. The letter ى is never found between the vowels *ŭ—ă*, *ŭ—ā*.

REM. In the first and second classes, the 3d pers. fem. sing. and dual of the Perf. Act. I. and II. might have been غَزَوَتْ, غَزَوَتَا, رَمَيَتْ, رَمَيَتَا, etc., after the analogy of رَضِيَتْ, خَزِيَتْ, and سَرُوَتْ ; but the Arabs followed in the sing. the masc. forms غَزَا, رَمَى (§ 167, *a*, *β*, a), and, not being able to say غَزَاتْ and رَمَاتْ or رَمَيْتْ (§ 25), they substituted غَزَتْ and رَمَتْ. In the dual, on the other hand, where they

might have said غَزَاتَا and رَمَاتَا, they followed the received fem. sing. A
in adopting غَزَتَا and رَمَتَا. The form رَمَاتَا is said to occur dialectically, but is condemned by the grammarians.

(*b*) The third radical is elided between a short vowel and the long vowels *ī* and *ū*, and the two vowels are contracted in one of two ways.

α. Into a long vowel; namely ـُوُو into ـُو, as سَرُوا for سَرُوُوا, يَغْزُونَ and يَغْزُوا for يَغْزُوُونَ and يَغْزُوُوا; ـِيُو into ـُو, as رَضُوا for رَضِيُوا, يَرْمُونَ and يَرْمُوا for يَرْمِيُونَ and يَرْمِيُوا; ـُوِى into ـِى, as B
تَغْزِينَ and تَغْزِى for تَغْزُوِينَ and تَغْزُوِى, اُغْزِى for اُغْزُوِى; ـِيِى into ـِى, as تَرْمِينَ and تَرْمِى for تَرْمِيِينَ and تَرْمِيِى, اِرْمِى for اِرْمِيِى.

Rem. The 2d pers. sing. fem. Imperat. اُغْزِى may be pronounced either *'uġzī*, with the pure sound of the *u* (as in the masc. *'uġzu*), or *'üġzī*, with the إِشْمَام (see §§ 123, rem., and 154, rem. *a*), owing to the influence of the *ī* in the second syllable.

β. Into a diphthong; namely ـَوُو into ـَوْ, as غَزَوْا for غَزَوُوا; C
ـَيُو into ـَوْ, as رَمَوْا for رَمَيُوا, يَرْضَوْنَ and يَرْضَوْا for يَرْضَيُونَ and يَرْضَيُوا, يُغْزَوْنَ and يُغْزَوْا for يُغْزَيُونَ and يُغْزَيُوا; ـَيِى into ـَىْ, as تَرْضَيْنَ and تَرْضَىْ for تَرْضَيِينَ and تَرْضَيِى, تُغْزَيْنَ and تُغْزَىْ for تُغْزَيِينَ and تُغْزَيِى, اِرْضَىْ for اِرْضَيِى.

167. At the end of a syllable, the third radical is either vocalised or elided. It may stand at the end of a syllable either naturally, as in غَزَوْتَ = فَعَلْتَ, or after dropping a short vowel, as in يَرْمِى for D
يَرْمِىُ = يَفْعِلُ. Hence arise the following cases.

(*a*) α. When standing naturally at the end of a syllable, the third radical is vocalised in two ways.

(a) If the preceding vowel be homogeneous (ـُ or ـِ), و and ى become letters of prolongation, that is to say, ـُوْ *uw* and ـِىْ *iy* pass into ـُو *ū* and ـِى *ī*. E.g. سَرُوتَ for سَرُوْتَ, خَزِيتَ for خَزِيْتَ, رَضِيتَ for رَضِيْتَ (from رَضِىَ for رَضِوَ, according to §§ 166, *a*, and 168).

A (b) If the preceding vowel be heterogeneous (ـَ), it forms with و and ى the diphthongs ـَوْ and ـَىْ. E.g. غَزَوْتَ, *ġazauta*, for *ġazawta* ; رَمَيْتَ, *ramaita*, for *ramayta*.

β. When the third radical stands at the end of a syllable, not naturally, but in consequence of a short vowel having been dropped (ـَوْ for ـَوَ, ـَىْ for ـَىَ and ـَىُ, ـُوْ for ـُوُ, ـِىْ for ـِىُ), it is vocalised in three different ways.

(a) ـَوْ *aw* and ـَىْ *ay* become *ā*, but for the sake of distinction
B we write ـَا for *aw*, and ـَى (§ 7, rem. *b*) for *ay*. E.g. غَزَا for غَزَوَ, رَمَى for رَمَيَ, يُغْزَى for يُغْزَيُ and يُغْزَيَ, يُرْمَى for يُرْمَيُ and يُرْمَيَ.

(b) ـُوْ *uw* becomes ـُو *ū* ; as يَغْزُو, يَسْرُو, for يَغْزُوُ, يَسْرُوُ.

(c) ـِىْ *iy* becomes ـِى *ī* ; as تَرْمِى for تَرْمِيُ.

(*b*) The third radical is elided :—

a. When standing naturally at the end of a syllable. This
C happens in the Jussive and Imperative, in which the signification of the form produces the abbreviation. E.g. يَغْزُ, اُغْزُ, for يَغْزُوْ (يَغْزُوْ), اُغْزُوْ (اُغْزُوْ) ; يَرْمِ, اِرْمِ, for يَرْمِى (يَرْمِىْ), اِرْمِى (اِرْمِىْ) ; يَرْضَ, اِرْضَ, for يَرْضَى (يَرْضَىْ), اِرْضَى (اِرْضَىْ)*.

β. When it does not naturally stand at the end of a syllable. This happens in the nomina agentis, فَاعِلٌ (§ 80), مُفَعِّلٌ, مُفْعِلٌ, etc. (see § 236), before the tènwīn of ḍamma and kèsra. These vowels are elided at the same time, but the tènwīn is thrown back upon the kèsra
D of the second radical. E.g. رَامٍ for رَامِيٌ and رَامِيٍ ; غَازٍ for غَازِيٌ and غَازِيٍ (غَازِوٌ, غَازِوٍ, § 166, *a*) ; رَاضٍ for رَاضِيٌ and رَاضِيٍ (رَاضِوٌ, رَاضِوٍ) ; مُغَنٍّ for مُغَنِّيٌ and مُغَنِّيٍ ; مُغْنٍ for مُغْنِيٌ and مُغْنِيٍ ; etc.

168. It has been already mentioned (§ 166, *a*) that when the third radical is و, it passes between the vowels *ĭ—ă* (ـِوَ) and *ĭ—ā*

---

* [At the end of a sentence the final vowel of the Imperative is often protected by a ه, as اِمْضِهْ *go on*, اُدْنُهْ *approach*. The Jussive is sometimes treated in the same manner (comp. Vol. ii. § 230). D. G.]

(ـِوا) into ى. After ى has been introduced in this manner into the A
3d pers. sing. masc. Perf., it maintains itself throughout the whole inflection, as far as the above rules permit. Consequently, we get from رَضِىَ (for رَضِوَ) the forms رَضِيتَ, يَرْضَى, اِرْضَ, تَرْضَيْنَ ; from غَزَى, غُزِيتَ, تُغْزَيْنَ.

169. Final و is changed into ى in all the derived forms of the
verb ; as غَزَّى, رَاضَى, أَغْزَى, تَجَلَّى, تَرَاضَى, اِنْجَلَى, اِغْتَزَى, اِسْتَرْضَى. B

REM. The ninth and eleventh forms conform to this rule, instead of contracting the two wāws into وّ. The Arabs say اِرْعَوَى *to abstain* or *refrain*, for اِرْعَوَوَ, and not اِرْعَوَّ (اِفْعَلَّ, see § 59, rem. *a*).

170. In the nomina patientis, مَفْعُولٌ (§ 80), of verba tertiæ rad. و, the و of the long vowel ـُو *ū* coalesces with the radical و into وّ ; as مَغْزُوٌّ for مَغْزُووٌ. In verba tertiæ rad. ى, the influence of the third radical converts this secondary و into ى, the two coalesce
into ىّ, and, in consequence, the preceding ḍamma becomes kèsra ; C
as مَرْمِىٌّ for مَرْمُىٌّ, مَرْمُوْىٌ. Such verbs as رَضِىَ, in which the final ى stands for و (§ 166, *a*), admit of either form, though مَرْضِىٌّ is far more common than مَرْضُوٌّ.

REM. *a*. The form مَغْزِىٌّ is occasionally found in verba tert. rad. و, instead of مَغْزُوٌّ ; e.g. أَرْضٌ مَسْنِيَّةٌ or أَرْضٌ مَسْنُوَّةٌ, *irrigated land*, from سَنَا *to irrigate*, Imperf. يَسْنُو ; أَنَا ٱللَّيْثُ مَعْدِيًّا عَلَيْهِ وَعَادِيَا,
I am (like) the lion, whether attacked or attacking, from عَدَا عَلَى *to* D
run at, to attack, Imperf. يَعْدُو (عَادِيَا in rhyme for عَادِيًا).

REM. *b*. For verbs final و and ى as compared with the corresponding forms in the other Semitic dialects see *Comp. Gr.* p. 255 *seq*.

3. *Verbs that are Doubly and Trebly Weak* (§ 129).

171. Doubly weak verbs are divisible into two classes, each of which comprises several varieties. The *first class* consists of those which have both an èlif hèmzatum and a و or ى among their radicals ; the *second* of those in which the letter و or ى occurs twice.

A REM. There is no triliteral verb that has more than one radical hèmza.

172. Of the first class there are three sorts :—

(*a*) Verba hèmzata and primæ rad. و or ى ;

(*b*) Verba hèmzata and secundæ rad. و or ى ;

(*c*) Verba hèmzata and tertiæ rad. و or ى.

Each of these admits of two varieties, according to the position of the èlif hèmzatum.

B **173.** The first sort consists of (α) verba secundæ rad. hèmzatæ, as وَأَرَ *to frighten*; and (β) verba tertiæ rad. hèmzatæ, as وَدَأَ *to smooth*, وَطِئَ *to tread upon*. Such words follow in their inflection both the classes to which they belong; e.g. Imperf. يَئِرُ, يَدَأُ, يَطَأُ (§§ 132—3, and 142, 144).

REM. The Imperf. of يَئِسَ, *to despair*, is يَيْأَسُ, more rarely يَيْئِسُ or يِيأَسُ, [also يَاءَسُ and يَايَسُ]; its Imperat. ايأَسْ, rarely ايئِسْ. See § 146, rem.

C **174.** The second sort is divided into (α) verba primæ rad. hèmzatæ, as آبَ or ءَآبَ (for أَوَبَ) *to return*, آلَ *or* ءَآلَ (for أَوَلَ) *to return*; and (β) verba tertiæ rad. hèmzatæ, as سَآءَ (for سَوَءَ) *to illtreat*, جَآءَ (for جَيَأَ) *to come*, شَآءَ (for شَيِءَ) *to wish*. Each variety unites the peculiarities of the two classes to which it belongs.

	α.		β.	
Perf. 3d p. s.	ءَآبَ	سَآءَ	جَآءَ	شَآءَ
2d p. s.	أُبْتَ	سُؤْتَ	جِئْتَ	شِئْتَ
Imperf.	يَؤُوبُ	يَسُوءُ	يَجِيءُ	يَشَآءُ
Imper.	أُبْ	سُؤْ	جِئْ	شَأْ
Perf. pass.	إِيبَ	سِيءَ	جِيءَ	شِيءَ

D

175. The third sort is divided into (α) verba primæ rad. hèmzatæ, as أَتَى *to come*, أَبَى *to refuse*, أَسِيَ *to grieve* or *mourn*; and (β) verba secundæ rad. hèmzatæ, as نَأَى *to be far off*, صَأَى *to utter a cry*. They are treated in their inflection like the two classes of verbs to which they belong.

a. أَتَى, أَتَتْ, أَتَيْتَ ; يَأْتِى ; اِيتِ (§ 132, rem. *b*) ; آتِ. A

أَبَى, أَبَتْ, أَبَيْتَ ; يَأْبَى ; اِيبَ ; آبِ.

β. نَأَى, نَأَتْ, نَأَيْتَ ; يَنْأَى ; اِنْأَ ; نَأَ.

Rem. *a*. The Imperat. of the verb أَتَى is not unfrequently shortened into تِ (compare § 137, and the Syriac form ܬܐ), which, at the end of a sentence, is written تِهْ. The same thing holds good in pause of all imperatives that consist of only one letter ; as رَهْ for B
رَ, from رَأَى *to see* (§ 176) ; فِهْ for فِ, from وَفَى *to keep faith* (§ 177).

Rem. *b*. The verb أَبَى, imperf. يَأْبَى, is an example of the rare forms mentioned in § 91, rem. *c*. Lexicographers mention the forms يَأْبِى, يِئْبَى, and يِئْبِى [§ 94, rem. *c*], as being occasionally used.

176. The èlif hèmzatum of the verb رَأَى is almost always elided in the Imperf. and Imperat.

Imperf. Indicative. C

	3. m.	3. f.	2. m.	2. f.	1. c.
S.	يَرَى	تَرَى	تَرَى	تَرَيْنَ	أَرَى
D.	يَرَيَانِ	تَرَيَانِ	تَرَيَانِ	تَرَيَانِ	
P.	يَرَوْنَ	يَرَيْنَ	تَرَوْنَ	تَرَيْنَ	نَرَى

Jussive.

S.	يَرَ	تَرَ	تَرَ	تَرَيْ	أَرَ
D.	يَرَيَا	تَرَيَا	تَرَيَا	تَرَيَا	
P.	يَرَوْا	يَرَيْنَ	تَرَوْا	تَرَيْنَ	نَرَ

D

Imperative.

S. m. رَ or رَهْ (§ 175, rem. *a*), f. رَيْ ; D. c. رَيَا ; P. m. رَوْا, f. رَيْنَ.

Rem. *a*. The Perf. Act. of رَأَى almost always retains the hèmza, which may however be transposed, رَآءَ ; [for رَأَيْتُ some say رَيْتُ]. The Imperf. يَرْأَى and the Imperat. اِرْءَ are used dialectically.

A REM. *b.* The Perf. Pass. is رُئِىَ (like رُمِىَ) or, by transposition, رِىءَ*. In the Imperf. Pass. the hèmza is elided, just as in the Active voice; e.g. يُرَى, يُرَ, for يُرْأَى, يُرْءَ.

REM. *c.* In the fourth form, when it signifies *to show,* the hèmza is always elided: أَرَى, أَرَتْ, أَرَيْتَ; يُرِى; يُرِ; أَرِ. Otherwise it is retained.

B **177.** Of the second class, in which و or ى occurs twice, there are two sorts: (*a*) those in which و or ى is the first and third radical, as وَقَى *to guard,* وَلِىَ *to be near,* وَجِىَ *to be sorefooted* (of a horse); and (*β*) those in which و or ى is the second and third radical, as شَوَى *to roast,* قَوِىَ *to be strong,* حَيِىَ (for حَيِوَ) *to live,* عَيِىَ *to have an impediment in one's speech.*

178. The first sort follows in its inflection the verbs of the two
C classes primæ and tertiæ rad. و or ى. E.g.

وَقَى, وَقَتْ, وَقَيْتَ; يَقِى; قِ or قِهْ (§ 175, rem. *a*).

وَلِىَ, وَلِيَتْ, وَلِيتَ; يَلِى; لِ or لِهْ.

وَجِىَ, وَجِيَتْ, وَجِيتَ; يَوْجَى; اِيجَ (for اِوْجَ).

179. In the second sort, the second radical undergoes no change whatever. E.g.

شَوَى, شَوَتْ, شَوَيْتَ; يَشْوِى; اِشْوِ

D قَوِىَ, قَوِيَتْ, قَوِيتَ; يَقْوَى; اِقْوَ.

حَيِىَ, حَيِيَتْ, حَيِيتَ; يَحْيَا; اِحْىَ.

عَيِىَ, عَيِيَتْ, عَيِيتَ; يَعْيَا; اِعْىَ.

REM. *a.* We write يَحْيَا, يَعْيَا, not يَحْيَى, يَعْيَى, to prevent the union of two ى, and also, in the former case, to distinguish the Imperf. of حَيِىَ from the proper name يَحْيَى *Yaḥyā* (John).

REM. *b.* حَيِىَ admits (1) of the *contraction* of the two ى, (*a*) in those persons of the Perf. I. in which the second ى has a vowel, as

* [A more recent form is رُؤِىَ; see the Gloss. to Tabarī. D. G.]

حَىَّ for حَيِيَ: (*b*) in the Imperf. I., as يَحَىُّ, يَحَىَّ, يَحَيَّنَ; (*c*) in the A
nomen actionis II. (§§ 80 and 202, rem.), تَحِيَّةٌ for تَحْيِيَةٌ; (2) of the *elision* of the second ى in the Perf. and Imperf. X., when it signifies *to feel shame*, as اِسْتَحَى, يَسْتَحِى, for اِسْتَحْيَا, يَسْتَحْيِى.—عَيِىَ also admits of being contracted into عَىَّ, and يَعْيَا into يَعَىُّ.—The forms حَىِّ and عَىِّ are said to occur (compare § 123, rem., and § 153, rem.).

180. Trebly weak verbs are divisible into two classes; namely B
(*a*) those in which one radical is hèmza and the other two و or ى; and (*b*) those in which all the three radicals are و or ى.

Rem. We pass over the second class, as it seems to consist of only one verb, which is hardly ever used; viz. يَيَّا *to write the letter* ى.

181. Verbs of the first class are of two sorts, namely (α) those in which the hèmza is the first radical, as أَوَى *to betake oneself to, to*
repair to; and (β) those in which the hèmza is the second radical, C
as وَأَى *to promise*. The former are inflected like أَسَرَ and شَوَى (§ 179), e.g. أَوَى, أَوَتْ, أَوَيْتَ, يَأْوِى, اِيوِ; the latter like سَأَلَ and وَقَى (§ 178), e.g.

Perfect.

	3. m.	3. f.	2. m.	2. f.	1. c.	
S.	وَأَى	وَأَتْ	وَأَيْتَ	وَأَيْتِ	وَأَيْتُ	
D.	وَأَيَا	وَأَتَا	وَأَيْتُمَا	وَأَيْتُمَا		D
P.	وَأَوْا	وَأَيْنَ	وَأَيْتُمْ	وَأَيْتُنَّ	وَأَيْنَا	

Imperf. Indicative.

S.	يَإِى	تَإِى	تَإِى	تَإِينَ	أَإِى
D.	يَإِيَانِ	تَإِيَانِ	تَإِيَانِ	تَإِيَانِ	
P.	يَأُونَ	يَإِينَ	تَأُونَ	تَإِينَ	نَإِى

A *Jussive.*

	3. m.	3. f.	2. m.	2. f.	1. c.
S.	يَإِ	تَإِ	تَإِ	تَإِى	أَإِ
D.	يَإِيَا	تَإِيَا	تَإِيَا	تَإِيَا	
P.	يَأُوا	يَإِينَ	تَأُوا	تَإِينَ	نَإِ

Imperative.

B S. m. إِ or إِهْ (§ 175, rem. *a*), f. إِى; D. c. إِيَا; P. m. أُوا, f. إِينَ.

APPENDIX A.

I. *The Verb* لَيْسَ.

182. The negative substantive verb لَيْسَ, *he is not*, has no Imperf. or Imperat., and is inflected like verba mediæ rad. و et ى.

	3. m.	3. f.	2. m.	2. f.	1. c.
S.	لَيْسَ	لَيْسَتْ	لَسْتَ	لَسْتِ	لَسْتُ
C D.	لَيْسَا	لَيْسَتَا	لَسْتُمَا	لَسْتُمَا	
P.	لَيْسُوا	لَسْنَ	لَسْتُمْ	لَسْتُنَّ	لَسْنَا

REM. *a.* لَيْسَ is compounded of لَا, *not*, and the unused أَيْسَ* = Heb. יֵשׁ, *he is*, Aramaic אִיתַי, אִית, ܐܝܬ; originally a substantive, signifying *being, existence,* as in the phrase لَا يَعْرِفُ أَيْسَ مِنْ لَيْسَ, *he does not know what is from what is not.* [Therefore the suffix of the 1st person sing. added to لَيْسَ is not only لَيْسَنِى (and لَيْسَ إِيَّاىَ), but also لَيْسِى (§ 185, rem. *a*, Vol. ii. § 186, *e*).]. The Assyrian D seems also to have the word *isu*, with its negative *lā isu*, in the double sense of 'to be' and 'to have'.

REM. *b.* Instead of لَيْسَ we find occasionally [as in the Ḳor'ānic phrase وَلَاتَ حِينَ مَنَاصٍ] the indeclinable لَاتَ, which corresponds to the Aramaic ܠܝܬ, לֵית, לָית, compounded of לָא and אִית, ܐܝܬ.

---

* [Or rather يَسَ according to Nöldeke, *Mand. Gramm.* p. 293, note 5.]

II. *The Verbs of Praise and Blame.* A

183. The *verbs of praise and blame* (أَفْعَالُ ٱلْمَدْحِ وَٱلذَّمِّ) are نِعْمَ, *to be good*, and بِئْسَ, *to be bad*. They are used as exclamations, and are generally indeclinable, though the fem. نِعْمَتْ and بِئْسَتْ (and, it is said, the dual نِعْمَا, نِعْمَتَا, and the plur. نِعْمُوا, نِعْمْنَ) occur. [The following noun must be defined by the article or a dependent genitive, as: نِعْمَ ٱلصَّاحِبُ زَيْدٌ, *Zèid is an excellent companion*, lit. B *excellent is the companion Zèid*, or else the indefinite accusative must be used نِعْمَ صَاحِبًا زَيْدٌ, *excellent as a companion is Zèid*.]

Rem. *a*. Instead of نِعْمَ we may say نِعِمَ, نَعْمَ, and نَعِمَ, which last is obviously the original form. In like manner بِئْسَ admits of the forms بِئِسَ, بَأْسَ, and بَئِسَ. If followed by مَا, we may write بِئْسَ مَا or بِئْسَمَا, and نِعْمَ مَا or, by contraction, نِعِمَّا.

Rem. *b*. These forms are to be explained as follows. (1) Every C Arabic verb of the form فَعِلَ or فَعُلَ may also be pronounced فَعْلَ; as بَذْخَ for بَذِخَ, دَبْرَ for دَبِرَ, ضَجْرَ for ضَجِرَ, عَلْمَ for عَلِمَ, رَضْيَ for رَضِيَ, شَهْدَ for شَهِدَ and شَهُدَ, حَسْنَ for حَسُنَ, قَرْبَ for قَرُبَ, قَصْرَ for قَصُرَ, كَرْمَ for كَرُمَ,—a contraction which is sometimes extended to the passive فُعِلَ, as مُطْيَ for مُطِيَ (from مَطَا). Hence نَعِمَ and بَئِسَ become نَعْمَ and بَأْسَ. (2) If the second radical be guttural, its vowel, instead of being elided, may be transferred to the first D radical; as شِهْدَ for شَهِدَ, ذِهْبَ for ذَهِبَ. Hence نِعْمَ for نَعِمَ, بِئْسَ for بَئِسَ. (3) The form فِعْلَ, which has been thus attained, may take an additional kèsra to lighten the pronunciation (فِعِلَ); as شِهِدَ, ذِهِبَ. Hence نِعِمَ, بِئِسَ [or rather, according to *Comp. Gr.* p. 166, شَهِدَ becomes شِهِدَ by assimilation of the vowels, and the latter may then be shortened to شِهْدَ, as the former may be shortened

A to شَهُدَ].—These observations cast light on the peculiar form of
intransitive verbs in Æthiopic; as *gabra* ("to do") for *gabĭra* (com-
pare عَمِلَ), and, when the second radical is guttural, *mĕḥra* ("to
have pity upon," رَحِمَ) for *maḥĭra*, *sĕḫna* ("to be hot," سَخُنَ) for
saḫĭna or *saḫŭna*, see *Comp. Gr.* l.c.

REM. *c.* Other verbs of this class are حَبَّ or حُبَّ, *to be pleasing*
or *charming* (contracted from حَبُبَ)*; حَسُنَ, usually contracted into
B حُسْنَ, *to be good* or *excellent*; سَآءَ, *to be bad* or *evil*; بَعُدَ, commonly
contracted into بُعْدَ, *to be far off*; and سَرُعَ or سُرْعَ, *to be quick*
(contracted from سَرُعَ). The first of these is frequently combined
with the demonstrative ذَا (§ 340), and forms the indeclinable حَبَّذَا,
lovely, charming, or *excellent, is* ——.

III. *The Forms expressive of Surprise or Wonder.*

184. The Arabic language possesses two forms of expression,
C called by the native grammarians أَفْعَالُ ٱلتَّعَجُّبِ or *verbs of surprise*
or *wonder*. The one is the 3d pers. sing. masc. Perf. Act. IV.,
preceded by مَا (مَا ٱلتَّعَجُّبِيَّةُ *the mā expressive of surprise*), and
followed by the accusative of the object that causes surprise; as
مَا أَفْضَلَ زَيْدًا, *what an excellent man Zèid is!* The other is the
2d pers. sing. masc. Imperat. IV., followed by the preposition بِ with
the genitive; as أَفْضِلْ بِزَيْدٍ, with the same signification as before.

REM. *a.* The first formula literally means: *what has made Zèid
excellent?* can anything make him more excellent than he is? The
D second: *make Z. excellent* (if you can,—you cannot make him more
excellent than he is); or, more literally: *try (your ability at) making
excellent upon* (بِ) *Zèid.* They are, of course, indeclinable. [For
أَكْثِرْ بِسَعْدٍ a poet says كَاثِرْ بِسَعْدٍ. *Hamāsa* p. 670; comp. § 43, rem.
c. D. G.]

REM. *b.* Verbs of surprise are, generally speaking, formed only
from triliteral verbs in the active voice, which are capable of being
fully inflected, and express an act or state in which one person may

* [You say حَبَّ زَيْدٌ إِلَيْنَا and, more commonly, حُبَّ بِزَيْدٍ إِلَيْنَا, *how beloved Zèid is to us!* D. G.]

vie with or surpass another. They cannot be formed from the A
passive voice; nor from quadriliterals; nor from verbs that are
defective in inflection, like نِعْمَ and بِئْسَ, or in meaning, like the
substantive verb كَانَ *to be* (from كَانَ زَيْدٌ قَآئِمًا, *Zèid was standing
up*, we cannot say مَا أَكْوَنَ زَيْدًا قَآئِمًا or أَكْوِنْ بِزَيْدٍ قَآئِمًا); nor
from verbs like مَاتَ *to die* and فَنِيَ *to perish*, expressing an act or
state in which one agent cannot excel another; nor from negatived
verbs (as مَا عَاجَ بِٱلدَّوَآءِ, *he did not heed the medicine*); nor from
verbs signifying colours and defects, whence are derived adjectives B
of the form أَفْعَلُ (as سَوِدَ *to be black*, أَسْوَدُ, حَوِلَ *to squint*, أَحْوَلُ).
The grammarians add that verbs of surprise cannot be formed from
the derived forms of the triliteral verb; but neither this limitation,
nor that with respect to the passive voice, is strictly observed (compare § 235). We find, for example, from the Passive مَا أَشْغَلَهُ, *how
much he is busied!* from شُغِلَ *to be busy;* مَا أَزْهَاهُ, *how proud* or
vain he is! from زُهِيَ *to be proud* or *vain;* مَا أَمْقَتَهُ عِنْدِي, *how
hateful he is to me!* from مُقِتَ *to be hated;* and from derived forms, C
especially the fourth, مَا أَعْطَاهُ, *how liberal he is!* from أَعْطَى *to
give*, IV. of عَطَا *to take in the hand;* مَا أَوْلَاهُ لِلْمَعْرُوفِ, *how liberal
he is in bestowing gratuities!* from أَوْلَى *to bestow*, IV. of وَلِيَ *to be
near;* مَا أَحْوَلَهُ, or مَا أَحْيَلَهُ, *how wily he is!* from اِحْتَالَ *to practise
an artifice* or *wile*, VIII. of حَالَ *to be shifted* or *changed;* مَا أَخْصَرَهُ,
how short, or *shortened, it is!* from اُخْتُصِرَ *to be shortened* or *abridged*, D
passive of VIII. from the rad. خصر. The rule with regard to verbs
expressing colours or defects is violated, for example, by مَا أَحْمَقَهُ,
how stupid he is! from حَمُقَ *to be stupid*, أَحْمَقُ, مَا أَبْيَضَ هٰذَا ٱلثَّوْبَ,
how white this piece of cloth is! from اِبْيَضَّ *to be white*, أَبْيَضُ.

Rem. *c*. When formed from verbs med. rad. gemin. or tert. rad.
و et ى, the verbs of surprise follow the inflection of these classes;
as مَا أَشَدَّ أَبَاهُ or أَشْدِدْ بِأَبِيهِ, *how strong his father is!* مَا أَحْلَاهُ, *how
sweet it is!* مَا أَغْنَاهُ, *how rich he is!* But if formed from verba med.

A rad. و et ى, they follow the inflection of the strong verb; as مَا أَقْوَلَهُ or أَقْوِلْ بِهِ, *how well he speaks!* مَا أَجْوَدَهُ or أَجْوِدْ بِهِ, *how excellent* or *generous he is!*

REM. *d.* When a verb of surprise cannot be formed directly from a root, recourse must be had to a circumlocution (compare § 235); as مَا أَشَدَّ حُمْرَتَهُ, *how red it is!* مَا أَنْقَى بَيَاضَهُ, *how pure white it is!* أَحْبِبْ بِسُمْرَتِهِ, *what a pretty brown it is!* مَا أَكْثَرَ قَائِلَتَهُ, *how often he takes a siesta!* مَا أَجْوَدَ جَوَابَهُ or أَجْوِدْ بِجَوَابِهِ, *how good*
B *his reply is!* and not مَا أَجْوَبَهُ, مَا أَقْيَلَهُ, أَسْمِرْ بِهِ, مَا أَبْيَضَهُ, مَا أَحْمَرَهُ or أَجْوِبْ بِهِ.

REM. *e.* To form the past tense of such verbs, كَانَ is prefixed to the Perfect form; as مَا كَانَ أَفْضَلَ زَيْدًا, *how excellent Zèid was!* But we may also say مَا أَفْضَلَ مَا كَانَ زَيْدٌ (literally, *what has made excellent that which Zèid was?* What has produced the past excellence of Zèid?).

C REM. *f.* مَا أَحْسَنَهُ, *how good,* or *goodly, he is!* مَا أَمْلَحَهُ, *how handsome he is!* and less frequently مَا أَحْلَاهُ, *how sweet it is!* admit of the diminutive forms (see § 269) مَا أُحَيْسِنَهُ, مَا أُمَيْلِحَهُ, and مَا أُحَيْلَاهُ.

APPENDIX B.

The Verbal Suffixes, which express the Accusative.

D **185.** The following are the verbal suffixes, which express the accusative:

Singular.

	Masc.	Common.	Fem.
3. p.	هُ *him.*	. . .	هَا *her.*
2. p.	كَ *thee.*	. . .	كِ *thee.*
1. p.	. . .	نِى *me.*	. . .

Dual. A

	Masc.	Common.	Fem.
3. p.	...	هُمَا *them both.*	...
2. p.	...	كُمَا *you both.*	...
1. p.	...	...	...

Plural.

	Masc.	Common.	Fem.
3. p.	هُمْ *them.*	...	هُنَّ *them.*
2. p.	كُمْ *you.*	...	كُنَّ *you.* B
1. p.	...	نَا *us.*	...

Rem. *a.* The same forms serve, when appended to the noun, to express the genitive; excepting that *my* is ـِى instead of نِى (see § 317). The ن of the suffix نِى is called by the grammarians نُونُ ٱلْوِقَايَةِ, *the guarding* or *preventive n*, because it prevents the final vowels of the verb from being absorbed by the long vowel ـِى, as happens with the noun (see § 316, *b*); and also نُونُ ٱلْعِمَادِ, *the supporting n*, because it serves as a sort of prop or support to the ـِى, which is regarded as the essential portion of the suffix.

Rem. *b.* The ḍamma of هُ, هُمَا, هُمْ, and هُنَّ, is changed after ـِ, ـِى, and ـَىْ, into kèsra; as يَأْتِيهِ, يَأْتِيهِمْ, *he will come to him, to them;* ايتِهِمَا, ايتِهِنَّ, *come to them* (dual m. and f.), *to them* (plur. fem.); لَمْ تَرْضَيْهِ *thou* (fem.) *hast not been pleased with him.*

Rem. *c.* The ى of the suffix 1st pers. sing. is sometimes dropped; as اتَّقُونِ for اتَّقُونِى, *fear me;* [comp. § 6, rem. *a*]. D

Rem. *d.* Old and poetic forms are: ـِيَ and نِيَ, هُمُ (هِمُ or هِمِ), كُمُ. See § 89, 1, rem. *c*, and § 20, *b* and *d.* [The pausal forms ـِيَهْ and نِيَهْ, see Vol. ii. § 228, rem. *b*. Instead of كِ some dialects have شِ; see Lane and the *Moḥīṭ*. D. G.]

Rem. *e.* The Hebrew and Aramaic suffixes, in general, closely resemble those of the *modern* Arabic; see *Comp. Gr.* p. 153 *seq.*

A **186.** Some forms of the verb are slightly altered by the addition of the accusative suffixes.

(*a*) Those persons which end in the êlif otiosum (see § 7, rem. *a*), reject it before the suffix, as being no longer necessary (since it was added only to prevent the possibility of the termination ـُو being in some cases mistaken for the conjunction وَ, *and*); as نَصَرُوا *they helped*, نَصَرُونِى *they helped me.*

B (*b*) The final consonant of the 2d pers. masc. plur. Perf. retains before the suffixes, to avoid cacophony, the long ḍamma which it had in an older stage of the language; as رَأَيْتُمْ *ye have seen*, رَأَيْتُمُونِى *ye have seen me.* The same thing takes place with the accusative suffix of the 2d pers. masc. plur. كُمْ, when it is followed by another suffix (see § 187); as يُرِيكُمُوهُمْ *he shews them to you.*

(*c*) The 2d and 3d pers. masc. plur. Imperf. occasionally reject C the termination نَ before the suffixes نِى and نَا; as تَأْمُرُونِى for تَأْمُرُونَنِى, *ye order me**, تَقْلُونَا for تَقْلُونَنَا, *ye hate us*, يَجِدُونِى for يَجِدُونَنِى, *they will find me.* The same thing happens to the 2d pers. sing. fem.; as تُشَوِّقِينِى, *thou makest me long*, for تُشَوِّقِينَنِى.

(*d*) The vowel ـِ in the termination of the 2d pers. fem. sing. Perf. is sometimes lengthened before the suffixes; as كَسَرْتِيهِ for كَسَرْتِهِ, *thou hast broken it.*

D (*e*) The ى of the 3d pers. masc. sing. Perf. in verba tertiæ rad. ى, may be retained before the suffixes, or (which is far more usual) be changed into ا; as رَمَيَهُ (§ 7, rem. *c*) or رَمَاهُ, *he threw*, or *shot, at him.*

[* In Sūra xxxix. 64 a third reading is recorded, viz. تَأْمُرُونِّى, and there are similar variations in other passages. So also with verbs third ن we occasionally find such contractions as مَكَّنِّى for مَكَّنَنِى (Sūr. xviii. 94), تَأْمَنَّا for تَأْمَنُنَا (Sūr. xii. 11).]

[Rem. In case of the suffixes كَ, كُمْ etc. being affixed to the Jussive of a verb tertiæ كْ, the two كْ are assimilated; the latter loses its ǵèzma, the كْ of the suffix takes tèšdīd, as يُدْرِكُّمْ.] A

187. A verbal form may take two suffixes, provided they do not indicate one and the same person. These two may both be appended to the verb, the suffix of the 1st pers. naturally preceding that of the 2d or 3d, and the suffix of the 2d pers. that of the 3d. E.g. أَعْطَانِيكَ, أَعْطَانِيهِ, *he gave thee, it, to me*; أَعْطَيْتُكَهُ, *I gave it to thee*; يَكْفِيكَهُمْ, *he will suffice thee against them* (will be sufficient to protect thee against them); أَنُلْزِمُكُمُوهَا, *shall we compel you (to receive) it?* B

[Rem. Combinations like أَعْطَاهَاهُ, *he gave him to her*, أَعْطَاهُوهَا, *he gave her to him*, are legitimate but rare. (Note the orthography in the latter case.) But أَعْطَاهُهُ is not used; see § 189, rem. *a*.]

188. Sometimes, however, we find the pronominal object expressed, not by the accusative suffixes attached to the verb, but by the genitive suffixes appended to the word إِيَّا *'īyā* (which never occurs alone). The following are the compound pronouns thus formed:

Singular. C

	Masc.	Common.	Fem.
3. pers.	إِيَّاهُ	...	إِيَّاهَا
2. pers.	إِيَّاكَ	...	إِيَّاكِ
1. pers.	...	إِيَّاىَ	...

Dual.

3. pers.	...	إِيَّاهُمَا	...
2. pers.	...	إِيَّاكُمَا	...
1. pers.	...	...	...

D

Plural.

3. pers.	إِيَّاهُمْ	...	إِيَّاهُنَّ
2. pers.	إِيَّاكُمْ	...	إِيَّاكُنَّ
1. pers.	...	إِيَّانَا	...

A REM. *a.* The suffix of the 1st p. sing. is in this case يَ, instead of ـِى, because all nouns ending in ـَا take that form. See § 317, rem. *a.*

REM. *b.* For the linguistic affinities of إِيَّا (dialectically هِيَّا) in the other Semitic languages, see *Comp. Gr.* p. 112 *seq.*

189. These suffixes compounded with إِيَّا are used in two cases.

(*a*) Very frequently, but not always (see § 187), when two suffixes
B would otherwise have to be appended to the same verb; as أَعْطَانِى إِيَّاهُ, instead of أَعْطَانِيهِ, *he gave it to me.*

(*b*) When the pronoun is, for the sake of emphasis, placed before the verb; as إِيَّاكَ نَعْبُدُ وَإِيَّاكَ نَسْتَعِينُ, *Thee* (none but Thee) *we worship, and to Thee we cry for help.* Compare in Heb. הַאוֹתִי לֹא־תִירָאוּ, Jerem. v. 22.

C REM. *a.* The suffix attached to إِيَّا is always that which would occupy the second place, if appended to the verb. In certain cases this form alone is used, either for the sake of precision or of euphony. Thus, *he gave me to him* must be worded أَعْطَاهُ إِيَّايَ, to distinguish it from أَعْطَانِيهِ *he gave him to me;* but it is euphony which requires أَعْطَاهُ إِيَّاهُ, *he gave it to him,* instead of أَعْطَاهُهُ.

REM. *b.* A very strong emphasis is expressed by prefixing the
D pronoun with إِيَّا, and at the same time appending the pronominal suffix to the verb; as وَإِيَّايَ فَاتَّقُونِ, *Me therefore, fear Me.*

II. THE NOUN.

190. The Noun, اَلِاسْمُ, *nomen,* is of six kinds.

(*a*) The *nomen substantivum,* or Substantive, more especially designated اَلِاسْمُ, and also اَلْمَوْصُوفُ, or اَلْمَنْعُوتُ, *qualificabile,* that is, a word which admits of being united with a descriptive epithet (adjective).

(*b*) The *nomen adjectivum*, or Adiective, اَلصِّفَةُ, اَلْوَصْفُ. or اَلنَّعْتُ, A
quality, descriptive epithet.

(*c*) The *nomen numerale*, or Numeral Adjective, اِسْمُ ٱلْعَدَدِ, *the noun of number.*

(*d*) The *nomen demonstrativum*, or Demonstrative Pronoun, اِسْمُ ٱلْإِشَارَةِ, *the noun of indication*, that is, by which some object is pointed out.

(*e*) The *nomen conjunctivum*, or Relative Pronoun, اَلِٱسْمُ ٱلْمَوْصُولُ B
or اَلْمَوْصُولُ ٱلِٱسْمِىُّ, *the noun that is united* (*with a relative clause*), as opposed to اَلصِّلَةُ, *the relative clause itself.*

(*f*) The *pronomen*, or Personal Pronoun, اَلضَّمِيرُ or اَلْمُضْمَرُ, *the word by which something is concealed* or *kept in, and so conceived of by, the mind,* as opposed to اَلظَّاهِرُ or اَلْمُظْهَرُ, *that which is apparent* or *manifested*, the substantive to which the pronoun refers. It is also C
called اَلْكِنَايَةُ, ἀντωνυμία.

Rem. *a.* Of the pronouns we have already treated in part in §§ 84—89 and 185—189, and some further remarks regarding them will be given in § 317. The numeral adjectives and the demonstrative and relative pronouns will be handled separately, after the nouns substantive and adjective (see §§ 318—353). The nouns substantive and adjective we shall treat of together, because, in regard to form, they are identical in almost every respect.

Rem. *b.* The names of the pronoun, اَلضَّمِيرُ and اَلْمُضْمَرُ, are D
elliptical expressions, for اَلضَّمِيرُ بِهِ and اَلْمُضْمَرُ بِهِ, as the above translation shows.

A

A. THE NOUNS SUBSTANTIVE AND ADJECTIVE.

1. *The Derivation of Nouns Substantive and Adjective, and their different Forms.*

191. Nouns are divisible, in respect of their origin, into two classes, *primitive* and *derivative*. The primitive nouns are all substantives; as رَجُلٌ *man*, فَرَسٌ *horse*, عَيْنٌ *eye*, مَآءٌ *water*. The derivative nouns may be substantives or adjectives, and are either
B *deverbal*, that is, derived from verbs, as تَقْسِيمٌ *division* (from قَسَمَ *to divide*), مِفْتَاحٌ *a key* (from فَتَحَ *to open*), مَرِيضٌ *sick* (from مَرِضَ *to be sick*); or *denominative*, that is, derived from nouns, as مَأْسَدَةٌ *a place which abounds in lions* (from أَسَدٌ *a lion*), إِنْسَانِيٌّ *human* (from إِنْسَانٌ *a human being*), كُلَيْبٌ *a little dog* (from كَلْبٌ *a dog*). At a later period, nouns were formed, in the language (or rather jargon) of the philosophical schools, from pronouns and particles (we might call
C them *departiculative*), as أَنَانِيَّةٌ *egotism* (from أَنَا *I*), كَيْفِيٌّ *qualitative*, and كَيْفِيَّةٌ *quality* (from كَيْفَ *how?*).

REM. *a*. In such Arabic Lexicons as are arranged according to the etymological principle, a verb is frequently given as the etymon of what are really primitive nouns, and a comparison of the meaning of the two shows that the former is in fact the derivative word. Thus مَآءٌ *water*, is not derived from مَاهَ *to be full of water*,
D which is given in the Dictionaries as its root, but, conversely, مَاهَ is a denominative verb, formed from مَآءٌ; nor is فَرُسَ, *to be skilled in horsemanship*, the root of فَرَسٌ, *a horse*, but a denominative from it.

REM. *b*. By the native grammarians nouns are classified as follows.

(1) اِسْمٌ جَامِدٌ, *a noun that is stationary* or *incapable of growth*, one that is not itself a nomen actionis or infinitive, nor derived from a nom. act., and which does not give birth to a nom. act. or verb,

as رَجُلٌ *a man*, بَطَّةٌ *a duck;* opposed to اِسْمٌ مُشْتَقٌّ, *a noun that is* A
derived from a nom. act. or verbal root, as كَاتِبٌ *a writer*, قَتِيلٌ *slain.*

(2) اِسْمٌ مُجَرَّدٌ, i.e. مُجَرَّدٌ عَنِ ٱلزِّيَادَةِ, *a noun that is bare of any accessory* or *increment*, which comprises merely the letters of the root and no more, as عِلْمٌ *knowledge*, سَفَرْجَلٌ *a quince;* opposed to اِسْمٌ مَزِيدٌ فِيهِ, *a noun that is augmented* by additional letters, as
عَلَّامَةٌ *a very learned man*, اِحْرِنْجَامٌ *the being gathered together in* B
a mass.

(3) اِسْمٌ عَلَمٌ, or اِسْمُ عَلَمٍ *a proper name*, the distinctive mark of an individual; opposed to اِسْمُ جِنْسٍ, *a generic* or *common noun*, designating a whole kind or genus (γένος, ܓܢܣܐ).

(4) The اِسْمُ ٱلْجِنْسِ may be either (*a*) اِسْمُ عَيْنٍ, a noun denoting *a concrete object*, as رَجُلٌ *a man*, فَرَسٌ *a horse;* or (*b*) اسْمُ
مَعْنًى, a noun denoting *an abstract idea*, as عِلْمٌ *knowledge*, جَهْلٌ C
ignorance. The same terms may be applied to adjectives; رَاكِبٌ, *riding*, is an اِسْمُ عَيْنٍ, but مَفْهُومٌ, *understood*, an اِسْمُ مَعْنًى.

(5) The اِسْمُ ٱلْعَلَمِ may be either (*a*) عَلَمُ جِنْسِيٌّ, *a proper name applicable to every individual of a whole kind*, as أُسَامَةُ *the lion*, جَعَارِ *the female hyæna* (like "Puss" for the cat, "Renard" for the
fox); or (*b*) عَلَمٌ شَخْصِيٌّ, *a proper name applicable to only one* D
individual of a kind, as دَاحِسٌ and ٱلْغَبْرَآءُ, names of horses, قَرُوبُ, the name of a camel, سَعْدٌ, عَوْفٌ, ثَعْلَبَةُ, names of men, أُمَيْمَةُ, ٱلْخَنْسَآءُ, names of women.

(6) The اِسْمُ ٱلْعَلَمِ may also be either (*a*) an اِسْمٌ, or *name*, in its strictest sense, as عَمْرٌو, جَعْفَرٌ, بُثَيْنَةُ; or (*b*) a كُنْيَةٌ, i.e. a name compounded with أَبُو, *father of*, as أَبُو ٱلْعَبَّاسِ, or أُمٌّ, *mother of* as أُمُّ كُلْثُومٍ, or اِبْنٌ, *son of*, as اِبْنُ حَيَّانَ, or اِبْنَةٌ or بِنْتٌ, *daughter of*,

A as بِنْتُ هِنْدٍ; or (*c*) a لَقَبٌ, *a surname*, which may be either a
nickname (نَبَزٌ), as بَطَّةُ *Duck* or *Bottle*, أَنْفُ ٱلنَّاقَةِ *Camel's-nose*,
بَبَّةُ *Bèbba* (imitation of a sound), or an honourable epithet, as
زَيْنُ ٱلْعَابِدِينَ, *the pride* or *glory of those that worship* (*God*), شَمْسُ
ٱلْمَعَالِى, *the sun of virtues*. The كُنْيَةُ is also employed in reference
to animals, as أَبُو أَيُّوبَ, *Job's father*, the "patient" camel; أَبُو
ٱلْحُصَيْنِ, *the father of the little fort*, the fox; أُمُّ عَامِرٍ, *the female
hyæna;* ابْنُ عِرْسٍ, *the weasel;* بِنْتُ طَبَقٍ, *the tortoise.*

B (7) An اِسْمُ عَلَمٍ may likewise be either (*a*) مُفْرَدٌ, *simple*,
consisting of a single word, as أَوْسٌ, عَنْتَرَةُ; or (*b*) مُرَكَّبٌ, *com-
pounded.* The مُرَكَّبٌ may be either (*α*) إِسْنَادِىٌّ, *predicative*, when
the words that compose it constitute a جُمْلَةٌ or proposition, as
بَرَقَ نَحْرُهُ (*his throat shone*), تَأَبَّطَ شَرًّا (*he carried mischief under his
arm*), شَابَ قَرْنَاهَا (*her two locks became gray*); or (*β*) a *mixed
compound*, مُرَكَّبٌ مَزْجِىٌّ, which is not a proposition (غَيْرُ جُمْلَةٍ), as
C بَعْلَبَكُّ, *Ba'al-bèk*, مَعْدِيكَرِبُ, *Ma'dī-karib*, سِيبَوَيْهِ, *Sība-wèih;* or
(*γ*) مُضَافٌ وَمُضَافٌ إِلَيْهِ, a substantive governing another in the
genitive, as عَبْدُ مَنَافٍ, اِمْرُؤُ ٱلْقَيْسِ, أَبُو ذُؤَيْبٍ, أُمُّ كُلْثُومٍ.

(8) Finally, an اِسْمُ عَلَمٍ may be either (*a*) مُرْتَجَلٌ *improvised,
extemporised, impromptu*, existing only as a proper name, as عِمْرَانُ,
فَقْعَسٌ, حَيْوَةُ; or (*b*) مَنْقُولٌ, *transferred* from some other use, *tro-*
D *pical.* The latter class is of six kinds, viz. (*α*) مَنْقُولٌ عَنِ ٱسْمِ عَيْنٍ,
as ثَوْرٌ (*a bull*), أَسَدٌ (*a lion*); (*β*) مَنْقُولٌ عَنِ ٱسْمِ مَعْنًى, as فَضْلٌ
(*excellence*), إِيَاسٌ (*giving, gift*); (*γ*) مَنْقُولٌ عَنْ صِفَةٍ, as حَاتِمٌ
(*judging*), نَائِلَةُ (*bestowing*); (*δ*) مَنْقُولٌ عَنْ فِعْلٍ, as شَمَّرُ, يَشْكُرُ,
يَحْيَى, تَغْلِبُ, إِصْمِتُ; (*ε*) مَنْقُولٌ عَنْ صَوْتٍ, as بَبَّةُ (see above, 6, *c*);
and (*ζ*) مَنْقُولٌ عَنْ مُرَكَّبٍ (see above, 7, *b*).

192. Deverbal nouns are divisible into two principal classes; A
namely:—

(*a*) *Nomina verbi* or *nomina actionis*, أَسْمَآءُ ٱلْفِعْلِ (*infinitives*).

(*b*) *Nomina agentis*, أَسْمَآءُ ٱلْفَاعِلِ, and *nomina patientis*, أَسْمَآءُ ٱلْمَفْعُولِ (*participles*).

The nomina verbi are by their nature substantives, but have come to be used also as adjectives; the nomina agentis et patientis are by their nature adjectives, but have come to be used also as B
substantives.

193. Connected with the nomina verbi are the four following classes of deverbal nouns.

(*a*) *Nomina vicis*, أَسْمَآءُ ٱلْمَرَّةِ, nouns that express the doing of an action *once*.

(*b*) *Nomina speciei*, أَسْمَآءُ ٱلنَّوْعِ, nouns of *kind* or *manner*.

(*c*) *Nomina loci et temporis*, أَسْمَآءُ ٱلْمَكَانِ وَٱلزَّمَانِ, also called
nomina vasis, أَسْمَآءُ ٱلظَّرْفِ, nouns of *place* and *time*. C

(*d*) *Nomina instrumenti*, أَسْمَآءُ ٱلْآلَةِ, nouns denoting the *instrument*.

194. Denominative nouns are divisible into six classes; namely:—

(*a*) *Nomen unitatis vel individualitatis*, اِسْمُ ٱلْوَحْدَةِ, the noun that denotes *the individual*.

(*b*) *Nomen abundantiæ vel multitudinis*, اِسْمُ ٱلْكَثْرَةِ, the noun D
that denotes the place where anything is found in *abundance*.

(*c*) *Nomen vasis*, اِسْمُ ٱلْوِعَآءِ, the noun that expresses the *vessel* which contains anything.

(*d*) *Nomen relativum*, ٱلِٱسْمُ ٱلْمَنْسُوبُ or ٱلنِّسْبَةُ (lit. *the referred noun*, *the reference* or *relation*), a particular class of derivative adjectives.

A (*e*) *Nomen abstractum qualitatis*, اِسْمُ ٱلْكَيْفِيَّةِ, the abstract noun of quality (see § 191).

(*f*) *Nomen deminutivum*, اَلِٱسْمُ ٱلْمُصَغَّرُ or اَلتَّصْغِيرُ (lit. *the lessened noun, the lessening*), the *diminutive*.

a. THE DEVERBAL NOUNS.

(α) *The Nomina Verbi.*

195. The nomina verbi, أَسْمَآءُ ٱلْفِعْلِ, are abstract substantives,
B which express the action, passion, or state indicated by the corresponding verbs, without any reference to object, subject, or time.

REM. The nomen verbi is also called اَلْمَصْدَرُ (lit. *the place whence anything goes forth, where it originates*), because most Arab grammarians derive the compound idea of the finite verb from the simple idea of this substantive. We may compare with it the Greek Infinitive used with the article as a substantive.

196. The nomina verbi, which may be derived from the ground-
C form of the ordinary triliteral verb, are very numerous. The following is a nearly complete list of them, the rarest forms being included within brackets.

1. فَعْلٌ, as ضَرْبٌ, رَدٌّ, عَجْزٌ, فَهْمٌ, قَوْلٌ, سَيْرٌ, غَزْوٌ, جَرْىٌ.
2. فَعَلٌ, as طَلَبٌ, هَرَبٌ, جَلَبٌ, نَظَرٌ, كَرَمٌ, عَمَلٌ, سَخَطٌ, فَرَحٌ, شَلَلٌ, جَوًى.
3. فَعِلٌ, as كَذِبٌ, ضَحِكٌ, حَرِمٌ, سَرِقٌ, حَلِفٌ.

D 4. فِعْلٌ, as حِفْظٌ, عِلْمٌ, ذِكْرٌ, فِسْقٌ.

5. فِعَلٌ, as كِبَرٌ, عِظَمٌ, صِغَرٌ, ثِقَلٌ, سِمَنٌ, رِضًى.
6. فُعْلٌ, as جُبْنٌ, شُغْلٌ, زُهْدٌ, شُكْرٌ, شُرْبٌ, سُخْطٌ, وُدٌّ.
7. فُعَلٌ, as هُدًى, سُرًى.
8. فَعْلَةٌ, as رَحْمَةٌ, كَثْرَةٌ, غَيْرَةٌ, حَيْرَةٌ.
9. فَعَلَةٌ, as غَلَبَةٌ, ضَبَعَةٌ, عَظَمَةٌ, شَكَاةٌ.

10. فَعِلَةٌ, as سَرِقَةٌ. A

11. فِعْلَةٌ, as حِمْيَةٌ, عِصْمَةٌ, نِشْدَةٌ.

12. فُعْلَةٌ, as أُدْمَةٌ, سُمْرَةٌ.

[13. فُعُلَّةٌ, as غُلُبَّةٌ (also written غَلُبَّةٌ).]

[13* فِعِلَّةٌ, as جِبِلَّةٌ.]

14. فَعْلَى, as دَعْوَى, تَقْوَى.

[15. فَعَلَى, as جَمَزَى, مَرَطَى.]

16. فِعْلَى, as ذِكْرَى. B

17. فُعْلَى, as بُشْرَى, رُجْعَى.

[18. فُعُلَّى, as غُلُبَّى (or غِلِبَّى).]

[19. فَعْلَآءُ, as رَغْبَآءُ, رَهْبَآءُ.]

[19* فُعْلَآءُ, as رُهْبَآءُ.]

[20. فَعْلَانٌ, as لَيَّانٌ, شَنْئَانٌ, زَيْدَانٌ.]

21. فَعَلَانٌ, as خَفَقَانٌ, جَوَلَانٌ, طَوَفَانٌ, هَيَجَانٌ, نَزَوَانٌ, شَنَئَانٌ.

22. فِعْلَانٌ, as حِرْمَانٌ, نِسْيَانٌ, رِضْوَانٌ. C

23. فُعْلَانٌ, as رُجْحَانٌ, شُكْرَانٌ, غُفْرَانٌ, كُفْرَانٌ.

[24. فَعَلُوتٌ, as جَبَرُوتٌ, رَحَمُوتٌ, رَهَبُوتٌ.]

[24* فَعَلُوتَى, as جَبَرُوتَى, رَحَمُوتَى, رَهَبُوتَى.]

25. فَعَالٌ, as صَلَاحٌ, فَسَادٌ, ذَهَابٌ, نَفَادٌ, نَفَاذٌ, رَوَاحٌ.

26. فِعَالٌ, as كِتَابٌ, حِجَابٌ, نِكَاحٌ, قِيَامٌ, إِيَابٌ, شِرَادٌ, نِفَارٌ, إِبَآءٌ. D

27. فُعَالٌ, as مُزَاحٌ, سُؤَالٌ, سُعَالٌ, زُكَامٌ, مُشَآءٌ, أُزَازٌ, نُعَاقٌ, نُعَابٌ.

28. فَعَالَةٌ, as ظَرَافَةٌ, نَظَافَةٌ, جَزَالَةٌ, فَصَاحَةٌ, ضَخَامَةٌ, زَهَادَةٌ.

29. فِعَالَةٌ, as كِتَابَةٌ, سِفَارَةٌ, عِبَادَةٌ, صِيَانَةٌ.

[30. فُعَالَةٌ, as بُغَايَةٌ, خُفَارَةٌ.]

31. فَعَالِيَةٌ, as كَرَاهِيَةٌ, طَمَاعِيَةٌ, عَلَانِيَةٌ, رَكَانِيَةٌ.

A 32. فَعُولٌ, as قَبُولٌ, وَلُوعٌ, وَقُودٌ, وَضُوءٌ.

33. فُعُولٌ, as خُرُوجٌ, دُخُولٌ, وُرُودٌ, غُدُوٌّ, جُحُودٌ, لُزُومٌ, قُدُومٌ.

[33*. فَعُولَةٌ, as أَلُوكَةٌ.]

34. فُعُولَةٌ, as سُهُولَةٌ, صُعُوبَةٌ, عُذُوبَةٌ.

[35. فَعُولِيَّةٌ, as خَصُوصِيَّةٌ, لَصُوصِيَّةٌ.]

[36. فُعُولِيَّةٌ, as خُصُوصِيَّةٌ, جُهُولِيَّةٌ, شُيُوخِيَّةٌ.]

37. فَعِيلٌ, as صَهِيلٌ, نَعِيقٌ, نَعِيبٌ, أَزِيزٌ, ذَمِيلٌ, رَحِيلٌ.

B 38. فَعِيلَةٌ, as شَكِيَّةٌ, حَمِيَّةٌ.

39. مَفْعَلٌ, as مَدْخَلٌ, مَحْبَسٌ, مَحْمَلٌ, مَفَرٌّ.

40. مَفْعِلٌ, as مَكْبِرٌ, مَرْجِعٌ, مَوْثِقٌ, مَوْعِدٌ, مَسِيرٌ, مَصِيرٌ, مَحِيضٌ, مَجِيءٌ.

[41. مَفْعُلٌ, as مَهْلُكٌ.]

42. مَفْعَلَةٌ, as مَحْمَدَةٌ, مَرَمَّةٌ, مَوَدَّةٌ, مَرْضَاةٌ.

43. مَفْعِلَةٌ, as مَحْمِدَةٌ, مَرْجِعَةٌ, مَعْرِفَةٌ, مَوْجِدَةٌ, مَسِيرَةٌ, مَأْوِيَةٌ, مَرْثِيَةٌ.

C [44. مَفْعُلَةٌ, as مَهْلُكَةٌ, مَقْدُرَةٌ.]

[REM. For the forms with prefix *ma-*, 39—44, the so-called مَصْدَرٌ مِيمِيٌّ, see further §§ 208, 221, rem. *c*, and the remarks to §§ 222—225.]

197. *All* these nouns cannot, however, be formed from *every* triliteral verb. The majority of verbs admit of but one form, very few of more than two or three. What these are, must be learned D from the Lexicon.

198. The five forms, which are most frequently used, are:

1. فَعْلٌ, 2. فَعَلٌ, 28. فَعَالَةٌ, 33. فُعُولٌ, 34. فُعُولَةٌ.

(*a*) فَعْلٌ is the abstract noun from *transitive* verbs of the forms فَعَلَ and فَعِلَ; as قَتَلَ *to kill*, قَتْلٌ *killing* or *being killed* (§ 201); فَهِمَ *to understand*, فَهْمٌ *understanding, insight*; خَطِفَ *to snatch*, خَطْفٌ.

(*b*) فُعُولٌ is the abstract noun from *intransitive* verbs of the form A
فَعَلَ; as قَعَدَ and جَلَسَ *to sit,* قُعُودٌ and جُلُوسٌ *sitting;* خَرَجَ *to go out,* خُرُوجٌ *going out.*

(*c*) فَعَلٌ is the abstract noun from *intransitive* verbs of the form فَعِلَ (§§ 38 and 92); as فَرِحَ *to be glad,* فَرَحٌ *joy;* مَرِضَ *to be sick,* مَرَضٌ *sickness.*

(*d*) فَعَالَةٌ and فُعُولَةٌ are the abstract nouns from verbs of the form فَعُلَ; as جَزُلَ *to be thick and large, to be of sound judgment,* جَزَالَةٌ *firmness* or *soundness of judgment;* سَرُوَ *to be generous,* سَرَاوَةٌ B
generosity; خَشُنَ *to be rough,* خُشُونَةٌ *roughness;* سَهُلَ *to be smooth,* سُهُولَةٌ *smoothness.*

REM. The abstract nouns of verbs which express FLIGHT, or REFUSAL, usually take the form 26. فِعَالٌ; as فَرَّ, نَفَرَ, شَرَدَ, *to flee,* فِرَارٌ, نِفَارٌ, شِرَادٌ; جَمَحَ *to become refractory, to run away* with his rider (of a horse), جِمَاحٌ; نَارَ *to flee from, shun with horror,* نِوَارٌ;
أَبَى *to refuse,* إِبَآءٌ. Those that express SICKNESS OR AILMENT of any C
kind have 27. فُعَالٌ, as عَطَسَ *to sneeze,* عُطَاسٌ; سَعَلَ *to cough,* سُعَالٌ; VIOLENT OR CONTINUOUS MOTION, 21. فَعَلَانٌ, as طَارَ *to fly,* طَيَرَانٌ; جَرَى *to run,* جَرَيَانٌ; خَطَرَ *to lash* the tail, *to brandish,* خَطَرَانٌ; بَرَقَ *to gleam,* بَرَقَانٌ; وَمَضَ *to flash,* وَمَضَانٌ; خَفَقَ *to palpitate,* خَفَقَانٌ; CHANGE OF PLACE, 37. فَعِيلٌ, as رَحَلَ *to travel,* رَحِيلٌ; دَبَّ *to creep,* دَبِيبٌ; رَسَمَ *to gallop* (of a camel), رَسِيمٌ; ذَمَلَ *to trot* (of a
camel), ذَمِيلٌ; وَجَفَ *to be agitated, palpitate, run quickly,* وَجِيفٌ; D
بَرَقَ *to gleam,* بَرِيقٌ; وَمَضَ *to flash,* وَمِيضٌ; SOUND, 27. فُعَالٌ and 37. فَعِيلٌ, as نَعَبَ *to croak,* نُعَابٌ and نَعِيبٌ; شَهَقَ *to sob, to bray,* شَهِيقٌ; صَهَلَ *to neigh,* صَهِيلٌ; نَهَقَ *to bray,* نُهَاقٌ and نَهِيقٌ; نَهَتَ *to roar,* نُهَاتٌ and نَهِيتٌ; صَاحَ *to cry out,* صُيَاحٌ; صَرَخَ *to cry out* for help, صُرَاخٌ; نَبَحَ *to bark,* نُبَاحٌ; بَكَى *to weep,* بُكَآءٌ; عَوَى *to*

A *howl,* عُوَآءٌ ; ثَغَا *to bleat,* ثُغَآءٌ ; رَغَا *to grumble* (of a camel), رُغَآءٌ ; OFFICE, TRADE OR HANDICRAFT, 29. فِعَالَةٌ, as خَلَفَ *to succeed,* خِلَافَةٌ *the office of successor* (خَلِيفَةٌ) or *caliph, the caliphate ;* أَمَرَ *to be chief* or *ĕmīr,* إِمَارَةٌ *the office of ĕmīr ;* وَلِيَ *to be in charge* or *command of,* وِلَايَةٌ, *governorship ;* نَابَ *to take one's place, act as deputy,* نِيَابَةٌ *deputyship ;* كَتَبَ *to write,* كِتَابَةٌ *the office of secretary ;* خَاطَ *to sew,* خِيَاطَةٌ *the trade of tailor ;* تَجَرَ *to trade,* تِجَارَةٌ *trade, traffic.*

B **199.** If the middle radical of a verb can be pronounced with two or three vowels, and its signification varies accordingly, that verb may have several abstract nouns, one for each form and meaning of the Perfect. Thus, فَرَقَ, *to part, divide,* has فَرْقٌ, but فَرِقَ, *to be afraid,* فَرَقٌ ; جَهَرَ, *to be plain, open* or *public,* has جَهْرٌ or جِهَارٌ, but جَهِرَ, *to be unable to see in the sunlight,* جَهَرٌ, and جَهُرَ, *to be loud,* جَهَارَةٌ ; شَرَفَ, *to surpass* or *excel in rank* or *nobility,* has شَرْفٌ, but شَرِفَ, *to be* C *high* or *prominent,* شَرَفٌ, and شَرُفَ *to be exalted, noble* or *eminent,* شَرَفٌ or شَرَافَةٌ.

200. If a verb has only one form, but several different significations, it often has different abstract nouns, one of which is peculiar to, or more generally used in, each of its meanings. E.g. حَكَمَ, *to judge,* has حُكْمٌ, but when it signifies *to curb (a horse),* حَكْمٌ ; خَرَّ, *to fall prostrate,* has خَرٌّ or خُرُورٌ, but when it means *to sound like rushing* D *water,* خَرِيرٌ ; رَفُعَ, *to be exalted* or *noble,* has رِفْعَةٌ, but in the sense of *to have a loud voice,* رَفَاعَةٌ ; وَجَدَ, *to find,* usually has وِجْدَانٌ, but when it means *to be wealthy,* جِدَةٌ, and *to be moved* by love, grief or anger, وَجْدٌ.

201. The nomina verbi are used both in an active and a passive sense ; as قَتْلُهُ *his killing (another)* or *his being killed himself ;* لَا تُفْسِدُوا فِى ٱلْأَرْضِ بَعْدَ إِصْلَاحِهَا *work no evil upon the earth after*

its having been well ordered; فِى هٰذِهِ ٱلسَّنَةِ أَظْهَرَ ٱلْمَأْمُونُ ٱلْقَوْلَ بِخَلْقِ A
ٱلْقُرْآنِ *in this year ăl-Ma'mūn publicly adopted the doctrine of the Ḳor'ān's having been created.*

Rem. There are also nomina verbi that have always a passive signification; as سُرُورٌ *joy, gladness,* from سُرَّ *to be glad;* وُجُودٌ *existence,* from وُجِدَ *to be found, to exist* (see § 200)*.

202. The nouns formed from the derived forms of the strong triliteral verb are as follows.

II. 1. تَفْعِيلٌ. B

2. تَفْعِلَةٌ, as تَذْكِرَةٌ, تَكْرِمَةٌ, تَقْدِمَةٌ, تَكْمِلَةٌ, تَفْرِقَةٌ, تَبْصِرَةٌ, تَسِرَّةٌ, تَضِرَّةٌ, تَهْنِئَةٌ, تَجْزِئَةٌ, تَذْكِيَةٌ, تَزْكِيَةٌ.

[3. تَفْعُلَةٌ, as تَهْلُكَةٌ, تَسُرَّةٌ, تَضُرَّةٌ.]

4. تَفْعَالٌ, as تَصْهَالٌ, تَهْطَالٌ, تَهْتَانٌ, تَصْدَاقٌ, تَرْدَادٌ, تَكْرَارٌ, تَوْمَاضٌ, تَجْوَالٌ, تَطْوَافٌ, تَسْيَارٌ.

[5. تِفْعَالٌ, as تِبْيَانٌ, تِلْقَآءٌ, تِمْشَآءٌ, تِشْرَابٌ, تِبْكَآءٌ, تِمْثَالٌ, C
تِنْضَالٌ. Of these examples some allow only the two first, pointing the others as examples of تَفْعَالٌ.]

[6. فِعَّالٌ, as كِذَّابٌ, كِلَّامٌ, عِلَّامٌ, فِسَّارٌ, خِرَّاقٌ, قِدَّامٌ, قِضَّآءٌ, حِمَّالٌ, كِبَّارٌ.]

[7. فِعِّيلَى, as حِثِّيثَى, خِصِّيصَى, خِلِّيفَى, قِلِّيلَى, خِطِّيبَى,
مِكِّيثَى, دِلِّيلَى, فِخِّيرَى, قِتِّيتَى, رِمِّيَّا.] D

[8. فِعِّيلَآءُ, as خِصِّيصَآءُ, مِكِّيثَآءُ.]

To these may be added تُفْعُولٌ, as تُهْلُوكٌ. Here the vowel of the

---

* [وُجُودٌ is also employed in the active signification; see the Gloss. to Bibl. Geogr. viii. and Lane. D. G.]

A first syllable seems to have been assimilated to that of the second; تُفُعُولٌ for تَفْعُولٌ.

III. 1. مُفَاعَلَةٌ. 2. فِعَالٌ.

[3. فِيعَالٌ, as ضِيرَابٌ, قِيتَالٌ]. [4. فِعَّالٌ, as قِتَّالٌ, مِرَّآءٌ.]

IV. إِفْعَالٌ.

V. 1. تَفَعُّلٌ. [2. تِفِعَّالٌ, as تِحِمَّالٌ, تِكِلَّامٌ, تِمِلَّاقٌ, تِنِقَّامٌ.]

B VI. 1. تَفَاعُلٌ. [2. تَفَاعَلٌ, as تَفَاوَتٌ.]

[3. تَفَاعِلٌ, as تَفَاوِتٌ.]

VII. اِنْفِعَالٌ. VIII. 1. اِفْتِعَالٌ. [2. فِعَّالٌ, as قِتَّالٌ, سِتَّارٌ.]

IX. اِفْعِلَالٌ. X. اِسْتِفْعَالٌ.

XI. اِفْعِيلَالٌ. XII. اِفْعِيعَالٌ.

XIII. اِفْعِوَّالٌ. XIV. اِفْعِنْلَالٌ.

C XV. اِفْعِنْلَآءٌ.

REM. *a.* In II. the form فِعَّالٌ is the original infinitive, but تَفْعِيلٌ is by far the most common; تَفْعِلَةٌ is chiefly used in verba tert. rad. hèmz. and tert. rad. و et ى (in which latter the form تَفْعِيلٌ is excessively rare, as تَنْزِيٌّ from نَزَا); فِعِّيلَى and فِعِّيلَآءٌ are usually ascribed to I., but as their use is لِقَصْدِ ٱلْمُبَالَغَةِ, *to express energy* or *intensity*, [or *frequency*,] they seem as deserving of a D place here as تَفْعَالٌ [which in like manner differ from the infin. of I., only by expressing greater energy or frequent repetition]. These forms with tèśdîd are akin to the Heb. infin. absol. קַטֹּל (קִטֹּל, קַטֵּל), to Heb. substantives like שִׁלּוּם, and to the Eastern Aramaic infin. קַטּוֹלֵי; whereas تَفْعَالٌ. تَفْعِيلٌ, تُفْعُولٌ and تَفْعِلَةٌ are, strictly speaking, the infinitives, not of فَعَّلَ, but of an obsolete تَفْعَلَ, akin to תַּפְעֵל, תִּפְעֵל, שַׁפְעֵל, and are represented in the

cognate dialects by such substantives as תַּכְרִיךְ, תַּגְמוּל, תַּבְלִית, A
תַּבְנִית, תַּרְבּוּת, ܬܰܘܕܺܝܬܳܐ, ܬܰܫܡܶܫܬܳܐ, ܬܰܫܥܺܝܬܳܐ, etc.*—In III. فِيعَالٌ is the original infinitive, which the great majority of the Arabs shortened into فِعَالٌ, whilst some compensated the loss of the long vowel by doubling the following consonant, فِعَّالٌ. The most common form of all is مُفَاعَلَةٌ ([in form identical with the] pass. particip. fem.).—In V. the original form is تِفِعَّالٌ, which has
however been almost entirely supplanted by تَفَعُّلٌ.—In VIII. those B
Arabs alone use فِعَّالٌ, who shorten the Perf. and Imperf. into فَعَّلَ, يَفَعِّلُ, or فِعَّلَ, يِفِعِّلُ, etc. in the cases mentioned in § 117*.—The form تِفْعَالٌ is sometimes ascribed to III., as تِرْمَآءٌ, تِنْضَالٌ; and فِعِّيلَى to VI., as حِجِّيزَى (تَحَاجَزُوا), هِجِّيرَى (تَهَاجَرُوا), رِمِّيَّا (تَرَامَوْا).

[Rem. *b*. For the مَصْدَرٌ مِيمِىٌّ of the derived conjugations see § 227, rem.]

203. The nouns formed from the quadriliteral verbs are :— C

I. 1. فَعْلَلَةٌ, as دَحْرَجَةٌ, سَرْهَفَةٌ, حَوْقَلَةٌ, جَهْوَرَةٌ, بَيْطَرَةٌ, سَلْقَاةٌ, قَلْقَلَةٌ, زَلْزَلَةٌ.

2. فِعْلَالٌ, as دِحْرَاجٌ, سِرْهَافٌ, حِيقَالٌ, سِلْقَآءٌ, زِلْزَالٌ, قِلْقَالٌ.

[3. فَعْلَالٌ, as زَلْزَالٌ, قَلْقَالٌ.]

II. تَفَعْلُلٌ, as تَدَحْرُجٌ.

III. اِفْعِنْلَالٌ, as اِحْرِنْجَامٌ. D

IV. اِفْعِلَّالٌ, as اِقْشِعْرَارٌ, اِطْمِئْنَانٌ. [The irregular form طُمَأْنِينَةٌ is rather to be considered as a substantive, اِسْمُ مَصْدَرٍ.]

Rem. In I. فَعْلَلَةٌ is the common form, whilst the employment of فِعْلَالٌ depends upon the *usus loquendi* (like that of فِعَالٌ in III.

---

* [Barth, *Nominalbildung*, § 180 disapproves of this theory. D. G.]

A of the triliteral verb). The form فَعْلَالٌ seems to be restricted to reduplicated verbs, like زَلْزَلَ.—A variation of the fourth form is presented to us in the word طِعِنَّانٌ, *mutual thrusting and stabbing with lances* = تَطَاعُنٌ, which comes from طَعَنَّنَ = اِطْعَنَنَ.

204. The abstract nouns of the verba mediæ rad. geminatæ are formed according to the rules given in § 120. Hence مَدٌّ for مَدْدٌ, مَرَدٌّ for مَرْدَدٌ (from رَدَّ), تَغِرَّةٌ for تَغْرِرَةٌ (from the second form of غَرَّ).

B REM. *a.* Those nouns, of which the first and second radicals are pronounced with fètḥa, undergo no contraction; as سَدَدٌ, عَلَلٌ, مَلَلٌ, غَصَصٌ.

REM. *b.* The nouns of the third and sixth forms may either be contracted or not; as مُمَادَدَةٌ or مُمَادَّةٌ, تَسَابُبٌ or تَسَابٌّ. See § 124.

205. The formation of nouns from the verba hèmzata takes place C according to the rules laid down in §§ 131—136.

206. Those verba primæ rad. و, that reject the و in the Imperf. and Imperat. (§§ 142 and 144), drop it also in the verbal noun. E.g.

عِدَةٌ	from	وَعَدَ,	Imperfect	يَعِدُ,	Imperat.	عِدْ
عِظَةٌ	„	وَعَظَ	„	يَعِظُ	„	عِظْ
دَعَةٌ	„	وَدَعَ	„	يَدَعُ	„	دَعْ
D زِنَةٌ	„	وَزَنَ	„	يَزِنُ	„	زِنْ
دِيَةٌ	„	وَدَى	„	يَدِى	„	دِ

The termination ـَةٌ, with which these nouns are furnished, is a compensation for the lost radical.

REM. *a.* Not a few verba primæ rad. و, however, have nouns of the form فَعْلٌ, though they drop the first radical in the Imperf.; e.g. وَجَرَ, يَجِرُ, وَجْرٌ; وَجَنَ, يَجِنُ, وَجْنٌ. Others have both forms;

e.g. وَضَعَ, يَضَعُ, وَضْعٌ and ضَعَةٌ ; وَزَنَ, يَزِنُ, وَزْنٌ and زِنَةٌ ; وَعَدَ, يَعِدُ, A
وَعْدٌ and عِدَةٌ.

Rem. *b.* Initial و, if pronounced with ḍamma or kèsra, may be changed into أ (see § 145, rem.), as أُجُودٌ, إِجْدَانٌ, for وُجُودٌ وِجْدَانٌ.

Rem. *c.* In nouns from verba primæ rad. و, this radical is changed into ى, if it be without a vowel, and kèsra precede; as إِيجَابٌ for إِوْجَابٌ, from the fourth form of وَجَبَ ; اِسْتِيفَآءٌ for اِسْتِوْفَآءٌ, from the tenth of وَفَى. See § 145. B

Rem. *d.* Compare in Hebrew, לֶדֶת (لِدَةٌ), רֶשֶׁת (رِثَةٌ), שֶׁבֶת, דַּעַת, from יָלַד, יָרַשׁ, יָשַׁב, יָדַע; עֵדָה (عِدَةٌ), עֵצָה (عِظَةٌ), שֵׁנָה (سِنَةٌ), from יָעַד, יָעַץ, יָשֵׁן. Corresponding forms in Syriac are ܝܪܬܐ (rad. ܝܪܬ), ܫܢܬܐ (rad. ܝܫܢ).

207. Nouns derived from verba mediæ rad. و et ى are subject to C
the same irregularities as those verbs (§ 150, etc.).

208. If the noun from a verb mediæ rad. و or ى be of the form فَعْلٌ, the و or ى remains unchanged ; as قَوْلٌ, سَيْرٌ. In the form فُعُولٌ from verba med. و, the و may be changed into ؤ, as ثُؤُوبٌ, حُؤُولٌ, دُؤُورٌ, رُؤُوبٌ, غُؤُورٌ, سُؤُورٌ, for ثُوُوبٌ, etc. Verba med. ى of the form فَعَلَ, Imperf. يَفْعِلُ (see § 157), frequently take kèsra in the مَصْدَرٌ مِيمِيٌّ, as مَبِيتٌ (for مَبْيِتٌ), مَبِيعٌ, مَجِىٓءٌ (or by assimilation مَجِيٌّ), مَزِيدٌ, مَسِيرٌ, مَصِيرٌ, مَعِيشٌ, and the like. [See § 223, rem.] D

209. If the letter و, pronounced with fètḥa, be preceded by kèsra, it is converted into ى ; as قِيَامٌ for قِوَامٌ, from قَامَ ; صِيَانَةٌ for صِوَانَةٌ, from صَانَ ; اِنْقِيَادٌ and اِقْتِيَادٌ for اِنْقِوَادٌ and اِقْتِوَادٌ, from the seventh and eighth forms of قَادَ. Except in the third form, where it remains

A unchanged ; as ثُوَارٌ from ثَاوَرَ, جِوَارٌ from جَاوَرَ, سِوَارٌ from سَاوَرَ, عِوَانٌ from عَاوَنَ, قِوَامٌ from قَاوَمَ, لِوَامٌ from لَاوَمَ, نِوَآءٌ from نَاوَأَ.

210. Peculiar to verba mediæ rad. و et ى is the nominal form فَعْلُولَةٌ, in which ى always takes the place of the second radical ; as دَيْمُومَةٌ from دَامَ (دوم), قَيْدُودَةٌ from قَادَ (قود), كَيْنُونَةٌ from كَانَ (كون), سَيْدُودَةٌ from سَادَ (سود), بَيْنُونَةٌ from بَانَ (بين), شَيْخُوخَةٌ from شَاخَ
B (شيخ), صَيْرُورَةٌ from صَارَ (صير), غَيْبُوبَةٌ from غَابَ (غيب), قَيْلُولَةٌ from قَالَ (قيل).

REM. Some grammarians regard فُعْلُولَةٌ as the original form. The impossible صُيْرُورَةٌ, شُيْخُوخَةٌ, were, they say, first changed into صِيرُورَةٌ, شِيخُوخَةٌ, and then altered, on account of the discord between ī and ū in successive syllables, into صَيْرُورَةٌ, شَيْخُوخَةٌ. Others look upon فَعْلُولَةٌ as a contraction for فَيْعَلُولَةٌ, so that
C دَيْمُومَةٌ was originally دَيْوَمُومَةٌ, by assimilation دَيَّمُومَةٌ, and then shortened دَيْمُومَةٌ (like مَيْتٌ for مَيِّتٌ) ; but there is no verbal form فَيْعَلَّ, with which such a nomen verbi could be connected. The rare substantive forms سُودَدٌ (or سُوْدَدٌ) from سَادَ, *to be chief* or *ruler*, and عُوطَطٌ from عَاطَ *to desire the male* (of a she-camel) ; the cognate forms فَوْضَى, فَوْضُوضَى and فَوْضُوضَآءُ, فَيُوضَى, فَيْضُوضَى and فَيْضُوضَآءُ, فَيْضِيضَى and فَيْضِيضَآءُ, *mixture, confusion ;* and the analogy of the
D Aramaic verbal form פַּעְלֵל (as ܪܰܘܪܶܒ, ܩܰܘܡܶܡ) and the Heb. פִּעְלֵל (as בּוֹנֵן, כּוֹנֵן, קוֹמֵם, רוֹמֵם),—all combine to prove that فَعْلُولَةٌ comes directly from a quadriliteral فَعْلَلَ.

211. In nouns of the fourth and tenth form of verba mediæ rad. و et ى, the second radical is elided, after throwing back its vowel upon the vowelless first radical ; and the termination ـَةٌ is appended to the noun by way of compensation (compare § 206). E.g. إِقَامَةٌ and اِسْتِقَامَةٌ for إِقْوَامٌ and اِسْتِقْوَامٌ ; إِفَادَةٌ and اِسْتِفَادَةٌ for إِفْيَادٌ and اِسْتِفْيَادٌ.

REM. Nouns of the fourth form without the ة very rarely A
occur; e.g. إِقَامٌ in the Ḳor'ān, Sūr. xxi. 73 (for إِقْوَامٌ, إِقْآمٌ or إِقَآمٌ); إِرَآءٌ (for إِرْءَآءٌ) from أَرَى *to make* or *let see, to show* (§ 176, rem. *c*).

212. In nouns formed from verba tertiæ rad. و et ى, the third radical is retained, when the second immediately precedes it and is vowelless; as غَزْوٌ, رَمْىٌ, زَهْوٌ, فَرْىٌ, رِضْوَانٌ, غِشْيَانٌ. If the second radical be و and the third ى, an assimilation takes place in the form فَعْلٌ, as حَىٌّ, زَىٌّ, طَىٌّ, لَىٌّ, for حَوْىٌ, زَوْىٌ, طَوْىٌ, لَوْىٌ.

213. In nouns from verba tertiæ rad. و et ى of the forms فَعَلٌ, B
فِعَلٌ, and فُعَلٌ, the third radical (which in this case always [if the root be of the latter, often if it be of the former class,] assumes the form of ى) rejects its ḍamma, throws back the tènwīn upon the fètḥa of the second radical, and becomes quiescent. E.g. جَلًا for جَلَىٌ (جَلَوٌ), لَظًى for لَظَىٌ, رِضًى [or رِضًا] for رِضَىٌ (رِضَوٌ), سُرًى for سُرَىٌ, هُدًى for هُدَىٌ (compare § 167, *a*, *β*, and *b*, *β*).

214. In nouns from verba tertiæ rad. و of the form فَعَلَةٌ, the و C
is changed, after the elision of its fètḥa, into èlif productionis; as صَلَاةٌ for صَلَوَةٌ, حَيَاةٌ for حَيَوَةٌ, زَكَاةٌ for زَكَوَةٌ, شَكَاةٌ for شَكَوَةٌ.

REM. *a.* We often find, however, the (etymologically more correct) orthography صَلٰوةٌ, حَيٰوةٌ, زَكٰوةٌ (§ 7, rem. *d*).

REM. *b.* In the same way as حَيَاةٌ for حَيَوَةٌ, we find مَرْضَاةٌ for مَرْضَيَةٌ (مَرْضَوَةٌ), مَرْثَاةٌ for مَرْثَيَةٌ, etc.

215. If the noun from a verb tertiæ rad. و be of the form D
فُعُولٌ or فُعُولَةٌ, the و productionis of the second syllable combines with the radical و into وٌّ; as دُنُوٌّ, عُلُوٌّ, for دُنُووٌ, عُلُووٌ. But, if these forms come from verba tertiæ rad. ى, the و productionis is changed, through the influence of the third radical, into ى, and combines with it into ىٌّ, whilst, at the same time, the ḍamma of the second radical becomes a kèsra; as أُوِىٌّ, رُقِىٌّ, مُضِىٌّ, for أُوُوىٌ, رُقُوىٌ,

A مُضُوِىٌّ (compare § 170). A further assimilation of the vowel of the first syllable sometimes takes place, as إِتِىٌّ for أُتِىٌّ, إِوِىٌّ for أُوِىٌّ, عِتِىٌّ for عُتِىٌّ; just as in the plural of substantives we find عِصِىٌّ, قِسِىٌّ, دِلِىٌّ, for عُصِىٌّ, قُسِىٌّ, دُلِىٌّ, from عَصًا, قَوْسٌ, دَلْوٌ.

216. If the noun from a verb tertiæ rad. ى be of the form فَعِيلٌ, the ى productionis of the second syllable combines with the
B radical ى into ىٌّ; as هَوِىٌّ for هَوِيىٌ, from هَوَى. In the same form from verba tertiæ rad. و, the third radical is converted into ى, and combines in the same manner with the ى productionis into ىٌّ.

217. In the nomina verbi of the forms فَعَالٌ, فِعَالٌ, and فُعَالٌ, the third radical of verba tertiæ rad. و et ى is changed into hèmza; as خَفَآءٌ, بِنَآءٌ, بُكَآءٌ. The same thing takes place in the verbal nouns of the fourth, seventh, and following forms, as إِعْطَآءٌ, اِنْجِلَآءٌ, اِرْتِجَآءٌ,
C اِرْعِوَآءٌ, اِسْتِدْعَآءٌ, اِحْوِيوَآءٌ; and in that of the third, when it has the form فِعَالٌ, as نِدَآءٌ from نَادَى. This change is caused by the preceding long fètḥa.

218. The nomina verbi of the second form of verba tert. rad. و et ى always take the form تَفْعِلَةٌ (§ 202, rem.), as تَسْلِيَةٌ, تَعْزِيَةٌ. In those of the fifth and sixth forms, the influence of the third radical
D (always ى, § 169) converts the ḍamma of the penult syllable into kèsra, and the syllables ـِىٌ are contracted into ـٍ (according to § 167, *b*, *β*). Hence تَجَلٍّ for تَجَلِّىٌ (تَجَلُّىٌ), تَوَالٍ for تَوَالِىٌ (تَوَالُىٌ).

(*β*) *The Nomina Vicis or Nouns that express the Doing of an Action once.*

219. That an act has taken place *once* (مَرَّةً), the Arabs indicate by adding the feminine termination ـَةٌ to the verbal noun. For this

purpose the form فَعْلٌ is always selected in the first form of the A
triliteral verb, تَفْعِيلٌ in the second, and فِعْلَالٌ in the first form of the quadriliterals. E.g. نَصْرَةٌ, قَعْدَةٌ, ضَرْبَةٌ, شَرْبَةٌ, فَرْحَةٌ, فَرَّةٌ, تَقْلِيبَةٌ, تَرْوِيحَةٌ, إِحْزَانَةٌ, إِكْرَامَةٌ, تَقَلُّبَةٌ, تَغَافُلَةٌ, إِنْكِشَافَةٌ, إِلْتِفَاتَةٌ, إِسْتِنْشَاقَةٌ, دِحْرَاجَةٌ, تَدَحْرُجَةٌ, إِقْشِعْرَارَةٌ, *the act of helping, sitting down, striking, drinking, rejoicing, fleeing, turning over, giving rest, vexing, honouring, rolling over, neglecting, being uncovered, turning round, inhaling* or B
snuffing, rolling, being rolled, shuddering, once. These nouns are called أَسْمَآءُ ٱلْمَرَّةِ, *nomina vicis,* or nouns that express the doing of an action once.

Rem. *a.* Nouns of this sort, derived from weak verbs, do not differ in form from those of the strong verbs; as وَعْدَةٌ, قَوْمَةٌ, عَدْوَةٌ, أَتْيَةٌ, رَمْيَةٌ, لَقْيَةٌ from وَعَدَ, قَامَ, عَدَا, أَتَى, رَمَى, لَقِيَ.

Rem. *b.* If the verbal noun happens to end in ـَةٌ, the feminine C
termination ـَةٌ cannot, of course, be appended to it, and the singleness of the action can only be expressed by adding the adjective وَاحِدَةٌ *one,* as رَحِمَهُ رَحْمَةً وَاحِدَةً, *he had pity* or *compassion upon him once;* and so with عَيْمَةٌ, تَسْلِيَةٌ, مُقَاتَلَةٌ, إِقَامَةٌ, إِسْتِعَانَةٌ, دَحْرَجَةٌ.

Rem. *c.* From these nouns a dual and a plural may be formed to express the doing of the act twice or oftener; as du. نَصْرَتَانِ, pl. نَصَرَاتٌ.

Rem. *d.* Other verbal nouns are but rarely used in this way; D
as حِجَّةٌ, رُؤْيَةٌ, لِقَآءَةٌ, إِتْيَانَةٌ, *the act of going on a pilgrimage, seeing, meeting, coming, once.*

(γ) *The Nomina Speciei or Nouns of Kind.*

220. The إِسْمُ ٱلنَّوْعِ or *noun of kind,* has always the form فِعْلَةٌ, and indicates the manner of doing what is expressed by the verb; as جِلْسَةٌ, رِكْبَةٌ, قِعْدَةٌ, طِعْمَةٌ, قِتْلَةٌ, مِيتَةٌ, نِيمَةٌ, *manner, mode,* or

A *way of sitting, riding, sitting, eating, killing, dying, sleeping.* E.g. هُوَ حَسَنُ ٱلْكِتْبَةِ *he is good as to his manner of writing, he writes a good hand,* قُتِلَ قِتْلَةَ سَوْءٍ *he was killed in a miserable way,* بِئْسَتِ ٱلْمِيتَةُ *'t is a wretched death!*

REM. *a.* The nom. speciei may, like the nom. verbi and nom. vicis, be used in a passive sense, as صِرْعَةٌ, *way of being thrown* (from horseback), e.g. سُوءُ ٱلِٱسْتِمْسَاكِ خَيْرٌ مِنْ حُسْنِ ٱلصِّرْعَةِ, *to sit fast*
B *badly is better than to be thrown easily.* Sometimes too it takes the meaning of one of the derived forms of the verb; as عِذْرَةٌ *manner of excusing oneself,* from اِعْتَذَرَ *to excuse oneself;* خِمْرَةٌ *mode of veiling oneself,* from اِخْتَمَرَتْ *she put on the* خِمَارٌ or *yashmak;* عِمَّةٌ *way of putting on a turban,* from تَعَمَّمَ or اِعْتَمَّ *to put on a turban* (عِمَامَةٌ).

REM. *b.* If the nom. verbi has the form فِعْلَةٌ, we must have
C recourse to a circumlocution to express the idea of the nom. speciei; as حَمَيْتُهُ حِمْيَةَ ٱلْمَرِيضِ *I made him observe a regimen like a sick man,* نَشَدْتُهُ نِشْدَةَ ٱلنَّفِيسِ *I searched for it as for something precious;* or else نَشَدْتُهُ نَوْعًا مِنَ ٱلنِّشْدَةِ, حَمَيْتُهُ نَوْعًا مِنَ ٱلْحِمْيَةِ. So too with the derived forms of the verb, أَكْرَمْتُهُ إِكْرَامَ ٱلصَّدِيقِ *I honoured him as a friend is honoured,* or أَكْرَمْتُهُ نَوْعًا مِنَ ٱلْإِكْرَامِ.

D (δ) *The Nomina Loci et Temporis or Nouns of Place and Time.*

221. The nouns called أَسْمَآءُ ٱلظَّرْفِ (*nomina vasis*), or أَسْمَآءُ ٱلْمَكَانِ وَٱلزَّمَانِ (*nomina loci et temporis*), are formed after the analogy of the Imperfect Active of the first form of the verb, by substituting the syllable مَ for the prefixes, and giving the second radical *fètḥa,* if the Imperfect has *fètḥa* or *ḍamma,* but *kèsra,* if the Imperfect has *kèsra.* E.g. مَشْرَبٌ *a place for drinking, a reservoir* or *water-trough,* from شَرِبَ *to drink,* imperf. يَشْرَبُ; مَنْهَلٌ *the time* or *place for watering*

(*camels*), from نَهِلَ *to drink*, imperf. يَنْهَلُ ; مَصْرَعٌ *the time when*, or A
place where, one is thrown down or *slain*, from صَرَعَ *to throw down*,
imperf. يَصْرَعُ ; مَكْتَبٌ *a place where writing is taught, a school*, from
كَتَبَ *to write*, imperf. يَكْتُبُ ; مَخْرَجٌ and مَدْخَلٌ, *a place of egress* and
ingress, from خَرَجَ *to go out*, imperf. يَخْرُجُ, and دَخَلَ *to go in*, imperf.
يَدْخُلُ ; مَجْلِسٌ *the place where*, or *time when, several persons sit, room,
assembly, party*, from جَلَسَ *to sit*, imperf. يَجْلِسُ ; مَقْصِدٌ *the place
aimed at* or *made for*, from قَصَدَ *to aim at, make for*, imperf. يَقْصِدُ. B

Rem. *a.* These nouns are called أَسْمَآءُ ٱلظَّرْفِ, because *time* and *place* are, as it were, the *vessels* in which the act or state is contained.

Rem. *b.* Twelve of these nouns, though derived from verbs in which the characteristic vowel of the Imperfect is *ḍamma*, take, notwithstanding, *kèsra*; viz.

1. مَجْزِرٌ *the place where animals are slaughtered, slaughterhouse* or *shambles*. C
2. مَرْفِقٌ . . . . *whereon one rests, the elbow.*
3. مَسْجِدٌ . . . . *of prostration in prayer, a mosque.*
4. مَسْقِطٌ . . . . *where anything falls.*
5. مَسْكِنٌ . . . . *where one dwells, habitation.*
6. مَشْرِقٌ . . . . *where the sun rises, the east.* D
7. مَطْلِعٌ . . . . *of ascent* or *rising.*
8. مَغْرِبٌ . . . . *where the sun sets, the west.*
9. مَفْرِقٌ . . . . *of division*, in particular, *where the hair divides in different directions, the crown of the head.*
10. مَنْبِتٌ . . . . *where a plant grows.*

A 11. مَنْخِرٌ *the place where the breath passes through the nose, the nostril.*

12. مَنْسِكٌ . . . . *where a sacrifice is offered during a religious festival.*

Of these, nos. 5, 7, 9, 11, and 12, may be pronounced with *fèt͟ha*, and the same license is extended by some grammarians to all the rest. Instead of مَنْخِرٌ some say مِنْخِرٌ, مُنْخُرٌ, and even مُنْخُورٌ. The verb جَمَعَ, *to collect*, which has *fèt͟ha* in the imperf., also makes
B مَجْمَعٌ or مَجْمِعٌ, *a place of collecting, meeting* or *assembling*. The vowel of the first syllable is variable in مَخْدَعٌ, also مُخْدَعٌ and مِخْدَعٌ, *a place of hiding* or *concealment, a small room* or *closet*. See § 228, rem. *a*; and compare the variations in مِجْسَدٌ *a garment worn (by a woman) next the skin;* مُصْحَفٌ *a book, a copy of the Ḳor'ān;* and مِطْرَفٌ *a robe with ornamental borders.*

C REM. *c.* The kèsra of the second syllable distinguishes in many cases the nomina temp. et loci from the مَصْدَرٌ مِيمِيٌّ, which, as a general rule, takes fèt͟ha in the second syllable. Thus مَجْلَسٌ, مَحْمَلٌ, مَحْبَسٌ, مَضْرَبٌ, مَفَرٌّ, are nomina verbi or infinitives; whilst مَجْلِسٌ, مَحْمِلٌ, مَحْبِسٌ, مَضْرِبٌ, مَفِرٌّ, are nomina temporis or loci.

REM. *d.* This class of nouns exists in the other Semitic languages. In Hebrew, the vowel of the first syllable has fre-
D quently been weakened into ִ and ֶ; as מַשְׁאָב, מַצָּב (מִנְצָב), מָקוֹם (מִקְוָם), מֶרְכָּב (مَرْكَبٌ), מִדְבָּר (ܡܰܕܒܪܐ), מִזְבֵּחַ (ܡܰܕܒܚܐ).

222. Nouns of time and place, formed from verba primæ rad. و et ى, retain the first radical, even though it be rejected in the Imperfect of the verb (§§ 142, 144), and have invariably *kèsra* in the second syllable. E.g. مَوْرِدٌ *watering-place,* from وَرَدَ *to go down* (*to draw water*), imperf. يَرِدُ; مَوْعِدٌ *the time* or *place of a promise* or *appointment, fixed time* or *place*, from وَعَدَ *to promise*, imperf. يَعِدُ;

مَوْضِعٌ *the place where anything is put, a place*, from وَضَعَ *to put down,* A
to place, imperf. يَضَعُ ; مَوْجِلٌ *a place that is dreaded*, from وَجِلَ *to be afraid*, imperf. يَوْجَلُ ; مَوْحِلٌ *a slough* or *quagmire*, from وَحِلَ *to stick in the mud*, imperf. يَوْحَلُ ; مَيْسِرٌ *a game at hazard*, from يَسَرَ *to play at hazard*, imperf. يَيْسِرُ.

Rem. Here the مَصْدَرٌ مِيمِىٌّ should, strictly speaking, have the same form as the nomina loci et temp., but the grammarians give B
some examples with fètḥa in the second syllable, as مَوْضَعٌ, مَوْحَلٌ.

223. Those formed from verba mediæ rad. و et ى undergo changes analogous to those suffered by the Imperfect of the verb (§ 150); that is to say, after the second radical has taken *fètḥa* or *kèsra*, according to § 221, this vowel is thrown back upon the vowelless first radical, and the و or ى is changed into the homogeneous letter of prolongation (ا or ى). E.g. مَقَامٌ (مَقْوَمٌ) *place of standing, place*, from قَامَ *to stand*, imperf. يَقُومُ (يَقْوُمُ) ; مَغَاصٌ (مَغْوَصٌ) *diving-place*, C
from غَاصَ *to dive*, imperf. يَغُوصُ (يَغْوُصُ) ; مَخَافٌ (مَخْوَفٌ) and مَهَابٌ (مَهْيَبٌ), *a place that is dreaded*, from خَافَ *to fear*, imperf. يَخَافُ (يَخْوَفُ), and هَابَ *to fear*, imperf. يَهَابُ (يَهْيَبُ) ; مَقِيلٌ (مَقْيِلٌ) *place of resting at mid-day*, from قَالَ *to sleep at mid-day*, imperf. يَقِيلُ (يَقْيِلُ).

Rem. The مَصْدَرٌ مِيمِىٌّ has in this case regularly the form with ā in the second syllable, as مَآبٌ, مَآلٌ, مَعَادٌ, *return* (from آبَ for D
أَوَبَ, etc.), مَشَاعٌ *being divulged* or *published* (from شَاعَ for شَيَعَ); but many verba med. ى take in preference the form with ī, as مَسَالٌ or مَسِيلٌ, مَحَاضٌ or مَحِيضٌ, مَبَاعٌ or مَبِيعٌ, مَبَاتٌ or مَبِيتٌ, مَمَالٌ or مَمِيلٌ, مَقَالٌ or مَقِيلٌ, مَكَالٌ or مَكِيلٌ, مَعَاشٌ or مَعِيشٌ. See § 208.

224. Those formed from verba tertiæ rad. و et ى violate the rule laid down in § 221, for they always take *fètḥa* in the second syllable,

A whatever be the vowel of the Imperfect. In regard to their contraction, they follow the analogy of the verbal nouns فُعَلٌ from the same verbs (§ 213). E.g. مَنْجًى (مَنْجَوٌ, مَنْجَىٌ) *place of refuge*, from نَجَا *to escape*, imperf. يَنْجُو ; مَرْعًى (مَرْعَىٌ) *pasture-ground*, from رَعَى, *to pasture* or *graze*, imperf. يَرْعَى ; مَثْوًى (مَثْوَىٌ) *the place where one stops*, from ثَوَى *to stop*, imperf. يَثْوِى ; مَأْوًى (مَأْوَىٌ) *do.*, from أَوَى *to go* or *resort to a place*, imperf. يَأْوِى ; مَطْوًى (مَطْوَىٌ) *a fold*, from
B طَوَى *to fold*, imperf. يَطْوِى ; مَثْنًى (مَثْنَىٌ) *a bend*, from ثَنَى *to bend*, imperf. يَثْنِى.

REM. The مَصْدَرٌ مِيمِىٌّ has the same form, as مَجْرًى from جَرَى, imperf. يَجْرِى ; مَسْرًى from سَرَى, imperf. يَسْرِى.

225. Nouns of time and place not unfrequently take the feminine
C form ـَةٌ ; as مَشْغَلَةٌ *time* or *place of occupation, business* ; مَشْرَعَةٌ *the place where cattle, etc., are watered* ; مَضْرِبَةٌ *the part of a sword with which the blow is struck, the edge* ; مَنْزِلَةٌ *a halting-place, a station* ; مَغَارَةٌ (مَغْوَرَةٌ) *a cave* ; مَرْعَاةٌ (مَرْعَيَةٌ) *pasture-ground*. If derived from a strong verb, the second rad. frequently has in this case *ḍamma* instead of *fetḥa* ; as مَقْبُرَةٌ *cemetery*, مَشْرُبَةٌ *place for drinking, banqueting-room*, مَشْرُعَةٌ *watering-place*. Some nouns have even three
D forms ; as مَشْرُقَةٌ *a place where one suns oneself* or *sits in the sunshine*, مَهْلُكَةٌ *a place where people perish, a desert*. Peculiar is مَظِنَّةٌ *the place where a thing is supposed to be*, from ظَنَّ *to think, suppose*, imperf. يَظُنُّ.

REM. The مَصْدَرٌ مِيمِىٌّ is liable to the same variations, though مَفْعَلَةٌ is the normal form, as مَسْغَبَةٌ *hunger*. For example: مَحْمَدَةٌ,

مَرْثِيَةٌ, مَغْفِرَةٌ, مَعْتِبَةٌ, مَظْلِمَةٌ ; مَذِمَّةٌ, مَحْمِدَةٌ in preference to مَذَمَّةٌ, A
مَقْدُرَةٌ, مَأْرُبَةٌ ; مَعْذُرَةٌ ; مَحْمِدَةٌ ; مَرْثَاةٌ (مَرْثِيَةٌ) or مَرْثَاةٌ.

226. Some nouns of time and place, derived from verba primæ rad. و et ى, take the form مِفْعَالٌ (see § 228). E.g. مِيلَادٌ *time of birth*, from وَلَدَ *to bear*; مِيعَادٌ *appointed time* [or *place*] for the fulfilment of a promise, from وَعَدَ *to promise*; مِيقَاتٌ *appointed time* [or *place* for the performance of some action], from وَقَتَ *to fix a time.* B

Rem. From the strong verb this form is very rare, as مِشْرَاقٌ or مِشْرِيقٌ = مَشْرِقَةٌ ; but in Æthiopic it is the usual form from all verbs, as *mĕsrāḳ* = مَشْرِقٌ, *mĕʻrāb* = مَغْرِبٌ, *mĕrʻāy* = مَرْعًى.

227. The nouns of time and place from the derived forms of the triliteral verb, or from the quadriliteral, are identical in form with the *nomina patientis* or passive participles. E.g. مُصَلًّى *a place* C
of prayer (صَلَّى *to pray*); مُصْبَحٌ, مُمْسًى, *the time of entering upon the morning* or *evening* (أَصْبَحَ, أَمْسَى, *to enter upon the time of morning* or *evening*); مُدْخَلٌ, مُخْرَجٌ *the place through which*, or *the time when, one is made to enter* (أَدْخَلَ *to make one enter*) or *go out* (أَخْرَجَ *to make go out*); مُنْصَرَفٌ *place* or *time of returning* (اِنْصَرَفَ *to return*); مُجْتَمَعٌ *a place where things are collected* (اِجْتَمَعَ *to be collected*); مُلْتَقًى *place* D
or *time of meeting* (اِلْتَقَى *to meet*); مُسْتَهَلٌّ *the first day of the month* (اُسْتُهِلَّ ٱلْهِلَالُ *the new moon appeared*); مُدَحْرَجٌ *a place where one rolls* anything (دَحْرَجَ *to roll*); مُحْرَنْجَمٌ *a place where* (camels) *are crowded together* (اِحْرَنْجَمَ *to be gathered together in a crowd*).

Rem. The same form is also used as a مَصْدَرٌ مِيمِىٌّ from the derived forms of the triliteral verb and from the quadriliteral; e.g. مُجَرَّبٌ *the being tried* or *tested* = تَجْرِيبٌ or تَجْرِبَةٌ ; مُنَدًّى *the*

A *letting* (camels) *graze in the interval of their being watered* = تَنْدِيَةٌ ; مُمَزَّقٌ *the rending in pieces* = تَمْزِيقٌ ; مُوَقًّى *the guarding carefully* = تَوْقِيَةٌ ; مُقَاتَلٌ *fighting* = قِتَالٌ or مُقَاتَلَةٌ ; مُغَارٌ *the making a raid* or *foray* = إِغَارَةٌ ; مُصَابٌ *affliction* = إِصَابَةٌ ; مُنْقَلَبٌ, مُتَقَلَّبٌ *turning* or *tossing to and fro* = اِنْقِلَابٌ, تَقَلُّبٌ ; مُتَحَامَلٌ *the pressing heavily on, wronging* = تَحَامُلٌ ; مُصَلْصَلٌ *to make a clashing* or *ringing sound* = صَلْصَلَةٌ ; إِلَى ٱللّٰهِ مِنْهَا ٱلْمُشْتَكَى وَٱلْمُعَوَّلُ, *to God is* (*our*) *complaint of this event* (وقيعة) *and* (*on Him*) *is* (*our*) *reliance.*

B

(ε) *The Nomina Instrumenti or Nouns that indicate the Instrument.*

228. The nouns which denote the instrument that one uses in performing the act expressed by a verb, are called in Arabic أَسْمَآءُ ٱلْآلَةِ, *nomina instrumenti.* They have the forms مِفْعَلٌ, مِفْعَالٌ, and مِفْعَلَةٌ, and are distinguished from the nouns of place and time
C by the kèsra with which the prefixed مِ is pronounced. When derived from verba med. rad. و et ى, they remain uncontracted. E.g. مِبْرَدٌ, *a file,* from بَرَدَ, *to file;* مِبْضَعٌ, *a lancet,* from بَضَعَ, *to cut;* مِشْرَطٌ and مِشْرَاطٌ, *a lancet;* مِقْرَاضٌ, *a pair of scissors;* مِفْتَحٌ or مِفْتَاحٌ, *a key;* مِسْرَحٌ and مِسْرَحَةٌ, *a comb;* مِحْجَمَةٌ, *a cupping-glass;* مِكْسَحَةٌ and مِكْنَسَةٌ, *a broom;* مِقَصٌّ (for مِقْصَصٌ), *a pair of scissors;* مِسَلَّةٌ, *a*
D *packing-needle;* مِئْثَرَةٌ, *an iron instrument for marking* a camel's foot (from أَثَرَ); مِيثَرَةٌ, *a pad placed under a horse's saddle* (from وَثَرَ); مِيسَمٌ, *a branding-iron* (from وَسَمَ); مِيزَانٌ, *a balance* or *pair of scales* (from وَزَنَ); مِرْوَحٌ and مِرْوَحَةٌ, *a fan;* مِقْوَدٌ, *a bridle* or *halter;* مِرْوَدٌ, *a small probe* for applying koḥl to the eyes; مِخْيَطٌ, *a needle;* مِصْيَدٌ and مِصْيَدَةٌ, *a net* or *snare;* مِرْقَاةٌ (for مِرْقَيَةٌ), *a staircase* or *ladder;* مِصْفَاةٌ, *a strainer;* مِكْوَاةٌ, *a branding-iron* or *cautery.*

REM. *a.* A very few have the form مُفْعُلٌ or مُفْعُلٌ; as مُنْخُلٌ, A *a sieve;* مُنْصُلٌ, *a sword;* مُغْزُلٌ = مِغْزَلٌ, *a spindle;* مُسْعُطٌ = مِسْعَطٌ, *an instrument for introducing medicine into the nose;* مُدُقٌّ = مِدَقٌّ, *a pestle* or *mallet;* مُجْمُرٌ = مِجْمَرٌ, *a censer.* The form مَغْزَلٌ is also used.

REM. *b.* The corresponding Hebrew nouns have ◌ַ and ◌ֶ, as well as ◌ִ, in the first syllable; e.g. מִזְרָק, מֶלְקָחַיִם, מַזְלֵג, מַפְתֵּחַ, B מַזְמֵרָה.

(ζ) *The Nomina Agentis et Patientis.*

229. The nouns which the Arab Grammarians call أَسْمَآءُ ٱلْفَاعِلِ, *nomina agentis,* and أَسْمَآءُ ٱلْمَفْعُولِ, *nomina patientis,* are *verbal* C *adjectives,* i.e. adjectives derived from verbs, and nearly correspond in nature and signification to what we call *participles.*

REM. These verbal adjectives often become in Arabic, as in other languages, substantives.

230. The verbal adjectives, derived from the first form of the triliteral verb, have two principal forms, namely, the nomen agentis, فَاعِلٌ, and the nomen patientis, مَفْعُولٌ. E.g. كَاتِبٌ *writing, a scribe* or *secretary,* from كَتَبَ *to write,* مَكْتُوبٌ *written, a letter,* from كَتَبَ; D خَادِمٌ *serving, a servant,* from خَدَمَ *to serve,* مَخْدُومٌ *served, a master,* from خَدَمَ; حَاكِمٌ *judging, a judge,* from حَكَمَ *to judge;* كَائِنٌ *being,* from كَانَ *to be;* مَوْجُودٌ *found, existing,* from وُجِدَ, *to be found, to exist;* مَجْنُونٌ *mad, a madman,* from جُنَّ, *to be possessed, to be mad.*

REM. *a.* When formed from فَعَلَ and the *transitive* فَعِلَ (as رَهِبَ *to fear,* رَكِبَ *to ride on,* عَلِمَ *to know,* مَسَّ *to touch*), these nomina agentis are not only real participles, indicating a temporary,

A transitory or accidental action or state of being, but also serve as adjectives or substantives, expressing a continuous action, a habitual state of being, or a permanent quality; e.g. خَادِمٌ, كَاتِبٌ, حَاكِمٌ (see above), عَالِمٌ *a scholar*, رَاهِبٌ *an ascetic*. But if from the *intransitive* فَعِلَ and from فَعُلَ, they have only the participial sense, the adjectival being expressed by one or other of the nominal forms enumerated in § 231. Thus فَارِحٌ or جَاذِلٌ *being glad*,
B *rejoicing*, جَابِنٌ *being cowardly*, جَائِدٌ *being liberal*, ضَائِقٌ *being narrow* or *confined*, are participles; the adjectives which indicate the corresponding permanent qualities or characteristics are فَرِحٌ and جَذِلٌ or جَذْلَانُ, *gladsome, cheery*, جَبَانٌ *cowardly*, جَوَادٌ *bountiful, generous*, and ضَيِّقٌ *narrow*. [Comp. however § 232, rem. *b*.]

REM. *b*. The nomen agentis فَاعِلٌ is said to be used occasionally in place of the nomen verbi or actionis, as in the phrase قُمْ قَائِمًا,
C for قُمْ قِيَامًا; but this is more frequently the case with the nomen patientis (compare § 227, rem.) مَفْعُولٌ. E.g. مَجْهُودٌ = جَهْدٌ, *labour, effort, one's utmost*; مَحْلُوفٌ = حَلْفٌ, *swearing, an oath*; مَرْدُودٌ = رَدٌّ, *giving* or *sending back, rejection*; مَعْقُولٌ = عَقْلٌ *understanding, intelligence*; مَشْعُورٌ = شِعْرٌ, *knowledge, perception*; مَوْعُودٌ = وَعْدٌ, *promising, a promise*; مَيْسُورٌ = يُسْرٌ *affluence*, opposed to مَعْسُورٌ = عُسْرٌ, *penury, distress*; مَرْفُوعٌ = رَفْعٌ, *to trot quickly* (of a camel); مَوْضُوعٌ =
D وَضْعٌ *to trot easily* (do.); مَخْفُوضٌ = خَفْضٌ, *to go gently* (do.); مَحْصُولٌ = حُصُولٌ, *being in existence, being got* or *acquired*; مَجْلُودٌ = جَلَادَةٌ, *hardiness, sturdiness, endurance*. The fem. مَفْعُولَةٌ is likewise occasionally so used, as مَحْلُوفَةٌ, مَشْعُورَةٌ, مَوْعُودَةٌ; مَصْدُوقَةٌ = صِدْقٌ, *the telling of the truth*, opposed to مَكْذُوبَةٌ = كَذِبٌ, *lying*; and also a cognate form مَفْعُولَآءُ, as مَحْلُوفَآءُ, مَشْعُورَآءُ.

REM. *c*. Conversely, the nomen actionis is sometimes used instead of the nomen agentis and patientis, or as an adjective. E.g. أَتَيْتُهُ رَكْضًا, *I came to him riding hard*, = رَاكِضًا; كَلَّمْتُهُ مُشَافَهَةً,

I spoke to him face to face (lit. *lip to lip*), = مُشَافَهًا ; لَقِيتُهُ عِيَانًا, A
I met him face to face (lit. *eye to eye*), = مُعَايَنًا . قَتَلْتُهُ صَبْرًا, *I slew him in cold blood* (lit. *bound, confined* or *held*, so that he could not resist or escape), = مَصْبُورًا ; رَجُلٌ عَدْلٌ, اِمْرَأَةٌ عَدْلٌ, رِجَالٌ عَدْلٌ, *a just man, a just woman, just men*, = عَادِلٌ, عَادِلَةٌ, عُدُولٌ ; مَآءٌ غَوْرٌ, *water which sinks into the ground*, = غَائِرٌ ; دِرْهَمٌ ضَرْبُ ٱلْأَمِيرِ, *a dirham struck by the ĕmīr*, = مَضْرُوبُ ٱلْأَمِيرِ ; هُمْ خَلْقُ ٱللّٰهِ, *they are* B
the creatures (lit. *the creation*) *of God*, = مَخْلُوقُ ٱللّٰهِ.

Rem. *d.* فَاعِلٌ is the Aram. קָטֵל, ܩܳܛܶܠ, and Heb. קֹטֵל (with *ō* for *ā*). The form مَفْعُولٌ does not occur in either of these languages, the Heb. using instead of it קָטוּל = فَعُولٌ, and the Aram. קְטִיל = فَعِيلٌ (see § 232, rem. *c*).

231. Besides these, there are other verbal adjectives derived from the first form of the verb, and called صِفَاتٌ مُشَبَّهَةٌ بِأَسْمَآءِ ٱلْفَاعِلِ وَٱلْمَفْعُولِ, *adjectives which are made like*, or *assimilated to, the participles*, viz. in respect of their inflection. Of these the following are the principal.

1. فَعْلٌ	9. فَعَالٌ
2. فَعَلٌ	10. فُعَالٌ
3. فَعِلٌ	11. فَعِيلٌ
4. فَعُلٌ	12. فَعُولٌ D
5. فِعْلٌ	13. فَعْلَانُ
6. فُعْلٌ	14. فِعْلَانٌ
7. فُعُلٌ	15. فُعْلَانٌ
8. فُعَلٌ	16. أَفْعَلُ

232. Most of these adjectives come from neuter verbs, and express, partly, a quality inherent and permanent in a person or

A thing,—which is their most usual signification (see § 38),—and, partly, a certain degree of intensity. Examples: 1. صَعْبٌ *difficult*, from صَعُبَ ; سَهْلٌ *easy*, from سَهُلَ ; عَذْبٌ *sweet*, from عَذُبَ ; ضَخْمٌ *large*, from ضَخُمَ ; طَفْلٌ *tender*, from طَفُلَ ; شَهْمٌ *strong, hardy, acute, clever*, from شَهُمَ ; شَأْزٌ *rough, rugged*, from شَئِزَ ; قَذْرٌ *unclean*, from قَذُرَ. 2. بَطَلٌ *brave*, from بَطُلَ ; حَسَنٌ *handsome*, from حَسُنَ ; قَذَرٌ from قَذُرَ. 3 and 4. فَرِحٌ, جَذِلٌ, *glad*, from فَرِحَ, جَذِلَ ; بَطِرٌ, أَشِرٌ, *proud*,

B *self-conceited and insolent*, from أَشِرَ and بَطِرَ ; وَجِعٌ *in pain*, from وَجِعَ ; حَبِطٌ *having a swollen stomach*, from حَبِطَ ; دَنِسٌ *dirty*, from دَنِسَ ; شَجٍ, جَوٍ (for شَجِيٌ, جَوِيٌ) *in grief*, from شَجِيَ, جَوِيَ ; رَدٍ (for رَدِيٌ) *perishing*, from رَدِيَ ; حَفٍ *having his foot* or *hoof chafed*, from حَفِيَ ; وَجٍ do., from وَجِيَ ; فَطِنٌ, فَطُنٌ, *clever, intelligent*, from فَطِنَ, فَطُنَ ; يَقِظٌ, يَقُظٌ, *awake*, from يَقِظَ, يَقُظَ ; حَزِنٌ, حَزُنٌ, *sorry*,

C from حَزِنَ ; حَذِرٌ, حَذُرٌ, *timid, cautious, wary*, from حَذِرَ ; نَدِسٌ, نَدُسٌ, *intelligent*, from نَدِسَ ; عَجِلٌ, عَجُلٌ, *quick, in haste*, from عَجِلَ ; قَذِرٌ, قَذُرٌ from قَذِرَ ; خَشِنٌ *rough, harsh*, from خَشُنَ ; طَهِرٌ *clean, pure*, from طَهُرَ. 5. خِرْقٌ *liberal* ; طِفْلٌ, *small, young*, from طَفُلَ *to be tender* ; جِلٌّ *large, coarse, fat*, from جَلَّ ; دِقٌّ *fine, thin*, from دَقَّ. 6 and 7. صُلْبٌ *hard*, from صَلُبَ ; حُلْوٌ *sweet*, from حَلُوَ ; مُرٌّ *bitter*, from مَرَّ ; غُمْرٌ, غُمُرٌ, *inexperienced, untaught*, from غَمُرَ ; جُنُبٌ *polluted*, from

D جَنُبَ. 8. حُطَمٌ *breaking, crushing, bruising*, from حَطَمَ ; غُدَرٌ *perfidious, treacherous*, from غَدَرَ *to forsake, abandon, betray* ; لُبَدٌ *remaining in one place, abundant*, from لَبِدَ, لَبَدَ ; زُكَنٌ *knowing*, from زَكِنَ. 9. جَبَانٌ *cowardly*, from جَبُنَ ; شَجَاعٌ *brave*, from شَجُعَ ; جَوَادٌ *liberal*, from جَادَ ; حَصَانٌ *chaste*, from حَصُنَتْ ; كَهَامٌ *blunt*, from كَهُمَ, كَهَمَ. 10. شُجَاعٌ *brave*, from شَجُعَ ; ضُخَامٌ *large*, from

فُرَاتٌ ; حَسُنَ from *handsome*, حُسَانٌ ; كَرُمَ from *noble*, كُرَامٌ ; ضَخُمَ A
sweet (of water), from فَرُتَ ; حُرَاقٌ *salt* (of water), from حَرَقَ *to burn* ;
طُوَالٌ *long, tall*, from طَالَ ; [قُدَارٌ *a cook*, from قَدَرَ *to cook*]. 11. بَخِيلٌ
stingy, niggardly, from بَخُلَ ; كَثِيرٌ *much, many, numerous*, from كَثُرَ ;
شَرِيفٌ *noble*. from شَرُفَ ; كَرِيمٌ *noble*, from كَرُمَ ; ضَعِيفٌ *weak*, from
ضَعُفَ ; ثَقِيلٌ *heavy*, from ثَقُلَ ; غَلِيظٌ *thick, coarse*, from غَلُظَ ; طَوِيلٌ
long, tall, from طَالَ ; رَحِيمٌ *compassionate, merciful*. from رَحِمَ ; سَلِيمٌ B
safe, from سَلِمَ ; سَقِيمٌ, مَرِيضٌ, *sick*, from سَقِمَ, مَرِضَ ; خَفِيفٌ *light*,
agile, from خَفَّ ; جَلِيلٌ *great, glorious*, from جَلَّ ; دَقِيقٌ *small, slender*,
paltry, from دَقَّ. 12. أَكُولٌ *gluttonous*, from أَكَلَ ; كَذُوبٌ *addicted*
to lying, from كَذَبَ ; صَدُوقٌ *veracious*, from صَدَقَ ; قَوُولٌ or قَؤُولٌ,
talkative [or *ready to speak*], from قَالَ ; [فَعُولٌ *ready to do*, from
فَعَلَ] ; دَفُوعٌ *pushing, thrusting* or *kicking violently*, from دَفَعَ ; عَطُوفٌ
moved by affection or *pity*, from عَطَفَ ; جَسُورٌ *daring*, from جَسَرَ ; C
جَهُولٌ *ignorant, foolish*, from جَهِلَ ; حَصُورٌ *continent, impotent*, from
حَصِرَ. 13. سَكْرَانُ *drunk*, from سَكِرَ ; غَضْبَانُ *angry*, from غَضِبَ ;
عَطْشَانُ, ظَمْآنُ, *thirsty*, from عَطِشَ, ظَمِئَ ; جَوْعَانُ, غَرْثَانُ, *hungry*,
from جَاعَ, غَرِثَ ; شَبْعَانُ *satisfied with food*, from شَبِعَ ; رَيَّانُ *satisfied*
with drink, from رَوِيَ ; خَزْيَانُ *ashamed*, from خَزِيَ. 14. نَدْمَانُ
repentant, from نَدِمَ. 15. عُرْيَانٌ *naked*, from عَرِيَ. 16. أَبْلَجُ *having* D
a clear space between the eyebrows, bright, open, cheerful in countenance,
from بَلِجَ ; أَشَمُّ *having a high, straight nose*, from شَمَّ ; أَهْيَفُ *having*
a slender waist, from هَيِفَ ; أَذْقَنُ *having a long chin* (ذَقَنٌ) ; أَحْدَبُ
humpbacked, from حَدِبَ ; أَعْوَرُ *one-eyed*, from عَوِرَ ; أَحْوَلُ *squinting*,
from حَوِلَ ; أَصَمُّ *deaf*, from صَمَّ ; أَحْمَقُ *foolish, stupid*, from حَمِقَ,
حَمُقَ ; أَخْرَقُ *unskilful, clumsy, stupid*, from خَرُقَ, خَرِقَ ; أَشْنَعُ *unseemly*,
ugly, foul, from شَنُعَ ; أَحْمَرُ *red*, أَسْوَدُ *black*, أَبْيَضُ *white*, أَصْفَرُ *yellow*.

A REM. *a.* As is shown by the above examples, the forms فَعْلٌ and فَعِيلٌ are principally derived from فَعُلَ; فَعِلٌ and فَعُلٌ come respectively from فَعِلَ intrans. and فَعُلَ, though the distinction is not always observed; فَعْلَانُ is principally formed from فَعِلَ intrans.; فَعَالٌ and فُعَالٌ mainly from فَعُلَ; أَفْعَلُ chiefly from فَعِلَ intrans., sometimes from فَعُلَ.

B REM. *b.* فَاعِلٌ is rarely used as a verbal adjective from فَعِلَ intrans. or فَعُلَ (see § 230, rem. *a*); e.g. آمِنٌ *safe, secure,* = أَمِينٌ or أَمِنٌ, from أَمِنَ; سَالِمٌ, *safe, sound,* = سَلِيمٌ, from سَلِمَ; عَاقِرٌ *barren,* from عَقُرَتْ; حَامِضٌ *sour, acid,* from حَمُضَ or حَمِضَ.

REM. *c.* فَعِيلٌ, when derived from *transitive* verbs, has usually a *passive* sense; as قَتِيلٌ *slain* = مَقْتُولٌ; جَرِيحٌ *wounded* = مَجْرُوحٌ;
C ذَبِيحٌ *slaughtered, a victim,* = مَذْبُوحٌ; خَضِيبٌ *dyed* = مَخْضُوبٌ; كَحِيلٌ *rubbed with kohl* = مَكْحُولٌ; أَسِيرٌ *bound, a prisoner,* = مَأْسُورٌ. The same is sometimes the case with فَعُولٌ, as رَكُوبٌ *ridden upon,* حَلُوبٌ *milked**.

REM. *d.* Adjectives of the forms فَعِيلٌ and فَعُولٌ, but more especially the latter, often indicate, as shown by some of the above examples, either a very high degree of the quality which their subject possesses, or an act which is done with frequency or violence
D by their subject; and hence they are called أَبْنِيَةُ ٱلْمُبَالَغَةِ, *intensive forms.* The form فَعِيلٌ is dialectically pronounced فِعِيلٌ, especially if the second radical be a guttural, as كِبِيرٌ, سِعِيدٌ, رِحِيمٌ, شِهِيدٌ, كِرِيمٌ, جِلِيلٌ; and so also in substantives, as بِعِيرٌ, رِغِيفٌ, شِعِيرٌ, ٱلْمِسِيحُ.

---

* [رَسُولٌ does not belong to this class; according to the native scholars, it is originally a nomen actionis like قَبُولٌ meaning *message.* Hence, as in the case of Latin *nuntius,* it got the signification of *bearer of a message.* D. G.]

Rem. e. Many of these forms exist in Hebrew and Aramaic. A
For example, in the former, فَعَلٌ, as חָדָשׁ = حَدَثٌ ; فَعِلٌ, as דָּשֵׁן = دَسِمٌ ; فَعُلٌ, as יָגֹר = وَجِرٌ, وَجِلٌ ; فَعَالٌ, as גָּדוֹל (ō for ā) ; فَعُولٌ, as אָסוּר, עָצוּם ; فَعِيلٌ, as אָסִיר, צָעִיר.

233. From verbal adjectives of the form فَاعِلٌ, as well as from some others, is derived an adjective فَعَّالٌ, which approaches very nearly in meaning to فَعُولٌ and فَعِيلٌ, since it adds to the signification B
of its primitive the idea of intensiveness or of habit. Hence it is called اِسْمُ ٱلْمُبَالَغَةِ, *the noun of intensiveness.* E.g. آكِلٌ *eating,* أَكَّالٌ *a glutton,* = أَكُولٌ ; كَاذِبٌ *lying,* كَذَّابٌ *a (habitual) liar,* = كَذُوبٌ ; دَافِعٌ *pushing, thrusting, repelling,* دَفَّاعٌ *pushing, etc., violently,* = دَفُوعٌ ; سَائِلٌ *asking,* سَأَّالٌ *importunate, a beggar,* = سَؤُولٌ ; شَارِبٌ *drinking,* شَرَّابٌ *drinking much, addicted to wine,* = شَرُوبٌ ; عَالِمٌ *knowing, learned,* C
عَلَّامٌ *very learned ;* بَاكٍ *weeping,* بَكَّآءٌ *weeping much ;* هَائِبٌ *fearing,* هَيَّابٌ *timid.*

Rem. a. The nouns which indicate professions and trades have usually this form ; as عَطَّارٌ *a druggist,* طَبَّاخٌ *a cook,* خَبَّازٌ *a baker,* خَيَّاطٌ *a tailor,* نَجَّارٌ *a carpenter,* سَقَّآءٌ *a water-carrier,* جَنَّانٌ *a gardener,* رَآَّسٌ *a seller of sheeps' heads,* صَرَّافٌ *a money-changer* or *banker,* بَنَّآءٌ *a builder* or *architect,* حَمَّالٌ *a porter.* Compare in
Hebrew and Aram. סַבָּל, מַלָּח, טַבָּח, גַּנָּב, חַטָּא, etc. D

Rem. b. Other intensive adjectives, less common than فَعَّالٌ are 1. فُعَّالٌ, 2. فِعِّيلٌ, 3. فَعُّولٌ or فُعُّولٌ, 4. فُعَّلٌ, and 5. فَاعُولٌ; as 1. حُسَّانٌ, وُضَّآءٌ, *very handsome,* كُرَّامٌ *very noble,* كُبَّارٌ *very large,* قُرَّآءٌ *one who devotes himself to reading (the sacred writings),* دُفَّاعٌ *a strong propeller* or *repeller, a great rush* (of water or of people) ; 2. خِمِّيرٌ, سِكِّيرٌ, شِرِّيبٌ, *addicted to wine, drunken,* ضِلِّيلٌ *going astray,*

A *wandering*; عِرِّيضٌ *fond of opposition*, فِخِّيرٌ *boastful*, صِدِّيقٌ *exceedingly veracious*, خِرِّيقٌ *very liberal*, صِرِّيعٌ *one who throws down often* or *violently, a wrestler*; دِرِّيٌّ *glistening intensely* (also دُرِّيٌّ, the only instance of the form فُعِّيلٌ, except مُرِّيقٌ); 3. فَرُوقٌ *timid*, قَيُّومٌ *everlasting*, سَتُّوقٌ or سُتُّوقٌ *bad* (of money), سَبُّوحٌ or سُبُّوحٌ *all-pure, all-glorious*, قَدُّوسٌ or قُدُّوسٌ *most holy*; 4. قُلَّبٌ, حُوَّلٌ,
B *shifting, turning, knowing, cunning*, خُلَّبٌ *deceitful*; 5. فَارُوقٌ *timid*, جَاسُوسٌ *a spy*.—On the other hand, مِفْعَلٌ, مِفْعَالٌ, and مِفْعِيلٌ, are, strictly speaking, substantives (nomina instrumenti, § 228), but used metaphorically as adjectives to mean "doing something like a machine, mechanically, and therefore invariably (habitually)." E.g. مِدْفَعٌ *thrusting* or *pushing much*, مِزْحَمٌ *pushing* or *pressing much*, مِصْدَمٌ *a brave warrior*, مِحْرَبٌ, مِحْرَابٌ, *do.*,
C مِطْعَنٌ, مِطْعَانٌ, *thrusting with the spear*, مِهْذَرٌ, مِهْذَارٌ, *talking nonsense*, مِطْعَمٌ, مِطْعَامٌ, *eating much* or *giving much to eat, hospitable*, مِقْوَلٌ, مِقْوَالٌ, *talkative, eloquent*, مِفْرَاحٌ *cheerful*, مِذْعَانٌ *docile, tractable*, مِخْرَاقٌ *very liberal*, مِقْدَامٌ *advancing boldly, daring*, مِكْسَالٌ *slothful*, مِذْكَارٌ *bearing male children*, مِئْنَاثٌ *bearing female children*, مِعْطَآءٌ *very liberal*, مِكْثَارٌ, مِكْثِيرٌ, *very talkative*, مِعْطَارٌ,
D مِعْطِيرٌ, *using perfumes*, مِسْكِينٌ *mean, poor* (מִסְכֵּן, ܡܣܟܢܐ)*.—Similar, too, is the use of such forms as تَفْعَالٌ or تِفْعَالٌ, تِفْعَلَةٌ, and تِفِعَّالٌ, which are abstract substantives (nomina actionis, § 202) used concretely; e.g. تَلْعَابٌ, تِلْعَابٌ, تِلِعَّابٌ, *given to play* or *sport*; تِلْقَامٌ, تِلِقَّامٌ, *swallowing big morsels, greedy*; تِضْرَابٌ *covered by the stallion* (of a she-camel), تِلِقَّاعٌ *talking much and foolishly*, تِكِذَّابٌ *mendacious*, تِلِمَّاظٌ *fickle*, تِقْوَلَةٌ *loquacious*, تِعْلِمَةٌ *very learned*.

---

* [To this class belongs also مِنْتِنٌ, مُنْتِنٌ, مُنْتُنٌ *stinking*. D. G.]

REM. *c.* Nearly all these adjectives and quasi-adjectives admit A
of being strengthened in their meaning by the addition of the
termination ةٌ, which is here used, as the grammarians say
لِلْمُبَالَغَةِ *to signify intensiveness*, or لِتَأْكِيدِ ٱلْمُبَالَغَةِ, *to strengthen the*
idea of intensiveness. For example, from فَاعِلٌ comes فَاعِلَةٌ, as
رَاوٍ *one who hands down poems* or *historical facts by oral tradition*,
رَاوِيَةٌ; دَاهٍ *crafty*, دَاهِيَةٌ; دَاعٍ *calling* or *summoning, an emissary* or
missionary, دَاعِيَةٌ; بَاقِعَةٌ *clever, crafty*; خَائِنَةٌ *treacherous, faithless*; B
بَاقِرَةٌ *a deep investigator* (compare in Heb. קֹהֶלֶת from קָהַל);
from فُعَلٌ, فُعَلَةٌ, as حُطَمَةٌ *breaking in pieces, crushing to bits*,
طُلَعَةٌ *always on the watch*, صُرَعَةٌ *throwing down* or *prostrating often*,
سُؤَلَةٌ *asking often, begging*, ضُحَكَةٌ *prone to laughter*, قُوَلَةٌ *loquacious*,
نُوَمَةٌ *given to sleep*, لُوَمَةٌ *abusive*, عُيَبَةٌ *finding fault*; from فَعِيلٌ,
فَعِيلَةٌ, as كَرِيمَةٌ, عَقِيلَةٌ, *noble, excellent*; from فَعُولٌ, فَعُولَةٌ, as
مَنُونَةٌ *taunting (one) with favours (conferred on him)*, كَذُوبَةٌ *lying*,
مَلُولَةٌ *tired of, disgusted with*, هَيُوبَةٌ, فَرُوقَةٌ, *timid*; from فَعَّالٌ, C
فَعَّالَةٌ, as عَلَّامَةٌ *very learned*, نَسَّابَةٌ *a great genealogist*, رَحَّالَةٌ *a*
great traveller, فَهَّامَةٌ *very quick of comprehension*, وَقَّاعَةٌ *ill-natured,*
slanderous, قَوَّالَةٌ *very talkative*, جَمَّاعَةٌ *a great collector*, صَنَّاجَةٌ *an*
excellent player on the cymbals or *harp* (صَنْجٌ); from فُعَّالٌ, فُعَّالَةٌ, as
صُرَّاعَةٌ *prostrating* or *throwing down very often*, كُرَّامَةٌ *very generous*
or *noble*, لُقَّاعَةٌ *talking much and rashly* or *foolishly*; from فِعِّيلٌ,
فِعِّيلَةٌ, as خِلِّيفَةٌ *very contrarious*; from فَعُّولٌ, فَعُّولَةٌ, as فَرُّوقَةٌ *very*
timid; from فَاعُولٌ, فَاعُولَةٌ, as حَاذُورَةٌ *very wary* or *cautious*, فَارُوقَةٌ D
very timid; from مِفْعَالٌ, مِفْعَالَةٌ, as مِلْحَادَةٌ *very unjust*, مِقْدَامَةٌ *very*
bold in attacking, مِهْذَارَةٌ *talking much and sillily*; from تِفْعَالٌ,
تِفْعَالَةٌ, as تِلْعَابَةٌ *addicted to play* or *sport*, تِقْوَالَةٌ *loquacious*, تِعْلَامَةٌ
very learned, تِعْجَابَةٌ *causing great wonder* or *marvel*, تِلْقَامَةٌ *swal-*
lowing big morsels, greedy (the cognate form تِفْعِيلَةٌ also occurs, as

A تِلْعِيبَةٌ *much addicted to play or sport*); from تِفِعَّالٌ, تِفِعَّالَةٌ, as تِلِعَّابَةٌ *much addicted to play* or *sport*, تِلِقَّامَةٌ *swallowing huge morsels, very greedy*, تِلِقَّاعَةٌ *talking much and foolishly*.

REM. *d.* Besides the forms incidentally noticed above, others of these intensive adjectives occur in Hebrew and Aramaic; for example, فَعُّولٌ, as חַנּוּן ,רַחוּם, and فِعِّيلٌ, but with the purer vowel *a* in the first syllable (فَعِّيلٌ), as עַלִּיז, צַדִּיק, אַבִּיר, ܢܰܟ݁ܺܝܦܳܐ,
B ܩܰܠܺܝܨ. Other forms are without exact equivalents in Arabic, as גִּבּוֹר = جَبَّارٌ, שִׁכּוֹר = سِكِّيرٌ, עִזּוּז (coming nearest to قُدُّوسٌ), יִלּוֹד = Aram. ܝܰܠܘܿܕ (فَعُّولٌ); and especially the form קִטֵּל, as גִּבֵּן (= حَدِبٌ), עִוֵּר (= أَعْوَرُ), חֵרֵשׁ (= أَخْرَسُ), which may be viewed as an intensive of فَعِلٌ (קִטֵּל for קַטֵּל, קַטֵּל = فَعِّلٌ).

C **234.** From verbal adjectives with three radicals*, or with three radicals and a letter of prolongation, are derived adjectives of the form أَفْعَلُ, which have the signification of our comparative and superlative, and are therefore called إِسْمُ ٱلتَّفْضِيلِ, *the noun of preeminence*, or أَفْعَلُ ٱلتَّفْضِيلِ, *the form 'af'alu denoting preeminence*. E.g. عَذْبٌ, حُلْوٌ, *sweet*, أَعْذَبُ, أَحْلَى, *sweeter, sweetest*; حَسَنٌ *beautiful*, أَحْسَنُ *more* or *most beautiful*; قَبِيحٌ *ugly*, أَقْبَحُ *uglier, ugliest*; جَلِيلٌ *great, glorious*, أَجَلُّ *more* or *most glorious*.

D REM. *a.* In the superlative sense, these adjectives must always have the article, or else be in the construct state, as ٱلْمَدِينَةُ ٱلْعُظْمَى *the greatest city*, كُبْرَى ٱلْمُدُنِ *the largest of the cities*.

---

* [A rare exception to this rule is أَعْلَقُ *bitterer*, as derived from عَلْقَمٌ *anything bitter*, spec. *the colocynth*, according to 'Ibn Durèid, *Kitāb el-iśtiḳāḳ*, 53, l. 6, 98, l. 16 *seq.* In the *Lisān*, however (xii. 142), it is differently explained. R. S.]

Rem. *b.* Of this form there remain only a very few traces in Hebrew, none in Aramaic. Such are: אַכְזָב *lying, false* (of a stream that dries up in summer), from כָּזַב = كَاذِبٌ ; אַכְזָר *fierce, cruel*, perhaps connected with كَاسِرٌ *breaking in pieces;* אֵיתָן (for אַיְתָן) *lasting, perennial,* = وَاتِنٌ ; and even these have lost their original signification, and are used as simple adjectives. A

235. No اِسْمُ ٱلتَّفْضِيلِ can, according to strict rule, be formed from the verbal adjectives of the passive voice and the derived forms of the verb, nor from verbal adjectives that denote colours or deformities, because they are themselves of the form أَفْعَلُ (compare § 184, rem. *b*). If we wish to say that one person surpasses another in the qualities expressed by such adjectives, we ought to prefix to the corresponding abstract or verbal nouns the comparatives أَشَدُّ *stronger*, أَحْسَنُ *more beautiful*, أَجْوَدُ *more excellent*, أَقْبَحُ *uglier*, خَيْرٌ *better*, شَرٌّ *worse*, and the like. E.g. أَشَدُّ حُمْرَةً (*stronger as to redness*) *redder;* أَحْسَنُ تَعْلِيمًا وَتَأْدِيبًا (*more excellent as to teaching and training*) *a better teacher and trainer;* أَجْوَدُ مِنْهُ جَوَابًا (*more excellent than he as to answering*) *more ready than he in answering*, or *giving a better answer than he;* أَسْرَعُ ٱنْطِلَاقًا (*more quick as to departing*) *departing more quickly;* أَقْبَحُ عَوَرًا *more deformed by blindness of one eye.* This form of expression is sometimes employed where a simple comparative might have been used; as ثُمَّ قَسَتْ قُلُوبُكُمْ مِنْ بَعْدِ ذٰلِكَ فَهِيَ كَٱلْحِجَارَةِ أَوْ أَشَدُّ قَسْوَةً, *then, after that, your hearts became hard, like stones, or even harder* (lit. *stronger as to hardness*), where أَشَدُّ قَسْوَةً = أَقْسَى (êl-Ḳor'ân ii. 69).—As a matter of fact, however, the strict rules laid down by the grammarians are constantly violated by usage. B C D

(*a*) Examples of أَفْعَلُ formed from the derived forms of the verb, especially from IV.: أَطْهَرُ *more cleansing* or *purifying* (أَكْثَرُ تَطْهِيرًا), from طَهَّرَ *to cleanse* or *purify*, II. of طَهُرَ *to be clean* or *pure;* أَصْفَى لِ

A *making clearer* or *purer*, from صَفَّى *to clarify* or *clear*, II. of صَفَا *to be*
clear; أَسْلَمُ لِ *preserving better*, from سَلَّمَ, II. of سَلِمَ *to be safe*;
أَقْوَمُ لِ *confirming* or *establishing better*, from أَقَامَ, IV. of قَامَ *to stand*
upright; أَثْبَتُ لِ *making more firm* or *sure*, from أَثْبَتَ, IV. of ثَبَتَ *to*
be firm; أَخْوَفُنِي عَلَى *causing me greater alarm about*, from خَوَّفَ or
أَخَافَ, II. or IV. of خَافَ *to fear*; أَعْوَنُ عَلَى *giving more help towards*,
from أَعَانَ *to help*, IV. of عَانَ; أَذْهَبُ لِ *making depart more quickly*,
B from أَذْهَبَ, IV. of ذَهَبَ *to go away*; أَرْخَاهُمَا لِ *that of the two which*
relaxes, or *loosens*, *more*, from أَرْخَى, IV. of رَخُوَ or رَخِيَ *to be flaccid*
or *flabby*; أَبْقَى لِ *causing to last longer*, أَبْقَى عَلَى *more merciful to*,
from أَبْقَى, IV. of بَقِيَ *to remain, last*; أَهْيَبُ لِ *inspiring more fear* or
respect, from أَهَابَ, IV. of هَابَ *to fear*; أَنْصَفُ مِنْ *more just than*,
from أَنْصَفَ *to be just*, IV. of نَصَفَ *to take the half, reach the middle*;
أَطْوَلُ لِ *causing to last longer*, from أَطَالَ, IV. of طَالَ *to be long*;
C أَحْيَى لِ *preserving alive better*, from أَحْيَى, IV. of حَيِيَ *to live*;
أَظَلُّ مِنْ *giving more shade than*, from أَظَلَّ *to give shade*, IV. of ظَلَّ;
أَجْوَدُ لِ *causing to be better*, from أَجَادَ, IV. of جَادَ *to be good, excellent*;
أَعْطَى لِ *giving more freely*, from أَعْطَى *to give*, IV. of عَطَا; أَوْلَى لِ
bestowing more liberally, from أَوْلَى *to bestow*, IV. of وَلِيَ; أَكْرَمُ لِ
D *showing greater honour to*, from أَكْرَمَ, IV. of كَرُمَ *to be noble*;
أَقْفَرُ مِنْ *more desert than*, from أَقْفَرَ *to be desert*, IV. of قَفِرَ; أَفْلَسُ مِنْ
poorer than, from أَفْلَسَ *to be poor*, IV. of فَلَسَ; أَحْوَلُ مِنْ *more crafty*
than, from اِحْتَالَ, *to be crafty*, VIII. of حَالَ; أَقْوَدُ مِنْ *more easily led*,
or *more docile, than*, from اِنْقَادَ, VII. of قَادَ *to lead*. (β) Examples of
أَفْعَلُ formed from the passive voice: أَهْيَبُ, أَخْوَفُ, أَخْشَى, *more feared*

or *formidable*; أَحْمَدُ *more praiseworthy* or *commendable*; أَعْرَفُ *better* A
known; أَلْوَمُ *more deserving of blame*; أَسَرُّ *more glad of* or *pleased by*; أَعْذَرُ *more to be excused*; أَوْجَدُ *more readily found*; أَشْغَلُ *more occupied*; أَزْهَى *prouder* (زُهِيَ *to be proud*); أَمْقَتُ *more hated* or *hateful*; أَعْنَى بِ *more occupied with* (عُنِيَ or VIII. اِعْتَنَى.); أَخْصَرُ *shorter* (from اُخْتُصِرَ, pass. of VIII.). (γ) Examples of أَفْعَلُ from words denoting colours or defects: أَبْيَضُ مِنْ *whiter than*; أَسْوَدُ مِنْ *blacker than*;
أَحْمَقُ مِنْ *more stupid than*. B

236. The verbal adjectives formed from the active and passive voices of the derived forms of the triliteral verb, and from the quadriliteral verb, are the following.

Triliteral Verb.

	Act.	Pass.		Act.	Pass.	
II.	مُفَعِّلٌ	مُفَعَّلٌ	VII.	مُنْفَعِلٌ	مُنْفَعَلٌ	C
III.	مُفَاعِلٌ	مُفَاعَلٌ	VIII.	مُفْتَعِلٌ	مُفْتَعَلٌ	
IV.	مُفْعِلٌ	مُفْعَلٌ	IX.	مُفْعَلٌّ	....	
V.	مُتَفَعِّلٌ	مُتَفَعَّلٌ	X.	مُسْتَفْعِلٌ	مُسْتَفْعَلٌ	
VI.	مُتَفَاعِلٌ	مُتَفَاعَلٌ	XI.	مُفْعَالٌّ	....	

Quadriliteral Verb. D

I.	مُفَعْلِلٌ	مُفَعْلَلٌ	III.	مُفْعَنْلِلٌ	مُفْعَنْلَلٌ
II.	مُتَفَعْلِلٌ	مُتَفَعْلَلٌ	IV.	مُفْعَلِلٌّ	مُفْعَلَلٌّ

Rem. *a.* The characteristic vowel of the second and third radicals is the same in all these verbal adjectives as in the corresponding Imperfects, excepting the active participles of the fifth and sixth forms of the triliteral verb and the second form of the

A quadriliteral, in which the second and third radicals have ـَ instead of ـُ.

REM. *b.* The preformative م takes in Arabic the vowel ـُ. in Heb. and Aram. ـְ (e.g. מְקַטֵּל, מְהַקְטִיל = מַקְטִיל, מִתְקַטֵּל = "מְהַת"), but the Æthiopic seems to have retained the original vowel in its prefix መ: *ma*, as መዐምፅ: (ma'ámmĕẓ) *oppressor*
B (חָמֵס, חֹמֵץ); መኰንን: (makwánnĕn) *judge* (מְכוֹנֵן); መናፍቅ: (manáfĕḳ) *sceptic, heretic* (مُنَافِق); መርዕድ: (már'ed) *causing to tremble, dreadful* (مُرْعِد, מַרְעִיד); መፍሪ: (máfrī) *fruitful* (מַפְרֶה); መስተምሕር: (mastámhĕr) *imploring mercy* (مُسْتَرْحِم); መተርጕም: (matárgwĕm) *an interpreter* (مُتَرْجِم).

237. In the formation of verbal adjectives from verba mediæ
C rad. geminatæ, the rules laid down in § 120 are to be observed. Hence مَادِدٌ becomes مَادٌّ (see § 13, rem.); أَشْدَدُ, أَشَدُّ; مُضْلِلٌ, مُضِلٌّ; etc.

238. In the formation of verbal adjectives from the verba hèmzata, the rules laid down regarding those verbs (§§ 131–6) are to be observed. Hence we write آثِرٌ for أَأْثِرٌ (§ 135), سَائِلٌ for سَاإِلٌ (§ 133), رَوُوفٌ or رَؤُوفٌ for رَأُوفٌ, لَئِيمٌ for لَإِيمٌ, مُوَاثِرٌ for مُأَاثِرٌ (§ 133), مُوثِرٌ for مُأْثِرٌ (§ 131).

D REM. *a.* أ preceded by kèsra becomes ئ; as هَانِئٌ for هَانِأٌ.

REM. *b.* Final hèmza, preceded by ī and ū, admits of assimilation; as رَدِيءٌ or رَدِيٌّ, دَرِيءٌ or دَرِيٌّ, مَقْرُوءٌ or مَقْرُوٌّ. See § 17, *b*, rem. *b*.

239. In the formation of verbal adjectives from verba primæ rad. ى, the rule laid down in § 147 must be observed; as مُوسِرٌ for مُيْسِرٌ.

240. In the nomina agentis of the first form of verba mediæ rad. و et ى, the place of the middle radical is occupied by a ى with hèmza (arising, according to § 133, out of ا); as قَآئِلٌ (for قَاإِلٌ), سَآئِرٌ (for سَاإِرٌ), instead of قَاوِلٌ, سَايِرٌ. A

Rem. *a.* This rule does not apply to the verbs mentioned in § 160, which retain their middle radical unchanged; as عَاوِرٌ, صَايِدٌ.

Rem. *b.* The form قَآئِمٌ admits in certain words of being contracted into قَامٌ (compare the Heb. קָם for קָוֵם), as شَاكٌ for شَآئِكٌ, B
in the phrase شَآئِكُ ٱلسِّلَاحِ or شَاكُ ٱلسِّلَاحِ, *bristling with weapons;* مَاهٌ for مَآئِهٌ, in the phrase مَآئِهُ ٱلْفُؤَادِ or مَاهُ ٱلْفُؤَادِ, *water-hearted, cowardly, stupid;* هَارٌ *feeble,* for هَآئِرٌ; هَاعٌ لَاعٌ *timid* or *greedy,* for هَآئِعٌ لَآئِعٌ; شَاهٌ *sharp* (*of sight*), for شَآئِهٌ; سَاسٌ *corroded* or *decayed* (of a tooth), for سَآئِسٌ; طَاعٌ *obedient,* for طَآئِعٌ; طَافٌ *going about,* for طَآئِفٌ; طَانٌ *clayey,* for طَآئِنٌ*. Sometimes the second radical C
is transposed; as شَاكِي ٱلسِّلَاحِ, مَاهِي ٱلْفُؤَادِ, هَارٍ, لَاعٍ, جَالٍ, شَاطٍ, شَاهٍ, لَاثٍ.

Rem. *c.* In the form فَعُولٌ the medial و is usually changed into ؤ; as قَؤُولٌ, صَؤُولٌ, نَؤُومٌ, for قَوُولٌ, صَوُولٌ, نَوُومٌ.

241. In the nomina patientis of the first form of verba mediæ rad. و, the middle radical is elided, after throwing back its ḍamma D
upon the preceding vowelless letter; as مَخُوفٌ, for مَخُوْوفٌ, from مَخْوُوفٌ. The same thing takes place in verba mediæ rad. ى, with this difference, that (to indicate the elision of the radical ى) the ḍamma is changed into kèsra, and, in consequence, the و productionis into a ى; as مَبِيعٌ, instead of مَبُوعٌ, from مَبْيُوعٌ.

---

* [A poet even allows himself to say سَارُهَا for سَآئِرُهَا (from سُؤْرٌ); see Abū Zèid, *Nawādir,* 26 infra. D. G.]

A REM. The forms مَدْوُوفٌ, مَصْوُونٌ, and مَقْوُودٌ, are said to be used dialectically. From verba med. ى the uncontracted forms are more common, but still rare; as مَزْيُوتٌ, مَدْيُونٌ, مَخْيُوطٌ, مَبْيُوعٌ, مَكْيُولٌ, مَغْيُومٌ, for مَبِيعٌ, مَخِيطٌ, etc.

242. Verbal adjectives of the form فَعِيلٌ, derived from verba mediæ rad. و et ى, become by transposition فَيْعِلٌ, and then pass into فَيِّلٌ, which is in its turn frequently shortened into فَيْلٌ. E.g. مَيِّتٌ
B or مَيْتٌ, *dead*, for مَيْوِتٌ, مَوِيتٌ (مَاتَ); [عَيِّلٌ *dependent for sustenance*, for عَيْوِلٌ (عَالَ)]; لَيِّنٌ or لَيْنٌ, *soft, easy*, for لَيْيِنٌ, لَيِينٌ (لَانَ); هَيِّنٌ or هَيْنٌ, *easy, contemptible* (هَوِينٌ); نَيِّفٌ or نَيْفٌ, *exceeding* (نَوِيفٌ); نَيِّرٌ, *bright* (نَوِيرٌ); سَيِّءٌ, *wicked* (سَوِيءٌ); بَيِّنٌ, *clear* (بَيِينٌ); خَيْرٌ, *good* (خَيِيرٌ). The verb قَامَ has قَوِيمٌ in the sense of *straight, right, tall*,
C and قَيِّمٌ in that of *having charge of, managing.*

243. Verbal adjectives from the derived forms of verba mediæ rad. و et ى follow the same rules as their Imperfects.

REM. The learner should observe that the participles of III. and VI. of verba med. ى are written and pronounced with ى, and on no account with hèmza; e.g. مُبَايِنٌ, مُتَبَايِنٌ, like يُبَايِنُ, يَتَبَايَنُ, and not مُبَائِنٌ, مُتَبَائِنٌ.

D **244.** The nomina agentis et patientis of the first form of verba ultimæ rad. و et ى have already been mentioned (§ 167, *b*, *β*, and § 170). Verbal adjectives of the forms فَعُولٌ and فَعِيلٌ are treated according to the same rules as the nomina patientis (§ 170); e.g. عَدُوٌّ *hostile, an enemy*, بَغِيٌّ *a harlot*, سَرِيٌّ *generous, noble*, صَبِيٌّ *a boy*, سَبِيٌّ *captive*, for عَدُووٌ, بَغُويٌ, سَرِيوٌ, صَبِيوٌ, سَبِييٌ.

245. In all adjectives derived from verba tertiæ rad. و et ى,

if the second radical be pronounced with fèthạ, the ى and و (which is converted into ى) reject their vowel or tènwīn, and assume the nature of the èlif maḳṣūra (§ 7, rem. *b*). If the form be one that admits of complete declension, the tènwīn is transferred to the second radical. According to this rule are formed: (*a*) the nomina patientis of the derived forms, as مُوَلًّى for مُوَلَّىٌ, مُعْطًى for مُعْطَىٌ (مُعْطَوٌ); (*b*) adjectives of the form أَفْعَلُ, as أَرْمَى for أَرْمَىُ, أَبْكَى for أَبْكَىُ, أَرْضَى for أَرْضَىُ (أَرْضَوُ), أَحْلَى for أَحْلَوُ (أَحْلَوُ). Compare § 167, *α*, *β*, a, and *b*, *β*. A

b. The Denominative Nouns. B

(*α*) *The Nomina Unitatis or Nouns that denote the Individual.*

246. The أَسْمَآءُ ٱلْوَحْدَةِ, or nouns of individuality, designate one individual out of a genus, or one part of a whole that consists of several similar parts. They are formed, like the analogous nomina vicis (§ 219), by adding the termination ـَةٌ to the nouns that express the genus or whole. E. g. حَمَامَةٌ *a pigeon* (*male* or *female*), from حَمَامٌ *pigeons*, with the article, اَلْحَمَامُ, *the genus pigeon* or *the whole number of pigeons spoken of;* بَطَّةٌ *a duck* or *drake*, from بَطٌّ *the duck;* بَقَرَةٌ *one head of cattle* (*bull* or *cow*), from بَقَرٌ *cattle;* ثَمَرَةٌ *a fruit*, from ثَمَرٌ *fruit;* تَمْرَةٌ *a date*, from تَمْرٌ *dates;* بَصَلَةٌ *an onion*, from بَصَلٌ *the onion;* ذَهَبَةٌ *a bit of gold, a nugget*, from ذَهَبٌ *gold;* تِبْنَةٌ *a straw*, from تِبْنٌ *straw**. C

Rem. *a*. The use of the nom. unit. is almost entirely restricted, as the above examples show, to created things or natural objects. D

---

* [A peculiar application of the اِسْمُ ٱلْوَحْدَةِ is its use for *a dish* or *portion of any food*, as أُرْزَّةٌ *a dish of rice*, سَمَكَةٌ *a dish of fish* (èl-Mubarrad 173, l. 4), لَحْمَةٌ *a portion of meat*, جُبْنَةٌ *a portion of cheese*, etc. Comp. Gloss. Fragm. Add. 129. This ة is called اَلتَّآءُ لِلتَّخْصِيصِ (Zamaḫšarī, *Fāiḳ*, i. 331, 417, ii. 323. D. G.]

A Examples of artificial or manufactured objects are very rare; e.g. لَبِنَةٌ or لِبْنَةٌ *a brick*, from لَبِنٌ or لِبْنٌ *bricks;* سَفِينَةٌ *a ship* or *boat*, from سَفِينٌ *shipping, boats.*

REM. *b.* Similar forms in Heb. are: נֵץ, נִצָּה; שֵׂעָר, שַׂעֲרָה; שׁוֹשָׁן, שׁוֹשַׁנָּה; אֳנִי, אֳנִיָּה; שִׁיר, שִׁירָה.

(β) The Nomina Abundantiæ vel Multitudinis.

B **247.** The أَسْمَاءُ ٱلْكَثْرَةِ, or nouns of abundance, designate the place where the object signified by the noun from which they are formed, is found in large numbers or quantities. They have the form مَفْعَلَةٌ, and are, consequently, a mere variety of the nouns of place (§ 221). E.g. مَأْسَدَةٌ, مَذْأَبَةٌ, مَسْبَعَةٌ *a place abounding in lions* (أَسَدٌ), *wolves* (ذِئْبٌ), *beasts of prey* (سَبُعٌ); مَحْيَاةٌ or مَحْوَاةٌ, مَفْعَاةٌ, *a place abounding in snakes* (حَيَّةٌ), *vipers* (أَفْعَى); مَبْطَخَةٌ, مَقْثَأَةٌ, *a bed of melons* (بِطِّيخٌ), *cucumbers* (قِثَّآءٌ); مَرْمَنَةٌ, *a place where pomegranates*
C (رُمَّانٌ) *grow abundantly.*

REM. *a.* From quadriliterals this formation is rare; as مَثْعَلَةٌ, مَعْقَرَةٌ, *a place abounding in foxes* (ثَعْلَبٌ, שׁוּעָל), *scorpions* (عَقْرَبٌ).

REM. *b.* Sometimes the fem. participle of the fourth form is used in this sense, with or without أَرْضٌ; as مُضِبَّةٌ, مُجْعِلَةٌ, *(a place) abounding in lizards* (ضَبٌّ), *black beetles* (جُعَلٌ),. مُقْثِئَةٌ *(a spot)*
D *producing cucumbers.* Similarly from quadriliterals, مُثَعْلِبَةٌ, مُعَقْرِبَةٌ, مُحَرْبِئَةٌ, مُوَرْنِبَةٌ *(a place) abounding in foxes, scorpions, chamæleons* (حِرْبَآءٌ), *hares.* Also from XII. مُغْلَوْلِبَةٌ *(a spot) producing many trees.*

REM. *c.* The use of nouns of the form مَفْعَلَةٌ to indicate the *cause* of a certain state or feeling, is only a tropical application of their ordinary meaning; as اَلْوَلَدُ مَجْبَنَةٌ مَبْخَلَةٌ *children are a cause*

of cowardice and niggardliness (in their parents); مَحْسَنَةٌ, مَطْيَبَةٌ, A
مَخْبَثَةٌ, *a cause of good health, joy* or *happiness, evil* or *ill-feeling;* مَجْلَبَةٌ لِلسَّقَامِ *a cause of bringing on* or *producing disease;* اَلْفُكَاهَةُ مَقْوَدَةٌ إِلَى ٱلْأَذَى *joking leads to annoyance;* and the like.

(γ) *The Nomina Vasis or Nouns denoting the Vessel which contains anything.*

248. The nomina vasis, أَسْمَاءُ ٱلْوِعَاءِ, have the same form as the
nomina instrumenti (§ 228); e.g. مِئْبَرٌ *a needle-case,* from إِبْرَةٌ *a needle;* B
مِحْلَبٌ *a milk-pail,* from حَلَبٌ or حَلِيبٌ *milk;* مِلْبَنٌ *a milk-pail,* from لَبَنٌ *milk,* or *a brick-mould,* from لَبِنَةٌ *a brick;* مِبْوَلَةٌ *a urinal,* from بَوْلٌ *urine;* مِبْزَقَةٌ *a spittoon,* from بُزَاقٌ *saliva.*

Rem. A very few take the form مُفْعُلٌ or مُفْعُلَةٌ (see § 228, rem.); as مُدْهُنٌ or مُدْهُنَةٌ *an oil-jar,* from دُهْنٌ *oil;* مُحْرُضَةٌ = مِحْرَضَةٌ *a vessel for keeping* حُرْضٌ, i.e. the plants from which alkali
or potash is obtained; مُكْحُلَةٌ *a phial for keeping kohl* or *eye-salve* C
(كُحْلٌ), to be carefully distinguished from مِكْحَلٌ, *the mīl* (مِيلٌ) or *instrument with which it is applied to the eye.*

(δ) *The Nomina Relativa or Relative Adjectives.*

249. The relative adjectives, اَلْأَسْمَاءُ ٱلْمَنْسُوبَةُ, or simply اَلنِّسَبَاتُ
(*relationes*), are formed by adding the termination ـِيٌّ to the words D
from which they are derived, and denote that a person or thing belongs to or is connected therewith (in respect of origin, family, birth, sect, trade, etc.). E.g. أَرْضِيٌّ *earthly,* from أَرْضٌ *the earth;* شَمْسِيٌّ *solar,* from شَمْسٌ *the sun;* جَوِّيٌّ *aërial,* from جَوٌّ *the air, the sky;* حَسَنِيٌّ *descended from el-Ḥasan* (اَلْحَسَنُ); تَمِيمِيٌّ *belonging to the tribe of Tèmīm* (تَمِيمٌ); دِمَشْقِيٌّ *born* or *living at Damascus* (دِمَشْقُ);

A مِصْرِيٌّ *Egyptian*, from مِصْرُ *Egypt*; سَعْدِيٌّ *a freedman of Sa'd* (سَعْدٌ); عِلْمِيٌّ *scientific*, from عِلْمٌ *knowledge, science*; حِسِّيٌّ *relating to sense* (حِسٌّ), *perceptible by one of the senses*; عَقْلِيٌّ *intellectual*, from عَقْلٌ *the intellect*; شَرْعِيٌّ *legal, legitimate*, from شَرْعٌ *the law*; عُرْفِيٌّ *according to common use and wont* (عُرْفٌ); قِيَاسِيٌّ *according to analogy* (قِيَاسٌ); مَجُوسِيٌّ *belonging to, or one of, the Maǵūs or fire-worshippers*
B (اَلْمَجُوسُ); مَالِكِيٌّ *belonging to, or one of, the sect of Mālik* (مَالِكٌ); طَوِيلِيٌّ from طَوِيلٌ *long*; خَيْرِيٌّ from خَيْرٌ *good*; إِنِّيٌّ from إِنَّ *truly, verily*.

REM. *a*. The nomina relativa are chiefly formed from substantives and adjectives, but in more modern Arabic, and especially in the language of the schools, also from the other kinds of nouns, and even from particles (see § 191).

REM. *b*. The nomina relativa derived from adjectives properly express "belonging to the class designated by such and such an
C adjective." [However, in such words as أَحْمَرِيٌّ, خَارِجِيٌّ, أَتَاوِيٌّ, دَوَّارِيٌّ the termination ـِيٌّ has, according to some, a corroborative or intensifying force (لِلْمُبَالَغَةِ). D. G.]

REM. *c*. This termination is common in Heb. (m. ִי, f. ִיָּה and ִית), as יִשְׂרְאֵלִי *Israelite*, עִבְרִי *Hebrew*, נָכְרִי *strange*. In Æthiopic, ī is generally used to form certain adjectives which are derived from other adjectives, as ሐራሲ: (ḥarrāsī) *a ploughman*,
D መሐሪ: (maḥḥārī) *compassionate*, from the obsolete ሐራስ: (= حَرَّاثٌ, חָרָשׁ) and መሐር:; whilst *āwī* and *āy* are the usual relative terminations, as ምድራዊ: (mĕdrāwī) *terrestrial*, ክርስቲያናዊ: (krĕstīyānāwī) *Christian*, አያዊ: ('aiyāwī) or አያይ: ('aiyāy) *like* (from አይ: 'ay, *of what kind? which?*). The Aram. has the last of these forms, viz. ָי, ـܳܝ, in general use; as מִצְרִי *Egyptian*, ܡܰܕܢܚܳܝ *eastern*.

250. In forming the nomina relativa, the primitive nouns undergo various changes in regard to the auxiliary consonants, to the final radicals و and ى, and to the vocalisation. A

I. *Changes of the Auxiliary Consonants.*

251. The feminine terminations ـَةُ, ـِيَةُ, and ـِيَّةُ are rejected; as مَكَّةُ *Mèkka,* مَكِّىٌّ; اَلْبَصْرَةُ *ʾl-Baṣra,* بَصْرِىٌّ; اَلْكُوفَةُ *ʾl-Kūfa,* كُوفِىٌّ; مَلَطْيَةُ *Malaṭya,* مَلَطِىٌّ; صِقِلِّيَةُ *Sicily,* صِقِلِّىٌّ; إِفْرِيقِيَةُ *Africa,* إِفْرِيقِىٌّ; B اَلسُّنَّةُ *the corpus of traditions relating to the ways and habits of Muḥammad,* سُنِّىٌّ; [اَلشِّيعَةُ *the party of ʿAlī,* شِيعِىٌّ*;] اَلْقِبْلَةُ *the ḳibla* or *direction of Mèkka,* to which the Muslim turns in praying, قِبْلِىٌّ; كَوَّةٌ *a window,* كَوِّىٌّ; خَاصِّىٌّ *refined,* عَامِّىٌّ *vulgar,* from اَلْخَاصَّةُ *distinguished persons, the higher classes,* and اَلْعَامَّةُ *the common people, the vulgar;* عِدَةٌ *a promise,* عِدِىٌّ; زِنَةٌ *weight, measure,* زِنِىٌّ. C

Rem. In the case of nouns which, like عِدَةٌ, have lost their first radical, if the third radical be a weak letter, the first ought to be restored and the second to take fètḥa; as شِيَةٌ (from وَشَى), [وِشَوِىٌّ or] وَشَوِىٌّ (on the second و see §§ 258 and foll.). The forms وِشْيِىٌّ [or وِشَيِىٌّ] are mentioned by the grammarians, and also the very irregular عِدَوِىٌّ from عِدَةٌ, [and شِيَوِىٌّ from شِيَةٌ (Ḥammād in ʾAnbārī's *Nozhat ʾl-ʾalibbā* 52. D. G.]. D

252. 1, (*a*) The feminine termination ـَى is rejected in nouns that have *four* or more letters, besides the ى; as حُبَارَى *a bustard,* حُبَارِىٌّ; جُمَادَى *Gumādā,* the name of two months, جُمَادِىٌّ. (*b*) But if the nouns ending in ـَى fem. have only *three* letters besides the

---

* [Lane has شِيَعِىٌّ; of this form, however, only a single instance has been mentioned in the T. A. D. G.]

A ى, two cases are to be distinguished. (*a*) If the second letter has a vowel, the ى is rejected; as جَمَزَى *a swift ass,* جَمَزِيٌّ ; بَرَدَى *Baradā,* the name of a river, بَرَدِيٌّ. (*β*) If the second letter is without a vowel, the ى may either be rejected (which is preferable), or changed into و ; as حُبْلَى *pregnant,* حُبْلِيٌّ or حُبْلَوِيٌّ ; قُرْبَى *relationship,* قُرْبِيٌّ or قُرْبَوِيٌّ ; اَلدُّنْيَا *the* (*present*) *world,* دُنْيِيٌّ or دُنْيَوِيٌّ.— 2, (*a*) The letter ى is likewise rejected in nouns that contain *four*
B or more letters besides the ى, if it belongs neither to the root nor to the feminine termination, but is what the Arab grammarians call أَلِفُ ٱلْإِلْحَاقِ or *the appended èlif* (i.e. which serves to give to the word to which it is appended the form of a quadriliteral or quinqueliteral word, e.g. ذِفْرَى to give it the form of دِرْهَمٌ, قُوبَآءُ to assimilate it to قُرْطَاسٌ); as حَبَرْكَى *a bug* or *tick,* حَبَرْكِيٌّ ; قَبَعْثَرَى *a big, stout camel* قَبَعْثَرِيٌّ ; بَاقِلَّى or بَاقِلَى, *the bean,* بَاقِلِّيٌّ or بَاقِلِيٌّ. (*b*) But if such
C nouns have only *three* letters besides the ى, it may either be changed into و (which is preferable), or rejected altogether; as عَلْقًى *a sort of heath,* عَلْقَوِيٌّ or عَلْقِيٌّ ; أَرْطًى *a sort of shrub* or *small tree,* أَرْطَوِيٌّ.

REM. In 1, *b*, *β*, and 2 *b*, a third form is admissible, viz. ـَاوِيٌّ as حُبْلَاوِيٌّ, قُرْبَاوِيٌّ, دُنْيَاوِيٌّ, عَلْقَاوِيٌّ, أَرْطَاوِيٌّ ; but دُنْيَائِيٌّ, with hèmza, is a vulgarism.

D **253.** The terminations ـِيٌّ and ـِيَّةٌ of relative adjectives fall away when new relative adjectives are to be formed from them; as مَكِّيٌّ, جُعْفِيٌّ *belonging to Mèkkī, Ǵuʿfī* (مَكِّيٌّ, جُعْفِيٌّ, names of men); شَافِعِيٌّ *a Šāfiʿite, one of the sect of ès-Šāfiʿī* (اَلشَّافِعِيُّ); مَرِيٌّ *belonging to Almeria* (اَلْمَرِيَّةُ) in Spain; إِسْكَنْدَرِيٌّ *a native of Alexandria* (اَلْإِسْكَنْدَرِيَّةُ). Similarly, from substantives like كُرْسِيٌّ *a chair, a seat,* and بَرْدِيٌّ *a bullrush,* the relative adjectives are كُرْسِيٌّ and بَرْدِيٌّ.

254. The plural terminations ـُونَ and ـَاتٌ, and the dual termi-

nation ـَانِ, are rejected; as اِثْنَانِ *two*, اِثْنِىٌّ *relating to two, dualistic*; A
اَلْحَرَمَانِ *the two ḥarams* (or sacred territories of Mèkka and êl-Medīna), حَرَمِىٌّ; قَيْسَانِ *two men named Ḳais*, قَيْسِىٌّ; اَلْمُسْلِمُونَ *the Muslims*, مُسْلِمِىٌّ; زَيْدُونَ *men of the name of Zèid*, زَيْدِىٌّ; هِنْدَاتٌ *women of the name of Hind*, هِنْدِىٌّ; عَرَفَاتٌ *ʻArafāt*, the name of a place, عَرَفِىٌّ.

Rem. *a.* It need hardly be remarked that this rule does not apply to proper names ending in ـَانُ and ـُونُ, as عِمْرَانُ *ʻImrān*, عِمْرَانِىٌّ; خَلِيلَانُ *Halīlān*, خَلِيلَانِىٌّ; زَيْدُونُ *Zèidūn*, زَيْدُونِىٌّ. B

Rem. *b.* It is only in later times that such forms are possible as عِشْرِينِىٌّ, from عِشْرُونَ *twenty*, instead of عِشْرِىٌّ; مِئِينِىٌّ, from مِئُونَ, plur. of مِئَةٌ *a hundred*, for مِئَوِىٌّ; اِثْنَيْنِىٌّ *dualistic*, from اِثْنَانِ *two*, instead of ثَنَوِىٌّ or اِثْنِىٌّ.

Rem. *c.* Foreign names of towns, ending in ـِينُ, sometimes change this termination in Arabic into ـُونَ, at other times retain C
it. In the former case the termination is rejected, in the latter it is preserved; as قِنَّسْرُونَ *Kinnèsrīn*, قِنَّسْرِىٌّ, but قِنَّسْرِينُ, قِنَّسْرِينِىٌّ; نَصِيبُونَ *Nisībis*, نَصِيبِىٌّ, but نَصِيبِينُ, نَصِيبِينِىٌّ; يَبْرُونَ *Yèbrīn*, يَبْرِىٌّ, but يَبْرِينُ, يَبْرِينِىٌّ.

Rem. *d.* Some proper names, chiefly foreign, are very irregular in their formations; e.g. اَلْبَحْرَيْنِ, بَحْرَانِىٌّ; دَارَيَّا, دَارَانِىٌّ; اَلْحِيرَةُ, D
حَارِىٌّ; بَغْشُورُ, بَغَوِىٌّ; اَلرَّىُّ, رَازِىٌّ; إِصْطَخْرُ, إِصْطَخْرَزِىٌّ; سِجِسْتَانُ, سِجْزِىٌّ; اَلْقَيْرَوَانُ, قَرَوِىٌّ; مَرْوُ (ٱلشَّاهِجَانِ), مَرْوَزِىٌّ; لُرِسْتَانُ, لُرِّىٌّ; طَبَرِسْتَانُ, طَبَرِىٌّ; طَبَرِيَّةُ *Tiberias*, طَبَرَانِىٌّ; أَذْرَبِيجَانُ, أَذْرِىٌّ or أَذْرَبِىٌّ. We may, however, use حِيرِىٌّ, إِصْطَخْرِىٌّ, مَرْوِىٌّ, قَيْرَوَانِىٌّ, سِجِسْتَانِىٌّ.—حَرَّانُ makes either حَرَّانِىٌّ or حَرْنَانِىٌّ;

A دَارَابَجِرْدُ or دَرَابَجِرْدُ has دَرَاوَرْدِىٌّ, as well as the regular formation; [مَانِى *Manes* makes مَنَانِىٌّ, مَنَوِىٌّ and مَانِىٌّ. D. G.]

REM. *e.* Quite peculiar are: تَهَامٍ (with the art. اَلتَّهَامِى), fem. تَهَامِيَةٌ, from تِهَامَةُ, *Tihāma;* شَآمٍ (with the art. اَلشَّآمِى), fem. شَآمِيَةٌ, from اَلشَّأْمُ *Syria;* and يَمَانٍ (with the art. اَلْيَمَانِى), fem. يَمَانِيَةٌ, from اَلْيَمَنُ *ĕl-Yèmèn;* instead of تِهَامِىٌّ, شَأْمِىٌّ, and يَمَنِىٌّ, which
B are also used. The forms تَهَامِىٌّ, شَآمِىٌّ, and يَمَانِىٌّ likewise occur. Comp. the words ثَمَانٍ, رَبَاعٍ and شَنَاحٍ (شَنَاحِىٌّ).

255. The letter ى in words of the forms فَعِيلَةٌ and فُعَيْلَةٌ, when not derived from verba mediæ rad. geminatæ or infirmæ (و or ى), is rejected, the kèsra of فَعِيلَةٌ being at the same time changed into fèthạ*;
C as فَرِيضَةٌ *a statute,* فَرَضِىٌّ; جَزِيرَةٌ *an island,* or اَلْجَزِيرَةُ *Mesopotamia,* جَزَرِىٌّ; اَلْمَدِينَةُ *ĕl-Medīna,* مَدَنِىٌّ; سَفِينَةٌ *a ship,* سَفَنِىٌّ; ضُبَيْعَةُ, جُهَيْنَةُ (tribes), ضُبَعِىٌّ, جُهَنِىٌّ. But, if they come from verba mediæ rad. geminatæ or mediæ و vel ى, they remain unchanged; as حَقِيقَةٌ *reality,* حَقِيقِىٌّ; حَدِيدَةٌ *a piece of iron, an iron tool,* حَدِيدِىٌّ; قُلَيْلَةٌ *a small jug,* قُلَيْلِىٌّ.—In the forms فَعِيلٌ and فُعَيْلٌ, the ى is rejected only when
D the third consonant of the radical is و or ى; as غَنِىٌّ, عَدِىٌّ (tribes), غَنَوِىٌّ, عَدَوِىٌّ; قُصَىٌّ, عَلِىٌّ (men), قُصَوِىٌّ, عَلَوِىٌّ. Otherwise it remains unchanged, as تَمِيمٌ (a tribe), تَمِيمِىٌّ; عَقِيلٌ (a man), عَقِيلِىٌّ; زَبِيدُ (a town), زَبِيدِىٌّ; نُمَيْرٌ, عُقَيْلٌ (tribes), نُمَيْرِىٌّ, عُقَيْلِىٌّ.

---

* [According to Zamahšarī, *Fāïk* i. 160 the same thing happens to the و of the form فَعُولَةٌ, as in شَنَائِىٌّ (شَنَئِىٌّ) from شَنُوءَةُ, غَضَبِىٌّ from غَضُوبَةُ. Comp. also *Mufaṣṣal* 90, l. 7 and Sībawèih ii. 66, § 319. D. G.]

Rem. *a.* There are, however, exceptions to these rules. E.g. A
طَبِيعَةٌ *nature,* طَبِيعِىٌّ ; مَدِينَةٌ *a city,* مَدِينِىٌّ (to distinguish it from مَدَنِىٌّ *belonging to ĕl-Medīna*), جَزِيرِىٌّ *belonging to Algeziras* in Spain (to distinguish it from جَزَرِىٌّ *Mesopotamian*); عَمِيرِىٌّ, سَلِيمِىٌّ, from عَمِيرَةُ, سَلِيمَةُ (tribes); خُرَيْبِىٌّ from خُرَيْبَةُ (a place); قُرَيْشٌ, ثَقِيفٌ ; عَتِيكٌ ; فُقَيْمٌ, سُلَيْمٌ, هُذَيْلٌ (tribes), قُرَشِىٌّ, هُذَلِىٌّ, سُلَمِىٌّ, فُقَمِىٌّ ; عَتَكِىٌّ, ثَقَفِىٌّ ; خَرِيفٌ *autumn,* خَرَفِىٌّ.—نَبِىءٌ, *a prophet,* B
makes نَبَوِىٌّ, from the assimilated form نَبِىٌّ.

Rem. *b.* Words of the form فَيِّلٌ (for فَيْعِلٌ, § 242) from radicals mediæ و et ى, reject the second ى along with its vowel kèsra, or in other words follow the shorter form فَيْلٌ ; as سَيِّدٌ *a lord* or *master,* سَيْدِىٌّ ; طَيِّبٌ *good,* طَيْبِىٌّ. But طَيِّءٌ (a tribe) has طَائِىٌّ.—The same remark applies to every penultimate double ى with kèsra (يِّ) ; as أُسَيِّدٌ, dimin. of أَسْوَدُ, *black,* أُسَيْدِىٌّ ; حُمَيِّرٌ, dimin. of حِمَارٌ, C
an ass, حُمَيْرِىٌّ. [But أُسَيِّدٌ as a tribal name has أُسَيْدِىٌّ.]

256. The ى productionis of the nomen patientis in verba tertiæ ى may be rejected, and the radical ى changed into و, whilst the kèsra of the second radical becomes fètḥa; as مَرْمِىٌّ *thrown,* مَرْمَوِىٌّ. But many grammarians prefer to reject both the ى productionis and the radical ى, so that the relative adjective coincides in form with the nomen patientis, مَرْمِىٌّ. D

257. Lastly, the و productionis in the form فَعُولَةٌ, derived from verba tertiæ و (§ 244), is rejected, and the second radical takes fètḥa instead of ḍamma; as عَدُوَّةٌ, *a female enemy,* عَدَوِىٌّ. Many, however, form عَدُوِّىٌّ from both عَدُوٌّ and عَدُوَّةٌ.

A ## II. *Changes of the Final Radicals* و *and* ى.

258. The *ĕlif maḳṣūra* (ا or ى, § 7, rem. *b*), as the third radical of a *triliteral* noun, is changed into و before adding the termination ـِىٌّ; as فَتًى *a youth*, فَتَوِىٌّ; رَحًى *a mill*, رَحَوِىٌّ; عَصًا *a staff*, عَصَوِىٌّ; قَذًى *a mote*, قَذَوِىٌّ. But if the noun has *four* letters, the final ى (ا does not occur in such words in good Arabic) may either be changed
B into و, which is the better form, or be rejected; as أَعْشَى *purblind*, أَعْشَوِىٌّ; مَلْهًى *play*, or مِلْهًى *a musical instrument*, مَلْهَوِىٌّ or مِلْهِىٌّ; مَعْنًى *meaning*, مَعْنَوِىٌّ or مَعْنِىٌّ. If the noun contains *five* or more letters, the ى is always rejected; as مُصْطَفًى *chosen*, مُصْطَفِىٌّ.—The same rules apply to the final ى of radicals tertiæ و et ى, which falls away in some nouns after kèsra (see § 167, *b*, *β*); but it must be borne in mind that the missing ى is to be counted as one of the letters
C of the word, and also, if it be changed into و, that the kèsra always becomes fètḥa. E.g. عَمٍ (for عَمِىٌ) *blind*, عَمَوِىٌّ; شَجٍ (for شَجِىٌ) *sorrowful*, شَجَوِىٌّ; قَاضٍ (for قَاضِىٌ) *a judge*, قَاضِىٌّ (which is the preferable form) or قَاضَوِىٌّ; مُعْتَدٍ (for مُعْتَدِىٌ), مُشْتَرٍ (for مُشْتَرِىٌ), مُسْتَعْلٍ (for مُسْتَعْلِىٌ), مُعْتَدِىٌّ, مُشْتَرِىٌّ, مُسْتَعْلِىٌّ.

REM. *a*. The addition of the feminine termination ـَةٌ does not
D affect the rule of formation; as دَوَاةٌ *an inkhorn* or *writing-case*, دَوَوِىٌّ *one who carries an inkhorn*; حَمَاةُ *Ḥamā* (חֲמָת), حَمَوِىٌّ; اَلشَّرَاةُ, a district in Palestine, شَرَوِىٌّ; مِرْقَاةٌ *a ladder*, مِرْقَوِىٌّ; حَانَاةٌ or حَانِيَةٌ *a wine-shop*, حَانَوِىٌّ or حَانِىٌّ *a vintner*.

REM. *b*. Such forms as دَوَاتِىٌّ for دَوَوِىٌّ, مَعْنَاوِىٌّ for مَعْنَوِىٌّ, and مُصْطَفَوِىٌّ for مُصْطَفِىٌّ, are modern and corrupt.

259. The hèmza of the termination ـَآءُ (the *èlif mèmdūda,* § 23, rem. *a*), is always changed into و; as عَذْرَآءُ *a virgin,* عَذْرَاوِيٌّ; اَلْبَيْضَآءُ (a town in Persia), بَيْضَاوِيٌّ; خُنْفَسَآءُ *the black beetle,* خُنْفَسَاوِيٌّ; زَكَرِيَّآءُ *Zachariah,* زَكَرِيَّاوِيٌّ. But in the termination ـَآءٌ, whether the hèmza be sprung from an original radical و or ى, or be not a radical but merely the so-called هَمْزَةُ ٱلْإِلْحَاقِ (see § 252, 2, *a*), it may either be retained unaltered (which is better) or be changed into و; as تَآءٌ the letter *tā,* رِدَآءٌ *a garment,* كِسَآءٌ *a robe,* سَمَآءٌ *the heaven,* تَآئِيٌّ, رِدَآئِيٌّ, كِسَآئِيٌّ, سَمَآئِيٌّ, or تَاوِيٌّ, رِدَاوِيٌّ, كِسَاوِيٌّ, سَمَاوِيٌّ; عِلْبَآءٌ *a large sinew in the neck,* حِرْبَآءٌ *a male chameleon,* بَاقِلَآءٌ *the bean,* بَاقِلَآئِيٌّ, حِرْبَآئِيٌّ, عِلْبَآئِيٌّ, or بَاقِلَاوِيٌّ, حِرْبَاوِيٌّ, عِلْبَاوِيٌّ. On the contrary, if the hèmza be an original أ, it always remains unaltered; as قُرَّآءٌ (rad. قَرَأَ), قُرَّآئِيٌّ.

Rem. The termination ـَآءُ is very rarely dropped in proper names; as جَلُولَآءُ, حَرُورَآءُ (places), جَلُولِيٌّ, حَرُورِيٌّ.—In a few cases too the letter ن is substituted for the hèmza; as رَوْحَآءُ (a place), رَوْحَانِيٌّ; بَهْرَآءُ (a tribe), بَهْرَانِيٌّ; صَنْعَآءُ (a city in èl-Yèmèn), صَنْعَانِيٌّ; with which compare the Hebrew forms שִׁילֹנִי, גִּילֹנִי, from שִׁילֹה, גִּילֹה.

260. Primitive defective substantives, i.e. those which have lost their third weak radical,—as أَبٌ, أَخٌ, حَمٌ, لُغَةٌ, لِثَةٌ, etc.,—necessarily recover it only in cases where it reappears in the dual and plural; but if this reappearance be not necessary, the third radical may be omitted in the relative adjective. In all cases where the third radical is restored, it appears as و, whether it was originally ى or not. E.g. أَبٌ (for أَبَوٌ, dual أَبَوَانِ) *a father,* أَبَوِيٌّ; أَخٌ (for أَخَوٌ, du. أَخَوَانِ) *a brother,* أَخَوِيٌّ; حَمٌ (for حَمَوٌ) *a husband's father* or *brother,* حَمَوِيٌّ;

A لُغَةٌ (rad. لغو) *a dialect*, لُغَوِيٌّ ; لِثَةٌ (rad. لثى) *the gum*, لِثَوِيٌّ ; مِئَةٌ (rad. مأى) *a hundred*, مِئَوِيٌّ ; أَمَةٌ (rad. امو) *a female slave*, أَمَوِيٌّ ; سَنَةٌ (rad. سنو) *a year*, سَنَوِيٌّ ; اِبْنٌ (for بَنَيٌ, du. اِبْنَانِ) *a son*, اِبْنِيٌّ or بَنَوِيٌّ ; اِسْمٌ (rad. سمو) *a name*, اِسْمِيٌّ or سُمَوِيٌّ (from سُمٌ) ; اِسْتٌ (rad. سته) *podex*, اِسْتِيٌّ or سَتَهِيٌّ (from سَتَهٌ) or سَهِيٌّ (from سَهٌ) ; يَدٌ (for يَدْيٌ, du. يَدَانِ) *a hand*, يَدِيٌّ or يَدَوِيٌّ ; دَمٌ *blood*, دَمِيٌّ or دَمَوِيٌّ ; غَدٌ *to-*
B *morrow*, غَدِيٌّ or غَدَوِيٌّ.

REM. *a.* أُخْتٌ, *a sister*, and بِنْتٌ, *a daughter*, make أُخْتِيٌّ and بِنْتِيٌّ, as well as أَخَوِيٌّ and بَنَوِيٌّ.—شَفَةٌ, *a lip*, has the three forms شَفَوِيٌّ, شَفَهِيٌّ, or شَفِيٌّ ; حِرٌ, *vulva*, makes حِرِيٌّ or حِرَحِيٌّ (from حِرْحٌ).—شَاةٌ (شَآءٌ) has شَاوِيٌّ, شَاهِيٌّ and شَاءِيٌّ.

REM. *b.* Where the original form was فَعْلٌ, some retain the
C gèzm; as يَدْيِيٌّ, دَمْوِيٌّ, غَدْوِيٌّ, سِمْوِيٌّ, حِرْحِيٌّ.

261. The third radical و or ى of the forms فُعْلٌ and فُعْلَةٌ is retained unchanged; as نَحْوٌ *grammar*, نَحْوِيٌّ *a grammarian*; ظَبْيٌ *a gazelle*, ظَبْيِيٌّ ; غَزْوَةٌ *a foray*, غَزْوِيٌّ ; رِشْوَةٌ *a bribe*, رِشْوِيٌّ ; عُرْوَةٌ *a handle*, عُرْوِيٌّ ; قَرْيَةٌ *a village*, قَرْيِيٌّ ; دُمْيَةٌ *an image*, دُمْيِيٌّ. But
D if the final ى of فُعْلَةٌ be changed into و, the second radical takes fètḥa, as قَرَوِيٌّ, دُمَوِيٌّ, قِنَوِيٌّ, from قَرْيَةٌ, دُمْيَةٌ, and قِنْيَةٌ *a possession*; a rule which is extended by some to words in which the third radical was originally و, as غَزَوِيٌّ, رِشَوِيٌّ, عُرَوِيٌّ, from غَزْوَةٌ, etc.—If the second radical in such nouns be a و or ى, combining with the third radical into ىّ, this ىّ is resolved into its original consonants, the second radical takes fètḥa, and final ى is converted into و ; as طَيٌّ (for طَوْيٌ) *a fold*, طَوَوِيٌّ ; حَيٌّ (for حَيْيٌ) *living*, حَيَوِيٌّ ; لَيَّةٌ *a*

twist or *turn*, لَوَوِىٌّ ; حَيَّةٌ *a snake*, حَيَوِىٌّ.—In words of the form فُعَالَةٌ, final و is retained, as شَقَاوَةٌ *misery*, شَقَاوِىٌّ ; but final ى is changed into hèmza, as سِقَايَةٌ *a drinking-vessel*, سِقَآئِىٌّ, عَظَايَةٌ *a sort of lizard*, عَظَآئِىٌّ.—Words of the form آيَةٌ *a sign*, ثَايَةٌ *a place where cattle, etc., rest at night*, رَايَةٌ *a banner*, make آيِىٌّ, آئِىٌّ, or آوِىٌّ, etc. A

Rem. *a.* بَدْوٌ, *a desert*, makes irregularly بَدَوِىٌّ (instead of بَدْوِىٌّ) *an inhabitant of the desert, a Bèdawī.* B

Rem. *b.* Nouns of the forms فَعِيلٌ, فَعِيلَةٌ, فُعَيْلٌ, فُعَيْلَةٌ, etc. from verba tertiæ rad. و et ى, reject the ى productionis and change a radical ى into و ; as غَنِىٌّ. غَنَوِىٌّ ; ضَرِيَّةٌ (a town), ضَرَوِىٌّ ; قُصَىٌّ, قُصَوِىٌّ ; أُمَيَّةُ (a man's name), أُمَوِىٌّ (rarely أُمَيِّىٌّ, and, though very incorrectly, أَمَوِىٌّ). See §§ 255–6. C

III. *Changes in the Vocalisation.*

262. In the forms فَعِلٌ and فَعِلَةٌ, the kèsra of the middle radical is changed into fètḥa; as مَلِكٌ *a king*, مَلَكِىٌّ ; كَبِدٌ *the liver*, كَبَدِىٌّ ; اَلنَّمِرُ, اَلصَّدِفُ (tribes), نَمَرِىٌّ, صَدَفِىٌّ ; شَقِرَةُ (a tribe), شَقَرِىٌّ. So also in فُعِلٌ, as اَلدُّئِلُ (a tribe), دُؤَلِىٌّ. But in فِعِلٌ, the kèsra may be retained, as إِبِلٌ *camels*, إِبَلِىٌّ or إِبِلِىٌّ. D

Rem. In nouns that consist of more than three consonants, the vowel of the penultimate letter is not altered. From تَغْلِبُ (a tribe) and يَثْرِبُ (the ancient name of ěl-Medīna) the forms تَغْلَبِىٌّ and يَثْرَبِىٌّ are admissible, though تَغْلِبِىٌّ and يَثْرِبِىٌّ are preferred; أَذْرِعَاتٌ makes أَذْرَعِىٌّ ; مَنْبِجُ, مَنْبَجَانِىٌّ and أَنْبَجَانِىٌّ, as well as مَنْبَجِىٌّ.

A **263.** Kèsra or ḍamma of the penultimate consonant is changed into fètḥa in all forms in which a و or ى has been rejected, or in which a final ى has been changed into و; as غَنِىٌّ ,جَزَرِىٌّ ,اَلْجَزِيرَةُ; غَنَوِىٌّ (see the preceding §§).

REM. Of rare and arbitrary changes, such as بُصْرِىٌّ from اَلْبَصْرَةُ, حِرْمِىٌّ from اَلْحَرَمُ *the sacred territory of Mèkka,* دُهْرِىٌّ from
B دَهْرٌ *time,* إِمْسِىٌّ from أَمْسِ *yesterday,* a grammar can take no account.

264. If a relative adjective is to be formed from a proper name which is compounded of *two words,* the following points must be attended to.—A. If the two words form a proposition (مُرَكَّبٌ إِسْنَادِىٌّ or تَرْكِيبٌ إِسْنَادِىٌّ), as تَأَبَّطَ شَرًّا (*he carried mischief under his arm,* the nickname of a celebrated poet and warrior), بَرَقَ نَحْرُهُ (*his throat*
C *shone*)*—or are contracted into one compound word (مُرَكَّبٌ مَزْجِىٌّ, *mixed compound*) as مَعْدِيكَرِبُ, a man's name, بَعْلَبَكُّ, قَالِيقَلَا, the towns of *Ba'albèk* and *Ḳālīḳalā,*—then the second word is omitted, and the termination ـِىٌّ appended to the first; as تَأَبَّطِىٌّ, بَرَقِىٌّ, مَعْدِىٌّ, بَعْلِىٌّ, قَالِىٌّ.—B. If the first word is in the status constructus, governing the second in the genitive, two cases arise. (1) If the governing word be
D one of the nouns أَبٌ *father,* اِبْنٌ *son,* أُمٌّ *mother,* or بِنْتٌ *daughter,* it is rejected, and ـِىٌّ appended to the governed word; as أَبُو بَكْرٍ, بَكْرِىٌّ; اِبْنُ ٱلزُّبَيْرِ; أَزْرَقِىٌّ, اِبْنُ ٱلْأَزْرَقِ; بَيْهَسِىٌّ, أَبُو بَيْهَسٍ; حَنَفِىٌّ, أَبُو حَنِيفَةَ, زُبَيْرِىٌّ. (2) If the first word be any other than these four, two secondary cases arise. (*a*) If the idea of definiteness through the status constructus still exists in the consciousness of the speaker,—as

* Compare the nickname of one of the Earls of Douglas, *Archibald Bell-the-cat.*

in غُلَامُ حُسَيْنٍ, *the slave of Ḥosèin*,—the first word is rejected, and the second takes ـِىٌّ; as حُسَيْنِىٌّ. (*b*) But if the idea of definiteness is no longer present to the mind of the speaker, then: (*α*) in cases where no uncertainty can arise as to the person intended, ـِىٌّ is attached to the first word, and the second is omitted; as فَخْرُ ٱلدِّينِ, فَخْرِىٌّ ; تَقِىُّ ٱلدِّينِ, تَقَوِىٌّ ; نِظَامُ ٱلْمُلْكِ, نِظَامِىٌّ ; عُبَيْدُ ٱللّٰهِ, عُبَيْدِىٌّ ; تَيْمُ ٱللَّاتِ, تَيْمِىٌّ ; أَنْفُ ٱلنَّاقَةِ (*Camel's-nose*, nickname of a man), أَنْفِىٌّ ; عَبْدُ ٱلْقَيْسِ, عَبْدِىٌّ ; ٱمْرُؤُ ٱلْقَيْسِ, ٱمْرَئِىٌّ or مَرْئِىٌّ ; سَعْدُ ٱلْعَشِيرَةِ, سَعْدِىٌّ ; [وَادِى ٱلْقُرَى, وَادِىٌّ]; but (β) if uncertainty might arise by so doing, the first is omitted, and the termination added to the second; as عَبْدُ ٱلْمُطَّلِبِ, مُطَّلِبِىٌّ ; عَبْدُ ٱلْأَشْهَلِ, أَشْهَلِىٌّ ; عَبْدُ مَنَافٍ, مَنَافِىٌّ ; وَادِى ٱلْحِجَارَةِ, *Guadalaxara* in Spain, حِجَارِىٌّ. أَزْدُ شَنُوءَةَ (a tribe) makes شَنَئِىٌّ or شَنَوِىٌّ (from the assimilated form شَنُوَّةَ). A B

Rem. *a*. In the case of the مُرَكَّبَاتٌ مَزْجِيَّةٌ, some allow a double formation, from both parts of the word; e.g. from رَامَهُرْمُزُ, رَامِىٌّ هُرْمُزِىٌّ. In later times it became very common to form the *nisba* from the whole compound word, as بَعْلَبَكِّىٌّ, رَامَهُرْمُزِىٌّ; and this license was extended to innumerable names which fall under the class B. For example: from بَيْتُ سَوَا, بَيْتَسَوَانِىٌّ, with the article ٱلْبَيْتَسَوَانِىٌّ; from تَلُّ عُكْبَرَا and تَلُّ مَنَّسَ, تَلَعُكْبَرِىٌّ and تَلَّمَنَّسِىٌّ; from عَيْنُ زَرْبَى, عَيْنَزَرْبِىٌّ; from دَارُ ٱلْقُطْنِ, دَارَقُطْنِىٌّ; from دَيْرُ ٱلْعَاقُولِ, دَيْرَعَاقُولِىٌّ; from نَهْرُ تِيرَى, نَهْرَتِيرِىٌّ; from مَرْوُ ٱلرُّوذِ, مَرْوَرُوذِىٌّ; from وَادِى آشَ, *Guadix* in Spain, وَادِيآشِىٌّ; from عَبْدُ ٱلْمَلِكِ, عَبْدَمَلِكِىٌّ; from تَاجُ ٱلْمُلْكِ, تَاجَمُلْكِىٌّ. To this stage of the language, too, belong such words as ذُنُّونِىٌّ from ذُو ٱلنُّونِ (a C D

A family in Spain); بُومَالِكِيٌّ from أَبُو مَالِكٍ; [بَلْعَدَوِيَّةٌ *a woman of the Bènū 'Adī* (§ 21, *c*, footn.)]; بُوجَدِيٌّ *an ignoramus* (Fr. *abécédaire*), from ابجد *'abuǵèd*, the first four letters of the alphabet (§ 32).

REM. *b*. In many cases falling under B, 2, *b*, *a* and *β*, strange forms arise by the rejection of some consonants, or the combination into one word of a few letters (generally four) selected from the two nouns. E.g. حَضْرَمِيٌّ from حَضْرَمَوْتُ *Ḥaḍramaut*; عَبْدَرِيٌّ
B from عَبْدُ ٱلدَّارِ (a family in Mèkka); عَبْقَسِيٌّ from عَبْدُ ٱلْقَيْسِ (a tribe); عَبْشَمِيٌّ from عَبْدُ شَمْسٍ (a tribe); رَسْعَنِيٌّ from رَأْسُ عَيْنٍ *Rās-'ain*; شُرُنْبُلَالِيٌّ from شُبْرَى بُلُولَةَ (a village in Egypt); اَلطَّبَرْخَزِيُّ, the name of a poet, whose mother was from طَبَرِسْتَانُ, and his father from خُوَارَزْمُ.

265. A relative adjective is never formed, in classical Arabic, from the plural, even where the sense might seem to demand it, but
C always from the singular; e.g. فَرَضِيٌّ *acquainted with the divine institutions*, from فَرِيضَةٌ, plur. فَرَائِضُ; حَصِيرِيٌّ *a seller of mats*, from حَصِيرٌ, plur. حُصُرٌ; صَحَفِيٌّ *one who makes mistakes in reading manuscript*, also *a learner* or *student*, from صَحِيفَةٌ *a written sheet, a letter, a book*, plur. صُحُفٌ or صَحَائِفُ. Such plurals, however, as are either really proper names, or approximate to them in sense, are excepted;
D e.g. أَنْمَارٌ (plur. of نَمِرٌ *a leopard*) the tribe of *'Anmār*, أَنْمَارِيٌّ; كِلَابٌ (plur. of كَلْبٌ *a dog*), the tribe of *Kilāb*, كِلَابِيٌّ; هَوَازِنُ (a tribe), هَوَازِنِيٌّ; مَعَافِرُ (a tribe), مَعَافِرِيٌّ; اَلْمَدَائِنُ (the name of a city, *Ctesiphon*, properly the plur. of مَدِينَةٌ), مَدَائِنِيٌّ; اَلْأَنْصَارُ *the Helpers* (of Muhammad, epithet of the tribes of *ĕl-'Aus*, اَلْأَوْسُ, and *ĕl-Ḫazraǵ*, اَلْخَزْرَجُ, at ĕl-Medīna), أَنْصَارِيٌّ; اَلْأَعْرَابُ *the Arabs of the desert*,

أَعْرَابِيٌّ; [اَلْأَحْلَافُ *the confederate tribes,* أَحْلَافِيٌّ, as 'Omar is called in a A
tradition; اَلْأَبْنَآءُ *the Persian colonists in el-Yèmèn,* أَبْنَاوِيٌّ. D. G.]

Rem. In more modern Arabic, on the contrary, a host of relative adjectives are formed from the plurals of nouns that indicate the object with which a person usually occupies himself in his trade, studies, etc. E.g. أَنْمَاطٌ (plur. of نَمَطٌ) *rugs,* أَنْمَاطِيٌّ *a maker* or *seller of rugs;* كُتُبٌ (plur. of كِتَابٌ) *books,* كُتُبِيٌّ *a bookseller;* حُصُرٌ (plur. of حَصِيرٌ) *mats,* حُصُرِيٌّ *a maker* or *seller of mats;* قَوَارِيرُ (plur. of قَارُورَةٌ) *glass bottles,* قَوَارِيرِيٌّ *a dealer in* B *bottles;* مَنَاخِلُ (plur. of مُنْخُلٌ) *sieves,* مَنَاخِلِيٌّ *a maker* or *seller of sieves;* سَاعَاتٌ (plur. of سَاعَةٌ) *watches,* سَاعَاتِيٌّ *a watchmaker;* مَشَاعِلِيٌّ *a bearer of the cresset called* مَشْعَلَةٌ; خَرَائِطُ (plur. of خَرِيطَةٌ) *pouches* or *bags,* خَرَائِطِيٌّ *one who makes* or *sells them;* جَرَائِحُ (pl. of جَرِيحَةٌ) *wounds,* جَرَائِحِيٌّ *a surgeon;* صِفَاتٌ (pl. of صِفَةٌ) *qualities, attributes,* صِفَاتِيٌّ *one who recognises in God attributes distinct from* C *His essential nature;* فَرَائِضِيٌّ = فَرَضِيٌّ ; صُحُفِيٌّ = صَحَفِيٌّ.—Similar forms in Syriac, of early date, are ܢܶܫ̈ܝܳܐ, *belonging to women,* from ܢܶܫ̈ܶܐ, plur. of ܐܰܢ̄ܬ݁ܬ݂ܳܐ, *a woman,* and ܡܕ݂ܺܝܢ̈ܳܝܳܐ from ܡܕ݂ܺܝܢ̈ܳܬ݂ܳܐ, plur. of ܡܕ݂ܺܝܢ݁ܬ݂ܳܐ.

266. Biliteral particles may double their second consonant or D not, at pleasure, if it be a strong letter; as كَمْ *how much?* كَمِّيٌّ or كَمِيٌّ; لَمْ *not,* لَمِّيٌّ or لَمِيٌّ. But if the second consonant be weak, the opinions of grammarians differ. In the case of و, the simple doubling is permitted, as لَوْ *if,* لَوِّيٌّ; or else a fètḥa is inserted between the two wâws, as لَوَوِيٌّ. In the case of ى, this latter form is alone admissible, the second ى being changed into و; as كَيْ *that,* كَيَوِيٌّ; فِي *in,*

A فِيَوِىٌّ. If the second letter be a quiescent ʼelif, there is inserted between it and the termination ـِىٌّ a hèmza, which may be changed into a و; as لَا *not*, لَآءِىٌّ or لَاوِىٌّ. The pronoun مَا *what?* forms مَآئِىٌّ and مَاهِىٌّ.

267. We have seen above (§§ 231, 232) that the termination ـَانُ or ـَانٌ in adjectives is one of those which imply a certain degree
B of intensity; and a few examples of rarer forms may here be given, as تَيَّهَانٌ *daring, reckless;* صِفَتَانٌ or صِفِتَّانٌ, *strong, robust;* جُلُبَّانٌ *clamorous, vociferous;* إِنْفِخَانٌ *corpulent;* أُسْحُلَانٌ or مُسْحُلَانٌ *tall* or *straight-haired;* مَلْكَعَانٌ *vile, sordid;* كُذُبْذُبَانٌ and مَكْذَبَانٌ or مَكْذَبَانَةٌ, *mendacious.* Hence we may form from many nouns a relative adjective ending in ـَانِىٌّ, as the grammarians say, لِتَأْكِيدِ ٱلنِّسْبَةِ, *to strengthen the relation;* e.g. from مَنْظَرٌ, *aspect, appearance,*
C the ordinary nisba is مَنْظَرِىٌّ, but مَنْظَرَانِىٌّ is = حَسَنُ ٱلْمَنْظَرِ *good-looking.* So: شَعْرَانِىٌّ *having much* or *long hair* (شَعْرٌ), لِحْيَانِىٌّ *having a long beard* (لِحْيَةٌ); جُمَّانِىٌّ *having a large head of hair* (جُمَّةٌ), رَقَبَانِىٌّ *bull-necked* (رَقَبَةٌ *the neck*), جُسْمَانِىٌّ *large in the body* (جِسْمٌ), إِنْفُخَانِىٌّ *corpulent,* إِسْحِلَانِىٌّ *tall* or *long-bearded,* مُسْحُلَانِىٌّ *tall* or *straight-haired,* حَوْصَلَانِىٌّ *having a large crop or craw* (حَوْصَلَةٌ), [نَفْسَانِىٌّ
D *smiting with the evil eye* (from نَفْسٌ in the sense of *eye*), صَيْدَلَانِىٌّ or صَيْدَنَانِىٌّ *a druggeller* (from original صَنْدَلَانِىٌّ *seller of sandalwood,* Fleischer, *Kl. Schr.* i. 245, n. 1). D. G.] In later times this termination was more extensively employed, both in common speech and in scientific writings (in the latter, perhaps, under the influence of the Aramaic); e.g. فَاكِهَانِىٌّ *a fruiterer,* بَاقِلَانِىٌّ *one who sells beans,* سِمْسِمَانِىٌّ *one who sells sesame,* instead of فَاكِهِىٌّ, بَاقِلِّىٌّ, بَاقِلَاَئِىٌّ or

بَاقِلَاوِيٌّ, and سِمْسِمِيٌّ ; جَوَّانِيٌّ *inner, interior, private,* بَرَّانِيٌّ *outward,* A
external, public ; فَوْقَانِيٌّ *upper,* تَحْتَانِيٌّ *lower ;* رُوحَانِيٌّ *spiritual*
(ܪܘܚܢܝܐ), نَفْسَانِيٌّ *relating to the soul,* (ܢܦܫܢܝܐ), جَسَدَانِيٌّ *corporeal,*
نُورَانِيٌّ *relating to light,* رَبَّانِيٌّ *learned and devout* (רַבָּן).

REM. A form expressing intensiveness, and applicable exclusively to the members of the body, is فُعَالِيٌّ ; as رُؤَاسِيٌّ *having a* B
large head ; أُنَافِيٌّ, أُذَانِيٌّ, عُضَادِيٌّ, *having a large* or *long nose, ears, arms ;* سُتَاهِيٌّ, أُيَارِيٌّ. Another rare form is exemplified by شُدْقُمٌ and سُتْهُمٌ = أَشْدَقُ and أَسْتَهُ.

(ε) *The Abstract Nouns of Quality,* أَسْمَآءُ ٱلْكَيْفِيَّةِ.

268. The feminine of the relative adjective serves in Arabic as a noun to denote the abstract idea of the thing, as distinguished from the concrete thing itself; and also to represent the thing or things signified by the primitive noun as a whole or totality. It corresponds therefore to German substantives in *heit, keit, schaft, thum,* and to English ones in *head, dom, ty,* etc. E.g. اَلْإِلٰهِيَّةُ [and اَلْأُلُهَانِيَّةُ D. G.] *the divine nature, Godhead* (اَلْإِلٰهُ *God*) ; إِنْسَانِيَّةٌ *humanity* (إِنْسَانٌ *a human being*) ; اَلرُّبُوبِيَّةُ *Lordship, Godhead* (اَلرَّبُّ) ; رُجُولِيَّةٌ *manhood ;* [خُصُوصِيَّةٌ or خَصُوصِيَّةٌ *particularity*] ; اِسْمِيَّةٌ, وَصْفِيَّةٌ, D
substantivity, adjectivity, from اِسْمٌ *a substantive,* and وَصْفٌ, *an adjective ;* أَمْكَنِيَّةٌ *the belonging to the fully-inflected class* (مُتَمَكِّنٌ أَمْكَنُ) *of nouns ;* مَاهِيَّةٌ *substance, quiddity* (مَا *what?*) ; مَائِيَّةٌ *wateriness* (مَآءٌ *water*) ; جَمْعِيَّةٌ *totality ;* شَاعِرِيَّةٌ *what constitutes the being a poet, the poetic mind* or *temperament ;* مَفْهُومِيَّةٌ *the capability of being understood, intelligibility ;* اَلْحَنَفِيَّةُ *what constitutes being a Ḥanefite, the school of*

A *the Ḥanîfites;* اَلنَّصْرَانِيَّةُ *Christendom, the Christian religion;* اَلْيَهُودِيَّةُ *Judaism.*

REM. In a few cases the termination ـُوتٌ borrowed from the Aramaic ܘܬ݂ـ, is similarly employed; as لَاهُوتٌ *divinity,* (ܐܰܠܳܗܽܘܬ݂ܳܐ), نَاسُوتٌ *humanity* (ܐ݈ܢܳܫܽܘܬ݂ܳܐ), مَلَكُوتٌ *kingdom* (מַלְכוּת, ܡܰܠܟܽܘܬ݂ܳܐ), جَبَرُوتٌ *pride, haughtiness, omnipotence,* etc. [These nouns are, in Arabic, of the masculine gender.]

B

(ζ) *The Diminutive.*

269. The diminutive, اَلِاسْمُ ٱلْمُصَغَّرُ or اَلتَّصْغِيرُ, and اَلِاسْمُ ٱلْمُحَقَّرُ or اَلتَّحْقِيرُ, when formed from a *triliteral* noun (اَلِاسْمُ ٱلْمُكَبَّرُ or اَلتَّكْبِيرُ), takes the form فُعَيْلٌ; as رَجُلٌ *a man,* رُجَيْلٌ; كَلْبٌ *a dog,* كُلَيْبٌ; عَمْرٌو *ʻAmr* (a man's name), عُمَيْرٌ; جَبَلٌ *a hill,* جُبَيْلٌ. When the noun is *quadriliteral,* it takes the form فُعَيْعِلٌ; as عَقْرَبٌ *a scorpion,*
C عُقَيْرِبٌ; دِرْهَمٌ *a dirham,* دُرَيْهِمٌ; مَسْجِدٌ *a mosque,* مُسَيْجِدٌ; أَرْطًى *a kind of tree,* أُرَيْطٍ (for أُرَيْطِيٌ). When the noun is *quinqueliteral,* but the fourth letter *weak,* the diminutive is فُعَيْعِيلٌ; as عُصْفُورٌ *a sparrow,* عُصَيْفِيرٌ; مِفْتَاحٌ *a key,* مُفَيْتِيحٌ.

REM. *a.* The diminutive is used, not merely in its literal sense, but also to express endearment (as بُنَيَّ, أُخَيَّ, أُبَيَّ) or contempt (as
D عُدَيٌّ), and even enhancement (لِلتَّعْظِيمِ, as دُوَيْهِيَةٌ *a great misfortune,* سُنَيَّةٌ *a terrible year of drought* or *dearth,* خُيَيْرٌ *the very best,* صُدَيِّقٌ *a special friend),* [اَلدُّهَيْمَآءُ *a very black calamity, a severe trial*].

REM. *b.* In forming a diminutive, it is not usual to fall back upon the root-consonants. On the contrary, the servile letters are generally taken into account, as long as the word does not exceed the form فُعَيْعِلٌ; as أَزْرَقُ *blue,* أُزَيْرِقُ; مِعْطَفٌ *a mantle,* مُعَيْطِفٌ. See however § 283.

Rem. *c.* The first syllable of the form فُعَيْلٌ is occasionally pronounced with kèsra instead of ḍamma, when the second radical of the primitive is ى; as بِيَيْتٌ, شِيَىْءٌ, شِيَيْخٌ, نِيَيْبٌ, for بُيَيْتٌ, شُيَىْءٌ, شُيَيْخٌ, نُيَيْبٌ, from بَيْتٌ, شَىْءٌ, شَيْخٌ, and نَابٌ (for نَيَبٌ). A

Rem. *d.* Traces of this diminutive form in Aramaic are עוּלֵימָא, ܥܠܝܡܐ, *a youth* (غُلَيِّمٌ, from غُلَامٌ), and ܥܘܙܠܐ *a fawn* (غُزَيِّلٌ, from غَزَالٌ). In Hebrew we may perhaps consider as such, זְעֵיר *little, a little* (صُغَيِّرٌ), פְּלֵיטָה *a band of fugitives*, שְׁפִיפֹן *the cerastes*, a sort of snake (سُفٌّ), and אֱמִינוֹן (from אַמְנוֹן, a con- B temptuous diminutive, like اَلْأُخَيْطِلُ). If so, the vowel ִי must be regarded as a weakening of ֵי (orig. ַי), like גְּלִית for גָּלִית (גָּלְיָת). This view derives some confirmation from the modern pronunciation of North Africa, where, for example, قُفَيْفَةٌ, the diminutive of قُفَّةٌ, *a basket*, is sounded *ḳ'fīfè* or *g'fīfè*,—in post-biblical Hebrew קוּפָּה and קְפִיפָה.

Rem. *e.* Diminutives may be formed not only from nouns C (substantive or adjective), but also (1) from the demonstrative pronoun ذَا and its derivatives, as well as the relative pronoun اَلَّذِى; (2) from certain prepositions, which are, however, obviously substantives in the accusative, as قُبَيْلَ *a little before*, بُعَيْدَ *a little after*, فُوَيْقَ *a little above*, دُوَيْنَ *a little below, a little nearer than*, etc.; and (3) from a few of the verbs of surprise or wonder (§ 184, rem. *f*). On the other hand, they cannot be formed from nouns D which have already the measure of a diminutive, as جُمَيْلٌ, *a kind of small bird*, كُمَيْتٌ *a bay horse.*

270. When the noun contains *five* letters, of which the fourth is *strong*, or more than five, the diminutive فُعَيْعِلٌ is commonly formed from the first four, and the rest are rejected; as سَفَرْجَلٌ *a quince*,

A سُفَيْرِجٌ ; عَنْدَلِيبٌ *a nightingale*, عُنَيْدِلٌ ; عَنْكَبُوتٌ *a spider*, عُنَيْكِبٌ. But if there be among the consonants several servile letters, these are rejected, or some of them; as إِسْتَبْرَقٌ *thick gold-brocade*, أُبَيْرِقٌ ; مُتَدَحْرِجٌ *rolling oneself*, دُحَيْرِجٌ ; مُسْتَكْمِلٌ *trying to render perfect*, مُكَيْمِلٌ ; مُخْتَارٌ *chosen*, مُخَيِّرٌ (for مُخَيْيِرٌ), and not مُخَيْتِرٌ ; مُقْعَنْسِسٌ *having a hump in front*, مُقَيْعِسٌ.

B Rem. *a*. The rule as to quinqueliterals like سَفَرْجَلٌ is not always strictly observed. Thus جَحْمَرِشٌ *a fat, lazy, old woman*, فَرَزْدَقٌ *a burnt cake*, and قُذَعْمِلٌ *a big camel* or *a little, ugly woman*, are said to make either جُحَيْمِرٌ, فُرَيْزِدٌ, قُذَيْعِمٌ, or جُحَيْرِشٌ, فُرَيْزِقٌ, قُذَيْعِلٌ.

Rem. *b*. If there be more servile consonants than must necessarily be cut off, their relative importance for the signification of the word is taken into account in choosing which is to be retained.
C In مُسْتَكْمِلٌ, for example, م is preserved in preference to س or ت, because it indicates the participial form. But if all the consonants are of equal value, we may select which we please, and therefore the diminutive of عَلَنْدًى, *a sort of thorn*, is either عُلَيْنِدٌ or عُلَيِّدٌ (for عُلَيْدِيٌ); of قَلَنْسُوَةٌ, *a sort of cap*, قُلَيْنِسَةٌ or قُلَيْسِيَةٌ; of حَبَنْطًى, *short and big-bellied*, حُبَيْنِطٌ or حُبَيِّطٌ (for حُبَيْطِيٌ).

Rem. *c*. The termination ـَانٌ, when appended to nouns of four
D or more letters, is not rejected, but remains attached to the diminutive, which is formed out of the preceding consonants; as زَعْفَرَانٌ *saffron*, زُعَيْفِرَانٌ ; أُفْعُوَانٌ *a male snake*, أُفَيْعِيَانٌ.

Rem. *d*. Nouns containing five or more consonants do not exceed the form فُعَيْعِلٌ, as قَرَعْبَلَانَةٌ *a tick*, قُرَيْعِبَةٌ ; and therefore a word which consists of four radical and one or more servile consonants, rejects the latter at once (except in the cases specified in rem. *b*, and in § 269). In place of the rejected consonants, however,

ى may be inserted immediately before the last letter; as سُفَيْرِيج, A
مُكَيْمِيل, عُنَيْكِيب, and the like.

271. The feminine terminations ـَة, ـَى, and ـَآء; the relative termination ـِىّ; the ending ـَانٌ in adjectives of which the feminine is فَعْلَى, and in proper names; the dual and plural terminations ـَانِ, ـُونَ, and ـَاتٌ; and the second syllable of the plural form أَفْعَالٌ; are all disregarded. The diminutives must be formed out of the B
preceding consonants, and these terminations added to them. E.g. قَلْعَةٌ *a castle,* قُلَيْعَةٌ; طَلْحَةُ (a man's name), طُلَيْحَةُ; مَسْلَمَةُ (a man's name), مُسَيْلِمَةُ; حُبْلَى *pregnant,* حُبَيْلَى; سَلْمَى (a woman's name), سُلَيْمَى; حَمْرَآءُ *red,* حُمَيْرَآءُ; عَبْقَرِىٌّ (from a place called عَبْقَرُ, supposed to be inhabited by the *ǵinn*) *demoniacal, mighty, perfect,* عُبَيْقِرِىٌّ; بَصْرِىٌّ *belonging to ĕl-Baṣra,* بُصَيْرِىٌّ; سَكْرَانُ (fem. سَكْرَى) *drunken,* C
سُكَيْرَانُ; سَلْمَانُ (a man's name), سُلَيْمَانُ; مُسْلِمَانِ *two Muslims,* مُسَيْلِمَانِ; مُسْلِمُونَ *Muslims,* مُسَيْلِمُونَ; مُسْلِمَاتٌ *Muslim women,* مُسَيْلِمَاتٌ; أَجْمَالٌ *camels,* أَصْحَابٌ *companions,* أَلْفَاظٌ *words,* أَبْيَاتٌ *verses,* أُجَيْمَالٌ, أُصَيْحَابٌ, أُلَيْفَاظٌ, أُبَيَّاتٌ.

Rem. *a.* The fem. ـَى is rejected, when the noun consists of five letters, the third of which is strong, or of more than five; as D
قَرْقَرَى *the back,* قُرَيْقِرٌ; لُغَيْزَى *a riddle,* لُغَيْغِيزٌ. But if, in the quinqueliteral noun, the third letter be a weak servile, either it, or the ى, may be omitted; as حُبَارَى *a bustard,* حُبَيْرَى or حُبَيِّرٌ (for حُبَيْبِيرٌ).

Rem. *b.* Other plurals, besides أَفْعَالٌ, of the class called جُمُوعُ ٱلْقِلَّةِ (see § 307) form their diminutives regularly; viz. فِعْلَةٌ, as وِلْدَةٌ *children,* وُلَيْدَةٌ; غِلْمَةٌ *boys, slaves,* غُلَيْمَةٌ; أَفْعُلٌ, as

A أَكْلُبٌ *dogs*, أُكَيْلِبٌ ; أَضْلُعٌ *ribs*, أُضَيْلِعٌ ; and أَفْعِلَةٌ, as أَجْرِبَةٌ *bags*,
أُجَيْرِبَةٌ ; أَعْمِدَةٌ *pillars*, أُعَيْمِدَةٌ ; أَغْلِمَةٌ *boys, slaves*, أُغَيْلِمَةٌ ; أَصْبِيَةٌ
children, أُصَيْبِيَةٌ. In regard to the جُمُوعُ ٱلْكَثْرَةِ (see § 307), two
courses may be adopted. We may fall back on the singular, adding
to its diminutive the appropriate plural termination; e.g. شُعَرَآءُ
poets, شُوَيْعِرُونَ, from شَاعِرٌ, شُوَيْعِرٌ (see § 277); دُورٌ *houses*, دُوَيْرَاتٌ,
B from دَارٌ, دُوَيْرَةٌ (see § 274). Or we may have recourse to the
جَمْعُ ٱلْقِلَّةِ, if such exist; e.g. فِتْيَانٌ *youths*, فُتَيُّونَ, from فَتًى, فُتَيٌّ,
or فُتَيَّةٌ, from the plural فِتْيَةٌ; أَذِلَّآءُ *base fellows*, ذُلَيِّلُونَ, from
ذَلِيلٌ, ذُلَيِّلٌ (see § 278), or أُذَيَّلَةٌ (for أُذَيْلِلَةٌ), from the plural أَذِلَّةٌ
(for أَذْلِلَةٌ).

272. The termination ـَانٌ in *triliteral* nouns, of which the femi-
C nine is *not* فَعْلَى, and which are not proper names, is regarded as
radical, and consequently the diminutive takes the form فُعَيْعِيلٌ; as
سُلْطَانٌ *power, a sultan*, سُلَيْطِينٌ; سِرْحَانٌ *a wolf*, سُرَيْحِينٌ; شَيْطَانٌ
a devil, شُيَيْطِينٌ; رَيْحَانٌ *sweet basil*, رُوَيْحِينٌ.

273. Proper names, consisting of two words (see § 264), form
their diminutives from the *first* word, the second remaining unchanged;
D as عَبْدُ ٱللّٰهِ ‘*Abdu 'llāh*, عُبَيْدُ ٱللّٰهِ ‘*Obèidu 'llāh*; مَعْدِيكَرِبُ, مُعَيْدِيكَرِبُ;
حَضْرَمَوْتُ, حُضَيْرَمَوْتُ; بَعْلَبَكُّ, بُعَيْلَبَكُّ.

274. If a diminutive be formed from a *triliteral feminine* noun,
which has not however a feminine termination, ـَةٌ is added to the
diminutive, provided that the primitive has no nomen unitatis (§ 246).
E. g. هِنْدٌ (a woman's name), هُنَيْدَةٌ; شَمْسٌ *the sun*, شُمَيْسَةٌ; دَارٌ *a house*,
دُوَيْرَةٌ; سِنٌّ *a tooth*, سُنَيْنَةٌ; إِبِلٌ *camels*, أُبَيْلَةٌ; غَنَمٌ *a flock of sheep* or
goats, غُنَيْمَةٌ; عَيْنٌ *an eye* or *fountain*, عُيَيْنَةٌ or عِيَيْنَةٌ (see § 269, rem. *c*).

But if the primitive has a nomen unitatis, ـَةٌ is not appended to the A
diminutive, in order to avoid ambiguity. E.g. شَجَرٌ *trees*, شُجَيْرٌ, but شَجَرَةٌ *a tree*, شُجَيْرَةٌ; بَقَرٌ *cattle*, بُقَيْرٌ, but بَقَرَةٌ *an ox* or *cow*, بُقَيْرَةٌ.

Rem. *a.* The diminutives of the fem. cardinal numbers, from 3 to 10 inclusive, do not take ـَةٌ for the same reason; e.g. خَمْسٌ *five* (fem.), خُمَيْسٌ, but خَمْسَةٌ *five* (masc.), خُمَيْسَةٌ. But see § 319, rem. *a*.

Rem. *b.* If the noun contains more than three consonants, ـَةٌ B
is not added to the diminutive.

Rem. *c.* There are a few exceptions to the rules of this § and rem. *b*. For example, حَرْبٌ, *war*, makes حُرَيْبٌ; دِرْعٌ *a coat of mail*, دُرَيْعٌ; ذَوْدٌ, *a herd of she-camels*, ذُوَيْدٌ; عَرَبٌ *Arabs*, عُرَيْبٌ; قَوْسٌ, *a bow*, قُوَيْسٌ; نَعْلٌ *a shoe*, نُعَيْلٌ; [عَرُوسٌ *a bride*, عُرَيِّسٌ; قَلُوصٌ *a young she-camel*, قُلَيِّصٌ, D. G.]; whilst قُدَّامٌ, *the front*, and وَرَآءُ, *the rear* or *back*, have قُدَيْدِيمَةٌ, and وُرَيِّئَةٌ (for وُرَيْيِئَةٌ).—قَوْمٌ
one's people or *tribe*, which is masc. and fem., has قُوَيْمٌ or قُوَيْمَةٌ; C
but رَهْطٌ and نَفَرٌ, though also of both genders, seem to make only رُهَيْطٌ and نُفَيْرٌ. عُرْسٌ, *a wedding-feast*, is usually masculine, and therefore has عُرَيْسٌ. بَحْرٌ *a sea*, which is masc., makes بُحَيْرَةٌ.

275. The double consonants in nouns formed from verba mediæ rad. geminatæ are resolved; as تَلٌّ *a hill*, تُلَيْلٌ; طَسٌّ *a cup* (Fr. *tasse*), طُسَيْسٌ; مُدَّةٌ *time*, مُدَيْدَةٌ.

276. If the second radical be a weak letter, and have been D
changed by the influence of the vowels into another, the original letter is restored in forming the diminutive. E.g. بَابٌ (بَوَبٌ) *a door*, بُوَيْبٌ; نَابٌ (نَيَبٌ) *an eye-tooth* or *canine tooth*, نُيَيْبٌ; رِيحٌ (رِوْحٌ) *wind*, رُوَيْحَةٌ; قِيمَةٌ (قِوْمَةٌ) *price*, *value*, قُوَيْمَةٌ; مُوسِرٌ (مُيْسِرٌ) *rich*, مُيَيْسِرٌ; مِيزَانٌ (مِوْزَانٌ) *a pair of scales*, مُوَيْزِينٌ.

A REM. شَىْءٌ, *a thing*, commonly makes شُوَىٌّ (for شُوَيْءٌ), and vulgarly شُوَيَّةٌ, instead of شُيَىْءٌ. From بَيْتٌ *a house*, شَيْخٌ *an old man*, عَيْنٌ *an eye* or *fountain*, بَيْضَةٌ *an egg*, and ضَيْعَةٌ *a farm*, may be formed بُوَيْتٌ, شُوَيْخٌ, عُوَيْنَةٌ, بُوَيْضَةٌ, and ضُوَيْعَةٌ, but the regular forms are preferable. Conversely, عِيدٌ, *a festival*, though derived from the radical عود, makes عُيَيْدٌ, following the plural أَعْيَادٌ.

277. If the second letter be either a servile ĕlif, or an ĕlif, the
B origin of which is unknown, it is changed into و; as شَاعِرٌ *a poet*, شُوَيْعِرٌ; دَاهِيَةٌ *a calamity*, دُوَيْهِيَةٌ; فَارِسٌ *a horseman*, فُوَيْرِسٌ; خَاتَمٌ *a signet-ring*, خُوَيْتِمٌ; دَابَّةٌ *an animal*, دُوَيْبَّةٌ (for دُوَيْبِبَةٌ); عَاجٌ *ivory*, عُوَيْجٌ; صَابَةٌ *a certain bitter tree*, صُوَيْبَةٌ.

REM. *a*. Words of the form فَاعِلٌ, in which the initial letter is و, change it into أ in forming the diminutive; e.g. وَاصِلٌ, أُوَيْصِلٌ, not وُوَيْصِلٌ. In other cases this change is optional, as in أُرَيْقٌ for
C وُرَيْقٌ, formed according to § 283 from أَوْرَقُ.

REM. *b*. Words of the form of دُوَيْبَّةٌ sometimes substitute ـَا for ـَيْ, to lighten the pronunciation, as دُوَابَّةٌ and شُوَابَّةٌ, the latter for شُوَيْبَّةٌ, from شَابَّةٌ *a young woman*. [Comp. § 13, rem.]

278. If the third letter be weak, it coalesces with the preceding ى of the diphthong ـَيْ into يّ; as غُلَامٌ *a youth, a slave*, غُلَيِّمٌ; طَعَامٌ *food*, طُعَيِّمٌ; أَكُولٌ *a glutton*, أُكَيِّلٌ; ظَلِيمٌ *a male ostrich*, ظُلَيِّمٌ;
D جَدْوَلٌ *a brook*, جُدَيِّلٌ; أَسْوَدُ *black*, أُسَيِّدُ; فَتًى *a youth*, فُتَيٌّ; عَصًا *a staff*, عُصَيَّةٌ; رَحًى *a mill*, رُحَيَّةٌ; عُرْوَةٌ *a handle*, عُرَيَّةٌ.

REM. *a*. The forms جُدَيْوِلٌ and أُسَيْوِدُ are also used.

REM. *b*. In words of which the second and third radicals are contracted into يّ, these letters must be separated, and treated according to this rule and § 276; e.g. طَيٌّ *a fold* (طَوْيٌ), طُوَيٌّ; حَيَّةٌ *a snake*, (حَيْيَةٌ), حُيَيَّةٌ.

279. A quadriliteral or quinqueliteral, of which the last two A
letters are *weak*, rejects one of them; as يَحْيَى *Yaḥyā* (*John*), يُحَيٌّ
(for يُحَيِّيٌ); أَحْوَى *black*, أُحَيٌّ (for أُحَيِّيٌ); صَبِيٌّ *a boy*, صُبَيٌّ (for
صُبَيِّيٌ); عَدُوٌّ *an enemy*, عُدَيٌّ (for عُدَيِّيٌ); عَطَآءٌ *a gift, pay*, عُطَيٌّ
(for عُطَيِّيٌ); سَمَآءٌ *the sky* or *heaven*, سُمَيَّةٌ; إِدَاوَةٌ *a small water-skin*,
أُدَيَّةٌ (for أُدَيِّيَةٌ); مُعَاوِيَةُ (a man's name), مُعَيَّةُ (for مُعَيِّيَةُ).

Rem. Instead of أُحَيٌّ, some say أُحَيْوٍ (accus. أُحَيْوِيَ, like B
أُسَيْوِدُ, § 278, rem. *a*), others أُحَيٍّ (accus. أُحَيَّ, for أُحَيِّيَ, like
أُسَيِّدُ, § 278), and others still, but irregularly, أُحَيٌّ.—From مُعَاوِيَةُ
the forms مُعَيْوَةُ and مُعَيِّيَةُ are also said to be in use.

280. The infinitives of verba primæ و, which reject the first
radical and take the fem. termination ـَةٌ in exchange (§ 206), resume C
the و in their diminutives; as عِدَةٌ *a promise*, وُعَيْدَةٌ; جِدَةٌ *affluence*,
وُجَيْدَةٌ; شِيَةٌ *being spotted, spots*, وُشَيَّةٌ.

Rem. They are distinguished by the ة from the diminutives of
the form فَعْلٌ in the same verbs; such as وُعَيْدٌ from وَعْدٌ, etc.

281. Nouns which have lost their third radical,—whether they
have the fem. termination ـَةٌ or not,—recover it in the diminutive. D
E.g. أَبٌ *a father* (ابو), أُبَيٌّ; أَخٌ *a brother* (اخو), أُخَيٌّ; دَمٌ *blood*,
دُمَيٌّ; يَدٌ *a hand*, يُدَيَّةٌ; حِرٌ *vulva*, حُرَيْحٌ; مَآءٌ *water*, مُوَيْهٌ and مُوَيٌّ;
شَاةٌ *a sheep* or *goat*, شُوَيْهَةٌ; شَفَةٌ *a lip*, شُفَيْهَةٌ; أَمَةٌ *a maidservant*,
أُمَيَّةٌ; لُغَةٌ *a dialect*, لُغَيَّةٌ; سَنَةٌ *a year*, سُنَيْهَةٌ and سُنَيَّةٌ; هَنَةٌ *a thing*,
هُنَيْهَةٌ, هُنَيْئَةٌ, and هُنَيَّةٌ.

Rem. *a*. فَمٌ, *mouth*, of which the radical is فُوهٌ or فَوَهٌ, forms its
diminutive accordingly, فُوَيْهٌ.

Rem. *b*. A lost first or second radical is not restored, if the

A word consists of three letters, exclusive of the feminine ة; as نَاسٌ (for أُنَاسٌ) *people*, نُوَيْسٌ; هَارٌ (for هَائِرٌ, § 240, rem. *b*) *feeble*, هُوَيْرٌ; شَاكٌ (for شَائِكٌ) *bristling* (*with weapons*), شُوَيْكٌ; مَيْتٌ (for مَيِّتٌ § 242) *dead*, مُيَيْتٌ; خَيْرٌ (for خَيِّرٌ) *good*, خُيَيْرٌ. Otherwise the diminutives would have been أُنَيِّسٌ, هُوَيْئِرٌ, شُوَيْئِكٌ, مُيَيِّتٌ, and خُيَيِّرٌ. [Words of the form فَاعِلٌ retain in the diminutive the termination ـٍ, as قُوَيْضٍ from قَاضٍ *a judge*, رُوَيْعٍ from رَاعٍ *a pastor*. D. G.]

B **282.** Those nouns which, after having lost their third radical, take a prosthetic elif, reject the elif, and recover their original letter. E.g. اِسْمٌ *a name*, سُمَيٌّ; اِبْنٌ *a son*, بُنَيٌّ; اِسْتٌ *the anus*, سُتَيْهَةٌ.

REM. The diminutives of أُخْتٌ *sister*, بِنْتٌ *daughter*, and هَنْتٌ *a thing*, are formed like those of أَخٌ, اِبْنٌ, and هَنَةٌ, and distinguished in the first two by the fem. termination; أُخَيَّةٌ, بُنَيَّةٌ, هُنَيَّةٌ (see
C § 281).

283. Another way of forming diminutives is to fall back upon the root. If this consists of *three* consonants, the diminutive is فُعَيْلٌ; if of *four*, فُعَيْعِلٌ (see § 269, rem. *b*). E.g. مِعْطَفٌ, عُطَيْفٌ; هُمَامٌ, هُمَيْمٌ; أَسْوَدُ, سُوَيْدٌ; قَاضٍ, قُضَيٌّ; حَامِدٌ, حُمَيْدٌ; حَارِثٌ, حُرَيْثٌ; قِرْطَاسٌ, قُرَيْطِسٌ; عُصْفُورٌ, عُصَيْفِرٌ; أَوْرَقُ, وُرَيْقٌ or أُرَيْقٌ; نَافِعٌ, نُفَيْعٌ;
D مُقْعَنْسِسٌ, قُعَيْسٌ; [مَعَدِّيٌّ, مُعَيْدِيٌّ]. This sort of diminutive is called تَصْغِيرُ ٱلتَّرْخِيمِ, *the softened* or *curtailed diminutive*.

284. With regard to this kind of diminutive the following rules are to be observed. (*a*) If a masc. noun ends in ـَةٌ, this termination falls away; e.g. حَارِثَةُ (a name), حُرَيْثٌ. (*b*) Fem. nouns in ـَى and ـَآءُ reject these terminations and take ـَةٌ; as حُبْلَى, حُبَيْلَةٌ; حَمْرَآءُ, حُمَيْرَةٌ.

REM. Very irregular diminutives are: رَجُلٌ *a man*, رُوَيْجِلٌ; A
دُخَانٌ *smoke*, دُوَيْخِنٌ; مَغْرِبٌ *sunset*, مُغَيْرِبَانٌ; عَشِيٌّ or عَشِيَّةٌ
nightfall, عُشَيْشَةٌ, عُشَيْشِيَةٌ, عُشَيَّانٌ, عُشَيْشَانٌ, and عُشَيْشِيَانٌ; إِنْسَانٌ
a human being, أُنَيْسِيَانٌ; لَيْلَةٌ *a night*, لُيَيْلِيَةٌ (compare the plur.
لَيَالٍ for لَيَالِيُ); بَنُونَ *sons* (plur. of ابْنٌ), أُبَيْنُونَ; أُصْلَانٌ (derived
from the plur. of أَصِيلٌ *the evening*), أُصَيْلَانٌ, أُصَيْلَالٌ, and أُصَيَّالٌ.
Further, دِينَارٌ *a dīnār*, دُنَيْنِيرٌ, and دِيوَانٌ *a register, an account-book,* B
a collection of poems, a public office or *bureau*, دُوَيْوِينٌ, as if from
دِنَّارٌ and دِوَّانٌ (see § 305, II., rem. *b*); دِيبَاجٌ *brocade*, دُيَيْبِيجٌ or
دُبَيْبِيجٌ, as if from دِبَّاجٌ.

(η) *Some other Nominal Forms.*

285. (*a*) The form فِعْلَةٌ frequently means a *small piece* of C
anything; as فِلْذَةٌ, قِطْعَةٌ, *a piece*, كِسْرَةٌ *a fragment*, جِذْوَةٌ *a firebrand,*
a live coal, خِرْقَةٌ *a rag*, فِرْقَةٌ *a sect*, حِصَّةٌ *a portion*, خِطَّةٌ *a piece of*
land, an allotment.—(*b*) The form فُعْلَةٌ is often used to signify a *small*
quantity, such as can be contained in a place at once; as قُبْضَةٌ *a*
handful; أُكْلَةٌ, لُقْمَةٌ, مُضْغَةٌ, *a morsel, a mouthful*; جُرْعَةٌ, بُلْعَةٌ, *a gulp,*
a sup or *sip*; شُرْبَةٌ *a draught* (*of water*). It also denotes *colour*; as
حُمْرَةٌ *redness*, صُفْرَةٌ *yellowness*, زُرْقَةٌ *a light blue*, دُكْنَةٌ *a blackish* D
brown.

286. (*a*) The form فِعَالٌ indicates *vessels* and *implements*; as
إِنَاءٌ, وِعَاءٌ, *a vessel*, جِرَابٌ *a bag*, حِلَابٌ *a milk-pail*, خِلَالٌ *a wooden pin,*
سِقَاءٌ *a water-skin*, شِرَاكٌ *the thong* or *strap of a sandal*, لِبَاسٌ *a garment,*
إِزَارٌ, رِدَاءٌ, certain garments, لِحَافٌ *a coverlet, a pelisse*.—(*b*) The form
فُعَالٌ denotes *diseases*; as حُمَامٌ *a fever*, زُكَامٌ *a cold*, سُعَالٌ *a cough,*

A صُدَاعٌ *a headache*, طُحَالٌ, كُبَادٌ, *disease of the spleen* (طِحَالٌ), *of the liver* (كَبِدٌ)*.

287. (*a*) The form فِعَالَةٌ indicates *a post* or *office;* as كِتَابَةٌ *the post of secretary* (كَاتِبٌ); عِمَالَةٌ, وِلَايَةٌ, *the post of governor* (عَامِلٌ, وَالٍ); إِمَارَةٌ *the office of ĕmīr* (أَمِيرٌ); خِلَافَةٌ *the caliphate;* نِيَابَةٌ *deputyship* B (نَائِبٌ); قِيَادَةٌ *the post of general* (قَائِدٌ); عِرَافَةٌ *the post of inspector, centurion*, etc. (عَرِيفٌ).—(*b*) The form فُعَالَةٌ denotes *small portions* which are broken off or thrown away; as بُرَادَةٌ, قُرَاضَةٌ, *filings;* بُرَايَةٌ *chips, shavings;* قُلَامَةٌ, قُصَاصَةٌ, *parings;* كُنَاسَةٌ, كُسَاحَةٌ, قُمَامَةٌ, *sweepings;* رُضَاضَةٌ *brayed* or *pounded fragments;* كُسَارَةٌ *broken pieces;* قُطَاعَةٌ *cuttings;* عُجَالَةٌ *a little food got ready in haste;* عُفَاوَةٌ *a small quantity* C *of broth* (left in a borrowed pot, when it is returned). Some of these words admit of a masculine collective form فُعَالٌ, indicating a larger quantity, as بُرَاءٌ, قُمَامٌ, رُضَاضٌ, كُسَارٌ, حُطَامٌ, دُقَاقٌ, فُتَاتٌ.

288. The form فَعَّالَةٌ (the feminine of فَعَّالٌ, § 233) is frequently employed to designate (*a*) an instrument or machine, as doing something, or by means of which something is done, regularly and constantly; or (*b*) the place where something is constantly obtained or prepared. D E.g. بَرَّادَةٌ *a vessel* or *stand for cooling water;* حَرَّاقَةٌ *a fire-ship, a galley;* رَعَّادَةٌ, عَرَّادَةٌ, دَبَّابَةٌ, *engines of war;* طَرَّاحَةٌ *a mattrass* or *cushion, a fishing-net;* زَرَّاقَةٌ *a short javelin;* طَرَّادَةٌ *a spear, a bolt;* حَرَّاضَةٌ *a*

---

* [According to D. H. Müller (Aṣmaʿī's *Kitāb al-Farḳ*, p. 26 *seqq.*) the forms فُعَالٌ, فُعَالَةٌ and فَعِيلٌ are often used to denote excretions, as *spittle* or *phlegm* بُصَاقٌ, لُعَابٌ, مُجَاجٌ, مُجَاجَةٌ, رُؤَالٌ, رُغَامٌ (رُغَامٌ), لُغَامٌ; *sweat* حُمَامٌ, حَمِيمٌ, رَشِيحٌ, صُوَاحٌ; *blood issuing from the nose* رُعَافٌ; *excrements* سُلَاحٌ; *sperma* سُلَالَةٌ; *drippings* قُطَارَةٌ. D. G.]

place where potash is made (by burning the plants called حُرْض); A
جَصَّاصَةٌ *a place where gypsum* or *plaster* (جِصّ) *is made;* كَلَّاسَةٌ *a chalk-pit* or *quarry* (كِلْس); مَلَّاحَةٌ *a salt-pan* or *salt-mine* (مِلْح); قَيَّارَةٌ *a well of bitumen* (قَار); جَبَّاسَةٌ *a place where gypsum is found* or *prepared;* زَرَّاعَةٌ *a land that is sown.* Hence the tropical application of this form to persons, as an intensive (§ 233, rem. *c*).

Rem. As فَعَّالَةٌ has been transferred from things to persons, as an intensive adjective, so also فَاعِلَةٌ (§ 233, rem. *c*); for سَاقِيَةٌ is B
a camel that draws water, an irrigating machine, a water-wheel; سَانِيَةٌ, *a water-wheel* and *the camel that works it;* رَاوِيَةٌ, *a water-skin, a camel that carries* or *draws water;* دَاعِيَةٌ, *a call* or *invitation;* عَادِيَةٌ, *a hindrance, an injury;* etc.

2. *The Gender of Nouns.*

289. In respect of gender, Arabic nouns are divisible into *three* C
classes; (*a*) those which are only *masculine* (مُذَكَّر); (*b*) those which are only *feminine* (مُؤَنَّث); (*c*) those which are both masc. and fem., or, as it is usually phrased, of the *common* gender.

Rem. *a.* None of the Semitic languages have what we call the *neuter* gender.

Rem. *b.* Feminines may be either *real* or *natural* (مُؤَنَّث حَقِيقِيّ), as امْرَأَةٌ *a woman,* نَاقَةٌ *a she-camel;* or *unreal, unnatural* (غَيْر حَقِيقِيّ), or *tropical* (مَجَازِيّ), as اَلشَّمْس *the sun,* نَعْل *a shoe* or D
sandal, ظُلْمَةٌ *darkness,* بُشْرَى *good news.*

290. That a noun is of the *fem.* gender may be ascertained either (*a*) from its *signification,* or (*b*) from its *form.*

a. Feminine by signification (اَلْمُؤَنَّث ٱلْمَعْنَوِيّ) are :—

(α) All common nouns and proper names which denote females, as أُمّ *a mother,* عَرُوس *a bride,* عَجُوز *an old woman,* [خَادِم *a female*

A *servant*]; مَرْيَمُ *Mary,* هِنْدٌ *Hind,* سُعَادُ *Su'ād,* زَيْنَبُ *Zèinèb* [; or that re represented as females, as شَعُوبُ *Death,* ذُكَاءُ *the Sun*].

(β) Proper names of countries and towns, because the common nouns أَرْضٌ, بُقْعَةٌ, مَدِينَةٌ, بَلْدَةٌ, and قَرْيَةٌ, are feminine*; as مِصْرُ *Egypt,* مُخَا *Mocha.* Those names, however, which belong to the triptote declension, are originally masculine, as اَلشَّأْمُ *Syria,* اَلْعِرَاقُ *el-'Irāk,* مِنًى, وَاسِطٌ, دَابِقٌ, فَلْجٌ, هَجَرٌ; but they may also be inflected

B as diptotes, and are then feminine, as مِنَى, وَاسِطُ, etc.

REM. The names of the quarters or directions, as قُدَّامُ, أَمَامُ, *the front,* خَلْفُ, وَرَآءُ, *the rear,* may also be treated as feminine, following the gender of جِهَةٌ.

(γ) The names of the winds and the different kinds of fire, because the common nouns رِيحٌ, *wind,* and نَارٌ, *fire,* are feminine; as قَبُولٌ *the east wind,* دَبُورٌ *the west wind,* شَمَالٌ *the north wind,* جَنُوبٌ

C *the south wind;* سَعِيرٌ, جَحِيمٌ, *blazing fire,* [جَهَنَّمُ,] سَقَرُ, لَظَى, *hell-fire.* Except إِعْصَارٌ *a dust-storm with whirlwinds,* which is masc.

(δ) The names of many parts of the body, especially those that are double; as يَدٌ *a hand,* رِجْلٌ *a leg* or *foot,* عَيْنٌ *an eye,* أُذُنٌ *an ear,* سِنٌّ *a tooth,* كَتِفٌ *a shoulder,* سَاقٌ *a shank,* رَحِمٌ *the womb,* اِسْتٌ *the anus.*

D REM. رَأْسٌ *the head,* وَجْهٌ *the face,* أَنْفٌ *the nose,* فَمٌ *the mouth,* صَدْرٌ *the breast,* ظَهْرٌ *the back,* [خَدٌّ *the cheek,*] and the names of the blood, muscles, sinews, and bones, are masc.; as also, in most instances, رَحِمٌ, when it means *relationship.* [قَدَمٌ is sometimes masc. and so كَفٌّ.]

---

* [Some admit also the use of the masculine gender, because the word مِصْرٌ is masc., بَلَدٌ masc. or fem. See Muḳaddasī, p. 7, l. 16 *seq.* D. G.]

(ε) Collective nouns (شِبْهُ ٱلْجَمْعِ, *resembling the plural*), which A
denote living objects that are destitute of reason, and do not form a nomen unitatis; as إِبِلٌ *camels*, ذَوْدٌ *a herd of she-camels*, غَنَمٌ *sheep* or *goats*.

b. Feminine by form (ٱلْمُؤَنَّثُ ٱللَّفْظِىُّ) are :—

(α) Nouns ending in ـَةٌ; as جَنَّةٌ *a garden*, ظُلْمَةٌ *darkness*, حَيَاةٌ, or حَيٰوةٌ, *life*.

(β) Nouns ending in ـَى or ـَا (élif maḳṣūra, § 7, rem. *b*), when B
that termination does not belong to the root; as دَعْوَى *a claim, a demand*, نَجْوَى *a secret*, لَوْمَى *blame*, أُرَبَى *misfortune*, ذِكْرَى *memory*, دِفْلَى *the oleander*, ذِفْرَى *the prominent bone behind the ear*, مِعْزَى *goats*, بُهْمَى *barley-grass*, اَلدُّنْيَا *the world*, رُؤْيَا *a vision* or *dream*, بُشْرَى *good news*, حُمَّى *a fever*.

Rem. But those who say دِفْلًى, ذِفْرًى, مِعْزًى, and بُهْمًى, regard C
them as masculine, the ى being considered as an أَلِفُ إِلْحَاقٍ [§ 252].

(γ) Nouns ending in ـَآءُ, when that termination does not belong to the root; as صَحْرَآءُ, بَيْدَآءُ, *a plain* or *desert*, ضَرَّآءُ *harm, mischief*, بَغْضَآءُ *hatred*, قَاصِعَآءُ *a jerboa's hole*, كِبْرِيَآءُ *glory* (of God), *pride* (of man), خُيَلَآءُ *vainglory, arrogance*, سِيَرَآءُ *a sort of striped cloth*.

Rem. A few nouns ending in ـَةٌ, and those verbal adjectives D
to which ـَةٌ is added to intensify their signification (§ 233, rem. *c*), are masc., because they apply to males; e.g. خَلِيفَةٌ *a successor, deputy*, or *caliph* (compare in Italian *il podestà*), عَلَّامَةٌ *very learned*, رَاوِيَةٌ *a traditionary*.

291. The following is a list of nouns which are feminine, not by form or signification, but merely by usage.

A أَرْضٌ *the earth, the ground, the floor.*
بِئْرٌ *a well.*
حَرْبٌ *war.*
خَمْرٌ *wine.*
دِرْعٌ *a coat of mail.*
دَلْوٌ *a bucket.*
B دَارٌ *a house.*
رَحًى *a mill.*
رِيحٌ *wind.*
اَلشَّمْسُ *the sun.*
ضَبُعٌ *a hyæna.*
[طَاغُوتٌ *idol.*]
عَرُوضٌ *metre.*
C عَصًا *a staff.*
عُقَابٌ *an eagle.*
عَقْرَبٌ *a scorpion.*
عِيرٌ *a caravan.*
فَأْسٌ *an axe.*
اَلْفِرْدَوْسُ *Paradise.*
أَفْعًى *a viper.*
[قَدُومٌ *an adze.*]
كَأْسٌ *a cup.*
[كَرْشٌ or كِرْشٌ *the maw.*]
مَنْجَنُونٌ *a water-wheel.*
مَنْجَنِيقٌ *a catapult.*
مُوسَى *a razor.*
نَارٌ *fire.*
نَعْلٌ *a shoe* or *sandal.*
نَفْسٌ *the soul.*
نَوًى *a traveller's destination.*

REM. Of these حَرْبٌ, خَمْرٌ, دِرْعٌ, دَارٌ, دَلْوٌ, رِيحٌ, ضَبُعٌ, مَنْجَنِيقٌ, and نَارٌ, are occasionally used as masculine; whilst دِرْعٌ *a woman's shift*, شَمْسٌ *a collar* or *pendant*, and فِرْدَوْسٌ *a garden* or *park*, are masculine. Those who say مُوسًى instead of مُوسَى, regard the word of course as masculine.

D **292.** Masculine or feminine are:—

(*a*) Collective nouns (أَسْمَآءُ الجِنْسِ), chiefly denoting animals and plants, which form a nomen unitatis; e.g. حَمَامٌ *pigeons*, شَآءٌ *sheep* or *goats*, بَقَرٌ *cattle*, جَرَادٌ *grasshoppers, locusts*, نَحْلٌ *bees*; شَجَرٌ *trees*, نَخْلٌ *palm-trees*, تَمْرٌ *dates*; [شَعِيرٌ *barley* (gen. masc.)]; سَحَابٌ *clouds*, لَبِنٌ or لِبْنٌ *bricks*, ذَهَبٌ *gold*. These are masc. by form, fem. by signification (اَلْجَمَاعَةُ *totality*).

[(*b*) Collective nouns (أَسْمَآءُ ٱلْجَمْعِ or أَشْبَاهُ ٱلْجَمْعِ), denoting A
rational beings and not forming a nomen unitatis; e.g. قَوْمٌ *one's people* or *tribe*, رَهْطٌ *do.*, نَفَرٌ *a small number of men* (3—7), نَاسٌ *men* (gen. masc.), تَجْرٌ *a company of merchants*, رَكْبٌ *a company of way-farers*, etc. But أَهْلٌ and آلٌ *one's family*, are masc. D. G.]

(*c*) The names of the letters of the alphabet, which are more usually feminine; as هٰذِهِ ٱلْأَلِفُ, or هٰذَا ٱلْأَلِفُ, *this èlif.*

[(*d*) The nomina verbi (*maṣdar*). One may say أَوْجَعَنِى ضَرْبُكَ B
and أَوْجَعَتْنِى ضَرْبُكَ *your striking caused me pain**. D. G.]

(*e*) Words regarded merely as such. These may be masculine, following the gender of لَفْظٌ, or feminine, following that of كَلِمَةٌ or لُغَةٌ. A noun may also be masculine, taking the gender of اِسْمٌ; a verb, taking that of فِعْلٌ; and a particle, taking that of حَرْفٌ. But a
particle is more usually feminine, following the gender of أَدَاةٌ. The C
verb كَانَ, *to be*, seems by common consent to be taken as feminine (كَانَ ٱلنَّاقِصَةُ, كَانَ ٱلتَّامَّةُ). Such mere words are treated like proper names, and therefore do not take the article, as مَآءُ هٰذَا or مَآءُ هٰذِهِ, *this word* مَآءُ (*water*).

(*f*) A considerable number of nouns, of which the following are those that most frequently occur.

[إِبْطٌ *the armpit* (gen. masc.).]
إِزَارٌ *an article of dress.*
آلٌ *the mirage.*
بَشَرٌ *a human being, human beings.*

بَطْنٌ *the belly* (gen. masc.). D
[بَعِيرٌ *camel* (gen. masc.).]
إِبْهَامٌ *the thumb* or *great toe* (gen. fem.).
ثَدْىٌ *a breast* (*mamma*).

* [This seems to be the explanation of صَوْتٌ being used as a fem. noun, *Ḥamāsa* 78, vs. 1, هٰذِهِ ٱلصَّوْتُ *this crying*. Comp. Lane. D. G.]

A ثَعْلَبٌ *a fox.*

جَنَاحٌ *a wing* (gen. masc.).

حَالٌ *state, condition* (gen. fem.).

حَانُوتٌ *a booth, a shop.*

[خَيَالٌ *a phantom.*]

أَرْنَبٌ *a hare* (gen. fem.).

دُكَّانٌ *a shop.*

B [ذِرَاعٌ *cubit* (gen. fem.).]

ذَنُوبٌ *a large bucket.*

رُوحٌ *spirit, soul* [when signifying *a celestial being* always masc.]

[زُقَاقٌ *a street* or *lane.*]

C زَنْدٌ *the upper of the two pieces of wood, used in producing fire* (gen. masc.).

سَبِيلٌ *a path, a road.*

سُرًى *journeying by night.*

سِكِّينٌ *a knife* (gen. masc.).

سِلَاحٌ *a weapon, weapons.*

D سُلْطَانٌ [prop. *authority,* hence] *power, a sovereign.*

سَلْمٌ *peace.*

سُلَّمٌ *a ladder.*

سَمَآءٌ *the sky* or *heaven, the clouds, rain.*

[سُورٌ *a wall* (gen. masc.).]

سُوقٌ *a market.*

إِصْبَعٌ *a finger* (gen. fem.).

صِرَاطٌ *a way, a road* (via *strata*).

صُلْحٌ *peace.*

صَاعٌ *a measure for corn, etc.*

ضُحًى *the forenoon.*

ضَرَبٌ *white honey.*

[ضِرْسٌ *a tooth.*]

طِبَاعٌ *nature, natural disposition* [gen. fem.].

طَرِيقٌ *a road.*

عَجُزٌ *the hinder part, the rump* [gen. fem.].

عُرْسٌ *a wedding, a marriage.*

عَسَلٌ *honey.*

[عَنْبَرٌ *ambergris.*]

عُنُقٌ *the neck.*

عَنْكَبُوتٌ *a spider* (gen. fem.).

فَرَسٌ *a horse* [gen. fem.].

فُلْكٌ *a ship.*

[فِهْرٌ *a stone for bruising perfume.*]

قِدْرٌ *a pot, a kettle* (gen. fem.).

قَفًا *the nape of the neck.*

قَلِيبٌ *a well.*

قَوْسٌ *a bow* (gen. fem.).

كَبِدٌ *the liver.*

كُرَاعٌ *the tibia* or *shin-bone.*	مِعًى *an intestine* (gen. masc.). A
لِسَانٌ *the tongue.*	مِلْحٌ *salt* (gen. fem.).
لَيْلٌ *the night* (gen. masc.).	[مُلْكٌ *dominion.*]
مِسْكٌ *musk* (gen. masc.).	[هُدًى *the right direction.*]

Rem. *a.* زَنْدٌ *the bone* (either *radius* or *ulna*) *of the fore-arm,* سَمَآءٌ *a roof* or *ceiling,* and usually عُرْسٌ *a wedding-feast,* are masculine. B

Rem. *b.* The above list, and that contained in § 291, cannot lay claim either to absolute completeness or to perfect accuracy, since the usage of the language has varied considerably at different periods. For example, in later times فَمٌ, *the mouth,* and مَرْكَبٌ, *a boat* or *ship,* are used as feminine; whilst عَضُدٌ, *the upper arm,* كَتِفٌ, *the shoulder,* [كَرِشٌ, *the maw,*] and بِئْرٌ, *a well,* become masculine. The masculine gender too preponderates in later times over the feminine in words which were anciently of both genders, as نَارٌ *fire,* كَبِدٌ *the liver.* C

293. From most adjectives and some substantives of the masculine gender, feminines are formed by adding the terminations ـَةٌ, ـَى, or ـَآءُ (§ 290, *b*).

Rem. Only ـَةٌ is appended to the masculine without farther affecting the form of the word; ـَى and ـَآءُ have forms distinct from the masculine, which must be learned by practice.

294. The most usual termination, by the mere addition of which to the masculine feminines are formed, is ـَةٌ; as عَظِيمٌ *great,* عَظِيمَةٌ; D فَرِحٌ glad, فَرِحَةٌ; نَدْمَانُ *repentant,* نَدْمَانَةٌ; ضَارِبٌ *striking,* ضَارِبَةٌ; مَضْرُوبٌ *struck,* مَضْرُوبَةٌ; جَدٌّ *a grandfather,* جَدَّةٌ *a grandmother;* فَتًى (for فَتَيٌ) *a young man,* فَتَاةٌ (for فَتَيَةٌ) *a young woman.*

[Rem. *a.* The hèmza of the termination آءٌ of nouns derived from verbs tertiæ و or ى may be replaced, before ة, by the radical letter, as سَمَاوَةٌ from سَمَآءٌ, سَقَّايَةٌ from سَقَّآءٌ, *a water-carrier,* but the

A forms with hèmza, as سَقَّآءَةٌ, غَزَّآءَةٌ, are preferable; comp. *Kāmil*, p. 87, l. 10—15, and below § 299, rem. *c*, § 301, rem. *e*.]

REM. *b*. ـَةٌ is a compromise in orthography between the original ـَتْ, *at*, the old pausal form ـَهْ, *ah*, and the modern ـَه, *a*, in which last the ه is silent (see the footnote to p. 7 supra). This view is confirmed by the comparison of the other Semitic languages; see *Comp. Gr.* 133—137.

B **295.** Feminines in ـَى are formed:—

(*a*) From adjectives of the form فَعْلَانُ, the feminine of which is فَعْلَى; as غَضْبَانُ *angry*, غَضْبَى; سَكْرَانُ *drunk*, سَكْرَى; شَبْعَانُ *sated*, شَبْعَى; غَرْثَانُ *hungry*, غَرْثَى; عَطْشَانُ, ظَمْآنُ, *thirsty*, عَطْشَى, ظَمْأَى; مَلْآنُ *full*, مَلْأَى; خَشْيَانُ *timid, fearing*, خَشْيَا.

(*b*) From adjectives of the form أَفْعَلُ, when they have the *superlative* signification, and are defined by the article or by a fol-
C lowing genitive, in which case the feminine is فُعْلَى; as ٱلْأَكْبَرُ *the largest*, ٱلْكُبْرَى; ٱلْأَصْغَرُ *the smallest*, ٱلصُّغْرَى; ٱلْأَعْظَمُ *the greatest*, ٱلْعُظْمَى; كُبْرَى ٱلْمُدُنِ *the largest of the cities*.

REM. *a*. Adjectives of the forms فَعْلَانُ and فُعْلَانُ form their feminine by adding ـَةٌ; as سَيْفَانُ *tall and slender*, سَيْفَانَةٌ; عُرْيَانُ *naked*, عُرْيَانَةٌ.

D REM. *b*. The feminine of ٱلْأَوَّلُ (for ٱلْأَوْأَلُ or ٱلْأَأْوَلُ) *the first*, is ٱلْأُولَى; that of آخَرُ (for أَأْخَرُ) *other, another*, أُخْرَى. The latter word can be used indefinitely, because it is superlative only in form, not in signification. The numeral أَحَدٌ, *one*, has إِحْدَى.

REM. *c*. There are some feminine adjectives of the form فُعْلَى, not superlatives, without any corresponding masculines; as أُنْثَى *female, feminine*, حُبْلَى *pregnant*, رُبَّى *which has recently yeaned* (of a ewe or she-goat).

296. Feminines in ـَاءُ are formed from adjectives of the form A
أَفْعَلُ, which have not the comparative and superlative signification: as أَصْفَرُ *yellow*, صَفْرَآءُ; أَجْهَرُ *of pleasing aspect*, جَهْرَآءُ; أَحْدَبُ *hump-backed*, حَدْبَآءُ. Many of these adjectives are not in actual use in the masculine; as هَطْلَآءُ *heavy and continuous (rain)*, حَسْنَآءُ *beautiful*, شَوْكَآءُ *rough to the feel* (a new dress), ٱلْعَرَبُ ٱلْعَرْبَآءُ *the Arabs of pure race.*

Rem. The form فَعْلَآءُ sometimes serves as feminine to فَعْلَانُ, B
e.g. جَذْلَانُ *joyful*, جَذْلَآءُ; حَيْرَانُ *perplexed, amazed*, حَيْرَى and حَيْرَآءُ.

297. All adjectives have not a separate form for the feminine. The following forms are of both genders.

(*a*) فَعُولٌ, when it has the meaning of فَاعِلٌ (transitive or intransitive), and is attached to a substantive in the singular, or serves
as predicate to a substantive or a pronoun in the singular; as C
رَجُلٌ صَبُورٌ وَشَكُورٌ *a patient and grateful man*, ٱمْرَأَةٌ صَبُورٌ وَشَكُورٌ *a patient and grateful woman;* رَجُلٌ كَذُوبٌ *a lying man*, ٱمْرَأَةٌ كَذُوبٌ *a lying woman;* كَانَتْ صَبُورًا *she was patient;* رَأَيْتُهَا صَبُورًا *I saw that she was*, or *I thought her, patient;* [بَقَرَةٌ شَبُوبٌ *a full grown antelope*]. But if no substantive or pronoun be expressed, فَعُولٌ makes a feminine فَعُولَةٌ, and also if it has the meaning of مَفْعُولٌ; as رَأَيْتُ صَبُورَةً *I saw*
a patient (*woman*); مَا لَهُ رَكُوبَةٌ وَلَا حَمُولَةٌ وَلَا حَلُوبَةٌ *he has not a* D
she-camel to ride, nor one to carry loads, nor one for milking, where رَكُوبَةٌ and حَلُوبَةٌ = مَرْكُوبَةٌ and مَحْلُوبَةٌ, whilst حَمُولَةٌ = حَامِلَةٌ.

Rem. *a*. Exceptions are rare; as عَدُوٌّ *hostile, an enemy*, fem. عَدُوَّةٌ; [and again, لَا حَلُوبَ فِى ٱلْبَيْتِ *there is no milch-ewe in the tent*, as we read in the tradition of Umm Ma'bad, نَاقَةٌ ضَبُوثٌ or نَاقَةٌ ضَغُوثٌ and شَاةٌ جَزُوزٌ *a shorn sheep*. D. G.]

A [REM. *b.* Hence the fem. nouns صَعُودٌ *an acclivity,* كَؤُودٌ *a mountain-road difficult of ascent,* حَدُورٌ and هَبُوطٌ *a declivity.* D. G.]

(*b*) فَعِيلٌ, when it has the meaning of مَفْعُولٌ, and under the same conditions as فَعُولٌ; e.g. عَيْنٌ كَحِيلٌ *an eye adorned with koḥl,* اِمْرَأَةٌ جَرِيحٌ *a wounded woman,* فَتَاةٌ قَتِيلٌ *a murdered woman;* but رَأَيْتُ قَتِيلَةَ ٱلْحَرُورِيَّةِ *I saw* (*the woman*) *whom the Ḥarūrīs had murdered;* هٰذِهِ أَكِيلَةُ سَبُعٍ *this is* (*a sheep*) *which has been* (*partly*)
B *eaten by a beast of prey.* If فَعِيلٌ has the meaning of فَاعِلٌ (transitive or intransitive), it forms a feminine in ـَةٌ; as نَصِيرٌ *a helper,* نَصِيرَةٌ; شَفِيعٌ *an intercessor,* شَفِيعَةٌ; عَفِيفٌ *temperate, chaste,* عَفِيفَةٌ; مَرِيضٌ *sick,* مَرِيضَةٌ.

REM. Exceptions in either case are rare. For example: فَعْلَةٌ حَمِيدَةٌ *a praiseworthy way of acting,* = مَحْمُودَةٌ; خَصْلَةٌ ذَمِيمَةٌ *a*
C *blameworthy habit,* = مَذْمُومَةٌ; and, on the other hand, مِلْحَفَةٌ جَدِيدٌ *a new wrapper,* إِنَّ رَحْمَةَ ٱللّٰهِ قَرِيبٌ مِنَ ٱلْمُحْسِنِينَ *verily God's mercy is nigh unto them who do well.*

(*c*) مِفْعَلٌ, مِفْعَالٌ, and مِفْعِيلٌ, which were originally nomina instrumenti (§ 228), but afterwards became intensive adjectives (§ 233, rem. *b*), under the same conditions as فَعُولٌ and فَعِيلٌ; e.g.
D اِمْرَأَةٌ مِغْشَمٌ *an obstinate, self-willed woman;* نَاقَةٌ مِذْعَانٌ *a docile she-camel;* جَارِيَةٌ مِعْطَارٌ, or جَارِيَةٌ مِعْطِيرٌ, *a young woman who uses much perfume;* but رَأَيْتُ مِعْطَارَةً *I saw* (*a woman*) *who uses much perfume.*

REM. Exceptions are rare; as مِسْكِينٌ *poor,* مِيقَانٌ *speaking the truth,* fem. مِسْكِينَةٌ, مِيقَانَةٌ [; but اِمْرَأَةٌ مِسْكِينٌ is allowed. D. G.]

[(*d*) Those adjectives that are properly infinitives (§ 230, rem. *c* A
and Vol. ii. § 136, *a*) e.g. قَلْبٌ, غَمٌّ, عَدْلٌ, دَنَسٌ, جُنُبٌ, جَدْبٌ, بُورٌ, وَغْرٌ, مَحْضٌ and some others as جَبَانٌ, عُضَالٌ etc. D. G.]

Rem. Adjectives which are, by their signification, applicable to females only, do not form a feminine in ـَةٌ, when they designate an action or state as natural and permanent, or, at any rate, as lasting for a certain period of time (صِفَةٌ ثَابِتَةٌ); as حَامِلٌ *pregnant,*
عَاقِرٌ, *barren,* كَاعِبٌ, نَاهِدٌ, *having swelling breasts,* حَائِضٌ, طَامِثٌ, B
عَارِكٌ, مُعْصِرٌ, [مِيلَاثٌ 'Ibn Hišām 15, last l. R. S.] *menstruating,* طَالِقٌ *divorced,* عَاطِلٌ *without ornaments,* حَاسِرٌ *with the head and bust naked,* مُرْضِعٌ *giving suck,* مُتْئِمٌ *bearing twins,* مُطْفِلٌ *having a child* or *a young one with her,* مُشْدِنٌ *having a fawn with her,* مُجْرٍ *having a whelp with her,* [حَصَانٌ *chaste,* رَزَانٌ *staid,* عَانِسٌ *unmarried and of middle age*] and likewise مُعَضِّلٌ, مُطَرِّقٌ, مُرَاسِلٌ. But if they
designate the said action or state as beginning, actually in progress, C
or about to begin (صِفَةٌ حَادِثَةٌ), they form a feminine in ـَةٌ; as هِىَ حَائِضَةٌ ٱلْيَوْمَ *she is menstruating to-day;* هِىَ طَالِقَةٌ غَدًا *she will be divorced to-morrow;* لِكُلِّ حَامِلَةٍ تَمَامٌ *every woman who is pregnant has her time* or *term;* يَوْمَ تَرَوْنَهَا تَذْهَلُ كُلُّ مُرْضِعَةٍ عَمَّا أَرْضَعَتْ *on the day when ye shall see it, every woman who is suckling* (in the act of giving suck) *shall become heedless of that which she has been*
suckling. D

3. *The Numbers of Nouns.*

298. Nouns have, like verbs, *three* numbers, the singular, dual, and plural (see § 81).

299. The *dual* is formed by adding ـَانِ to the singular (omitting, of course, the tènwīn); as كِتَابٌ *a book,* كِتَابَانِ ; رَشَأٌ *a fawn,* رَشَأَانِ or رَشَآنِ.

A REM. *a.* If the singular ends in ـَةٌ, ة is changed into ت (see § 294, rem.); as أُمَّةٌ *a nation*, أُمَّتَانِ. But أَلْيَةٌ *a buttock*, and خُصْيَةٌ *a testicle*, usually make أَلْيَانِ and خُصْيَانِ.

REM. *b.* If the singular ends in a quiescent ى (ـًى or ـَى), which was originally ى *mobile* (compare § 167, *a*, *β*, a), it becomes so again in the dual; as فَتًى *a youth*, for فَتَيٌ, فَتَيَانِ; رَحًى *a mill*, رَحَيَانِ; حِمًى *interdicted ground*, حِمَيَانِ; مَرْمًى *a butt for shooting*,
B مَرْمَيَانِ; فَتْوَى *a legal opinion*, فَتْوَيَانِ; حُبْلَى *pregnant*, حُبْلَيَانِ; حُبَارَى *a bustard*, حُبَارَيَانِ. From حِمًى the form حِمَوَانِ is said to occur. If the singular ends in a quiescent ا (ـًا or ـَا), which was originally و *mobile* (compare § 167, *a*, *β*, a), the و is restored in the dual; as عَصًا *a staff*, for عَصَوٌ, عَصَوَانِ; قَفًا *the nape of the neck*, قَفَوَانِ.—If the singular of a quadriliteral noun ends in a quiescent ى, which was originally a و, the و is *not* restored in the dual, but
C becomes ى *mobile*, as مِلْهًى *a musical instrument* (from لَهَا for لَهَوَ), مِلْهَيَانِ; أَعْشَى *purblind* (from عَشِيَ for عَشِوَ), أَعْشَيَانِ; مُسَمًّى *named* (from اِسْمٌ for سِمْوٌ), مُسَمَّيَانِ; مُرْضًى *rendered contented* (from رَضِيَ for رَضِوَ), مُرْضَيَانِ. A solitary exception seems to be مِذْرَوَانِ *the upper parts of the two buttocks*, the singular of which, if used, would be مِذْرًى.

REM. *c.* The hèmza of the termination ـَاءُ, denoting the femi-
D nine (§ 296), becomes و; as بَطْحَاءُ *a wide water-course* or *bottom*, بَطْحَاوَانِ; صَحْرَاءُ *a desert*, صَحْرَاوَانِ; حَمْرَاءُ *red*, حَمْرَاوَانِ; صَفْرَاءُ *yellow*, صَفْرَاوَانِ. Forms like حَمْرَاءَانِ, صَحْرَاءَانِ, and even صَحْرَايَانِ, are, however, said by some to be admissible.—In the termination ـَآءٌ, when sprung from a radical و or ى, the hèmza may either be retained or changed into و, though the former is preferable; as كِسَآءٌ *a dress* (for كِسَاوٌ), كِسَآءَانِ or كِسَاوَانِ; رِدَآءٌ *a mantle* (for رِدَايٌ), رِدَآءَانِ or رِدَاوَانِ. Some, however, admit the forms رِدَايَانِ

and كِسَايَانِ (comp. § 294, rem. *a*). In the case of a هَمْزَةُ ٱلْإِلْحَاقِ A
(see § 259), the better course is to change it into و; as عِلْبَآءٌ, عِلْبَاوَانِ or عِلْبَآءَانِ; حِرْبَآءٌ, حِرْبَاوَانِ or حِرْبَآءَانِ. If the hèmza of ـَآءٌ be radical, it cannot be changed into و; as قُرَّآءٌ (from قَرَأَ), قُرَّآءَانِ; وُضَّآءٌ (from وَضُؤَ), وُضَّآءَانِ.—In words of five or more letters, the rejection of the terminations ى and ـَآءٌ is admissible; as خَوْزَلَى *a sluggish mode of walking*, خَوْزَلَانِ; زِبَعْرَى *having a hairy face*,
زِبَعْرَانِ; قَبَعْثَرَى *a big, stout camel*, قَبَعْثَرَانِ; قَاصِعَآءٌ *a jerboa's hole*, B
قَاصِعَانِ; خُنْفُسَآءٌ *a black beetle*, خُنْفُسَانِ; instead of خَوْزَلَيَانِ, زِبَعْرَيَانِ, قَبَعْثَرَيَانِ, قَاصِعَاوَانِ, and خُنْفُسَاوَانِ.

Rem. *d*. If a ى has been elided in the singular after a kèsra and before a ḍamma with tènwīn (see § 167, *b*, β), it is restored in the dual; as رَامٍ, for رَامِىٌ, رَامِيَانِ; رَاضٍ, for رَاضِىٌ, رَاضِيَانِ; شَجٍ,
for شَجِىٌ, شَجِيَانِ (compare § 166, *a*).—In like manner, an elided و C
is restored in the dual of some words; as أَبٌ, أَخٌ, حَمٌ (for أَبَوٌ, أَخَوٌ, حَمَوٌ), أَبَوَانِ, أَخَوَانِ (rarely أَخَانِ), حَمَوَانِ. اِبْنٌ and اِسْمٌ (for بَنَىٌ and سِمْوٌ) have اِبْنَانِ, اِسْمَانِ; بِنْتٌ or اِبْنَةٌ makes بِنْتَانِ or اِبْنَتَانِ. يَدٌ, دَمٌ, and فَمٌ, have يَدَانِ, دَمَانِ, and فَمَانِ, rarely يَدَيَانِ, دَمَيَانِ, فَمَوَانِ, still more rarely دَمَوَانِ and فَمَيَانِ. حِرٌ makes حِرَانِ; هَنٌ, هَنَوَانِ or هَنَانِ.

Rem. *e*. If the third radical has been elided before ة in the D
singular, it is not restored; as أَمَةٌ, for أَمَوَةٌ, أَمَتَانِ; لُغَةٌ, for لُغْوَةٌ, لُغَتَانِ; لِثَةٌ, for لِثْيَةٌ, لِثَتَانِ; شَفَةٌ, for شَفْهَةٌ, شَفَتَانِ; سَنَةٌ, for سَنْهَةٌ, سَنَتَانِ; هَنَةٌ, for هَنَوَةٌ, هَنَتَانِ.

Rem. *f*. The dual is commonly employed in Arabic to signify two individuals of a class, as رَجُلَانِ *two men*, or a pair of anything, as جَلَمَانِ, or مِقَصَّانِ, *a pair of scissors*. When two objects are

A constantly associated, in virtue either of natural connection or opposition, a dual may be formed from one of them, which shall designate both, and the preference given to the one over the other is termed تَغْلِيبٌ, *the making it prevail over the other*. For example: أَبَوَانِ *father and mother*, from أَبٌ *father*; أَخَوَانِ *brother and sister*, from أَخٌ *brother*; اَلْقَمَرَانِ *the sun and moon*, from اَلْقَمَرُ *the moon*; اَلْمَشْرِقَانِ *the east and west*, from اَلْمَشْرِقُ *the east*; [اَلْعِرَاقَانِ *Baṣra*
B *and Kūfa*; اَلرَّقَّتَانِ *Rakka and Rāfika*; اَلْفُرَاتَانِ *the Euphrates and Tigris**;] اَلْحَسَنَانِ *ĕl-Ḥasan and ĕl-Ḥosèin*, from اَلْحَسَنُ *ĕl-Ḥasan* (the elder son of ‘Alī); اَلْعُمَرَانِ *‘Omar ’ibn ĕl-Ḫaṭṭāb and ’Abū Bèkr*, from عُمَرُ *‘Omar*. Compare in Sanskrit *pitarau*, "father and mother," *bhrātarau*, "brother and sister," *rōdasī*, "heaven and earth," *ahanī*, "day and night," *uśāsau*, "morning and evening," *Mitrā*, "Mitra and Varuṇa," etc.

[REM. *g*. The Arabs like to designate two different objects by
C the dual of an adjective used as a substantive and denoting a quality that the two have in common, as اَلْأَبْرَدَانِ *the two coolest* (of things) for *morning and evening*; اَلْأَطْيَبَانِ *the two best ones* for *eating and coitus*; اَلْأَحْمَرَانِ *the two red ones* for *meat and wine*; اَلْأَسْوَدَانِ *dates and water*; اَلْأَبْيَضَانِ *milk and water*; اَلْجَدِيدَانِ or اَلْأَجَدَّانِ *the two new ones* for *the night and the day*; اَلْأَصْغَرَانِ *the heart and the tongue*; اَلْكَرِيمَتَانِ *the two eyes*; اَلْأَخْبَثَانِ *urine and*
D *dung* or *sleeplessness and disquietude of mind*; اَلرَّافِدَانِ *the Tigris and Euphrates*. D. G.]

REM. *h*. The dual is sometimes formed from broken plurals (§ 300, *b*), or from أَشْبَاهُ ٱلْجَمْعِ (§ 290, *a*, ε), to designate two bodies or troops (جَمَاعَتَانِ or فِرْقَتَانِ) of the objects in question. E.g. إِبِلَانِ *two herds of camels* (إِبِلٌ), غَنَمَانِ *two flocks of sheep* or

---

* [The dual of place-names in poetry sometimes means only the two sides of the town; see Schol. on ’Ibn Hiśām, p. 121, l. 16. R. S.]

goats (غَنَمٌ), جِمَالَانِ *two herds of he-camels* (from جِمَالٌ, pl. of A
جَمَلٌ), لِقَاحَانِ *two herds of milch-camels* (from لِقَاحٌ, pl. of لِقْحَةٌ);
بَيْنَ رِمَاحَىْ مَالِكٍ وَنَهْشَلٍ *between the* (*collected*) *spears of* (*the tribes of*) *Mālik and Nahšal* (from رِمَاحٌ, pl. of رُمْحٌ); اَلْأُصُولَانِ *the fundamental principles of theology* (أُصُولُ ٱلدِّينِ) *and of law* (أُصُولُ ٱلْفِقْهِ), from أُصُولٌ, pl. of أَصْلٌ *a root;* [comp. in Hebrew חֹמֹתַיִם]. B

Rem. *i.* Proper names of the class مُرَكَّبٌ مَزْجِيٌّ (§ 264) vary in their mode of forming the dual. If the first part of the compound be indeclinable and the second declinable, the latter takes the termination ـَانِ; as مَعْدِىكَرِبُ, مَعْدِىكَرِبَانِ. But if both parts be indeclinable, as in سِيبَوَيْهِ,—or, when taken together, form a proposition, as in تَأَبَّطَ شَرًّا,—recourse must be had to a periphrasis with ذُو *possessor of;* as ذَوَا سِيبَوَيْهِ, ذَوَا تَأَبَّطَ شَرًّا, *two men called* C
Sībawèih or *Ta'abbaṭa šarran.* If the first part be in the status constructus, it is simply put in the dual, as عَبْدَا مَنَافٍ *two men called* عَبْدُ مَنَافٍ *'Abd Menāf,* أَبَوَا زَيْدٍ *two men called* أَبُو زَيْدٍ *'Abū Zèid,* ٱبْنَا ٱلزُّبَيْرِ *two men called* ٱبْنُ ٱلزُّبَيْرِ *'Ibnu 'z-Zubèir.* But in the case of compounds with أَبٌ, ٱبْنٌ, etc., it is allowable to put the second part in the dual likewise, as أَبَوَا زَيْدَيْنِ.

300. There are two kinds of *plurals* in Arabic. D

(*a*) The one, which has only a single form, is called اَلْجَمْعُ ٱلصَّحِيحُ, or اَلْجَمْعُ ٱلْمُصَحَّحُ, *the sound* or *perfect plural* (*pluralis sanus*), and اَلْجَمْعُ ٱلسَّالِمُ, or جَمْعُ ٱلسَّلَامَةِ, *the complete* or *entire plural,* because all the vowels and consonants of the singular are retained in it.

(*b*) The other, which has various forms, is called اَلْجَمْعُ ٱلْمُكَسَّرُ,

A or جَمْعُ ٱلتَّكْسِيرِ, *the broken plural* (*pluralis fractus*), because it is more or less altered from the singular by the addition or elision of consonants, or the change of vowels.

301. The pluralis sanus of masculine nouns is formed by adding the termination ـُونَ to the singular; as سَارِقٌ *a thief*, سَارِقُونَ. The pluralis sanus of feminine nouns, which end in ـَةٌ, is formed by changing ـَةٌ into ـَاتٌ, as سَارِقَةٌ, سَارِقَاتٌ; of those which do not
B end in ـَةٌ, by adding ـَاتٌ to the sing., as مَرْيَمُ *Mary*, مَرْيَمَاتٌ.

REM. *a.* If the singular ends in èlif maḳṣūra, with or without tènwīn (ـًى or ـَى),—or in kèsra with tènwīn (ـٍ), arising out of ـِيٌ (§ 167, *b*, *β*),—or in a quiescent ى preceded by kèsra (ـِى), arising out of ـِيُ,—then the rules laid down in § 166, *b*, *a* and *β*, and § 167, *a*, *β*, c, are to be observed. E.g. مُصْطَفًى, for مُصْطَفَىٌ (§ 245), *chosen*, مُصْطَفَوْنَ, for مُصْطَفَيُونَ, and in the oblique cases
C مُصْطَفَيْنَ, for مُصْطَفَيِينَ; مُوسَى *Moses*, مُوسَوْنَ for مُوسَيُونَ; قَاضٍ, for قَاضِيٌ, *a judge*, قَاضُونَ, for قَاضِيُونَ, and in the oblique cases قَاضِينَ, for قَاضِيِينَ; اَلْحَافِى, for اَلْحَافِىُ, *the barefooted*, اَلْحَافُونَ, for اَلْحَافِيُونَ; حُبْلَى *pregnant*, حُبْلَيَاتٌ; اَلصُّغْرَى *the smallest*, اَلصُّغْرَيَاتُ; سُمَانَى *a quail*, سُمَانَيَاتٌ.

REM. *b.* The gèzma of the middle radical in feminine substantives of the forms فَعْل and فَعْلَة, فِعْل and فِعْلَة, فُعْل and فُعْلَة,
D derived from roots which are not mediæ radicalis geminatæ or mediæ و vel ى, passes in forming the plural into a vowel, which may either be the same as that of the first syllable, or in all cases fètḥa. E.g. دَعْدٌ *Da'd*, دَعَدَاتٌ; أَرْضٌ *the earth, the ground*, أَرَضَاتٌ (אֲרָצוֹת); عَبْلَةُ *'Abla*, عَبَلَاتٌ; قَصْعَةٌ, جَفْنَةٌ, *a dish*, قَصَعَاتٌ, جَفَنَاتٌ; قَرْيَةٌ *a village*, قَرَيَاتٌ; غَدْوَةٌ *a coming in the morning*, غَدَوَاتٌ; هِنْدٌ *Hind*, هِنَدَاتٌ or هِنِدَاتٌ; كِسْرَةٌ *a fragment*, كِسَرَاتٌ or كِسِرَاتٌ, سِدْرَةٌ *the lotus-tree*, سِدَرَاتٌ or سِدِرَاتٌ; جُمْلٌ *Ǵuml*, جُمُلَاتٌ or

جُمَلَاتٌ ; ظُلْمَةٌ *darkness*, ظُلُمَاتٌ or ظُلَمَاتٌ ; غُرْفَةٌ *an upper chamber*, A
غُرُفَاتٌ or غُرَفَاتٌ. In the forms فُعْلٌ and فُعْلَةٌ, the ǵèzma may also be retained, as كِسْرَاتٌ, ظُلْمَاتٌ, [غُرْفَاتٌ]; but in فَعْلَةٌ this can be done only by poetic license, as رَفْضَاتٌ from رَفْضَةٌ *looseness* or *slackness (of the joints)*, زَفْرَاتٌ from زَفْرَةٌ *a sigh*. Names of men of the form فَعْلَةٌ have likewise فَعَلَاتٌ, as طَلْحَةُ *Ṭalḥa*, طَلَحَاتٌ ; حَمْزَةُ *Ḥamza*, حَمَزَاتٌ. The word عُرْسٌ or عُرُسٌ, *a wedding* or
marriage, has عُرُسَاتٌ.—In فِعْلَةٌ, if the third radical be و, the form B
فِعِلَاتٌ is not admissible, as ذِرْوَةٌ *a summit*, ذِرْوَاتٌ or ذِرَوَاتٌ (but not ذِرِوَاتٌ). A rare exception is جِرِوَاتٌ from جِرْوَةٌ *a whelp*. [If the third radical be ى, the form فِعِلَاتٌ is likewise disapproved. One may say لِحْيَاتٌ, as كِسْرَاتٌ, but not لِحِيَاتٌ, instead of which one uses لِحًى. R. S.]—In فُعْلَةٌ, if the third radical be ى, the form
فُعُلَاتٌ is inadmissible, as رُقْيَةٌ *a charm*, كُلْيَةٌ *a kidney*, رُقَيَاتٌ, C
كُلَيَاتٌ (but not رُقُيَاتٌ, كُلُيَاتٌ).—If the middle radical be و or ى, the ǵèzma of these three forms is retained; as جَوْزَةٌ *a nut*, جَوْزَاتٌ ; رَوْضَةٌ *a garden*, رَوْضَاتٌ ; بَيْضَةٌ *an egg, a helmet*, بَيْضَاتٌ ; عَيْبَةٌ *a fault*, عَيْبَاتٌ ; دِيمَةٌ (for دِوْمَةٌ) *a lasting, still rain*, دِيمَاتٌ ; بِيعَةٌ (for بِيْعَةٌ) *a church*, بِيعَاتٌ ; دُولَةٌ (for دُوْلَةٌ) *a turn of fortune, a vicissitude*, دُولَاتٌ. The vowel fètḥa is, however, admitted dialectically*,
especially in the form فَعْلَةٌ, as جَوَزَاتٌ, بَيَضَاتٌ, دِيَمَاتٌ, بِيَعَاتٌ, D
دُوَلَاتٌ.—Substantives of the forms فُعْلَةٌ, derived from verbs med. rad. gemin. always retain the ǵèzma; as ذَرَّةٌ *a mote*, ذَرَّاتٌ ; شَدَّةٌ *a charge* or *attack*, شَدَّاتٌ ; عِدَّةٌ *a certain number, a few*, عِدَّاتٌ ; سُرَّةٌ *a navel*, سُرَّاتٌ. The same is the case with all adjectives, as ضَخْمَةٌ *big*, ضَخْمَاتٌ (not ضَخَمَاتٌ); سَهْلَةٌ *easy*, سَهْلَاتٌ ; عِلْجَةٌ *fat*

* [Viz. in the dialect of Huḏèil, according to Zamaḫśari, *Fāïḳ*, i. 43. D. G.]

A *and strong,* عِلْجَاتٌ ; حُلْوَةٌ *sweet,* حُلْوَاتٌ. Exceptions are, رَبْعَةٌ *of middle stature,* رَبَعَاتٌ or رَبْعَاتٌ, and لَجْبَةٌ *having little milk* (of a sheep or goat), لَجَبَاتٌ.

REM. *c.* If و and ى, as third radicals, reject their fètḥa in the fem. singular, and become quiescent before ة, passing into ا (§ 214, and § 7, rem. *c* and *d*), they are restored in the plural along with the vowel. E.g. صَلوٰةٌ or صَلَاةٌ, *prayer* (for صَلَوَةٌ), صَلَوَاتٌ ; قَنَاةٌ,
B *a cane, spear, tube* (for قَنَوَةٌ), قَنَوَاتٌ ; فَتَاةٌ, *a young woman* (for فَتَيَةٌ), فَتَيَاتٌ ; مُرْمَاةٌ, *thrown* (for مُرْمَيَةٌ), مُرْمَيَاتٌ (compare § 167, *a*, *β*, a, with § 166, *a*).

REM. *d.* If the third radical has been elided in the sing. before ـَةٌ, it may be restored in the plural or not, according to usage. E.g. عِضَةٌ (for عِضْوَةٌ or عِضْهَةٌ) *a thorny tree,* عِضَوَاتٌ and عِضَهَاتٌ ; سَنَةٌ (for سَنْوَةٌ or سَنْهَةٌ) *a year,* سَنَوَاتٌ and سَنَهَاتٌ ; شَفَةٌ (for شَفْهَةٌ
C or شَفْوَةٌ) *a lip,* شَفَهَاتٌ or شَفَوَاتٌ ; أَمَةٌ (for أَمَوَةٌ) *a female slave,* أَمَوَاتٌ or أَمَاتٌ ; هَنَةٌ (for هَنَوَةٌ), *a thing,* هَنَوَاتٌ or هَنَاتٌ ; ظُبَةٌ (for ظُبْوَةٌ) *the point of a weapon,* ظُبَاتٌ ; بُرَةٌ (for بُرْوَةٌ) *an armlet, a ring,* بُرَاتٌ ; ثُبَةٌ (for ثُبْوَةٌ) *a troop* or *band,* ثُبَاتٌ ; لِثَةٌ (for لِثْيَةٌ) *the gum,* لِثَاتٌ ; رِئَةٌ (for رِئْيَةٌ) *a lung,* رِئَاتٌ ; مِئَةٌ (for مِئْيَةٌ) *a hundred,* مِئَاتٌ.—بِنْتٌ or ابْنَةٌ (for بَنَيَةٌ), *a daughter,* makes بَنَاتٌ ; and أُخْتٌ (for أَخَوَةٌ), *a sister,* أَخَوَاتٌ.

D REM. *e.* The hèmza in the terminations ـَآءٌ and ـَآءِ is subject to the same rules in the plural as in the dual (§ 299, rem *c*). Hence from صَحْرَآءُ, دَكَّآءُ, بَرْقَآءُ. سَمَآءٌ, are formed صَحْرَاوَاتٌ, دَكَّاوَاتٌ, بَرْقَاوَاتٌ, سَمٰوَاتٌ or سَمَاوَاتٌ.—Words of five or more letters sometimes reject the terminations ى and ـَآءُ (see § 299, rem. *c*); as حُبَارَى, حُبَارَيَاتٌ or حُبَارَاتٌ ; قَاصِعَآءُ *a jerboa's hole,* قَاصِعَاتٌ.

302. The pluralis sanus masc. is formed from :—

(*a*) Proper names of men (excepting those which end in ـَةٌ, as

طَلْحَةُ), their diminutives, and the diminutives of common nouns A
which denote rational beings; as عُثْمٰنُ *'Othmān*, عُثْمَانُونَ; عُبَيْدٌ
'Obèid (dimin. of عَبْدٌ *'Abd*), عُبَيْدُونَ; رُجَيْلٌ (dimin. of رَجُلٌ *a man*),
رُجَيْلُونَ; شُوَيْعِرٌ (dimin. of شَاعِرٌ) *an inferior poet*, شُوَيْعِرُونَ.

(*b*) Verbal adjectives which form their fem. by adding ـَةٌ.

(*c*) Adjectives of the form أَفْعَلُ, which have the comparative and superlative signification. [The corroboratives of كُلٌّ viz. أَجْمَعُ, أَكْتَعُ, etc. have also the plur. san. masc., though by their fem. sing. جَمْعَاءُ, B
كَتْعَاءُ, etc. they might seem to belong rather to the class of adjectives exemplified by أَصْفَرُ, etc. § 296. For the plur. fem. see § 304, II. 2, rem. D. G.]

(*d*) The relative adjectives in ـِىٌّ.

(*e*) The words اِبْنٌ (for بَنَىٌ) *a son*, عَالَمٌ *one of the four classes of created beings*, أَرْضٌ *the earth*, أَهْلٌ *one's family*, إِوَزٌّ *the goose*, ذُو *the possessor* (of a thing); which make بَنُونَ, عَالَمُونَ, أَرَضُونَ C
(rarely أَرْضُونَ), أَهْلُونَ, إِوَزُّونَ and ذَوُونَ (used only in the construct state ذَوُو, see § 340, rem. *c*)*.

Rem. *a*. Adjectives, however, have the plur. sanus masc. only when joined to substantives denoting rational beings.

Rem. *b*. Plurales fracti are also formed from substantives and adjectives that have the plur. sanus masc., but more especially from adjectives when used substantively. D

Rem. *c*. To the words enumerated under (*e*) may be added عِلِّيُّونَ, *the highest heavens*, and أُولُو or أُلُو (construct form of

---

* In a poem of ĕn-Nābiġa (Ahlw. App. 13, vs. 5) we find تُبَّعُونَ from تُبَّعٌ, and in the commentary on the Dīw. of Huḏèil, p. 120, last l. بُوهُونَ from بُوهٌ. We ought to mention also the expressions عَمِلَ بِهِ ٱلْعِمِلِّينَ and بَلَغْتَ مِنَّا ٱلْبُلَغِينَ, لَقِيتُ مِنْهُ ٱلْبِرَحِينَ.

A أُولُونَ, with the first syllable short, see § 340, rem. *c*), *possessors*, which have no singular; as also the numerals denoting the *tens*, from 20 up to 90 (§ 323). Further, حُشٌّ *a privy*, حُشُّونَ; هَنٌ *a thing*, هَنُونَ; حِرٌ *vulva*, حِرُونَ; and the rarer forms أَبُونَ, أَخُونَ, from أَبٌ and أَخٌ.

REM. *d.* Some fem. nouns in ـَةٌ, especially those of which the third radical (و, ى, ه) has been elided, have a plur. sanus masc., the termination ـَةٌ disappearing entirely; as حَرَّةٌ *a stony, volcanic*
B *district*, حَرُّونَ (and, very irregularly, أَحَرُّونَ); عِضَةٌ *a thorny tree*, عِضُونَ; رِئَةٌ *a lung*, رِئُونَ; كُرَةٌ *a ball, a sphere*, كُرُونَ; قُلَةٌ *a stick used by children at play*, قُلُونَ [cas. obliq. قِلِينَ]; سَنَةٌ *a year*, سِنُونَ. From the oblique case of this last word, viz. سِنِينَ, arises a secondary formation سِنِينٌ, [like مِئِينٌ § 325, rem. *a*. Comp. also ii. § 108].

REM. *e.* In proper names of the class مُرَكَّبٌ مَزْجِيٌّ (§ 264),
C the formation of the plural is analogous to that of the dual (§ 299, rem. *h*). Thus مَعْدِيكَرِبُ, in which the second member only is declinable, makes مَعْدِيكَرِبُونَ; but سِيبَوَيْهِ and تَأَبَّطَ شَرًّا, which are wholly indeclinable, form ذَوُو سِيبَوَيْهِ and ذَوُو تَأَبَّطَ شَرًّا, *men called Sībawèih* and *Ta'abbaṭa šarran.* Construct compounds, like عَبْدُ مَنَافٍ, أَبُو زَيْدٍ, and اِبْنُ ٱلزُّبَيْرِ, form عَبْدُو مَنَافٍ, آبَاءُ زَيْدٍ, and أَبْنَاءُ ٱلزُّبَيْرِ, *men called 'Abd Menāf, 'Abū Zèid*, and *'Ibnu 'z-Zubèir;*
D but in the case of compounds with أَبٌ, اِبْنٌ, etc., it is also allowable to say آبَاءُ زَيْدِينَ and the like.—It may be added that compounds with اِبْنٌ, when they are the names, not of persons, but of animals or other objects (see § 191, rem. *o*, 6), take the feminine plural بَنَاتٌ (from بِنْتٌ or اِبْنَةٌ); e.g. اِبْنُ عِرْسٍ *a weasel*, اِبْنُ مَآءٍ *a water-fowl*, اِبْنُ نَعْشٍ *any one of the stars in the tail of the Great Bear*, بَنَاتُ عِرْسٍ, etc.

[Rem. *f.* If a word in the status constructus is put in the plural, the following genitive of possession may be put also in the plural, as شِبْهُ ٱلْجَمْعِ pl. أَشْبَاهُ ٱلْجُمُوعِ or أَشْبَاهُ ٱلْجَمْعِ ; فِعْلُ ٱلْقَلْبِ, A
. أَفْعَالُ ٱلْقُلُوبِ or أَفْعَالُ ٱلْقَلْبِ ; صَاحِبُ البَرِيدِ, أَصْحَابُ البُرُدِ or
أَصْحَابُ ٱلْبَرِيدِ ; لَيْلَةُ ٱلْجُمْعَةِ has لَيَالِي ٱلْجُمَعِ ; بَيْتُ ٱلْمَالِ,
بُيُوتُ ٱلْأَمْوَالِ ; etc. D. G.]

303. The pluralis sanus fem. is formed from :— B

(*a*) Proper names of women, and such names of men as end in ـَةٌ ; as زَيْنَبُ *Zèinèb*, زَيْنَبَاتٌ ; هِنْدٌ *Hind*, هِنَدَاتٌ ; عَزَّةُ *'Azza*, عَزَّاتٌ ; طَلْحَةُ *Ṭalḥa* (a man's name), طَلَحَاتٌ (§ 301, rem. *b*).

Rem. According to some grammarians the plur. sanus fem. may be formed from *any* word ending in ـَةٌ ; as ظَبْيَةٌ *a gazelle*, ظَبَيَاتٌ ; قَرْيَةٌ *a village*, قَرَيَاتٌ ; عَلَّامَةٌ *a very learned man*, عَلَّامَاتٌ.

(*b*) Feminine adjectives, the masculine gender of which has the pluralis sanus.

(*c*) Feminine nouns in ـَى and ـَآءُ ; as حُبْلَى *pregnant*, حُبْلَيَاتٌ ; ذِكْرَى *memory*, ذِكْرَيَاتٌ ; ضَرَّآءُ *distress*, ضَرَّاوَاتٌ (§ 301, rem. *e*); حُبَارَى *a bustard*, حُبَارَيَاتٌ.

(*d*) The names of the letters, which are usually feminine (§ 292, *b*); as أَلِفٌ *an elif*, أَلِفَاتٌ ; مِيمٌ *an m*, مِيمَاتٌ.

(*e*) The names of the months; as ٱلْمُحَرَّمُ *the Moḥarram*, D
مُحَرَّمَاتٌ ; رَمَضَانُ *Ramaḍān*, رَمَضَانَاتٌ ; شَوَّالٌ *Sauwāl*, شَوَّالَاتٌ.

(*f*) The feminine nomina verbi (§ 196), and all nomina verbi of the derived forms (§ 202); as تَعْرِيفٌ *a definition*, تَعْرِيفَاتٌ ; إِقْطَاعٌ *a feof*, إِقْطَاعَاتٌ ; اِصْطِلَاحٌ *a technical term*, اِصْطِلَاحَاتٌ.

Rem. The nomina verbi of the second and fourth forms, when used in a concrete sense, admit also of a pluralis fractus; as تَصْنِيفٌ,

A تَأْلِيفٌ, *a literary composition, a book,* تَصَانِيفُ, تَوَالِيفُ (compare § 136); تَأْرِيخٌ *a date, an era, a chronicle,* تَوَارِيخُ; تَبَارِيحُ *distresses, difficulties;* تَبَاشِيرُ *annunciations, prognostics;* تَعَاجِيبُ *wonders, marvels;* إِرْجَافٌ *a false rumour,* أَرَاجِيفُ; إِسْنَادٌ *a chain* or *series of authorities,* أَسَانِيدُ.

B (*g*) Substantives of foreign origin, even when they denote persons; as سُرَادِقٌ *an awning, a tent,* سُرَادِقَاتٌ; بِيمَارِسْتَانٌ *a hospital,* بِيمَارِسْتَانَاتٌ; شَاذُرْوَانٌ *a jet d'eau, a fountain,* شَاذُرْوَانَاتٌ; أَغَا *an Aga,* أَغَوَاتٌ; بَاشَا *a Pasha,* بَاشَوَاتٌ; أُسْتَا (for أُسْتَاذٌ) *a teacher,* أُسْتَوَاتٌ.

(*h*) Many masc. substantives, which have no plur. fractus; and some fem. nouns, which have not a fem. termination; as سِبَحْلٌ *a stout camel,* سِبَحْلَاتٌ; حَمَّامٌ *a warm bath,* حَمَّامَاتٌ; جَمَادٌ *an*
C *inanimate* or *inorganic thing,* جَمَادَاتٌ; حَيَوَانٌ *a living thing, an animal,* حَيَوَانَاتٌ; عَقَارٌ *landed property,* عَقَارَاتٌ; مَاجَرَى *an event* or *occurrence* (lit. مَا جَرَى *what happened* or *occurred*), مَاجَرَيَاتٌ; أَهْلٌ *one's family* or *relations,* أَهْلَاتٌ or أَهَلَاتٌ, which some, however, derive (according to § 301, rem. *b*) from أَهْلَةٌ; عِيرٌ *a caravan of loaded camels,* عِيرَاتٌ or عِيَرَاتٌ; سَمَآءٌ *the sky* or *heavens,* سَمَاوَاتٌ (though this word is also masc.); أَرْضٌ *the earth* or *ground,* أَرَضَاتٌ (see § 301,
D rem. *b*); مَنْجَنُونٌ *a waterwheel,* مَنْجَنُونَاتٌ; عُرْسٌ or عُرُسٌ *a wedding* or *marriage,* عُرُسَاتٌ. From أَرْبَعِينَ *a collection of forty traditions* is formed أَرْبَعِينَاتٌ.

(*i*) Verbal adjectives, which are used in the plural as substantives; as كَائِنَاتٌ *entities* (from كَائِنٌ *being*); مَوْجُودَاتٌ *beings* (from مَوْجُودٌ *found, existing*); مَخْلُوقَاتٌ *creatures* (from مَخْلُوقٌ *created*); مُصَنَّفَاتٌ *literary compositions, works* (from مُصَنَّفٌ *arranged, classified*);

مُجَلَّدَاتٌ *bound books, volumes* (from مُجَلَّدٌ *covered with skin,* A
bound).

(*j*) All diminutives, except those specified in § 302, *a*; as جُبَيْلٌ *a hillock,* جُبَيْلَاتٌ; كُتَيِّبٌ *a little book,* كُتَيِّبَاتٌ.

304. The more common forms of the plur. fractus of substantives and adjectives, which are derived from triliteral roots, and in none of which (excepting أَفْعُلٌ) does any letter precede the first radical, are B
twenty-nine in number. The following is a list of these forms, with the principal corresponding singulars, and examples.

Plur. Fract.

I. فُعَلٌ. *Sing.*

1. فُعْلَةٌ; as تُحْفَةٌ *a present,* تُحَفٌ; رُكْبَةٌ *a knee,* رُكَبٌ; غُرَّةٌ *the white spot,* or *blaze* (Germ. *Blässe*), on a horse's forehead, غُرَرٌ; أُمَّةٌ *a nation,* أُمَمٌ; قُبَّةٌ [*a leather tent,*] *a dome,* قُبَبٌ; صُورَةٌ *a form,* صُوَرٌ; كُورَةٌ *a district* (Gr. χώρα), كُوَرٌ; جُذْوَةٌ *a* C
fire-brand, جُذًى (for جُذَيٌ or جُذَوٌ, § 213); كُلْيَةٌ *a kidney,* كُلًى (for كُلَيٌ); [بُهْمَةٌ *courageous,* بُهَمٌ].

2. فُعْلَى, fem. of أَفْعَلُ as a superlative (§ 234 and § 295, *b*); as اَلْكُبْرَى *the largest,* اَلْكُبَرُ; اَلصُّغْرَى *the smallest,* اَلصُّغَرُ; اَلْعُظْمَى *the greatest,* اَلْعُظَمُ; اَلْأُولَى *the first* (fem. of اَلْأَوَّلُ), اَلْأُوَلُ; اَلْعُلْيَا *the highest,* اَلْعُلَى.

Rem. Similarly أُخْرَى *other, another* (fem. of آخَرُ, see D
§ 295, rem. *b*), أُخَرُ, without tènwīn.

3. فُعْلَةٌ (especially from verba mediæ rad. و), فِعْلَةٌ, rare; as دَوْلَةٌ *a turn of fortune, a dynasty,* دُوَلٌ; نَوْبَةٌ *a turn,* نُوَبٌ; قَرْيَةٌ *a village,* قُرًى (for قُرَيٌ, § 213); لِحْيَةٌ *a beard,* لُحًى (for لُحَيٌ); حِلْيَةٌ *a trinket,* حُلًى (for حُلَيٌ).

A *Plur. Fract.*

II. فُعْلٌ. *Sing.*

1. أَفْعَلُ, not comparative and superlative (§§ 232 and 235); as أَحْمَرُ *red*, حُمْرٌ; أَحْدَبُ *humpbacked*, حُدْبٌ; أَصَمُّ *deaf*, صُمٌّ; أَبْيَضُ *white*, بِيضٌ (for بُيْضٌ); أَسْوَدُ *black*, سُودٌ (for سُوْدٌ); أَعْمَى *blind*, عُمْيٌ.

2. فَعْلَآءُ, fem. of أَفْعَلُ, not comparative and superlative (§ 296);
B as صَفْرَآءُ *yellow*, صُفْرٌ; عَرْجَآءُ *lame*, عُرْجٌ; etc. [Accordingly بَيْدَآءُ *a desert* has بِيدٌ.]

REM. جَمْعَآءُ, كَتْعَآءُ, بَصْعَآءُ, and بَتْعَآءُ (fem. of أَجْمَعُ, etc., corroboratives of كُلٌّ *all*), make جُمَعُ, كُتَعُ, بُصَعُ, بُتَعُ, without tènwīn [§ 309, *a*, δ], *all together*. [Comp. § 302, *c*, and vol. ii. § 137 and rem. *c*.]

3. فَعَالٌ, فِعَالٌ, فُعَالٌ, derived from verba med. rad. و; as عَوَانٌ
C *a middle-aged married woman*, عُونٌ (for عُوْنٌ); نَوَارٌ *timid, retiring* (of a woman), نُورٌ; بِوَانٌ *the pole of a tent*, بُونٌ; خِوَانٌ *a table, a plate*, خُونٌ; سِوَارٌ *a bracelet*, سُورٌ; أُوَارٌ *heat*, أُورٌ. [They may be contractions from original فُعُلٌ, as e.g. سِوَاكٌ *a tooth-stick*, has certainly both سُوكٌ and سُوُكٌ. R. S.]

4. فَاعِلٌ, derived from verba med. rad. و; as عَآئِذٌ *having newly had young*, عُوذٌ (for عُوْذٌ); عَآئِطٌ [and حَائِلٌ *farrow*,] *not bearing*
D *young for some years*, عُوطٌ [or عِيطٌ, حُولٌ]. [Also in some other cases, as فُرْهٌ from فَارِهٌ and بُزْلٌ from بَازِلٌ. They may, however, be contractions from فُرُهٌ and بُزُلٌ (comp. III. 5, rem.). D. G.]

[REM. نَاقَةٌ *a she-camel* has نُوقٌ.]

III. فُعُلٌ.

1. فَعَالٌ, فِعَالٌ, فُعَالٌ, not derived either from verba mediæ rad.

Plur. Fract. A

III. فُعُلٌ continued. *Sing.*

geminatæ or verba tertiæ rad. و et ى ; as رَدَاحٌ *a large bowl* or *dish*, رُدُحٌ ; قَذَالٌ *the neck*, قُذُلٌ ; سَيَالٌ *a mimosa tree*, سُيُلٌ ; كِتَابٌ *a book*, كُتُبٌ ; فِرَاشٌ *a bed*, فُرُشٌ ; خِمَارٌ *a veil*, خُمُرٌ ; حِصَانٌ *a stallion*, حُصُنٌ ; سِوَاكٌ *a tooth-stick*, سُوُكٌ ; شِيَارٌ *Saturday*, شُيُرٌ ; كُرَاعٌ *the shinbone of an animal*, كُرُعٌ ; قُرَادٌ *a tick*, قُرُدٌ. B

Rem. Exceptions are حِجَاجٌ *the bone over the eye*, حُجُجٌ ; عِنَانٌ *a rein*, عُنُنٌ. [A rare case is أُنُثٌ from أُنْثَى *female*, as though it were formed from إِنَاثٌ.]

2. فَعِيلٌ, فَعِيلَةٌ, فَعُولٌ, not derived from verba tertiæ rad. و et ى ; as قَضِيبٌ *a twig* or *rod*, قُضُبٌ ; كَثِيبٌ *a sandhill*, كُثُبٌ ; سَرِيرٌ *a seat, throne, bier*, سُرُرٌ ; سَفِينَةٌ *a ship*, سُفُنٌ ; مَدِينَةٌ *a city*, C مُدُنٌ ; صَحِيفَةٌ *a leaf* or *page*, صُحُفٌ ; عَمُودٌ *a pillar*, عُمُدٌ ; رَسُولٌ *a message, a messenger*, رُسُلٌ.

3. فَعِيلٌ, فَعُولٌ, verbal adjectives not having a passive signification, and not derived from verba tertiæ rad. و et ى ; as نَذِيرٌ *one who warns*, نُذُرٌ ; صَبُورٌ *patient*, صُبُرٌ ; ذَلُولٌ *docile*, [*a dromedary*,] ذُلُلٌ ; غَيُورٌ *jealous*, غُيُرٌ ; بَيُوضٌ *laying many eggs*, بُيُضٌ.

4. فَعْلٌ, فَعَلٌ, فَعَلَةٌ, فَعِلٌ, فَعُلٌ, rare ; as سَقْفٌ *a roof*, سُقُفٌ ; سَحْلٌ D *a thin, white piece of cloth*, سُحُلٌ ; أَسَدٌ *a lion*, أُسُدٌ ; فَلَكٌ *a sphere, the heavens*, فُلُكٌ ; وَثَنٌ *an idol*, وُثُنٌ ; بَدَنَةٌ *a victim for sacrifice*, بُدُنٌ ; خَشَبَةٌ *a piece of wood*, خُشُبٌ ; أَجَمَةٌ *a brake* or *thicket*, أُجُمٌ ; نَمِرٌ *a leopard*, نُمُرٌ ; خَشِنٌ *rough*, خُشُنٌ ; ضَبُعٌ *a hyæna*, ضُبُعٌ.

A *Plur. Fract.*

III. فُعُلٌ continued. *Sing.*

5. فَاعِلٌ, rare; as تَاجِرٌ *a merchant*, تُجُرٌ; بَازِلٌ *a full-grown camel*, بُزُلٌ.

REM. The form فُعْلٌ is admissible in all these cases*, unless the word comes from a radical mediæ geminatæ; e.g. كُتْبٌ, قُضْبٌ, رُسْلٌ, أُسْدٌ, [بُشْرٌ, غُدْرٌ], شِيرٌ (for شُيْرٌ), بِيضٌ (for
B بُيْضٌ, instead of which بُوضٌ is sometimes used), نِيبٌ *full-grown she-camels* (for نُيْبٌ), from نَابٌ (for نَيَبٌ). Forms like لَذِيذٌ *pleasant*, لُذٌّ, ذُبَابٌ *the common fly*, ذُبٌّ, are rare. Sometimes the ḍamma of words med. rad. gemin. is changed into fètḥa, as سَرِيرٌ, سُرَرٌ; جَدِيدٌ *new*, جُدُدٌ or جُدَدٌ.

IV. فِعَلٌ.

C 1. فِعْلَةٌ; as قِطْعَةٌ *a piece*, قِطَعٌ; حِكْمَةٌ *a maxim*, حِكَمٌ; لِمَّةٌ *a lock of hair*, لِمَمٌ; سِيرَةٌ *mode of walking, manner of living, character*, سِيَرٌ; إِسْوَةٌ *an example* or *pattern*, إِسًى (for إِسَيٌ); بِنْيَةٌ *a building*, بِنًى; [رِشْوَةٌ *a bribe*, رِشًا or رِشًى].

2. فَعْلَةٌ, فَعَلَةٌ, rare; as خَيْمَةٌ *a tent*, خِيَمٌ; ضَيْعَةٌ *a farm*, ضِيَعٌ; بَدْرَةٌ *a skin for milk*, بِدَرٌ; هَضْبَةٌ *a shower of rain*, هِضَبٌ;
D تَارَةٌ *a time*, تِيَرٌ; قَامَةٌ *a fathom*, قِيَمٌ; [ثَلَّةٌ *a flock of sheep*, ثِلَلٌ].

V. فِعَالٌ.

1. فَعْلٌ (not primæ or secundæ rad. ى), فِعْلٌ, فُعْلٌ; as بَحْرٌ *a sea*,

---

* [Again, شُدُفٌ *Persian curved bows* (Ṭabarī, i. 957, l. 1) is said to be the plural of شَدْفَآءُ. R. S. It may be a poetical license for شُدْفٌ. For, as a rule, just as the form فُعُلٌ may be changed into فُعْلٌ (عَلَى مَذْهَبِ ٱلتَّعْوِيضِ), so فُعْلٌ may be replaced by فُعُلٌ.]

Plur. Fract. A

V. فِعَالٌ continued. *Sing.*

بِحَارٌ ; ثَوْبٌ *a piece of cloth, a dress,* ثِيَابٌ ; ظَبْيٌ *a gazelle,* ظِبَآءٌ ; قِدْحٌ *an arrow,* قِدَاحٌ ; ذِئْبٌ *a wolf,* ذِئَابٌ ; رِيحٌ *a wind,* رِيَاحٌ ; ظِلٌّ *a shade, a shadow,* ظِلَالٌ ; رُمْحٌ *a spear,* رِمَاحٌ ; خُفٌّ *a boot,* خِفَافٌ.

2. فَعْلَةٌ, فِعْلَةٌ (rare), فُعْلَةٌ ; as قَصْعَةٌ *a dish,* قِصَاعٌ ; مَرَّةٌ *an occasion, a time,* مِرَارٌ ; رَوْضَةٌ *a garden,* رِيَاضٌ ; ضَيْعَةٌ *a farm,* ضِيَاعٌ ; لِقْحَةٌ *a milch-camel,* لِقَاحٌ ; رُقْعَةٌ *a scrap of cloth* or *paper, a note,* رِقَاعٌ ; بُقْعَةٌ *a low-lying, level district,* بِقَاعٌ ; قُبَّةٌ *a dome,* قِبَابٌ. B

REM. اِمْرَأَةٌ, *a woman,* has a plural of this form, نِسَآءٌ.

3. فَعَلٌ, فَعَلَةٌ, not derived from verba mediæ rad. geminatæ or tertiæ rad. و et ى ; as جَبَلٌ *a hill,* جِبَالٌ ; جَمَلٌ *a he-camel,* جِمَالٌ ; رَقَبَةٌ *the neck,* رِقَابٌ ; ثَمَرَةٌ *a fruit,* ثِمَارٌ ; حَسَنٌ, fem. حَسَنَةٌ, *handsome,* حِسَانٌ. C

4. فَعُلٌ ; as رَجُلٌ *a man,* رِجَالٌ ; سَبُعٌ *a beast of prey,* سِبَاعٌ ; ضَبُعٌ *a hyæna,* ضِبَاعٌ.

5. فُعْلٌ, fem. فُعْلَةٌ, verbal adjectives ; as صَعْبٌ *difficult,* صِعَابٌ ; عَذْبٌ *sweet,* عِذَابٌ ; صُلْبٌ *hard,* صِلَابٌ. D

6. فُعَلٌ ; as رُطَبٌ *fresh ripe dates,* رِطَابٌ ; رُبَعٌ *an early born camel's colt,* رِبَاعٌ ; هُبَعٌ *a late born camel's colt,* هِبَاعٌ.

7. فُعْلَى, not fem. superlatives ; as أُنْثَى *female,* إِنَاثٌ ; خُنْثَى *a hermaphrodite,* خِنَاثٌ.

A *Plur. Fract.*

V. فِعَالٌ continued. *Sing.*

8. فُعْلَانٌ, fem. فُعْلَانَةٌ, verbal adjectives; as نَدْمَانٌ *repentant*, نِدَامٌ; خُمْصَانٌ *lean, slim*, خِمَاصٌ.

9. فَعْلَانُ, fem. فَعْلَى, verbal adjectives; as عَطْشَانُ *thirsty*, عِطَاشٌ; غَضْبَانُ *angry*, غِضَابٌ; رَيَّانُ, f. رَيَّا, *satisfied with*
B *drink*, رِوَآءٌ.

10. فَعِيلٌ, fem. فَعِيلَةٌ, verbal adjectives, not having a passive signification; as كَبِيرٌ *large, old*, كِبَارٌ; كَرِيمٌ, شَرِيفٌ, *noble*, كِرَامٌ, شِرَافٌ; مَرِيضٌ *sick*, مِرَاضٌ; [ضَعِيفٌ *feeble*, ضِعَافٌ]; طَوِيلٌ *long*, طِوَالٌ (rarely طِيَالٌ); لَئِيمٌ *base*, لِئَامٌ; جَيِّدٌ (for جَوِيدٌ) *good*, جِيَادٌ; خَيْرٌ (for خَيِّرٌ, خَيِيرٌ) *good*, خِيَارٌ.

C REM. From words tertiæ rad. و et ى this form is rarely used; as نَقِىٌّ *pure*, نِقَآءٌ. An example of the passive signification is فَصِيلٌ *a weanling*, فِصَالٌ.

11. فَاعِلٌ, verbal adjectives; as صَاحِبٌ *a companion*, صِحَابٌ; تَاجِرٌ *a merchant*, تِجَارٌ; نَاهِلٌ *drinking, thirsty*, نِهَالٌ; قَآئِمٌ *standing*, قِيَامٌ; نَآئِمٌ *sleeping*, نِيَامٌ; رَاعٍ (for رَاعِىٌ) *a shepherd*,
D رِعَآءٌ; نَاوٍ *fat*, نِوَآءٌ.

[REM. *a*. Rare cases are جِيَادٌ from جَوَادٌ *a courser*; بِطَاحٌ from بَطْحَآءُ *the channel of a torrent*; عِجَافٌ from أَعْجَفُ fem. عَجْفَآءُ *lean*; عِشَارٌ and نِفَاسٌ from عُشَرَآءُ and نُفَسَآءُ.]

[REM. *b*. The plural فُعَالٌ is said to occur in a few words (see Harīrī, *Dorrat*, ed. Thorb. 97 *seq*. and H̱afāgī's comm.

Plur. Fract. A

V. فِعَالٌ continued. *Sing.*

141 *seq.*) as بُسَاطٌ from بُسْطٌ *a she-camel with her own calf*, ثُنَآءٌ from ثَنِىٌّ *a sheep* or *goat in the second year*, رُخَالٌ from رِخْلٌ or رَخِلٌ *a ewe lamb*, رُذَالٌ from رَذْلٌ *mean*, رُعَآءٌ from رَاعٍ *a shepherd*, صُبَآءٌ from صَابِئٌ *a Sabian* (see the Gloss. to
Ṭabarī). Some say that it is another form for فِعَالٌ, others B
that it is really a collective (اِسْمُ جَمْعٍ). D. G.]

VI. فُعُولٌ.

1. فَعْلٌ, فِعْلٌ, فُعْلٌ; as بَحْرٌ *a sea*, بُحُورٌ; نَفْسٌ *the soul*, نُفُوسٌ; كَهْلٌ *a middle-aged man*, كُهُولٌ; ضِرْسٌ *a molar tooth* or
grinder, ضُرُوسٌ; جِلْدٌ *a skin*, جُلُودٌ; جُنْدٌ *a military force*, C
جُنُودٌ; بُرْدٌ *a robe*, بُرُودٌ; جَيْشٌ *an army*, جُيُوشٌ; جِيدٌ *the neck*, جُيُودٌ; ظَبْىٌ *a gazelle*, ظُبِىٌّ (for ظُبُوىٌ); دَلْوٌ *a bucket*, دُلِىٌّ (for دُلُوىٌ); and, by assimilation of the vowels, ظِبِىٌّ, دِلِىٌّ (comp. § 215).

Rem. *a.* From words med. rad. و of the forms فَعْلٌ and فِعْلٌ this plural is rare; e.g. فَوْجٌ *a troop*, فُوُوجٌ; حَوْلٌ *a year*,
حُوُولٌ (or حُؤُولٌ). قَوْسٌ *a bow*, usually makes قُسِىٌّ or قِسِىٌّ, D
as if from قَسْوٌ.

Rem. *b.* In words med. rad. ى the vowel of the first syllable is sometimes assimilated to the second radical, as بَيْتٌ *a house*, بُيُوتٌ or بِيُوتٌ; شَيْخٌ *an old man, a chief, a doctor*, شُيُوخٌ or شِيُوخٌ; عَيْنٌ *an eye*, عُيُونٌ or عِيُونٌ (comp. § 269, rem. *c*).

2. فَعَلٌ, فَعِلٌ; as أَسَدٌ *a lion*, أُسُودٌ; نَدَبٌ *a scar*, نُدُوبٌ; كَبِدٌ

A *Plur. Fract.*

VI. فُعُولٌ continued. *Sing.*

the liver, كُبُودٌ ; وَعِلٌ *a mountain-goat*, وُعُولٌ ; مَلِكٌ *a king*, مُلُوكٌ ; نَابٌ (for نَيَبٌ) *a canine tooth*, نُيُوبٌ ; عَصًا *a staff*, عُصِيٌّ (for عُصُوىٌ), or by assimilation عِصِيٌّ ; دَمٌ *blood* (for دَمْوٌ, دَمَىٌ), دُمِيٌّ or دِمِيٌّ.

B REM. From words med. rad. و of the form فَعَلٌ this plural is rare; as سَاقٌ (for سَوَقٌ) *a stem* or *trunk*, سُوُوقٌ (or سُؤُوقٌ).

3. فُعْلَةٌ, فَعَلَةٌ, rare; as بَدْرَةٌ *a skin for milk, a purse of money*, بُدُورٌ ; حِقْبَةٌ *a period of time*, حُقُوبٌ ; خُرْبَةٌ *a hole*, خُرُوبٌ ; حُقَّةٌ *a casket*, حُقُوقٌ ; شَعَفَةٌ *a top* or *summit*, شُعُوفٌ ; دَوَاةٌ
C *an inkhorn*, دُوِيٌّ or دِوِيٌّ.

4. فَاعِلٌ, verbal adjectives, not mediæ rad. gemin. or med. rad. و vel ى ; as وَاقِفٌ *standing*, وُقُوفٌ ; قَاعِدٌ, جَالِسٌ, *sitting*, جُلُوسٌ, قُعُودٌ ; شَاهِدٌ *a witness*, شُهُودٌ ; عَاتٍ *proud, wicked*, عُتِيٌّ (for عُتُوىٌ) or عِتِيٌّ ; بَاكٍ *weeping*, بُكِيٌّ or بِكِيٌّ.

[REM. Rare cases are ضُلُوعٌ from ضِلَعٌ (ضِلْعٌ) *a rib*;
D أُرُومٌ from إِرَمٌ (أَرِمٌ) *a stone set up*; ظُرُوفٌ from ظَرِيفٌ *elegant*.]

VII. فُعَّلٌ.

1. فَاعِلٌ, verbal adjectives, not derived from verba tertiæ rad. و et ى (with rare exceptions); as سَاجِدٌ *prostrating oneself*, سُجَّدٌ ; سَامِرٌ *conversing at night*, سُمَّرٌ ; نَائِمٌ *sleeping*, نُوَّمٌ and نُيَّمٌ ; صَائِمٌ *fasting*, صُوَّمٌ and صُيَّمٌ ; شَائِلٌ *pregnant*, شُوَّلٌ and شُيَّلٌ ;

Plur. Fract. A

VII. فُعَّلٌ continued. *Sing.*

[حَائِضٌ *menstruating*, حُيَّضٌ; طَالِقٌ *repudiated*, طُلَّقٌ]; غَائِبٌ *absent*, غُيَّبٌ; غَازٍ *a soldier*, غُزًّى (for غُزَّىٌ or غُزَّوٌ, § 213).

2. فَاعِلَةٌ, fem. of the preceding; as نَائِحَةٌ *mourning*, نُوَّحٌ.

Rem. *a.* The substitution of *kèsr* for *ḍamm* is allowable in the first syllable of فُعَّلٌ from verba med. و et ى, in which B case the و must be changed into ى; as خِيَّفٌ for خُيَّفٌ, خُوَّفٌ, from خَائِفٌ *fearing*; صِيَّمٌ, from صَائِمٌ *fasting*; etc.

[Rem. *b.* Anomalous is عُزَّلٌ from أَعْزَلُ *having no weapon.*]

VIII. فُعَّالٌ.

فَاعِلٌ, verbal adjectives, not derived from verba tertiæ rad. و et ى [or med. gem.] (with rare exceptions); as حَاكِمٌ *a judge*, حُكَّامٌ; تَابِعٌ *a follower*, تُبَّاعٌ; صَانِعٌ *an artisan*, صُنَّاعٌ; كَافِرٌ *an* C *unbeliever*, كُفَّارٌ; جَاهِلٌ *ignorant*, جُهَّالٌ; نَائِبٌ *a deputy*, نُوَّابٌ; نَائِمٌ *sleeping*, نُوَّامٌ; غَازٍ *a soldier*, غُزَّاءٌ; جَانٍ *an offender*, جُنَّاءٌ; [صَادٌّ *avoiding*, صُدَّادٌ]*.

IX. فَعَلَةٌ.

1. فَاعِلٌ, verbal adjectives, denoting rational beings, and not derived from verba tertiæ rad. و et ى; as فَاعِلٌ *a workman*, D فَعَلَةٌ; كَافِرٌ *an unbeliever*, كَفَرَةٌ; كَامِلٌ *perfect*, كَمَلَةٌ; سَاحِرٌ *a conjuror*, سَحَرَةٌ; بَارٌّ *pious, dutiful*, بَرَرَةٌ; طَائِعٌ *obedient*, طَاعَةٌ (for طَوَعَةٌ); بَائِعٌ *selling*, بَاعَةٌ (for بَيَعَةٌ).

---

* [فُلَّالٌ *defeated, fugitives*, properly pl. of فَالٌّ, is by usage pl. of فَلٌّ. R. S.]

A *Plur. Fract.*

IX. فَعَلَةٌ continued. *Sing.*

REM. فَاعِلٌ from verba med. و sometimes remains uncontracted in the plural; as جَآئِرٌ *acting wrongly*, جَوَرَةٌ or جَارَةٌ; حَآئِكٌ *a weaver*, حَوَكَةٌ or حَاكَةٌ; خَآئِنٌ *treacherous*, خَوَنَةٌ or خَانَةٌ.

B [2. فَعِيلٌ rare, as خَبِيثٌ *bad*, خَبَثَةٌ; ضَعِيفٌ *feeble*, ضَعَفَةٌ; سَرِيٌّ *generous*, سَرَاةٌ; سَيِّدٌ *a chief*, سَادَةٌ.]

X. فُعَلَةٌ.

فَاعِلٌ, verbal adjectives, denoting rational beings, and derived from verba tertiæ rad. و et ى; as غَازٍ *a soldier*, غُزَاةٌ (for غُزَوَةٌ), قَاضٍ *a judge*, قُضَاةٌ (for قُضَيَةٌ); رَاوٍ *a reciter, rehearser,*

C or *traditionary*, رُوَاةٌ (for رُوَيَةٌ); جَانٍ *a sinner*, جُنَاةٌ (for جُنَيَةٌ); سَاعٍ *a manager*, سُعَاةٌ. [And so in the dialect of Ḥijāz اَلصُّبَاةُ (*Sabians*) for اَلصَّابِئُونَ, a nickname given to the first Muslims. R. S.]

[REM. An exception is بُزَاةٌ from بَازٍ *a falcon.*]

D XI. فِعَلَةٌ.

1. فُعْلٌ, not derived from verba tertiæ rad. و et ى; as قُرْطٌ *an earring*, قِرَطَةٌ; دُرْجٌ *a case* or *casket*, دِرَجَةٌ; غُصْنٌ *a branch*, غِصَنَةٌ; دُبٌّ *a bear*, دِبَبَةٌ; كُوزٌ *a jug*, كِوَزَةٌ; صُلْبٌ *a rugged place*, صِلَبَةٌ; تُرْسٌ *a shield*, تِرَسَةٌ.

2. فَعْلٌ, فِعْلٌ, with the same restriction, rare; as ثَوْرٌ *an ox*, ثِوَرَةٌ or ثِيَرَةٌ; زَوْجٌ *a husband* or *wife*, زِوَجَةٌ; شَيْخٌ *an old*

Plur. Fract. A

XI. فِعَلَةٌ continued. *Sing.*

man, شِيَخَةٌ ; غَرْدٌ *a truffle,* غِرَدَةٌ ; رَطْلٌ *soft, lax, flaccid,* رِطَلَةٌ ; قِرْدٌ *an ape,* قِرَدَةٌ ; هِرٌّ, قِطٌّ *a tom-cat,* قِطَطَةٌ, هِرَرَةٌ ; دِيكٌ *a cock,* دِيَكَةٌ ; فِيلٌ *an elephant,* فِيَلَةٌ.

XII. فِعْلَةٌ. B

1. فَعْلٌ ; as ثَوْرٌ *a bull,* ثِيرَةٌ ; شَيْخٌ *an old man,* شِيخَةٌ.

2. فَعَلٌ ; as وَلَدٌ *a child,* وِلْدَةٌ ; جَارٌ (for جَوَرٌ) *a neighbour,* جِيرَةٌ ; قَاعٌ *level ground,* قِيعَةٌ ; أَخٌ (for أَخَوٌ) *a brother,* إِخْوَةٌ ; فَتًى (for فَتَيٌ) *a youth,* فِتْيَةٌ.

3. فَعَالٌ, فُعَالٌ ; as غَزَالٌ *a gazelle,* غِزْلَةٌ ; غُلَامٌ *a youth, a slave,* غِلْمَةٌ ; شُجَاعٌ *brave,* شِجْعَةٌ. C

4. فَعِيلٌ ; as صَبِيٌّ (for صَبِيوٌ) *a boy,* صِبْيَةٌ ; جَلِيلٌ *thick, coarse, big, great,* جِلَّةٌ ; خَصِيٌّ *a gelding, a eunuch,* خِصْيَةٌ.

REM. اِمْرَأَةٌ *a woman,* has a plural of this form, نِسْوَةٌ.

[The plural فِعْلَةٌ varies in almost all cases with فِعْلَانٌ. R.S.]

XIII. أَفْعُلٌ. D

1. فَعْلٌ, not derived from verba mediæ rad. و et ى ; as بَحْرٌ *a sea,* أَبْحُرٌ ; نَفْسٌ *the soul,* أَنْفُسٌ ; فَلْسٌ *a copper coin,* أَفْلُسٌ ; [سَطْرٌ *a line of writing,* أَسْطُرٌ] ; ضَبٌّ *a lizard,* أَضُبٌّ (for أَضْبُبٌ) ; وَجْهٌ *the face,* أَوْجُهٌ ; دَلْوٌ *a bucket,* أَدْلٍ (for أَدْلُيٌ or أَدْلُوٌ) ; ظَبْيٌ *an antelope,* أَظْبٍ (for أَظْبُيٌ) ; يَدٌ (for يَدْيٌ) *the hand,* أَيْدٍ (for أَيْدُيٌ).

A *Plur. Fract.*

XIII. أَفْعُلٌ continued. *Sing.*

REM. Exceptions are, for example, ثَوْبٌ *a piece of cloth, a garment,* أَثْوُبٌ or أَثْؤُبٌ; قَوْسٌ *a bow,* أَقْوُسٌ or أَقْؤُسٌ; سَيْفٌ *a sword,* أَسْيُفٌ; عَيْنٌ *an eye, a fountain,* أَعْيُنٌ.

2. Feminine quadriliterals, not ending in ـَةٌ, which have a quiescent letter (long vowel) between the second and third radicals; as ذِرَاعٌ *the arm,* أَذْرُعٌ; عَنَاقٌ *a female kid,* أَعْنُقٌ;

B يَمِينٌ *the right hand, an oath,* أَيْمُنٌ; شِمَالٌ *the left hand,* أَشْمُلٌ; لِسَانٌ *the tongue**, أَلْسُنٌ; عُقَابٌ *an eagle,* أَعْقُبٌ.

3. فَعَلٌ, فِعْلٌ, فُعْلٌ, not derived from verba mediæ rad. و et ى, rare; as جَبَلٌ *a hill,* أَجْبُلٌ; زَمَنٌ *time,* أَزْمُنٌ; عَصًا (for عَصَوٌ) *a staff,* أَعْصٍ (for أَعْصُىٌ or أَعْصُوٌ); رِجْلٌ *a leg* or *foot,* أَرْجُلٌ; شِبْلٌ *a lion's cub,* أَشْبُلٌ; ذِئْبٌ *a wolf,* أَذْؤُبٌ; قُفْلٌ *a lock,* أَقْفُلٌ.

C REM. بِئْرٌ, *a well,* has أَبْؤُرٌ and, by transposition, آبُرٌ. From radicals mediæ و et ى occur, for example, دَارٌ *a house,* أَدْوُرٌ, أَدْؤُرٌ, and, by transposition, آدُرٌ; سَاقٌ *the shank,* أَسْوُقٌ, أَسْؤُقٌ; نَارٌ *fire,* أَنْوُرٌ; نَابٌ (for نَيَبٌ) *a canine tooth,* أَنْيُبٌ.

4. فَعَلَةٌ, rare; as أَكَمَةٌ *a hillock,* آكُمٌ; رَقَبَةٌ *the neck,* أَرْقُبٌ; أَمَةٌ *a maidservant,* (for أَمَوَةٌ), آمٍ (for أَأْمُىٌ); نَاقَةٌ *a she-camel,* أَنْوُقٌ, أَنْؤُقٌ, and أَنْيُقٌ, whence, by transposition, أَيْنُقٌ and,

D dialectically, أَوْنُقٌ.

REM. أَفْعُلٌ occurs now and then in a few other forms; as نَمِرٌ *a leopard,* أَنْمُرٌ; سَبُعٌ *a beast of prey,* أَسْبُعٌ; ضِلَعٌ *a rib,* أَضْلُعٌ; نَهَارٌ *day,* أَنْهُرٌ; غُرَابٌ *a raven,* أَغْرُبٌ; etc.

---

* [If fem.; for if masc. it has أَلْسِنَةٌ (XV. 1), according to El-Mubarrad 50, l. 5 *seq.* D. G.]

Plur. Fract. A

XIV. أَفْعَالٌ. *Sing.*

1. Triliterals of all forms, especially فَعَلٌ, rarely فَعْلٌ (see no. 2) and فُعَلٌ; as قَدَمٌ *a footstep,* أَقْدَامٌ; طَلَلٌ *a vestige* or *trace,* أَطْلَالٌ; مَطَرٌ *rain,* أَمْطَارٌ; بَابٌ (for بَوَبٌ) *a door,* أَبْوَابٌ; نَابٌ (for نَيَبٌ) *a canine tooth, an old she-camel,* أَنْيَابٌ; اِبْنٌ (for بَنَىٌ) *a son,* أَبْنَاءٌ; أَبٌ (for أَبَوٌ) *a father,* آبَاءٌ; بِئْرٌ *a well,* أَبْآرٌ
or, by transposition, آبَارٌ; رَأْىٌ *idea, belief, opinion,* أَرْآءٌ or آرَآءٌ; B
حِمْلٌ *a load,* أَحْمَالٌ; عِيدٌ *a festival,* أَعْيَادٌ; إِبْطٌ *the armpit,* آبَاطٌ; قُفْلٌ *a lock,* أَقْفَالٌ; حُكْمٌ *a judgment,* أَحْكَامٌ; أُذْنٌ or أُذُنٌ *an ear,* آذَانٌ; حُرٌّ *free,* أَحْرَارٌ; اِسْمٌ (for سِمْوٌ) *a name,* أَسْمَآءٌ; عَضُدٌ *the arm,* أَعْضَادٌ; عِنَبٌ *grapes,* أَعْنَابٌ; إِبِلٌ *a herd of camels,* آبَالٌ; نَمِرٌ *a leopard,* أَنْمَارٌ; فَخِذٌ *a thigh,* أَفْخَاذٌ; فَرْخٌ *the young of a bird,* أَفْرَاخٌ; أَلْفٌ *a thousand,* آلَافٌ;
بَرٌّ *pious, dutiful,* أَبْرَارٌ; فَنٌّ *a branch,* أَفْنَانٌ; رُطَبٌ *fresh* C
ripe dates, أَرْطَابٌ.

2. فَعْلٌ, from verba mediæ rad. و et ى, and primæ rad. و; as ثَوْبٌ *a dress,* أَثْوَابٌ; سَيْفٌ *a sword,* أَسْيَافٌ; يَوْمٌ *a day,* أَيَّامٌ (for أَيْوَامٌ); وَقْتٌ *time,* أَوْقَاتٌ; وَهْمٌ *a fancy, a notion, a mistake,* أَوْهَامٌ.

Rem. شَيْءٌ, *a thing,* makes أَشْيَآءُ, and not (as one would D
naturally expect) أَشْيَآءٌ.

3. فَاعِلٌ, rare; as نَاصِرٌ *a helper,* أَنْصَارٌ; شَاهِدٌ *a witness,* أَشْهَادٌ; طَاهِرٌ *pure,* أَطْهَارٌ; صَاحِبٌ *a companion, a friend,* أَصْحَابٌ; فَاتِرٌ *tepid,* أَفْتَارٌ.

4. فَعِيلٌ, verbal adjectives, not having a passive signification,

A *Plur. Fract.*

XIV. أَفْعَالٌ continued. *Sing.*

rare; as شَرِيفٌ *noble*, أَشْرَافٌ; مَيِّتٌ or مَيْتٌ (for مَوِيتٌ, § 242), *dead*, أَمْوَاتٌ.

REM. أَفْعَالٌ occurs now and then in a few other forms; as عَدُوٌّ *an enemy*, أَعْدَآءٌ; فَلُوٌّ *a weaned foal, a colt*, أَفْلَآءٌ; يَمِينٌ *a right hand, an oath*, أَيْمَانٌ; جَنَانٌ *the heart*, أَجْنَانٌ.

B XV. أَفْعِلَةٌ.

1. Quadriliterals, of which the penult letter is quiescent (a long vowel), especially nouns of the forms فَعَالٌ, فِعَالٌ, and فُعَالٌ; as جَنَاحٌ *a wing*, أَجْنِحَةٌ; طَعَامٌ *food*, أَطْعِمَةٌ; زَمَانٌ *time*, أَزْمِنَةٌ; دَوَآءٌ *physic*, أَدْوِيَةٌ; غِذَآءٌ *food*, أَغْذِيَةٌ; لِسَانٌ *the tongue**, أَلْسِنَةٌ; حِمَارٌ *an ass*, أَحْمِرَةٌ; إِلٰهٌ *a god*, آلِهَةٌ (for أَأْلِهَةٌ); إِمَامٌ
C *an 'imām* or *priest*, أَيِمَّةٌ or أَئِمَّةٌ (for أَأْمِمَةٌ); فِنَآءٌ *a courtyard*, أَفْنِيَةٌ; فُؤَادٌ *the heart*, أَفْئِدَةٌ; غُرَابٌ *a raven*, أَغْرِبَةٌ; غُلَامٌ *a youth*, أَغْلِمَةٌ; زُقَاقٌ *a lane, a strait*, أَزِقَّةٌ; عَمُودٌ *a pillar*, أَعْمِدَةٌ; رَغِيفٌ *a cake of bread*, أَرْغِفَةٌ; قَضِيبٌ *a branch, a rod*, أَقْضِبَةٌ; كَثِيبٌ *a sand-hill*, أَكْثِبَةٌ; قَفِيزٌ *a certain measure*, أَقْفِزَةٌ.

2. فَعِيلٌ, verbal adjectives, derived from verba mediæ rad.
D geminatæ or ultimæ rad. و et ى; as عَزِيزٌ *mighty, glorious*, أَعِزَّةٌ (for أَعْزِزَةٌ); عَفِيفٌ *temperate, chaste*, أَعِفَّةٌ; شَحِيحٌ *niggardly, stingy*, أَشِحَّةٌ; حَبِيبٌ *dear*, أَحِبَّةٌ; صَبِيٌّ *a boy* (for صَبِيوٌ), أَصْبِيَةٌ; نَجِيٌّ *a confidant*, أَنْجِيَةٌ; عَيِيٌّ *stammering, stuttering*, أَعْيِيَةٌ.

---

* [If masc.; see the footnote to XIII. 2.]

Plur. Fract. A

XV. أَفْعِلَةٌ continued. *Sing.*

3. فَعْلٌ, فِعْلٌ, فُعْلٌ, rare; as فَرْخٌ *the young of a bird,* أَفْرِخَةٌ; نَعْلٌ *a shoe,* أَنْعِلَةٌ; نَجْدٌ *a high land,* أَنْجِدَةٌ; زِرٌّ *a button,* أَزِرَّةٌ (for أَزْرِرَةٌ); بُرْجٌ *a tower,* أَبْرِجَةٌ; جُحْرٌ *the hole of a reptile,* أَجْحِرَةٌ. B

4. فَعَلٌ, فُعَلٌ, rare; as طَبَقٌ *a cover* or *lid,* أَطْبِقَةٌ; زَادٌ (for زَوَدٌ) *provisions,* أَزْوِدَةٌ; خَالٌ (for خَوَلٌ) *an uncle* (*by the mother's side*), أَخْوِلَةٌ; قَفًا (for قَفَىٌ or قَفَوٌ) *the back of the neck,* أَقْفِيَةٌ; [حَيًا *vulva,* أَحْيِيَةٌ]; نَدًى *moisture, dew,* أَنْدِيَةٌ; خُزَزٌ *a buck-hare,* أَخِزَّةٌ (for أَخْزِزَةٌ).

Rem. أَفْعِلَةٌ is rarely used in some other forms; as سِحَاءَةٌ or سِحَايَةٌ *a sealed strip of paper* (with which a letter is bound), أَسْحِيَةٌ; وَادٍ *a watercourse,* أَوْدِيَةٌ; نَادٍ *an assembly,* أَنْدِيَةٌ. C

XVI. فَوَاعِلُ*.

1. فَاعَلٌ; as خَاتَمٌ *a signet-ring,* خَوَاتِمُ; طَابَعٌ *a seal,* طَوَابِعُ; طَابَقٌ *a pot, a crucible,* طَوَابِقُ; قَالَبٌ *a mould,* قَوَالِبُ.

2. فَاعِلٌ, substantives; بَاعِثٌ *a motive* or *cause,* بَوَاعِثُ; حَافِرٌ D *a hoof* (of a horse or ass), حَوَافِرُ; جَانِبٌ *a side,* جَوَانِبُ; كَاهِلٌ *the space between the shoulders,* كَوَاهِلُ; غَارِبٌ *the top of a*

* [By the influence of و the preceding Fètḥa often, in vulgar pronunciation, passes into ḍamma, as طُوَارِق *Touareg,* جُوَارٍ *female slaves.* In the old language there are some instances of it in proper names, e.g. صُوَائِقُ, عُوَارِضُ, عُوَاهِمُ, كُوَاكِبُ. D. G.]

A *Plur. Fract.*

XVI. فَوَاعِلُ continued. *Sing.*

camel's hump, of a wave, etc., غَوَارِبُ ; سَاحِلٌ *the seashore,* سَوَاحِلُ ; شَاهِدٌ *an example,* شَوَاهِدُ.

3. فَاعِلٌ, verbal adjectives, applicable to men, rare; as فَارِسٌ *a horseman,* فَوَارِسُ ; تَابِعٌ *a follower,* تَوَابِعُ ; نَاكِسٌ *hanging*
B *the head,* نَوَاكِسُ ; هَالِكٌ *perishing,* هَوَالِكُ ; خَالِفٌ *remaining behind,* خَوَالِفُ.

4. فَاعِلٌ, verbal adjectives, applicable by their signification only to females (§ 297, *d*, rem.); as حَامِلٌ *pregnant,* حَوَامِلُ ; حَائِضٌ *menstruating* حَوَائِضُ ; طَالِقٌ *divorced,* طَوَالِقُ ; نَاهِدٌ *having swelling breasts,* نَوَاهِدُ.

C 5. فَاعِلَةٌ, substantives and fem. verbal adjectives; as فَاكِهَةٌ *fruit,* فَوَاكِهُ ; صَاعِقَةٌ *a thunderbolt,* صَوَاعِقُ ; نَادِرَةٌ *a rarity, a witticism, a joke,* نَوَادِرُ ; آنِسَةٌ *cheerful, sociable,* أَوَانِسُ ; صَاحِبَةٌ *a female companion,* صَوَاحِبُ ; خَاصَّةٌ *distinguished people, the upper classes,* خَوَاصُّ (for خَوَاصِصُ) ; عَامَّةٌ *common people, the vulgar,* عَوَامُّ (for عَوَامِمُ) ; فَائِدَةٌ *gain, profit,* فَوَائِدُ ; جَارِيَةٌ
D *a girl,* جَوَارٍ (for جَوَارِيُ, see no. XXIII., rem.) ; نَاحِيَةٌ *a quarter of the sky, a region, a district,* نَوَاحٍ (for نَوَاحِيُ).

REM. Initial و is changed into أ ; as وَاصِلَةٌ *joining* or *adding, a proximate cause,* أَوَاصِلُ (for وَوَاصِلُ) ; وَاقِيَةٌ *custody, a guard,* أَوَاقٍ (for وَوَاقٍ , وَوَاقِيُ), which is also the plural of أُوقِيَّةٌ = وَاقِيَةٌ *an ounce.*

Plur. Fract. A

XVI. فَوَاعِلُ continued. *Sing.*

6. فَاعِلَآءُ ; as حَاثِيَآءُ, دَامَّآءُ, قَاصِعَآءُ, نَافِقَآءُ, *holes of the jerboa*, حَوَاثٍ (for حَوَاثِىُ), دَوَامُّ (for دَوَامِمُ), قَوَاصِعُ, نَوَافِقُ ; سَابِيَآءُ *a caul*, سَوَابٍ (for سَوَابِىُ).

XVII. فَعَآئِلُ.

Fem. quadriliterals, of which the third letter is servile or quiescent (a long vowel), whether they have the fem. termination ـَةٌ , or not; as سَحَابَةٌ *a cloud*, سَحَآئِبُ ; رِسَالَةٌ *an embassy, a letter, a treatise*, رَسَآئِلُ ; ذُؤَابَةٌ *a lock of hair*, ذَوَآئِبُ ; جُعَالَةٌ or جَعِيلَةٌ *wages*, جَعَائِلُ ; جَزِيرَةٌ *an island*, جَزَآئِرُ ; صَحِيفَةٌ *a written leaf, a letter, a book*, صَحَآئِفُ ; صَفِيحَةٌ *a board* or *plank, a slab*, صَفَآئِحُ ; كَرِيمَةٌ *noble*, كَرَآئِمُ ; ذَبِيحَةٌ *slaughtered, a victim*, ذَبَآئِحُ ; حَلُوبَةٌ *a milch-camel*, حَلَآئِبُ ; شَمَالٌ *the north wind*, شَمَآئِلُ ; شِمَالٌ *the left hand*, شَمَآئِلُ ; جَزُورٌ *a she-camel for slaughter**, جَزَآئِرُ ; عَجُوزٌ *an old woman*, عَجَآئِزُ ; ذَنُوبٌ *a large bucket*, ذَنَآئِبُ. B C

Rem. فَعَآئِلُ occurs rarely in a few other cases; as أَفِيلٌ *a young camel*, أَفَآئِلُ ; ضَمِيرٌ *a pronoun*, ضَمَآئِرُ ; [دَلِيلٌ *a proof*, دَلَآئِلُ ; وَصِيدٌ *a court*, وَصَآئِدُ] ; حَاجَةٌ *a want* or *need, a thing, affair* or *business*, حَوَآئِجُ ; ضَرَّةٌ *a second wife*, ضَرَآئِرُ ; حُرَّةٌ *a free woman*, حَرَآئِرُ ; [كَنَّةٌ *a daughter in law*, كَنَائِنُ ; مَرَائِرُ ٱلشَّجَرِ *bitter kinds of trees*, from مُرَّةٌ] ; لَيْلٌ *the night*, لَيَآئِلُ. D

* [Also applied to the male, but nevertheless fem. gen. D. G.]

A *Plur. Fract.*

XVIII. فِعْلَانٌ. *Sing.*

1. فُعْلٌ, from radicals mediæ و; as حُوتٌ, نُونٌ, *a fish*, حِيتَانٌ, نِينَانٌ; سُورٌ *a wall*, سِيرَانٌ; عُودٌ *a piece of wood, a branch*, عِيدَانٌ; دُودٌ *a worm*, دِيدَانٌ.

B 2. فَعَلٌ; as خَرَبٌ *a male bustard*, خِرْبَانٌ; وَصَعٌ *a kind of small bird*, وِصْعَانٌ; وَرَلٌ *a lizard*, وِرْلَانٌ; تَاجٌ (for تَوَجٌ) *a crown*, تِيجَانٌ; بَابٌ *a door*, بِيبَانٌ; جَارٌ *a neighbour*, جِيرَانٌ; نَارٌ *fire*, نِيرَانٌ; فَتًى (for فَتَيٌ) *a youth*, فِتْيَانٌ; أَخٌ (for أَخَوٌ) *a brother*, إِخْوَانٌ.

3. فُعَلٌ; as صُرَدٌ *a kind of bird*, صِرْدَانٌ; نُغَرٌ *a nightingale*,
C نِغْرَانٌ; جُرَدٌ *a field-rat*, جِرْذَانٌ; خُزَزٌ *a buck-hare*, خِزَّانٌ; جُعَلٌ *a black beetle*, جِعْلَانٌ.

4. فُعَالٌ, and more rarely فَعَالٌ and فِعَالٌ; as غُلَامٌ *a boy, a slave*, غِلْمَانٌ; غُرَابٌ *a raven*, غِرْبَانٌ; عُقَابٌ *an eagle*, عِقْبَانٌ; ذُبَابٌ *a fly*, ذِبَّانٌ; غَزَالٌ *a gazelle*, غِزْلَانٌ; شِهَابٌ *a firebrand, a meteor*, شِهْبَانٌ; صِوَارٌ *a herd of wild cattle*, صِيرَانٌ.

D 5. فَعْلٌ and فِعْلٌ, rare; as عَبْدٌ *a slave*, عِبْدَانٌ; وَغْدٌ *a slave*, وِغْدَانٌ; ثَوْرٌ *a bull*, ثِيرَانٌ; ضَيْفٌ *a guest*, ضِيفَانٌ; فَأْرٌ *a mouse*, فِئْرَانٌ; رَأْلٌ *a young ostrich*, رِئْلَانٌ; صِنْوٌ *one of two or more trees growing from a single root*, صِنْوَانٌ; قِنْوٌ *a bunch of dates*, قِنْوَانٌ; نِيرٌ *a yoke*, نِيرَانٌ.

6. فَعِيلٌ, rare; as قَضِيبٌ *a branch*, قِضْبَانٌ; ظَلِيمٌ *a male ostrich*,

Plur. Fract. A

XVIII. فِعْلَانٌ continued. *Sing.*

ظِلْمَانٌ ; صَبِىٌّ (for صَبِيوٌ) *a boy* or *child*, صِبْيَانٌ ; خَصِىٌّ *a gelding, a eunuch*, خِصْيَانٌ.

. [7. فَعُولٌ, rare ; as خَرُوفٌ *a lamb*, خِرْفَانٌ.]

8. فُعَيْلٌ, فُعَيْلَةٌ, not diminutives, rare ; as جُمَيْلٌ, كُعَيْتٌ, *a nightingale*, جِمْلَانٌ, كِعْتَانٌ ; تُمَيْلَةٌ *a sort of wild cat*, تِمْلَانٌ. B

9. فَعَلَانٌ, rare ; as شَقَذَانٌ *a male chamæleon*, شِقْذَانٌ ; كَرَوَانٌ *a bustard*, كِرْوَانٌ ; وَرَشَانٌ *a wood-pigeon*, وِرْشَانٌ.

10. فَاعِلٌ, rare ; as حَآئِطٌ *a wall*, حِيطَانٌ ; جَانٌّ *a spiritual being of the class called* اَلْجِنُّ, جِنَّانٌ.

REM. أَمَةٌ (for أَمَوَةٌ), *a maidservant*, has إِمْوَانٌ ; and C
اِمْرَأَةٌ, *a woman*, an irregular plural نِسْوَانٌ.

XIX. فُعْلَانٌ.

1. فَعْلٌ, more rarely فِعْلٌ ; as سَقْفٌ *a roof*, سُقْفَانٌ ; وَغْدٌ *a slave*, وُغْدَانٌ ; عَبْدٌ *a slave*, عُبْدَانٌ ; ظَهْرٌ *the back, the short side of a wing-feather*, ظُهْرَانٌ ; بَطْنٌ *the belly, the long side of a wing-feather*, بُطْنَانٌ ; [حَبٌّ *grain*, حُبَّانٌ ;] ذِئْبٌ *a wolf*, ذُؤْبَانٌ ; D
قِنْوٌ *a bunch of dates*, قُنْوَانٌ ; زِقٌّ *a skin for water, etc.*, زُقَّانٌ.

2. فَعَلٌ ; as بَلَدٌ *a town*, بُلْدَانٌ ; بَرَقٌ, حَمَلٌ, *a lamb*, بُرْقَانٌ, حُمْلَانٌ ; ذَكَرٌ *a male*, ذُكْرَانٌ.

3. فُعَالٌ, rare ; as زُقَاقٌ *a lane, a strait*, زُقَّانٌ ; شُجَاعٌ *brave*, شُجْعَانٌ ; شِهَابٌ *a firebrand, a meteor*, شُهْبَانٌ ; حُوَارٌ *an unweaned foal of a camel*, حُورَانٌ.

A *Plur. Fract.*

XIX. فُعْلَانٌ continued. *Sing.*

4. فَعِيلٌ; as رَغِيفٌ *a cake of bread,* رُغْفَانٌ; قَضِيبٌ *a twig* or *rod,* قُضْبَانٌ; كَثِيبٌ *a sand-hill,* كُثْبَانٌ; ظَلِيمٌ *a male ostrich,* ظُلْمَانٌ; خَلِيلٌ *a friend,* خُلَّانٌ; قَرِيٌّ *a channel for irrigation,* قُرْيَانٌ; صَبِيٌّ *a boy* or *child,* صُبْيَانٌ.

B 5. فَاعِلٌ, verbal adjectives, used as substantives and not derived from verba mediæ rad. و et ى; as رَاكِبٌ *a rider,* رُكْبَانٌ; صَاحِبٌ *a companion,* صُحْبَانٌ; فَارِسٌ *a horseman,* فُرْسَانٌ; رَاهِبٌ *a Christian ascetic* or *recluse,* رُهْبَانٌ; شَابٌّ *a youth,* شُبَّانٌ; رَاعٍ *a shepherd,* رُعْيَانٌ.

6. أَفْعَلُ, fem. فَعْلَآءُ; as أَحْمَرُ *red,* حُمْرَانٌ; أَصْلَعُ *bald,* صُلْعَانٌ;
C أَصَمُّ *deaf,* صُمَّانٌ; أَعْوَرُ *blind of one eye,* عُورَانٌ; أَبْيَضُ *white,* بِيضَانٌ (for بُيْضَانٌ); أَعْمَى *blind,* عُمْيَانٌ.

REM. The forms فِعْلَانٌ and فُعْلَانٌ are, as some of the above examples show, used conjointly or interchangeable, even in cases where we should hardly expect it. For example, instead of عُورَانٌ, *blind of one eye,* from أَعْوَرُ, and حُورَانٌ, *unweaned foals of camels,* from حُوَارٌ, we find عِيرَانٌ and
D حِيرَانٌ. [حَشٌّ or حُشٌّ *a garden* has حُشَّانٌ and حِشَّانٌ.]

XX. فُعَلَآءُ.

1. فَعِيلٌ, verbal adjectives, applicable to rational beings, which have not the passive signification, and are not derived from verba mediæ rad. geminatæ or tertiæ rad. و et ى; as فَقِيرٌ *poor,* فُقَرَآءُ; أَمِيرٌ *a commander* or *chief,* أُمَرَآءُ; رَئِيسٌ *a chief,* رُؤَسَآءُ; بَخِيلٌ *stingy,* بُخَلَآءُ; ظَرِيفٌ *witty,* ظُرَفَآءُ; حَكِيمٌ *wise,*

Plur. Fract. A

XX. فُعَلَآءُ continued. *Sing.*

a philosopher or *sage, a physician,* حُكَمَآءُ ; نَجِيبٌ *noble,* نُجَبَآءُ ; بَيِّنٌ *clear, plain, eloquent,* بُيَنَآءُ.

2. فَاعِلٌ, some masc. adjectives, with the same restrictions as above; as عَالِمٌ *learned,* عُلَمَآءُ ; جَاهِلٌ *ignorant,* جُهَلَآءُ ; شَاعِرٌ *a poet,* شُعَرَآءُ ; عَاقِلٌ *wise,* عُقَلَآءُ ; صَالِحٌ *good, right,* صُلَحَآءُ. B

Rem. Examples of rarer cases are: سَمْحٌ *liberal,* سُمَحَآءُ ; جَوَادٌ *liberal,* جُوَدَآءُ ; جَبَانٌ *cowardly,* جُبَنَآءُ (from جَبِينٌ); شُجَاعٌ *brave,* شُجَعَآءُ (from شَجِيعٌ); قَتِيلٌ *slain,* قُتَلَآءُ ; أَسِيرٌ *a prisoner,* أُسَرَآءُ ; [وَدُودٌ *loving,* وُدَدَآءُ].—خَلِيفَةٌ, *a successor, a deputy, a caliph,* usually makes خَلَآئِفُ in the former senses, and خُلَفَآءُ in the last. C

XXI. أَفْعِلَآءُ.

فَعِيلٌ, masc. adjectives of the same kind as XX. 1, but mostly derived from verba mediæ rad. geminatæ or mediæ or tertiæ rad. و et ى ; as صَدِيقٌ *a friend,* أَصْدِقَآءُ ; قَرِيبٌ *a relative,* أَقْرِبَآءُ ; حَبِيبٌ, خَلِيلٌ, *a friend,* أَحِبَّآءُ, أَخِلَّآءُ (for أَحْبِبَآءُ, أَخْلِلَآءُ); طَبِيبٌ *a physician,* أَطِبَّآءُ ; شَدِيدٌ *strong,* أَشِدَّآءُ ; هَيِّنٌ (for هَوِينٌ) D *light, easy,* أَهْوِنَآءُ ; لَيِّنٌ (for لَيِينٌ) *smooth, easy,* أَلْيِنَآءُ ; بَيِّنٌ *clear, plain, eloquent,* أَبْيِنَآءُ ; غَنِيٌّ *rich,* أَغْنِيَآءُ ; عَيِيٌّ *stuttering, stammering,* أَعْيِيَآءُ ; وَلِيٌّ *a friend, a welī* or *saint,* أَوْلِيَآءُ ; شَقِيٌّ *wretched,* أَشْقِيَآءُ ; سَخِيٌّ *liberal,* أَسْخِيَآءُ ; تَقِيٌّ *pious,* أَتْقِيَآءُ ; and similarly, بَرِيٌّ for بَرِيٓءٌ, *quit of, exempt from,* أَبْرِيَآءُ ; نَبِيٌّ, for نَبِيٓءٌ, *a prophet,* أَنْبِيَآءُ.

A *Plur. Fract.*

XXII. فَعْلَى. *Sing.*

1. فَعِيلٌ, فَعِلٌ, فَاعِلٌ, أَفْعَلُ, verbal adjectives, denoting injuries, defects, etc., of body or mind; as قَتِيلٌ *slain*, قَتْلَى; جَرِيحٌ *wounded*, جَرْحَى; لَدِيغٌ *bitten by a snake, stung by a scorpion*, لَدْغَى; أَسِيرٌ *a prisoner*, أَسْرَى; كَسِيرٌ *broken*, كَسْرَى; مَيِّتٌ
B (for مَوِيتٌ) *dead*, مَوْتَى; مَرِيضٌ *sick*, مَرْضَى; غَرِيقٌ *drowned*, غَرْقَى; هَالِكٌ *perishing*, هَلْكَى; عَائِلٌ *poor*, عَيْلَى; زَمِنٌ *paralytic*, زَمْنَى; هَرِمٌ *decrepit through age*, هَرْمَى; وَجِعٌ *in pain*, وَجْعَى; حَمِقٌ, or أَحْمَقُ, *silly*, حَمْقَى*; جَرِبٌ, or أَجْرَبُ, *mangy, scabby*, جَرْبَى; أَنْوَكُ *a fool*, نَوْكَى.

2. فَعْلَانُ, verbal adjectives; as كَسْلَانُ *lazy*, كَسْلَى; غَضْبَانُ
C *angry*, غَضْبَى; غَرْثَانُ *hungry*, غَرْثَى; سَكْرَانُ *drunken*, سَكْرَى.

REM. The plural فِعْلَى is said to occur in only two words; viz., حَجَلٌ *a partridge*, حِجْلَى, and ظَرِبَانٌ *a polecat*, ظِرْبَى.

XXIII. فَعَالٍ.

1. فَعْلَاءُ; as عَذْرَاءُ *a virgin*, عَذَارٍ; صَحْرَاءُ *a plain* or *desert*, صَحَارٍ; فَيْفَاءُ *a desert*, فَيَافٍ.

D 2. فَعْلَى, فِعْلَى; as فَتْوَى *a judicial opinion*, فَتَاوٍ; دَعْوَى *a claim*, دَعَاوٍ; ذِفْرَى *the prominent bone behind the ear*, ذَفَارٍ.

3. فِعْلَاةٌ, فِعْلِيَةٌ, فَعْلُوَةٌ; as سِعْلَاةٌ *a female gūl* (غُولٌ) or *goblin, an old hag*, سَعَالٍ; حِذْرِيَةٌ *rough ground*, حَذَارٍ; عِفْرِيَةٌ *the*

---

* [كَيِّسٌ *clever* has كَيْسَى in order that it may resemble (لِلْاِزْدِوَاجِ) its contrary حَمْقَى.]

Plur. Fract. A

XXIII. فَعَالٍ continued. *Sing.*

hackles of a cock, عَفَارٍ ; تَرْقُوَةٌ *the collar-bone,* تَرَاقٍ ; عَرْقُوَةٌ *the cross-handle of a bucket,* عَرَاقٍ.

Rem. فَعَالٍ stands in the nom. and genit. for فَعَالِيُ and فَعَالِيِ (both with the art. اَلْفَعَالِي). The accus., however, is always فَعَالِيَ, with the art. اَلْفَعَالِيَ.—In the same way لَيْلٌ, B
night, makes لَيَالٍ (acc. لَيَالِيَ) ; أَهْلٌ *one's people* or *family,* أَهَالٍ (acc. أَهَالِيَ) ; and أَرْضٌ, *the earth,* أَرَاضٍ (acc. أَرَاضِيَ).

XXIV. فَعَالَى.

1. فَعْلَاءُ ; as عَذْرَاءُ *a virgin,* عَذَارَى ; صَحْرَاءُ *a plain* or *desert,* صَحَارَى ; فَيْفَاءُ *a desert,* فَيَافَى.
2. فَعْلَى, فِعْلَى ; as فَتْوَى *a judicial opinion,* فَتَاوَى ; حَلْوَى *sweetmeat,* حَلَاوَى ; دَعْوَى *a claim,* دَعَاوَى ; ذِفْرَى *the prominent* C
bone behind the ear, ذَفَارَى ; شَكْوَى *a complaint,* شَكَاوَى.
3. فُعْلَى, feminine adjectives, not superlatives ; as أُنْثَى *female, feminine,* أَنَاثَى ; حُبْلَى *pregnant,* حَبَالَى ; خُنْثَى *a hermaphrodite,* خَنَاثَى.
4. فِعْلِيَةٌ ; as حِذْرِيَةٌ *rough ground,* حَذَارَى ; عِفْرِيَةٌ *the hackles* of a cock, عَفَارَى.

Rem. In nos. 1, 2, and 4, the forms فَعَالٍ and فَعَالَى are D
interchangeable.

5. فَعْلَانُ, fem. فَعْلَى, and فَعِيلٌ, verbal adjectives ; as سَكْرَانُ *drunken,* سَكَارَى ; غَضْبَانُ *angry,* غَضَابَى ; غَرْثَانُ *hungry,* غَرَاثَى ; كَسْلَانُ *lazy,* كَسَالَى ; حَيْرَانُ *perplexed,* حَيَارَى ; غَيْرَانُ *jealous,* غَيَارَى ; أَسِيرٌ *a prisoner,* أَسَارَى ; كَسِيرٌ *broken,* كَسَارَى ;

A *Plur. Fract.*

XXIV. فَعَالَى continued. *Sing.*

يَتِيمٌ *an orphan*, يَتَامَى ; نَدِيمٌ *a boon-companion*, نَدَامَى ; أَيِّمٌ (for أَيْيِمٌ) *unmarried*, أَيَامَى ; [خَزْيَانُ *covered with shame*, خَزَايَا].

6. فَعِلٌ, فَعُلٌ, verbal adjectives; as حَبِطٌ *having a swollen belly*, حَبَاطَى ; وَجِعٌ *in pain*, وَجَاعَى ; حَذِرٌ *cautious, wary*, حَذَارَى ;
B حَزِنٌ *sad*, حَزَانَى.

REM. Instead of فَعَالَى we find, in nos. 5 and 6, فُعَالَى and even فعالى ; as أُسَارَى, غُيَارَى, عُجَالَى, حُيَارَى, سُكَارَى, كِسَالَى or كُسَالَى, وُجَاعَى ; رَدِيفٌ has only رُدَافَى and عَاظِلٌ only عُظَالَى.

7. فَعِيلَةٌ, fem. substantives from verba tertiæ rad. و et ى ; as
C هَدِيَّةٌ *a present*, هَدَايَا ; مَنِيَّةٌ *fate*, مَنَايَا ; رَعِيَّةٌ *subjects*, رَعَايَا ; بَلِيَّةٌ *a trial* or *calamity*, بَلَايَا ; مَطِيَّةٌ *an animal for riding*, مَطَايَا ; سَجِيَّةٌ *nature, disposition*, سَجَايَا ; خَطِيَّةٌ (for خَطِيئَةٌ) *a sin*, خَطَايَا ; [عَشِيَّةٌ *evening*, عَشَايَا*].

REM. We write هَدَايَا instead of هَدَايَى, etc., to prevent the repetition of the letter ى (see § 179, rem. *a*).—Many
D grammarians regard these words as being of the form فَعَائِلُ (see XVII.), for هَدَائِى (هَدَاءٍ), etc.

8. فُعَالَةٌ, from verba tertiæ rad. و et ى ; as جُدَايَةٌ *a young gazelle*, جَدَايَا ; إِتَاوَةٌ *a tax*, أَتَاوَى ; إِدَاوَةٌ *a small water-skin*, أَدَاوَى ; عِلَاوَةٌ *the upper part, something over and above*, عَلَاوَى ; هِرَاوَةٌ

* [In conjunction with عشايا, for the sake of conformity (لِلْاِزْدِوَاجِ) غُدْوَةٌ has غَدَايَا.]

Plur. Fract. A

XXIV. فَعَالَى continued. *Sing.*

a stout stick, هَرَاوَى ; نُقَاوَةٌ *plants of the kind called* حَمْض, *used for washing clothes,* نَقَاوَى ; نُقَايَةٌ *the pick and choice of anything,* نَقَايَا.

Rem. Here too فَعَالَى is thought to stand for فَعَآئِلُ ; as جَدَايَا for جَدَآئِىُ (جَدَآءِ), etc. B

9. فَاعِلَةٌ, from verba mediæ rad. و and tertiæ rad. و et ى ; as رَاوِيَةٌ *a camel used in drawing water, a large water-skin,* رَوَايَا ; حَاوِيَةٌ *an intestine,* حَوَايَا ; زَاوِيَةٌ *a corner,* زَوَايَا.

Rem. *a.* Here فَعَالَى is thought to stand for فَوَاعِلُ ; as رَوَايَا for رَوَائِىُ (رَوَآءِ), etc.

[Rem. *b.* Anomalous is نَصَارَى from نَصْرَانِىٌّ *a Christian.*] C

XXV. فَعِيلٌ (rare).

1. فَعْلٌ, فَعَلٌ ; as عَبْدٌ *a slave,* عَبِيدٌ ; كَلْبٌ *a dog,* كَلِيبٌ ; بَقَرٌ *cattle,* بَقِيرٌ ; رَحًى *a mill,* رَحِىٌّ.

2. فِعَالٌ ; as حِمَارٌ *an ass,* حَمِيرٌ.

3. فَاعِلٌ ; as حَاجٌّ *a pilgrim,* حَجِيجٌ ; غَازٍ (for غَازِوٌ) *a soldier,* غَزِىٌّ (for غَزِيوٌ) ; مَاعِزٌ *a goat,* مَعِيزٌ ; ضَآئِنٌ *a sheep,* ضَئِينٌ. D

XXVI. فُعُولَةٌ (rare).

فَعْلٌ, فَعَلٌ ; as بَعْلٌ *a husband,* بُعُولَةٌ ; عَمٌّ *an uncle (by the father's side),* عُمُومَةٌ ; عَيْرٌ *a wild ass,* عُيُورَةٌ ; خَالٌ *an uncle (by the mother's side),* خُؤُولَةٌ (comp. § 240, rem. *c*) ; فَحْلٌ *a stallion,* فُحُولَةٌ ; [خَيْطٌ *a thread,* خُيُوطَةٌ ; نَمِرٌ *a panther,* نُمُورَةٌ ; صَقْرٌ *a hawk,* صُقُورَةٌ ; عَلَفٌ *fodder,* عُلُوفَةٌ].

A *Plur. Fract.*

XXVII. فِعَالَةٌ (rare). *Sing.*

1. فَعْلٌ, فَعَلٌ ; as ثَوْرٌ *a bull,* ثِيَارَةٌ ; [فَحْلٌ *a stallion,* فِحَالَةٌ ; جَمَلٌ *a camel,* جِمَالَةٌ (also جُمَالَةٌ)] ; ذَكَرٌ *male,* ذِكَارَةٌ ; حَجَرٌ *a stone,* حِجَارَةٌ.

2. فَاعِلٌ ; as صَاحِبٌ *a companion,* صِحَابَةٌ (also [the more common]
B صَحَابَةٌ).

XXVIII. فَعَلٌ (rare).

1. فَعْلَةٌ, فَعَلَةٌ ; as حَلْقَةٌ *a ring, a circle,* حَلَقٌ ; بَكْرَةٌ *a pulley,* بَكَرٌ.

2. فَاعِلٌ, as نَاهِلٌ *drinking for the first time* (of camels), نَهَلٌ ; طَالِبٌ *seeking,* طَلَبٌ ; خَادِمٌ *a servant,* خَدَمٌ ; تَابِعٌ *a follower, an attendant,* تَبَعٌ ; رَاصِدٌ *lying in wait, watching,* رَصَدٌ ; حَارِسٌ
C *a guardian, a keeper,* حَرَسٌ ; جَالِبٌ *a driver, an importer,* جَلَبٌ.

XXIX. فَعْلٌ (rare).

فَاعِلٌ ; as شَارِبٌ *drinking,* شَرْبٌ ; نَاصِرٌ *a helper,* نَصْرٌ ; تَاجِرٌ *a merchant,* تَجْرٌ ; صَاحِبٌ *a companion,* صَحْبٌ ; رَاكِبٌ *a rider,* رَكْبٌ ; سَافِرٌ *a traveller,* سَفْرٌ ; [زَائِرٌ *a visitor,* زَوْرٌ].

REM. *a.* The above rules regarding the correspondence of certain forms of the pluralis fractus and of the singular, are subject
D to many exceptions*. The dictionaries also give various forms

* [Many scholars do not admit the forms XXV., XXVIII. and XXIX. as plur. fracta, but call them quasi-plurals (أَشْبَاهُ ٱلْجَمْعِ), making a distinction between them and the real collectives (أَسْمَآءُ ٱلْجَمْعِ), as قَوْمٌ etc., and the generic collectives (أَسْمَآءُ ٱلْجِنْسِ), which form a nomen unitatis, as نَحْلٌ. The forms فَعِيلٌ, فَعَلٌ and فَعْلٌ are

which we have not thought it necessary to notice; for instance, A
مَفْعَلَةٌ, rarely مَفْعِلَةٌ and مَفْعُلَةٌ (as ضَبُعٌ *a hyæna*, مَضْبَعَةٌ; عَبْدٌ *a slave*, مَعْبَدَةٌ; وَعِلٌ *a mountain-goat*, مَوْعِلَةٌ; شَيْخٌ *an old man, a chief, a doctor*, مَشْيَخَةٌ, مَشِيخَةٌ and مَشْيُخَةٌ; سَيْفٌ *a sword*, مَسْيَفَةٌ and مَسِيفَةٌ), and مَفْعُولَآءُ, of which the principal examples in use are: أَتَانٌ *a she-ass*, مَأْتُونَآءُ; بَغْلٌ *a mule*, مَبْغُولَآءُ; تَيْسٌ *a he-goat*, مَتْيُوسَآءُ; حِمَارٌ *a he-ass*, مَحْمُورَآءُ; شَيْخٌ *an old man*, مَشْيُوخَآءُ; عَبْدٌ B
a slave, مَعْبُودَآءُ; عِلْجٌ *a Christian* (or *other not Muḥammadan*) *captive* or *slave*, مَعْلُوجَآءُ; عَيْرٌ *a wild ass*, مَعْيُورَآءُ; كَبِيرٌ *large, stout*, مَكْبُورَآءُ.

Rem. *b*. Many forms of the pluralis fractus seem to be derived, not from the singular forms in actual use, but from others, which are obsolete or of rare occurrence. E.g. فَاعِلٌ, pl. فُعَلَآءُ, (as شَاعِرٌ *a poet*, شُعَرَآءُ,) from an obsolete فَعِيلٌ (شَعِيرٌ); and فَاعِلٌ, pl. فَعْلَى, C
(as هَالِكٌ *perishing*, هَلْكَى,) also from an obsolete فَعِيلٌ (هَلِيكٌ).

Rem. *c*. From the preceding table it is obvious that one sing. may have several forms of the pluralis fractus; e.g. بَحْرٌ *a sea*, بِحَارٌ, بُحُورٌ, أَبْحُرٌ; ثَوْرٌ *a bull*, أَثْوَارٌ, ثِيرَةٌ, ثِيَرَةٌ or ثِوَرَةٌ, ثِيرَانٌ, ثِيَارٌ, ثِيَارَةٌ; عَبْدٌ *a slave*, عُبُدٌ, عِبَادٌ, عُبُودٌ, أَعْبَادٌ, أَعْبِدَةٌ, عَبِيدٌ, أَعْبُدٌ, عِبْدَانٌ (besides عُبُدٌ, عُبْدَانٌ, عِبِدَّآءُ, عِبِدَّى, عِبِدَّةٌ, مَعْبَدَةٌ, مَعْبُودَآءُ, see rem. *a*); صَاحِبٌ *a companion*, صَحْبٌ, صِحَابٌ, أَصْحَابٌ, صَحَابَةٌ, صُحْبَانٌ D
(besides صُحْبَةٌ, see rem. *a*). Or one sing. may have several plurales fracti and a pluralis sanus besides; e.g. شَاهِدٌ *one who is present*,

---

masculine by form, feminine by signification. The forms XXVI. فُعُولَةٌ and XXVII. فِعَالَةٌ seem to be derived respectively from فُعُولٌ and فِعَالٌ with the termination ة to reinforce the collective meaning (تَآءٌ لِتَأْكِيدِ مَعْنَى ٱلْجَمْعِ).]

A *an eye-witness, a witness,* شَاهِدُونَ, شَهْدٌ, شُهَّدٌ, شُهُودٌ, أَشْهَادٌ; عَابِدٌ *serving, worshipping,* عَابِدُونَ, عُبَّادٌ, عَبَدَةٌ. In such cases, if the sing. has several meanings, it often happens that each of them has one or more forms of the pluralis fractus which are peculiar to it, or used in preference to the rest. For example, شَاهِدٌ, in the sense of *an evidential example,* has شَوَاهِدُ. The word بَيْتٌ means: (1) *a tent* or *house,* (2) *a verse of poetry;* in the former sense the
B plur. fract. is بُيُوتٌ or أَبْيَاتٌ, in the latter almost always أَبْيَاتٌ. Again, عَيْنٌ signifies: (1) *an eye,* (2) *a fountain,* (3) *peculiar nature* or *essence,* (4) *a distinguished man;* its plur. fract. in the first sense is عُيُونٌ, أَعْيُنٌ, or أَعْيَانٌ; in the second, عُيُونٌ or أَعْيُنٌ; in the third and fourth, أَعْيَانٌ. Or, to take another instance, بَطْنٌ means: (1) *the belly,* (2) *a valley,* (3) *a tribe,* (4) *the interior,* (5) *the inner* or *wider side of a wing-feather;* its plur. fract. in the first sense is بُطُونٌ, أَبْطُنٌ, or بُطْنَانٌ; in the second, بُطُونٌ, أَبْطِنَةٌ, or
C بُطْنَانٌ; in the third, بُطُونٌ or أَبْطُنٌ; in the fourth and fifth, بُطْنَانٌ.

305. The forms of the plur. fract. of substantives and adjectives, which consist of *four* or more consonants, are exhibited, along with the corresponding singulars, in the following table.

Plur. Fract.

I. فَعَالِلُ (أَفَاعِلُ, تَفَاعِلُ, مَفَاعِلُ). *Sing.*

1. Quadriliteral substantives and adjectives (ة not being counted as a letter), the consonants of which are all radical; as ثَعْلَبٌ *a fox,* ثَعَالِبُ; ضِفْدِعٌ *a frog,* ضَفَادِعُ; دِرْهَمٌ *a dirham,* دَرَاهِمُ;
D بُرْثُنٌ *a claw* of a lion, بَرَاثِنُ; جُنْدَبٌ *a locust,* جَنَادِبُ; قَنْطَرَةٌ *a bridge,* قَنَاطِرُ; زِعْنِفَةٌ *a fin* of a fish, زَعَانِفُ; جَوْهَرٌ *gems,* جَوَاهِرُ; كَوْكَبٌ *a star,* كَوَاكِبُ; جَدْوَلٌ *a streamlet, a column* or *table* (in a book), جَدَاوِلُ.

2. Quadriliterals (ة not included), formed from triliteral roots by prefixing ا, ت, or م; as إِصْبَعٌ, *a finger,* أَصَابِعُ; [أَنْمُلَةٌ *the end*

Plur. Fract. A

I. فَعَالِلُ (مَفَاعِلُ, تَفَاعِلُ, أَفَاعِلُ) cont. *Sing.*

of a finger, أَنَامِلُ]; آدَمُ *Adam*, أَوَادِمُ; أَفْعَى *a viper*, أَفَاعٍ (for أَفَاعِيُ, compare § 304, no. XXIII., rem.); تَجْرِبَةٌ *trial, experience*, تَجَارِبُ; مِخْلَبٌ *a claw* or *talon*, مَخَالِبُ; مَنْزِلَةٌ *a halting-place, a station*, مَنَازِلُ; مَحَلَّةٌ *a place where one stops* or *dwells, a quarter of a town*, مَحَالُّ; مَعِيشَةٌ *means of subsistence*, مَعَايِشُ; مَعْنًى *meaning*, مَعَانٍ (for مَعَانِيُ); مَرْثِيَةٌ B *an elegy*, مَرَاثٍ (for مَرَاثِيُ); [مُرْضِعٌ *suckling*, مَرَاضِعُ].

Rem. *a.* In the plur. fract. of the form مَفَاعِلُ from verba mediæ rad. ى, the ى is not converted after the èlif productionis into hèmza (ئ),—as happens, for instance, in form XVII. of the triliterals (فَعَآئِلُ), or in the nomen agentis (فَاعِلٌ, § 240),—but it remains unchanged; e.g. مَسَاحَةٌ, مَسَاحٌ, *an open space for walking* (from سَاحَ for سَيَحَ), مَسَايِحُ; C whereas مَسَآئِحُ is the plural of مَسِيحَةٌ *a curl* (from مَسَحَ). In the same form from verba mediæ rad. و, the و is usually retained, as مِقْوَسٌ *a bowcase*, مَقَاوِسُ; مَفَازَةٌ (from فَازَ for فَوَزَ) *a desert*, مَفَاوِزُ; مَلَامَةٌ *a reproof*, مَلَاوِمُ; مَغَاصٌ (from غَاصَ for غَوَصَ) *a place for diving*, مَغَاوِصُ; but in one or two instances into hèmza (ئ), e.g. مُصِيبَةٌ (from صَابَ for صَوَبَ) *a misfortune*, مَصَاوِبُ, and usually مَصَآئِبُ; مَنَارَةٌ *a* D *candlestick, a lighthouse, a minaret*, مَنَاوِرُ, and usually مَنَآئِرُ. The changing of the و into ى is vulgar, as مَنَايِرُ, مَغَايِرُ.

Rem. *b.* Adjectives of the form أَفْعَلُ, especially with the superlative meaning, make, when used as substantives [and, in that case, often taking the form أَفْعَلٌ, as أَجْدَلٌ; see § 309, *b*, γ], a plur. أَفَاعِلُ; e.g. أَدْهَمُ *a shackle* or *fetter*,

A *Plur. Fract.*

IIa فَعَالِلُ (أَفَاعِلُ, تَفَاعِلُ, مَفَاعِلُ) cont. *Sing.*

أَدَاهِمُ ; أَرْقَمُ *a mottled snake,* أَرَاقِمُ ; ٱلْأَكْبَرُ *the greatest,* ٱلْأَكَابِرُ, *grandees, nobles.*

II. فَعَالِيلُ (أَفَاعِيلُ, تَفَاعِيلُ, مَفَاعِيلُ, يَفَاعِيلُ, فَوَاعِيلُ).

Quinqueliteral substantives and adjectives (ة not included), of
B which the penultimate letter is a litera productionis (ا, و, ى);
as شَيْطَانٌ *a devil,* شَيَاطِينُ ; سِرْحَانٌ *a wolf,* سَرَاحِينُ ; سُلْطَانٌ
a sultan, سَلَاطِينُ ; تُبَّانٌ *short drawers,* تَبَابِينُ ; نُوَّارٌ *white
flowers,* نَوَاوِيرُ ; فُقَّاعَةٌ *a bubble,* فَقَاقِيعُ ; سِكِّينٌ *a knife,* سَكَاكِينُ ;
قِنْدِيلٌ *a lamp,* قَنَادِيلُ ; شُؤْبُوبٌ *a heavy shower of rain,* شَآبِيبُ ;
كُرْسِيٌّ *a chair,* كَرَاسِيُّ (for كَرَاسِيىُ*) ; [مَكُّوكٌ a measure,
C مَكَاكِيكُ and مَكَاكِيُّ] ; بَرِّيَّةٌ *a desert,* بَرَارِيُّ (for بَرَارِيىُ) ;
تِمْثَالٌ *a statue,* تَمَاثِيلُ ; تَصْوِيرٌ *a picture,* تَصَاوِيرُ ; تَأْرِيخٌ *a
chronicle,* تَوَارِيخُ (compare § 303, *f,* rem.) ; مِفْتَاحٌ *a key,*
مَفَاتِيحُ ; مِسْكِينٌ *poor,* مَسَاكِينُ ; مَشْؤُومٌ *unlucky, inauspicious,*
مَشَائِيمُ ; مَيْمُونٌ *lucky, auspicious,* مَيَامِينُ ; مَلْعُونٌ *accursed,*
مَلَاعِينُ ; إِعْصَارٌ *a dust-storm with whirlwinds,* أَعَاصِيرُ ; إِكْلِيلٌ
a garland or *crown,* أَكَالِيلُ ; أُرْجُوزَةٌ *a poem in the metre
D rağez,* أَرَاجِيزُ ; أُدْحِيٌّ (for أُدْحُوىٌ) or إِدْحِيٌّ, *an ostrich's nest,*
أَدَاحِيُّ ; أُمْنِيَّةٌ (for أُمْنُويَةٌ) *a wish,* أَمَانِيُّ ; [آخِيَّةٌ *a tent-rope,*

---

* [This may be lightened also to كَرَاسٍ, as إِنْسِيٌّ *a human being,* has أَنَاسِيُّ and أَنَاسٍ, بُخْتِيٌّ *a Bactrian camel,* بَخَاتِيُّ and بَخَاتٍ, مَهْرِيٌّ *a camel from Mahrah,* مَهَارِيُّ and مَهَارٍ. The two latter words have also the irregular plurals بَخَاتَى and مَهَارَى.]

Plur. Fract. *Sing.* A

II. فَعَالِيلُ (أَفَاعِيلُ, تَفَاعِيلُ, مَفَاعِيلُ, يَفَاعِيلُ, فَوَاعِيلُ) cont.

a sacred claim, أَوَاخِىُّ ; آرِيَّةٌ *a stall,* أَوَارِىُّ]; يَنْبُوعٌ *a spring,* يَنَابِيعُ ; يَعْسُوبٌ *the queen-bee* (rex apum), يَعَاسِيبُ ; جَامُوسٌ *a buffalo,* جَوَامِيسُ ; بَاسُورٌ *hæmorrhoids,* بَوَاسِيرُ.

Rem. *a.* The plur. فَعَالِيلُ is sometimes found in cases where a quinqueliteral sing. form is either rare or does not exist; as خَوَاتِيمُ *signet-rings,* from خَاتَمٌ = خَاتَامٌ (pl. خَوَاتِمُ); دَرَاهِيمُ *dirhams,* from دِرْهَمٌ = دِرْهَامٌ (pl. دَرَاهِمُ); قَنَاطِرُ = قَنَاطِيرُ *bridges,* from قَنْطَرَةٌ; مُفْطِرٌ *one who breaks his fast,* مَفَاطِيرُ; مُشْدِنٌ *having a fawn with her,* مَشَادِنُ and مَشَادِينُ; مُطْفِلٌ *having a young one with her,* مَطَافِلُ and مَطَافِيلُ; مُنْكَرٌ *clever, cunning,* مَنَاكِيرُ. Conversely, فَعَالِلُ is used, chiefly by poetical license, instead of فَعَالِيلُ; as مَقَاصِرُ = مَقَاصِيرُ, plur. of مَقْصُورَةٌ *a space partitioned* or *railed off, a closet;* أَعَاصِيرُ = أَعَاصِرُ, plur. of إِعْصَارٌ *a dust-storm.* B

Rem. *b.* دِينَارٌ *a dīnār,* قِيرَاطٌ *a carat,* دِيوَانٌ *a register, an account-book, a collection of poems, a public office* or *bureau,* and إِيوَانٌ *an arched* or *vaulted portico, vestibule* or *apartment,* make دَنَانِيرُ, قَرَارِيطُ, دَوَاوِينُ, and أَوَاوِينُ (as if from singular forms دِنَّارٌ, قِرَّاطٌ, دِوَّانٌ, and إِوَّانٌ). دِيبَاجٌ, *brocade,* has دَيَابِيجُ and دَبَابِيجُ; دَيْمَاسٌ or دِيمَاسٌ (δημόσιον), *a dungeon, a bath,* دَيَامِيسُ and دَمَامِيسُ; شِيرَازٌ or شِتْرَازٌ, *curds,* شَوَارِيزُ, شَآرِيزُ and شَرَارِيزُ; أَتُّونٌ, *a furnace,* أَتَاتِينُ and perhaps also أَتَانِينُ (as if from a form أَتْنُونٌ); خُنَاقٌ (خُنَّاقٌ) *quinsy,* has خَوَانِيقُ and, in modern Arabic, خَنَانِيقُ. Compare § 284, rem. D

A *Plur. Fract.*

III. فَعَالِلَةٌ. *Sing.*

1. Occasionally substantives and adjectives of five or more letters (principally foreign words), of which the penultimate letter is a litera productionis; as أُسْتَاذٌ (Pers. أُسْتَاذ) *a master, a teacher,* أَسَاتِيذُ and أَسَاتِذَةٌ; تِلْمِيذٌ (Heb. תַּלְמִיד, Syr. ܬܠܡܝܕܐ) *a*
B *disciple, a pupil,* تَلَامِيذُ and تَلَامِذَةٌ; فَيْلَسُوفٌ (φιλόσοφος) *a philosopher,* فَلَاسِفَةٌ; بِطْرِيقٌ *a Grecian general* (patricius, πατρίκιος), بَطَارِيقُ and بَطَارِقَةٌ; مِطْرَانٌ *a metropolitan bishop* (μητροπολίτης), مَطَارِينُ and مَطَارِنَةٌ; تَرْجُمَانٌ *an interpreter,* تَرَاجِمُ and تَرَاجِمَةٌ.

2. Substantives and adjectives of four or more letters, which have not a litera productionis before the last radical,—especially
C when they are words of foreign origin,—and a great many relative adjectives, consisting of more than four letters. E.g. مَلْأَكٌ *an angel,* مَلَائِكَةٌ; صَيْقَلٌ *a polisher of swords,* صَيَاقِلُ and صَيَاقِلَةٌ; تُبَّعٌ *a king of ĕl-Yĕmĕn,* تَبَابِعَةٌ; قُمَّسٌ *a nobleman* (comes, κόμης), قَمَامِسَةٌ; بَطْرَكٌ *a patriarch* or *archbishop* (πατριάρχης), بَطَارِيكُ and بَطَارِكَةٌ; جَوْرَبٌ *a stocking* or *sock* (Pers. گورب), جَوَارِبُ and جَوَارِبَةٌ; مُلْحِدٌ *a heretic,* مَلَاحِدَةٌ;
D أُسْقُفٌ (ἐπίσκοπος) *a bishop,* أَسَاقِفُ and أَسَاقِفَةٌ; قَيْصَرُ (*Cæsar,* Καῖσαρ) *the Byzantine emperor,* قَيَاصِرَةٌ; فِرْعَوْنُ (פַּרְעֹה) *Pharaoh,* فَرَاعِنَةٌ; صَيْرَفٌ and صَيْرَفِيٌّ, *a money-changer,* صَيَارِفُ and صَيَارِفَةٌ; مَغْرِبِيٌّ *a Moor,* مَغَارِبَةٌ; بَغْدَادِيٌّ *a native of Bagdād,* بَغَادِدَةٌ; مَصْمُودِيٌّ *a man of the Bĕrbĕr tribe of Maṣmūda,* مَصَامِدَةٌ; مُهَلَّبِيٌّ *a descendant of ĕl-Muhallĕb,* مَهَالِبَةٌ.—From كِسْرَى (Pers. خُسْرَوْ, *Chosroes*) *the king of*

Plur. Fract. A

III. فَعَالِلَةٌ continued. *Sing.*

Persia, are formed irregularly أَكَاسِرُ, أَكَاسِرَةٌ, and كَسَاسِرَةٌ; and سَوَآءٌ or سِيٌّ, *a like, an equal*, has, besides أَسْوَآءٌ, the irregular سَوَاسِوَةٌ, سَوَاسِيَةٌ, and سَوَاسٍ (for سَوَاسِيُ).

Rem. *a.* This form is also found, though rarely, in quadriliterals which have a litera productionis before the last radical; B as جَبَّارٌ *a tyrant, a giant*, جَبَابِرَةٌ; شَمَّاسٌ *a deacon* (Syr. ܡܫܡܫܢܐ), شَمَامِسَةٌ.

Rem. *b.* In forming the plur. fract. of nouns which contain five or more letters (exclusive of ة and the letters of prolongation), one of the radicals is rejected, generally the last. E.g. عَنْكَبُوتٌ *a spider*, عَنَاكِبُ; عَنْدَلِيبٌ *a nightingale*, عَنَادِلُ; جَحْمَرِشٌ *a fat, lazy old woman*, جَحَامِرُ; سَفَرْجَلٌ *a quince*, سَفَارِجُ; but فَرَزْدَقٌ *a burnt cake*, فَرَازِقُ; قَلَنْسُوَةٌ *a sort of cap*, قَلَانِسُ, قَلَاسٍ (for قَلَاسِيُ), or C قَلَاسِيُّ; أُسْطُوَانَةٌ *a pillar*, أَسَاطِينُ; بَطْلَمِيُوسُ *Ptolemy*, بَطَالِسَةٌ; دُمُسْتُقٌ *a Byzantine governor* (domesticus, δομεστικός), دَمَاسِقُ. Here may also be mentioned such plurals as عَبَادِلَةٌ from عَبْدُ ٱللّٰهِ *'Abdu 'llāh* (compare § 264, rem. *b*).

Rem. *c.* The forms of the plur. fract. of quadriliterals and quinqueliterals are also used in forming plurals from other plurals (جَمْعُ ٱلْجَمْعِ *the plur. of the plur.*, or secondary plural). In particular, forms XIII. أَفْعُلٌ and XV. أَفْعِلَةٌ make أَفَاعِلُ, and XIV. D أَفْعَالٌ, أَفَاعِيلُ; more rarely V. فِعَالٌ, فَعَائِلُ, and XVIII. and XIX. فُعْلَانٌ, فَعَالِينُ. E.g. XIII. كَلْبٌ *a dog*, أَكْلُبٌ, أَكَالِبُ; نَاقَةٌ *a she-camel*, أَنْيُقٌ, أَيَانِقُ; رَهْطٌ *one's people* or *tribe*, أَرْهُطٌ, أَرَاهِطُ; ضِلَعٌ *a rib*, أَضْلُعٌ, أَضَالِعُ; يَدٌ *a hand, a benefit*, أَيْدٍ (for أَيْدِيٌ), أَيَادٍ (for أَيَادِيُ); XV. سِوَارٌ *a bracelet*, أَسْوِرَةٌ, أَسَاوِرُ; مَكَانٌ *a place*, أَمْكِنَةٌ,

A أَمَاكِنُ ; إِنَآءٌ *a vessel*, آنِيَةٌ, أَوَانٍ (for أَوَانِيُ) ; XIV. نَعَمٌ *camels*, أَنْعَامٌ, أَنَاعِيمُ ; زَهْرٌ *a (yellow) flower*, أَزْهَارٌ, أَزَاهِيرُ ; قَوْلٌ *a saying, a speech*, أَقْوَالٌ, أَقَاوِيلُ ; ظُفْرٌ *a nail*, أَظْفَارٌ, أَظَافِيرُ ; جَلَدٌ *she-camels having neither young ones nor milk*, أَجْلَادٌ, أَجَالِيدُ ; V. جَمَلٌ *a he-camel*, جِمَالٌ, جَمَائِلُ ; XVIII. XIX. مَصِيرٌ *an intestine*, مُصْرَانٌ, مَصَارِينُ ; حُشٌّ *a garden (of palm trees)*, حُشَّانٌ, حَشَاشِينُ ; عُقَابٌ *an eagle*,
B عُقْبَانٌ, عَقَابِينُ. Again, XV. أَفْعِلَةٌ forms a pluralis sanus أَفْعِلَاتٌ ; as شَرَابٌ *a drink*, أَشْرِبَةٌ, أَشْرِبَاتٌ ; دُخَانٌ *smoke*, أَدْخِنَةٌ, أَدْخِنَاتٌ ; بِنَآءٌ *a building*, أَبْنِيَةٌ, أَبْنِيَاتٌ ; عَطَآءٌ *a gift, pay*, أَعْطِيَةٌ, أَعْطِيَاتٌ. A pluralis sanus in ـَاتٌ may also be derived from V. فِعَالٌ, VI. فُعُولٌ, III. فُعُلٌ, XVII. فَعَائِلُ, and a few other forms ; as جَمَلٌ *a he-camel*, جِمَالٌ, جِمَالَاتٌ ; رَجُلٌ *a man*, رِجَالٌ, رِجَالَاتٌ ; كَلْبٌ *a dog*, كِلَابٌ, كِلَابَاتٌ ; بَيْتٌ *a house*, بُيُوتٌ, بُيُوتَاتٌ, *houses, families* ; طَرِيقٌ
C *a road*, طُرُقٌ, طُرُقَاتٌ ; جَزُورٌ *a she-camel for slaughter*, جُزُرٌ, جُزُرَاتٌ ; حِمَارٌ *a he-ass*, حُمُرٌ, حُمُرَاتٌ ; حَدِيدَةٌ *an iron tool*, حَدَائِدُ, حَدَائِدَاتٌ ; نَسِيجَةٌ *anything woven* or *plaited*, نَسَائِجُ, نَسَائِجَاتٌ ; دَارٌ *a house*, دُورٌ, دُورَاتٌ ; [صَاحِبَةٌ *a female companion*, صَوَاحِبُ, صَوَاحِبَاتٌ] ; نَاقَةٌ *a she-camel*, pl. نِيَاقٌ, نِيَاقَاتٌ, and أَيْنُقٌ, أَيْنُقَاتٌ (with the dimin. أُيَيْنِقَاتٌ) ; etc. Sometimes there is even a treble formation ; as فِرْقَةٌ *a band, a party or sect*, فِرَقٌ, أَفْرَاقٌ, أَفَارِيقُ. Such secondary
D plurals can be properly used only when the objects denoted are at least nine in number, or when their number is indefinite.

REM. *d.* Plurals [or rather collectives] are formed from a great many relative adjectives,—especially those that indicate the relations of sect, family, or clientship,—by adding the termination ـَةٌ ; as شَافِعِيٌّ *a follower of eš-Šâfi'î* (ٱلشَّافِعِيُّ), ٱلشَّافِعِيَّةُ *the sect of the Šâfi'ites* ; صُوفِيٌّ *a Ṣûfî*, ٱلصُّوفِيَّةُ *the sect of the Ṣûfîs* ; ٱلْمَرْوَانِيَّةُ,

اَلزُّبَيْرِيَّةُ, *the partisans of Marwân, of Ibnu 'z-Zubêir.* See § 268. A
Sometimes ـَةٌ is added with the same effect to other adjectives, especially of the forms فَاعِلٌ and فَعَّالٌ; as شَارِبَةٌ *those who live on the bank and drink the water of* (*a certain stream*); وَارِدَةٌ [and وَرَّادَةٌ] (*men*) *drawing water* or (*cattle*) *drinking*; سَابِلَةٌ *travellers*; جَمَّالَةٌ, حَمَّارَةٌ, خَيَّالَةٌ, بَغَّالَةٌ, *persons who own* or *keep camels, asses, horses, mules*; سَيَّارَةٌ *a company of persons journeying together, a caravan* (Syr. ܫܝܪ̈ܬܐ); رَجَّالَةٌ *pedestrians*; نَظَّارَةٌ *spectators*; [نَهَّابَةٌ *plunderers*]. B

Rem. *e.* The plural of some nouns is anomalous, or derived from other forms or roots than the sing. in use; as أُمٌّ *a mother*, أُمَّهَاتٌ (Syr. ܐ̈ܡܗܬܐ, ܐܡ̈ܗܬܐ), rarely أُمَّاتٌ; فَمٌ *a mouth*, أَفْوَاهٌ (from a sing. فُوهٌ or فَوْهٌ); مَآءٌ *water, a spring*, مِيَاهٌ, أَمْوَاهٌ (from a sing. مَاهٌ); شَفَةٌ *a lip*, شِفَاهٌ; اِسْتٌ *the anus*, أَسْتَاهٌ; شَاةٌ *a sheep* or *goat*, شَآءٌ, شِيَاهٌ, شَوِيٌّ; اِمْرَأَةٌ *a woman*, نِسَآءٌ, نِسْوَةٌ, نِسْوَانٌ (from the rad. أنس, whence Heb. אִישׁ, אִשָּׁה, for אִנְשׁ, אִנְשָׁה); خُلْدٌ *a mole*, مَنَاجِذُ (from C
the rad. نجذ). إِنْسَانٌ, *a human being* (Heb. אִישׁוֹן, for אִשְׁוֹן, אִנְשׁוֹן), has usually نَاسٌ [especially with the article اَلنَّاسُ], instead of the older and poetic أُنَاسٌ (Heb. אֱנוֹשׁ, Aram. אֱנָשָׁא, ܐ̱ܢܫܐ).

306. As regards their meaning, the plurales fracti differ entirely from the sound plurals; for the latter denote several *distinct* individuals of a genus, the former a number of individuals viewed *collectively*, the idea of individuality being wholly suppressed. For D
example, عَبْدُونَ are *slaves* (*servi*), i.e. several individuals who are slaves, عَبِيدٌ *slaves* collectively (*servitium* or *servitus*); شُبَّانٌ *young men, youth* (*juventus*), = شَبَابٌ; مَشْيَخَةٌ *old men* in general. The plurales fracti are consequently, strictly speaking, *singulars* with a *collective* signification, and often approach in their nature to *abstract nouns.* Hence, too, they are all of the *feminine* gender, and can be used as masc. only by a constructio ad sensum.

A REM. We must distinguish from the plurales fracti those nouns which are called أَسْمَآءُ ٱلْجِنْسِ (*generic nouns*), as نَحْلٌ *bees*, on which see § 246 and § 292, *a*. The former may be styled *abstract*, the latter *concrete collectives*. A third class of collectives is formed by those nouns, to the meaning of which the idea of collectiveness attaches; as قَوْمٌ, رَهْطٌ, *people* or *tribe*, عَسْكَرٌ *an army*; [إِبِلٌ *camels*, غَنَمٌ *sheep*]. These are called أَسْمَآءُ ٱلْجَمْعِ or أَشْبَاهُ ٱلْجَمْعِ (*like the plural*), and differ from the أَسْمَآءُ ٱلْجِنْسِ in not admitting of the
B formation of nomina unitatis (§ 246).

307. The pluralis sanus and the plurales fracti of the forms XII. فِعْلَةٌ, XIII. أَفْعُلٌ, XIV. أَفْعَالٌ, and XV. أَفْعِلَةٌ, are used only of persons and things which do not exceed *ten* in number (3 to 10), and are therefore called جُمُوعُ قِلَّةٍ, *plurals of paucity*, whilst the rest are named جُمُوعُ كَثْرَةٍ, *plurals of abundance*. This observation applies,
C of course, only to such nouns as have also other plurals, for if one of the forms alone be used, it is necessarily employed without any limitation as to number.

4. *The Declension of Nouns.*

I. *The Declension of Undefined Nouns.*

308. (1) Undefined substantives and adjectives are, in the *singular* number, either *triptotes* or *diptotes*. Triptotes are those which have *three* terminations to indicate the different cases; viz. ـٌ
D (Nom.), ـٍ (Gen.), and اً or ـً (Acc., see § 8, rem. *a*). Diptotes are those which have only *two* terminations; viz. ـُ (Nom.) and ـَ (Gen., Acc.)*.—(2) The *dual* number has only *two* case-endings, which are

* A noun may be مُعْرَبٌ, *declinable*, or مَبْنِىٌّ, *indeclinable*. A declinable noun may be مُنْصَرِفٌ, *declined with tènwīn*, or غَيْرُ مُنْصَرِفٍ, *declined without tènwīn*. The term مُتَمَكِّنٌ فِى ٱلْأِسْمِيَّةِ, *established in*, or *possessed of, the nominal character* or *nature*, or simply مُتَمَكِّنٌ is synonymous with مُعْرَبٌ, and غَيْرُ مُتَمَكِّنٍ with مَبْنِىٌّ; whi…

common to both genders; viz. ـَانِ (Nom.) and ـَيْنِ (Gen., Acc.)*.— A
(3) The *pluralis sanus* has likewise only *two* case-endings for each

---

مُتَمَكِّنٌ أَمْكَنُ, *possessed of (the nominal character) to the fullest extent*, is equivalent to مُنْصَرِفٌ, and مُتَمَكِّنٌ غَيْرُ أَمْكَنَ to غَيْرُ مُنْصَرِفٍ.— The vowel *u* of the nominative is called اَلرَّفْعُ, *the raising (of the voice)*, and is عَلَمُ ٱلْفَاعِلِيَّةِ, *the sign of agency*; the vowel *i* is termed اَلْخَفْضُ *the depression (of the voice)*, or اَلْجَرُّ, *the being drawn along* or *attracted* B
(by a governing word, اَلْجَارُّ*)*, and is عَلَمُ ٱلْإِضَافَةِ, *the sign of annexation*; the vowel *a* is designated اَلنَّصْبُ, *the uplifting* or *elevation (of the voice)*, and is عَلَمُ ٱلْمَفْعُولِيَّةِ, *the sign of objectivity*.—The tènwīn may be (*a*) اَلتَّنْوِينُ ٱلدَّالُّ عَلَى ٱلْمَكَانَةِ, *the nunation which shows that a noun is fully declinable*, also called تَنْوِينُ ٱلتَّمْكِينِ, and found in the singular and the pluralis fractus, as رَجُلٌ, رِجَالٌ; (*b*) تَنْوِينُ ٱلْمُقَابَلَةِ, *the nunation of correspondence*, found in the plural feminine, as مُسْلِمَاتٌ,
because it corresponds to the ن of مُسْلِمِينَ; (*c*) تَنْوِينُ ٱلتَّنْكِيرِ, *the* C
nunation which distinguishes, in the case of an indeclinable noun, between the definite, اَلْمَعْرِفَةُ, *and the indefinite*, اَلنَّكِرَةُ, as مَرَرْتُ بِسِيبَوَيْهِ وَسِيبَوَيْهٍ آخَرَ, *I passed by Sībawèih and another (man called) Sībawèih*; and (*d*) تَنْوِينُ ٱلْعِوَضِ, *the nunation of compensation*. This last may be of three kinds: (α) of compensation for the omission of an entire proposition, as in وَأَنْتُمْ حِينَئِذٍ تَنْظُرُونَ *and ye are then looking on*, where حِينَئِذٍ stands for حِينَ إِذْ بَلَغَتِ ٱلرُّوحُ ٱلْحُلْقُومَ, *at the time when*
the spirit has reached the throat; (β) of compensation for a governed D
word, as when the genitive is omitted after كُلٌّ or بَعْضٌ, as كُلٌّ قَائِمٌ for كُلُّ إِنْسَانٍ قَائِمٌ or كُلُّهُمْ قَائِمٌ; (γ) of compensation for a letter, as in جَوَارٍ, plural of جَارِيَةٌ, for جَوَارِيُ in the nominative or جَوَارِيٍ in the genitive.

* The form ـَيْنَ is used dialectically, as in the hemistich عَلَى أَحْوَذِيَّيْنَ ٱسْتَقَلَّتْ عَشِيَّةً, *at eve it* (a bird) *rose on two nimble (wings)*.

A gender; viz. for the *masculine*, ـُونَ (Nom.) and ـِينَ (Gen., Acc.)*; for the *feminine*, ـَاتٌ (Nom.) and ـَاتٍ (Gen., Acc.).—(4) The *plurales fracti* are either diptotes or triptotes, exactly like the singular (see § 309, *a*).—The following is the paradigm of the declension of undefined substantives and adjectives.

TRIPTOTE OR FIRST DECLENSION.

Substantives.

B

	Masc.		Fem.	
	Proper.	Common.	Proper.	Common.
	Sing.		*Sing.*	
N.	زَيْدٌ *Zèid.*	رَجُلٌ *a man.*	هِنْدٌ *Hind.*	جَنَّةٌ *a garden.*
G.	زَيْدٍ	رَجُلٍ	هِنْدٍ	جَنَّةٍ
Ac.	زَيْدًا	رَجُلًا	هِنْدًا	جَنَّةً
	Dual.		*Dual.*	
C N.	زَيْدَانِ	رَجُلَانِ	هِنْدَانِ	جَنَّتَانِ
G. Ac.	زَيْدَيْنِ	رَجُلَيْنِ	هِنْدَيْنِ	جَنَّتَيْنِ

The existence of the form ـَانَ is doubtful, despite the verse أَعْرِفُ مِنْهَا ٱلْجِيدَ وَٱلْعَيْنَانَا وَمَنْخِرَيْنِ أَشْبَهَا ظَبْيَانَا, *I know of her the neck, and the two eyes, and two nostrils which resemble two gazelles,* in which
D ٱلْعَيْنَانَ and ظَبْيَانَ (written in rhyme نَا) are used instead of ٱلْعَيْنَيْنِ and ظَبْيَيْنِ.

* The form ـِينِ is said by some to be dialectical, whilst others consider it due only to poetic license (ضَرُورَةُ ٱلشِّعْرِ); e.g. وَأَنْكَرْنَا زَعَانِفَ آخَرِينِ, *and we ignore the riffraff of other* (*tribes*); وَمَا ذَا تَبْتَغِى ٱلشُّعَرَآءُ مِنِّى وَقَدْ جَاوَزْتُ حَدَّ ٱلْأَرْبَعِينِ, *and what is it pray that the poets want of me, since I have already passed the limit of forty* (*years*)? where آخَرِينِ and ٱلْأَرْبَعِينِ are used instead of آخَرِينَ and ٱلْأَرْبَعِينَ.

TRIPTOTE OR FIRST DECLENSION. A

Substantives.

	Masc. Proper.	Masc. Common.	Fem. Proper.	Fem. Common.
	Plur. sanus.		*Plur. sanus.*	
N.	زَيْدُونَ	. . .	هِنْدَاتٌ	جَنَّاتٌ
G. Ac.	زَيْدِينَ	. . .	هِنْدَاتٍ	جَنَّاتٍ
	Plur. fract.		*Plur. fract.*	
N.	زُيُودٌ	رِجَالٌ	هُنُودٌ	جِنَانٌ
G.	زُيُودٍ	رِجَالٍ	هُنُودٍ	جِنَانٍ
Ac.	زُيُودًا	رِجَالًا	هُنُودًا	جِنَانًا

B

Adjectives.

	Masc.	Fem.
	Sing.	
N.	جَالِسٌ *sitting.*	نَائِحَةٌ *mourning.*
G.	جَالِسٍ	نَائِحَةٍ
Ac.	جَالِسًا	نَائِحَةً
	Dual.	
N.	جَالِسَانِ	نَائِحَتَانِ
G. Ac.	جَالِسَيْنِ	نَائِحَتَيْنِ
	Plur. sanus.	
N.	جَالِسُونَ	نَائِحَاتٌ
G. Ac.	جَالِسِينَ	نَائِحَاتٍ
	Plur. fract.	
N.	جُلَّاسٌ	نُوَّحٌ
G.	جُلَّاسٍ	نُوَّحٍ
Ac.	جُلَّاسًا	نُوَّحًا

C

D

A

DIPTOTE OR SECOND DECLENSION.

Substantives.

	Masc.	Fem.
	Sing.	
N.	عُثْمَانُ *‘Othmān.*	زَيْنَبُ *Zeineb.*
G. Ac.	عُثْمَانَ	زَيْنَبَ
	Dual.	
N.	عُثْمَانَانِ	زَيْنَبَانِ
B G. Ac.	عُثْمَانَيْنِ	زَيْنَبَيْنِ
	Plur. sanus.	
N.	عُثْمَانُونَ	زَيْنَبَاتٌ
G. Ac.	عُثْمَانِينَ	زَيْنَبَاتٍ

Plur. fract.

(of دِرْهَمٌ *a dirham*)		(of جَارِيَةٌ *a young woman*)	
N.	دَرَاهِمُ	N. G.	جَوَارٍ*
C G. Ac.	دَرَاهِمَ	A.	جَوَارِيَ

Adjectives.

	Masc.		Fem.
		Sing.	
N.	أَسْوَدُ *black.*	أَفْضَلُ *more excellent.*	سَوْدَآءُ *black.*
G. Ac.	أَسْوَدَ	أَفْضَلَ	سَوْدَآءَ
		Dual.	
N.	أَسْوَدَانِ	أَفْضَلَانِ	سَوْدَاوَانِ
D G. Ac.	أَسْوَدَيْنِ	أَفْضَلَيْنِ	سَوْدَاوَيْنِ
		Plur. sanus.	
N.	. . .	أَفْضَلُونَ	. . .
G. Ac.	. . .	أَفْضَلِينَ	. . .

* جَوَارٍ stands in the Nom. for جَوَارِيُ, in the Gen. for جَوَارِيِ (identical in form with the Acc.). See p. 235, at the end of the note.

DIPTOTE OR SECOND DECLENSION. A

Adjectives.

	Masc.		Fem.
		Plur. fract.	
	(of فَقِيرٌ *poor*)		(of نَآئِحَةٌ *mourning*)
N.	فُقَرَآءُ	. . .	نَوَآئِحُ
G. Ac.	فُقَرَآءَ	. . .	نَوَآئِحَ

REM. *a.* There are two words in Arabic, in which the final flexional vowel of the singular affects the last vowel of the radical part of the substantive; viz. امْرُؤٌ, *a man*, and ابْنُمٌ, *a son*, for امْرَأٌ and ابْنَمٌ, which are also used (see § 19, *d*). B

Sing. Nom.	امْرُؤٌ or امْرُءٌ,	ابْنُمٌ
Gen.	امْرِئٍ or امْرِءٍ,	ابْنِمٍ
Acc.	امْرَءًا or امْرَءً,	ابْنَمًا

[According to ên-Naḍr ibn Śomèil, as quoted by Zamaḫśarī, *Fāïḳ* i. 524, فَمٌ *the mouth* is also doubly declined, فُمٌ, فِمٍ, فَمًا, as رَأَيْتُ فَمَهُ, أَخْرَجَ لِسَانَهُ مِنْ فِمِهِ and هٰذَا فُمُهُ. Comp. Lane and Fleischer, *Kl. Schr.* I. 180. D. G.] C

REM. *b.* For the comparison of the Arabic Declension with that of the other Semitic Languages see *Comp. Gr.* p. 139 *seqq.*

309. The following nouns are diptote. D

a. Several forms of the pluralis fractus; viz.

(α) Quadrisyllabic plurales fracti, the first and second syllables of which have fètḥa and the third kèsra, that is to say, the forms فَوَاعِلُ (XVI.), فَعَائِلُ (XVII.), فَعَالِلُ etc., and فَعَالِيلُ etc. (I. and II. of nouns which have more than three radical letters); as بَوَاعِثُ *causes*, عَجَائِبُ *wonders*, قَنَاطِرُ *bridges*, سَلَاطِينُ *sultans*.

(β) Plurales fracti which end in hèmza preceded by êlif mèmdūda

A (ـَآءُ), viz. فُعَلَآءُ (XX.) and أَفْعِلَآءُ (XXI.); as حُكَمَآءُ *wise men*, أَوْلِيَآءُ *friends* (compare *b*, α and *c*, β).

(γ) Plurales fracti which end in ـٍ and ـَى, viz. فَعَالٍ (XXIII.), فَعْلَى (XXII.), and فَعَالَى (XXIV.); as عَذَارٍ *virgins*, جَرْحَى *wounded men*, أَسَارَى *prisoners*, هَدَايَا *presents* (compare *b*, β and *c*, β).

(δ) أُوَلُ, plur. fract. of أَوَّلُ, and of its fem. أُولَى, *first*; أُخَرُ, plur. fract. of آخَرُ, and of its fem. أُخْرَى, *other*, *another*; جُمَعُ,
B كُتَعُ, بُصَعُ, بُتَعُ, plur. fract. of جَمْعَآءُ, كَتْعَآءُ, بَصْعَآءُ, بَتْعَآءُ, fem. of أَجْمَعُ, etc., *all together*.

[(ε) أَشْيَآءُ, the irregular plural of شَيْءٌ (comp. XIV. 2, rem.).]

b. Various common nouns and adjectives; viz.

(α) Common nouns and adjectives which end in hèmza preceded by èlif mèmdūda (ـَآءُ); as عَذْرَآءُ *a virgin*, بَيْضَآءُ *white* (§ 296).
C Compare *a*, β and *c*, β.

REM. This rule does not apply to cases in which the hèmza is *radical*, as قُرَّآءٌ from قَرَأَ (compare § 299, rem. *c*, and § 301, rem. *e*).

(β) Common nouns and adjectives ending in èlif maḳṣūra (ـَى); as ذِكْرَى *memory*, سَكْرَى *drunken* (§ 295, *a*). Compare *a*, γ and *c*, β.

REM. Excepting those in which the èlif maḳṣūra is *radical*; as
D هُدًى *guidance* (for هُدَيٌ, § 213).

(γ) Adjectives of the form أَفْعَلُ (§§ 232, 16, and 234—5), of which the fem. is فُعْلَى and فَعْلَآءُ (§§ 295, *b*, and 296); as أَعْجَبُ *more wonderful*; أَحْمَرُ *red*.—But adjectives of the form أَفْعَلٌ, f. أَفْعَلَةٌ, are triptote; as أَرْمَلٌ *poor*, *needy*, *without a wife*, f. أَرْمَلَةٌ *poor*, *needy*, *without a husband*, *a widow*.—Substantives of this form are usually regarded as triptote, e.g. أَجْدَلٌ *a hawk*, أَخْيَلٌ *a green woodpecker*, أَرْنَبٌ *a hare*, أَزْمَلٌ *a humming*; but the diptote form is admissible in such as were originally adjectives, e.g. أَجْدَلُ, أَخْيَلُ.

Rem. *a.* Some good authorities give أَرْمَلُ as the masculine of A
أَرْمَلَةٌ, which would be very irregular.

Rem. *b.* Adjectives of the form أَفْعَلُ, when used as substantives, retain the diptote inflection; e.g. أُدْهَمُ *a fetter* (properly *blackish, dun*), أَسْوَدُ *a serpent* (prop. *black*), أَبْرَقُ *stony land* (prop. *mottled*), أَبْطَحُ *a wide, gravelly water-course*, أَجْرَعُ *a tract of land without herbage.*

(δ) Adjectives of the form فَعْلَانُ, of which the fem. is فَعْلَى B
(§ 295, *a*); as سَكْرَانُ, f. سَكْرَى, *drunken.*—But those of which the fem. is فَعْلَانَةٌ (§ 295, rem. *a*) are triptote; as نَدْمَانٌ, f. نَدْمَانَةٌ, *a boon companion.*—Adjectives of the form فُعْلَانُ are all triptote, their fem. being formed by adding ـَةٌ (§ 295, rem. *a*); as عُرْيَانٌ, f. عُرْيَانَةٌ, *naked.*

Rem. *a.* Adjectives of the form فَعْلَانٌ, f. فَعْلَانَةٌ, are rare. The principal examples in the language are: أَلْيَانٌ *having a large fat tail* (of a sheep); حَبْلَانٌ *angry;* دَخْنَانٌ *stiflingly hot;* سَخْنَانٌ *hot;* C
سَيْفَانٌ *tall and slender;* ضَحْيَانٌ *exposed to the sun, eating in the forenoon* (اَلضُّحَى); صَوْجَانٌ and صَوْحَانٌ *dry, withered;* عَلَّانٌ *stupid, ignorant;* قَشْوَانٌ *thin, slender;* مَصَّانٌ *sucking* (sheep or cows) *out of greed, mean, vile;* مَوْتَانٌ *stupid, stolid;* نَدْمَانٌ *a boon companion;* نَصْرَانٌ *Christian.* Some of these, however, have also the form فَعَلَانٌ, فُعْلَانٌ, or فَعْلَانُ; as أَلَيَانٌ and أَلْيَانُ; سَخَنَانٌ, سُخْنَانٌ, or سَخْنَانُ; صُوحَانٌ; قُشْوَانٌ. The word صَوْجَانٌ may perhaps be merely a mistake for صَوْحَانٌ or صُوحَانٌ.

Rem. *b.* فُلَانٌ *so and so, such and such a one*, makes irregularly D
in the feminine فُلَانَةُ, [because it takes the place of a proper name (*c*, ζ)].

(ε) The masculine numerals as mere abstract numbers; e.g. ثَمَانِيَةُ ضِعْفُ أَرْبَعَةَ 8 *is the double of* 4; سِتَّةُ أَكْثَرُ مِنْ خَمْسَةَ بِوَاحِدٍ 6 *is more than* 5 *by one.*

(ζ) Distributive numerals of the forms فُعَالُ and مَفْعَلُ (§ 333); as ثُنَاءَ and مَثْنَى, *two by two*, ثُلَاثُ and مَثْلَثُ, *three by three.*

A (η) The grammatical paradigms formed from the root فعل, when used without the article as a sort of definite proper names. For example: أَفْعَلُ صِفَةً لَا يَنْصَرِفُ (*the form*) *'af'al*, (*used*) *as an adjective, is declined without tènwīn* (e.g. أَحْمَرُ *red*); أَفْعَلُ إِذَا كَانَ ٱسْمًا نَكِرَةً فَإِنَّهُ يَنْصَرِفُ (*the form*) *'af'al, when it is an indefinite noun, is declined with tènwīn* (e.g. أَفْكَلٌ *tremor,* أَجْدَلٌ *a hawk*); وَزْنُ طَلْحَةَ وَإِصْبَعٍ فَعْلَةٌ وَإِفْعَلُ *the measure of Ṭalḥa and 'iṣba' is fa'la and 'if'al.* But if we

B say كُلُّ أَفْعَلٍ يَكُونُ صِفَةً لَا يَنْصَرِفُ, *every* (*word of the form*) *'af'al, which is an adjective, is declined without tènwīn*, we must employ the nunation, because كُلٌّ, in the sense of *each, every*, requires an *indefinite* word after it in the genitive; and so in other cases.

[(θ) The diminutives of all diptote nouns, as أُسَيِّدُ, with the exception of the softened diminutives (§ 283) and of those that are derived from the distributive numerals of the form فُعَالُ (§ 333), as أُحَيِّدُ, ثُلَيِّثُ.]

C *c.* Many proper names; viz.

(α) Foreign names of men, as إِبْرَاهِيمُ *Abraham,* إِسْحٰقُ *Isaac,* يُوسُفُ *Joseph,* دَاوُدُ *David;* excepting such as consist of three letters, the second of which has ǵèzma or is a litera productionis, as نُوحٌ *Noah,* لُوطٌ *Lot.*

(β) Proper names which end in èlif maḳṣūra (compare *a*, γ and *b*, β) and èlif mèmdūda (compare *a*, β and *b*, α), whether Arabic or

D foreign; as يَحْيَى *John,* عَادِيَا or عَادِيَاءُ *'Ādiyā,* زَكَرِيَّاءُ *Zachariah,* يَعْلَى *Ya'lā,* لَيْلَى *Lèilā,* سَلْمَى *Sulmā.*

(γ) Proper names in ـَانُ, whether Arabic or foreign; as غَطَفَانُ *Ġaṭafān* (a tribe), عُثْمٰنُ *'Othmān,* حِطَّانُ *Ḥiṭṭān,* سُفْيَانُ *Sufyān,* سُلَيْمٰنُ *Solomon,* عِمْرَانُ *'Imrān* (*'Amram*), [with the exception of those that were originally common nouns of the forms فِعَالٌ and فِعْلَانٌ, as سِنَانٌ and رِضْوَانٌ].

(δ) Proper names which resemble in form the verbal forms فَعَّلَ A
and فُعِلَ, or any of the persons of the Imperfect; as شَمَّرُ *Šammar*,
شَلَّمُ *Jerusalem*, ضُرِبُ *Ḍorib*, أَحْمَدُ *Aḥmèd*, يَزِيدُ *Yèzīd*, يَشْكُرُ *Yèškur*,
تَدْمُرُ *Tadmur* (Palmyra), تَغْلِبُ *Taġlib*, يُبْنَى *Yubnā*, تُمَاضِرُ *Tumāḍir*,
يُرَامِلُ *Yurāmil*.

(ε) Common nouns of the feminine gender, consisting of more than three letters, when used as proper names; e.g. عَقْرَبٌ *a scorpion*, B
عَقْرَبُ *ʿAḳrab* (a man's name).

(ζ) Proper names which end in ـَةُ, whether masculine or feminine; as مَكَّةُ *Mèkka*, فَاطِمَةُ *Fāṭima* (a woman), دُغَةُ *Doġa* (a woman), طَلْحَةُ *Ṭalḥa*, قَتَادَةُ *Ḳatāda* (men). [Fem. proper names in ات keep their tènwīn, as أَذْرِعَاتٌ gen. acc. أَذْرِعَاتٍ; عَرَفَاتٌ gen. acc. عَرَفَاتٍ. Dialectic forms are عَرَفَاتُ gen. acc. عَرَفَاتِ and even عَرَفَاتَ.]

(η) Fem. proper names, which do not end in ـَةُ, but are either of C
foreign origin, or consist of more than three letters, or, though consisting of only three letters, are trisyllabic, owing to their middle radical having a vowel; e.g. مِصْرُ *Egypt*, جُورُ *Ġūr*, صُورُ *Tyre*, زَيْنَبُ *Zèinèb*, سُعَادُ *Suʿād*, شَتَرُ *Šatar*, سَقَرُ *Hellfire* (as the name of a particular part of hell).—But fem. proper names which consist of only three letters, the second of which has ġèzma, may be either diptote or triptote (though the former is preferred); as هِنْدُ or هِنْدٌ *Hind*,
دَعْدُ or دَعْدٌ *Daʿd*. D

(θ) Proper names, which are actually or seemingly derived from common substantives or adjectives; especially masculine names of the form فُعَلُ (from فَاعِلٌ), as عُمَرُ *ʿOmar*, زُفَرُ *Zufar*, جُشَمُ *Ġušèm*, زُحَلُ *the planet Saturn*, قُثَمُ *the male hyæna*; and feminine names of the form فَعَالِ (from فَاعِلَةٌ), as قَطَامِ *Ḳaṭām*, رَقَاشِ *Raḳāš*, حَذَامِ *Ḥaḏām*, بَرَاحِ *the sun*, صَلَاحِ *Ṣalāḥ* (a name of Mekka). These latter, however, have

A more usually and correctly the form فَعَالِ, and are wholly indeclinable; s قَطَامِ, رَقَاشِ, حَذَامِ, بَرَاحِ, صَلَاحِ, ظَفَارِ *Ẓafār* (a city), قَثَامِ *the female hyæna,* حَلَاقِ *death,* صَرَامِ *war,* أَزَامِ *a year of famine.*

REM. *a.* Words of the form فَعَالِ, of which the last letter is *r*, as جَعَارِ *the female hyæna,* حَضَارِ *Ḥaḍār* (a star in the Centaur), are almost invariably indeclinable, even in the dialect of those Arabs
B who in other cases use the form فَعَالُ.

REM. *b.* Besides being used as proper names, the forms فُعَلُ and فَعَالِ are often employed as vocatives, in terms of abuse; e.g. يَا خُبَثُ *O improbe!* f. يَا خَبَاثِ ; يَا فُسَقُ *O sceleste!* f. يَا فَسَاقِ ; يَا لُكَعُ *O vilis!* f. يَا لَكَاعِ.

REM. *c.* In compound proper names of the class called مُرَكَّبٌ مَزْجِيٌّ (§ 264), the first word is usually not declined at all, and the
C second follows the diptote declension; nom. حَضْرَمَوْتُ, بَعْلَبَكُّ, رَامَهُرْمُزُ, gen. and acc. حَضْرَمَوْتَ, بَعْلَبَكَّ, رَامَهُرْمُزَ*. Each word may, however, be declined separately, the second being in the genitive, and the first losing the tènwīn because it is defined by the second (see § 313, foll.); nom. حَضْرُمَوْتٍ, بَعْلُبَكٍّ, رَامُهُرْمُزٍ, gen. حَضْرِمَوْتٍ, acc. حَضْرَمَوْتٍ, etc. The proper name مَعْدِى كَرِب admits of three forms, for we may say مَعْدِى كَرِبٍ (like حَضْرُمَوْتٍ); or مَعْدِى كَرِبُ,
D gen. and acc. مَعْدِى كَرِبَ (like حَضْرَمَوْتُ, حَضْرَمَوْتَ); or مَعْدِى كَرِبَ in all three cases (like رَامَهُرْمُزُ).—Proper names of men ending in وَيْهِ are wholly indeclinable; as سِيبَوَيْهِ, نِفْطَوَيْهِ, عَمْرَوَيْهِ, بُوَيْهِ.

---

* [The kunya is sometimes considered as a single compound noun. A letter of the Prophet begins مِنْ مُحَمَّدٍ إِلَى ٱلْمُهَاجِرِ بْنِ أَبُو أُمَيَّةَ (*Fāiḳ* i. 5), some Ḳor'ān readers read in Sūr. cxi., تَبَّتْ يَدَا أَبُو لَهَبٍ, and well known are عَلِيُّ بْنُ أَبُو طَالِبٍ and مُعَاوِيَةُ بْنُ أَبُو سُفْيَانَ. Compare Belāḏorī 60, last l. and Baiḍāwī ii. 421, l. 10. D. G.]

Rem. *d.* Proper names, when used *indefinitely* [as is always A
the case when they are employed in the dual or plural], are
naturally declined with tènwīn; as رُبَّ إِبْرٰهِيمٍ لَقِيتُهُ *many an*
Abraham have I met; [فَكُلُّ دَوْرٍ مَخْصُوصٌ بِآدَمٍ وَحَوَّآءٍ *and each*
period has its peculiar Adam and Eve]; and so رُبَّ عِمْرَانٍ وَأَحْمَدٍ
وَفَاطِمَةٍ وَسُعَادٍ وَعُمَرٍ وَقَطَامٍ وَسِيبَوَيْهٍ. There is, however, a doubt as
to the admissibility of the *ṣarf* in the form أَفْعَلٍ.

Rem. *e.* The أَسْبَابُ ٱلِٱمْتِنَاعِ مِنَ ٱلصَّرْفِ, or reasons why a noun B
is debarred from taking the tènwīn, are usually reckoned by the
grammarians to be nine in number; viz. اَلْعَلَمِيَّةُ *its being a proper*
name; اَلْوَصْفِيَّةُ *its being an adjective*; اَلْعُجْمَةُ *its being a foreign*
word; اَلتَّرْكِيبُ *its being a compound of the class* اَلْمُرَكَّبُ ٱلْمَزْجِيُّ;
اَلتَّأْنِيثُ ٱللَّازِمُ لَفْظًا أَوْ مَعْنًى *its being necessarily feminine by form*
or meaning; اَلْأَلِفُ وَٱلنُّونُ ٱلْمُضَارِعَتَانِ لِأَلِفَيِ ٱلتَّأْنِيثِ *its ending in*
the termination ـَانِ, *which resembles the feminine termination* ـَآءُ; C
كَوْنُهُ جَمْعًا لَيْسَ عَلَى زِنَتِهِ وَاحِدٌ *its being a plural of a form which*
does not occur in the language as a singular (e.g. مَسَاجِدُ *mosques*,
مَصَابِيحُ *lamps*, for there is no singular noun of the form مَفَاعِلُ or
مَفَاعِيلُ); اَلْعَدْلُ عَنْ صِيغَةٍ إِلَى أُخْرَى *its being turned from one form*
into another (as عُمَرُ, which is مَعْدُولٌ, or *transformed*, from عَامِرٌ,
or قَطَامِ, which is مَعْدُولَةٌ from قَاطِمَةٌ); and وَزْنُ ٱلْفِعْلِ *its resembling*
in form a part of the verb. Any two or more of these causes in D
combination prevent a noun from being declined with tènwīn; e.g.
(1) اَلْعَلَمِيَّةُ + the termination ـَانِ, as عُثْمَانُ. Hence we say حَسَّانُ
Ḥassān, if we derive this name from the radical حَسٌّ; but if we
derive it from حُسْنٌ, it is triptote, حَسَّانٌ. (2) اَلْعَلَمِيَّةُ + اَلتَّرْكِيبُ,
as بَعْلَبَكُّ. (3) اَلْعَلَمِيَّةُ + اَلتَّأْنِيثُ, viz. (*a*) لَفْظًا وَمَعْنًى *in form and*
meaning, as فَاطِمَةُ; (*β*) مَعْنًى لَا لَفْظًا *in meaning but not in form*,

A as زَيْنَبُ ; (γ) لَفْظًا لَا مَعْنًى *in form but not in meaning*, as طَلْحَةُ (which, though feminine in form, yet is the name of a man). Except feminine proper names of the form فُعْل, in *c*, *η*. (4) اَلْعَلَمِيَّةُ + وَزْنُ ٱلْفِعْلِ, as يَزِيدُ. (5) اَلْعَلَمِيَّةُ + اَلْعَدْلُ, as عُمَرُ. (6) اَلْعَلَمِيَّةُ + اَلْعُجْمَةُ, as بُطْرُسُ *Petrus*. Except the case of نُوحٌ and similar names in *c*, *α*. (7) اَلْوَصْفِيَّةُ + اَلْعَدْلُ, as أُخَرُ, which is مَعْدُولٌ from آخَرُونَ, or جُمَعُ, which is مَعْدُولٌ from جَمْعَاوَاتٌ. (8) اَلْوَصْفِيَّةُ +

B the termination ـَانُ, in adjectives of the form فَعْلَانُ, fem. فَعْلَى. (9) اَلْوَصْفِيَّةُ + وَزْنُ ٱلْفِعْلِ, in adjectives of the form أَفْعَلُ.

310. Nouns ending in ـًى or ـًا, for ـَيٌ or ـَوٌ (§§ 213 and 245), which follow the first declension, and those in ـَى and ـَا, for ـَيُ, which follow the second (§ 309, *a*, *γ*; *b*, *β*; *c*, *β*), retain in the oblique cases the termination of the nominative, so that their declension is only *virtual* (تَقْدِيرِيٌّ), not expressed (لَفْظِيٌّ) or external (ظَاهِرٌ).

C E.g. عَصًا for عَصَوٌ, عَصَوٍ, and عَصَوًا ; رَحًى for رَحَيٌ, رَحَيٍ, and رَحَيًا ; بُشْرَى for بُشْرَيُ and بُشْرَيَ.

311. Nouns ending in ـٍ, for ـِيٌ or ـِوٌ (§ 167, *b*, *β*, and the Paradigms of the Verb, Tab. XVIII.) and ـِيٌ or ـُيٌ (see the same Tab. and § 218), have the same termination in the nom. and gen., but in the acc. ـِيًا (according to § 166, *a*). E.g. غَازٍ for غَازِوٌ, acc. غَازِيًا ;

D رَامٍ for رَامِيٌ, acc. رَامِيًا ; مُغْزٍ for مُغْزِيٌ, acc. مُغْزِيًا ; مُرْمٍ for مُرْمِيٌ, acc. مُرْمِيًا ; تَغَزٍّ for تَغَزِّيٌ (تَغَزُّيٌ), acc. تَغَزِّيًا ; تَمَنٍّ for تَمَنِّيٌ (تَمَنُّيٌ), acc. تَمَنِّيًا ; شَجٍ (verbal adj.) for شَجِيٌ, acc. شَجِيًا ; عَمٍ (verbal adj.) for عَمِيٌ, acc. عَمِيًا.

312. All plurals of the second declension, which ought regularly to end in ـِي, for ـِيُ, follow in the nom. the first declension instead of the second, and substitute ـٍ (for ـِى). They moreover retain, according to § 311, the same termination in the genit., and consequently follow the first declension in that case too; but in the acc. they remain true to the second declension, and have ـِىَ. E.g. جَارِيَةٌ, plur. nom. and gen. جَوَارٍ, for جَوَارِيٌ (instead of جَوَارِىُ), acc. جَوَارِىَ; مَعْنًى, plur. nom. and gen. مَعَانٍ, for مَعَانِيٌ (instead of مَعَانِىُ), acc. مَعَانِىَ; صَحْرَآءُ, plur. nom. and gen. صَحَارٍ, for صَحَارِيٌ (instead of صَحَارِىُ), acc. صَحَارِىَ. A B

II. *The Declension of Defined Nouns.*

313. Undefined nouns become defined: 1. by prefixing the article أَلْ; 2. (*a*) by adding a noun in the genitive, or (*b*) by adding a pronominal suffix.

[Rem. Only proper names and words used as proper names are in themselves definite (§ 309, *b*, *η*, vol. ii. § 78); if, therefore, they are not originally appellatives (as اَلْحَسَنُ properly *the beautiful*) they never have the article, unless they be used as generic nouns (as in رُبَّ إِبْرٰهِيمَ, § 309, *c*, rem. *d*), اَلزَّيْدُ ٱلْأَوَّلُ *the first Zèid.*—A defined noun is called مَعْرِفَةٌ or مُعَرَّفٌ (تَعْرِيفٌ means *defining*), an undefined noun نَكِرَةٌ or مُنَكَّرٌ (تَنْكِيرٌ means *leaving undefined*).] C

314. If an undefined noun be defined by the article, the following cases arise. D

(*a*) If it belongs to the first declension, it loses the tènwīn.

Nom.	اَلرَّجُلُ	اَلْحَسَنُ	اَلْمَدِينَةُ	اَلْمُحْصَنَةُ	اَلرِّجَالُ
	the man.	*Ĕl-Ḥasan.*	*the city.*	*the chaste (woman).*	*the men.*
Gen.	اَلرَّجُلِ	اَلْحَسَنِ	اَلْمَدِينَةِ	اَلْمُحْصَنَةِ	اَلرِّجَالِ
Acc.	اَلرَّجُلَ	اَلْحَسَنَ	اَلْمَدِينَةَ	اَلْمُحْصَنَةَ	اَلرِّجَالَ

Rem. The final ا of the acc. disappears along with the tènwīn.

A (*b*) If it belongs to the second declension, it assumes the terminations of the first, and becomes triptote.

Nom.	اَلْأَسْوَدُ	اَلسَّوْدَآءُ	اَلْأَكَابِرُ
	the black (m.).	*the black* (f.).	*the nobles.*
Gen.	اَلْأَسْوَدِ	اَلسَّوْدَآءِ	اَلْأَكَابِرِ
Acc.	اَلْأَسْوَدَ	اَلسَّوْدَآءَ	اَلْأَكَابِرَ

(*c*) If it be a plur. sanus fem., it loses the tènwīn.

B Nom.	اَلظُّلُمَاتُ	اَلْمَخْلُوقَاتُ	اَلْمُؤْمِنَاتُ
	the darknesses.	*the creatures.*	*the believing (women).*
Gen. Acc.	اَلظُّلُمَاتِ	اَلْمَخْلُوقَاتِ	اَلْمُؤْمِنَاتِ

REM. *a.* The plur. sanus masc. and the dual undergo no change when the article is prefixed; as اَلضَّارِبُونَ *those who beat,* اَلرَّجُلَانِ *the two men,* gen. acc. اَلضَّارِبِينَ, اَلرَّجُلَيْنِ.

REM. *b.* Nouns ending in ـٍ drop the tènwīn and resume their
C original ى; as اَلرَّامِى from رَامٍ, اَلْمَعَانِى from مَعَانٍ, اَلتَّمَنِّى from تَمَنٍّ, اَلْجَوَارِى from جَوَارٍ (see §§ 311, 312).

315. If a noun in the genitive is appended to an undefined noun, the following changes are produced.

(*a*) The singulars and broken plurals of both declensions are declined in the same way as if they were defined by the article (§ 314).

Nom.	كِتَابُ ٱللّٰهِ	أَسْفَلُ ٱلْأَرْضِ	رِجَالُ ٱلْمَدِينَةِ
D	*the book of God.*	*the lowest part of the earth.*	*the men of the city.*
Gen.	كِتَابِ ٱللّٰهِ	أَسْفَلِ ٱلْأَرْضِ	رِجَالِ ٱلْمَدِينَةِ
Acc.	كِتَابَ ٱللّٰهِ	أَسْفَلَ ٱلْأَرْضِ	رِجَالَ ٱلْمَدِينَةِ

Nom.	عَجَائِبُ ٱلْمَخْلُوقَاتِ	كُلُّ يَوْمٍ
	the wonders of creation.	*every day.*
Gen.	عَجَائِبِ ٱلْمَخْلُوقَاتِ	كُلِّ يَوْمٍ
Acc.	عَجَائِبَ ٱلْمَخْلُوقَاتِ	كُلَّ يَوْمٍ

Rem. *a.* The words أَبٌ *a father,* أَخٌ *a brother,* حَمٌ *a father-in-law,* and less frequently هَنٌ *a thing,* after rejecting the tènwīn, lengthen the preceding vowel. A

Nom.	أَبُو,	أَخُو,	حَمُو,	هَنُو;	for أَبٌ, etc.
Gen.	أَبِى,	أَخِى,	حَمِى,	هَنِى;	for أَبٍ, etc.
Acc.	أَبَا,	أَخَا,	حَمَا,	هَنَا;	for أَبًا, etc.*

The word ذُو, *the owner* or *possessor* of a thing, which is always connected with a following substantive in the genitive, has in the B gen. ذِى, in the acc. ذَا; whilst فَمٌ, *the mouth* (Aram. פּוּם), which is used instead of فُوهٌ or فَوَهٌ, makes either:

Nom.	فَمٌ,	Gen. فَمٍ,	Acc. فَمًا;
or:	فُو,	فِى,	فَا†.

Rem. *b.* Proper names of the first declension lose their tènwīn, when followed by the word ٱبْنٌ in a genealogical series; as مُحَمَّدُ

* The same is the case in the other Semitic languages; see *Comp. Gr.* p. 142 *seq.*—In Arabic the short vowels are used dialectically, as C in the verse بِأَبِهِ ٱقْتَدَى عَدِىٌّ فِى ٱلْكَرَمْ وَمَنْ يُشَابِهْ أَبَهُ فَمَا ظَلَمْ *'Adī has imitated his father in generosity, and whoever tries to resemble his father, does not do wrong;* where we find بِأَبِهِ and أَبَهُ for بِأَبِيهِ and أَبَاهُ. Some of the Arabs employ the forms أَبَا, etc., in all the three cases [أَبًا being, according to some lexicographers a dial. var. of أَبٌ. Comp. vol. ii. § 39, *a*, rem. *a*], as in the verse إِنَّ أَبَاهَا وَأَبَا أَبَاهَا قَدْ بَلَغَا فِى ٱلْمَجْدِ غَايَتَاهَا, *verily their* (the family's) *father and their father's* D *father have reached in glory their utmost limit;* where the first أَبَاهَا is the accus. after إِنَّ, and the second أَبَاهَا the genit., instead of أَبِيهَا, whilst غَايَتَاهَا stands by poetic license (in this case ٱلْإِشْبَاعُ) for غَايَتَهَا. [The genuineness of this verse is not free from suspicion. Comp. Nöldeke in *Zeitschr. D. M. G.* xlix. 321.]

† With these latter forms [which are employed only in connexion with a following pronoun or noun in the genitive] compare in Heb. פֶּה, constr. פִּי, with suffix פִּיךָ.

A بْنُ جَعْفَرِ بْنِ خَالِدِ بْنِ مُحَمَّدٍ, *Muhammad, the son of Ǵa'far, the son of Ḫālid, the son of Muhammad.* On the elision of the ا in اِبْنٌ, see § 21, *b*.

REM. *c*. Instead of بِنْتٌ, *a daughter*, we may use, when a genitive follows, the form اِبْنَةٌ. [The latter was formerly preferred, except at the beginning of a sentence. The form ابنت occurs in the Ḳor'ān (Sūr. lxvi. 12) and often in old Mss.]

(*b*) The dual loses the termination نِ.

B Nom. جَآءَ عَبْدَا ٱلسُّلْطَانِ *the two slaves of the sultan came;* لَنَا مَسْجِدَا ٱللّٰهِ ٱلْحَرَامَانِ *to us belong the two holy temples of God.*

Gen. رَوَى عَنْ أَبَوَىْ بَكْرٍ ٱبْنِ طَلْحَةَ وَٱبْنِ قَسُّومٍ *he learned and transmitted* (*traditions, poems, etc.*) *from the two 'Abū Bèkrs,* (viz. *'Abū Bèkr*) *'ibn Ṭalḥa and* (*'Abū Bèkr*) *'ibn Ḳassūm* (see § 299, rem. *h*).

Acc. رَأَيْتُ جَارِيَتَىْ أَبِى *I saw the two female slaves of my father.*

C REM. If an èlif conjunctionis follows the oblique cases of the dual, the final ى takes a kèsra instead of a ǵèzma; as مَرَرْتُ بِجَارِيَتَىِ ٱلْمَلِكِ *I passed by the two female slaves of the king* (see §§ 19 and 20, *c*); ٱلْمَنْسِمَانِ ظُفْرَا خُفَّىِ ٱلْبَعِيرِ *the two mansims are the extremities* (*nails*) *of the camel's hoofs.*

(*c*) The pluralis sanus loses the termination نَ.

D Nom. جَآءَ بَنُو ٱلْمَلِكِ *the sons of the king came;* مُجَرِّدُو أَسْيَافِهِمْ *drawing their swords.*

Gen. عِبْرَةٌ لِأُولِى ٱلْأَلْبَابِ *an example,* or *warning, for those who are possessed of intelligence* (see § 302, rem. *c*).

Acc. رَأَيْتُ بَنِى ٱلْمَلِكِ *I saw the king's sons;* كُنَّا مُوقِدِى ٱلنَّارِ *we were kindling the fire.*

REM. If the plur. ends in ـَوْنَ, acc. ـَيْنَ (for ـَيُونَ, ـَيِينَ), A
these terminations become, before a following gen., ـَوْ, ـَيْ; and if the genit. begins with an èlif conjunct., the final و takes ḍamma, and the final ى kèsra, instead of the ǵèzma; as مُصْطَفَوُ ٱللّٰهِ, مُصْطَفَيِ ٱللّٰهِ (§ 20, *c*).—Regarding the ا otiosum which is often, though incorrectly, added to the nominal term. ـُو and ـَوْ, see § 7, rem. *a*.

316. If a pronominal suffix is added to an undefined noun, the following changes take place. B

(*a*) Triptotes and the plur. sanus fem. lose the tènwīn, the dual and plur. sanus masc. the terminations نِ and نَ; as كِتَابٌ *a book*, كِتَابُهُ *his book;* ظُلُمَاتٌ *darkness*, ظُلُمَاتُهَا *its darkness;* كِتَابَانِ *two books*, كِتَابَاكَ *thy two books;* بَنُونَ *sons*, بَنُوكَ *thy sons;* لِبَائِعِيهِ *to its purchasers.*

(*b*) Before the pronominal suffix of the 1st p. sing. ـِى (see C
§ 185, rem. *a*, and § 317), the final vowels of the sing., plur. fractus, and plur. sanus fem. are elided; as كِتَابِى *my book*, from كِتَابٌ; كِلَابِى *my dogs*, from كِلَابٌ, plur. fract. of كَلْبٌ; تَوَابِعِى *my followers*, from تَوَابِعُ, plur. fract. of تَابِعٌ; جَنَّاتِى *my gardens*, from جَنَّاتٌ, plur. sanus of جَنَّةٌ.

(*c*) If the noun ends in ة, this letter is changed into (or rather, resumes its original form of) ت; as نِعْمَةٌ *a favour* or *benefit*, نِعْمَتِى. D

(*d*) If the noun ends in èlif mobile or hèmza, this letter passes before the suffixes into ؤ, when it has ḍamma (Nom.), and into ئ, when it has kèsra (Gen.); as نِسَآءٌ *women*, nom. with suffix نِسَآؤُهُ, *his women*, gen. نِسَآئِهِ. But when it has fètḥa (Acc.), it remains unchanged, as acc. نِسَآءَهُ.

REM. Of the words mentioned in § 315, rem. *a*, أَبٌ, أَخٌ and

A حَمٌ, take the suffixes thus: nom. أَبُوكَ, أَبُوهُ; gen. أَبِيكَ, أَبِيهِ; acc. أَبَاكَ, أَبَاهُ; but أَبِى, أَخِى, حَمِى, in all the three cases.—هَنٌ makes هَنِى; هَنُوكَ or هَنُكَ; هَنِيكَ or هَنِكَ; هَنَاكَ or هَنَكَ.—فَمٌ has regularly فَمِى; فَمُكَ; فَمُهُ, فَمِهِ; but more usually, nom. فُوكَ, فُوهُ; gen. فِيكَ, فِيهِ; acc. فَاكَ, فَاهُ; and فِىَّ, *my mouth*, in all the three cases.—ذُو is not used with suffixes.—On some dialectical varieties of أَبٌ
B see § 315, rem. *a*, note *.

APPENDIX.

The Pronominal Suffixes, which denote the Genitive.

317. The pronominal suffixes attached to nouns to denote the genitive, are exactly the same as those attached to verbs to denote the accusative (§ 185), with the single exception of the suffix of the
C 1st p. sing., which is ـِى, and not نِى.

REM. *a*. The suffix of the 1st p. sing. ـِى, when attached to a word ending in èlif maḳṣūra (ـَى), in the long vowels ـَا, ـِى, ـُو, or in the diphthongs ـَىْ and ـَوْ, becomes ىَ, the kèsra of the original form ـِىَ (see § 185, rem. *d*) being simply elided. Further, when the word ends in ـِى or ـَىْ, the final ى unites with the ى of the suffix into ىّ; and when it ends in ـُو or ـَوْ, the و is changed into ى, and likewise forms ىّ. E.g. هَوَاىَ *my love*, for هَوَاءِىَ,
D from هَوًى; خَطَايَاىَ *my sins*, for خَطَايَاءِىَ, from خَطَايَا, plur. fract. of خَطِيَّةٌ; غُلَامَاىَ *my two slaves*, for غُلَامَاءِىَ, from غُلَامَانِ, nom. dual of غُلَامٌ; قَاضِىَّ *my judge*, for قَاضِيىَ (قَاضِيِئِىَ), from قَاضٍ; مُسْلِمِىَّ *my Muslims*, for مُسْلِمُوىَ (مُسْلِمُوءِىَ) or مُسْلِمِيىَ (مُسْلِمِيِئِىَ), from مُسْلِمُونَ, مُسْلِمِينَ, plur. sanus of مُسْلِمٌ; غُلَامَىَّ *my two slaves*, for غُلَامَيْىَ (غُلَامَيْئِىَ), from غُلَامَيْنِ, genit. dual of غُلَامٌ; مُصْطَفَىَّ *my elect*, for مُصْطَفَوْىَ (مُصْطَفَوْئِىَ) or مُصْطَفَيْىَ

(مُصْطَفَيِّىَ), from مُصْطَفَوْنَ, مُصْطَفَيْنَ, plur. sanus of مُصْطَفًى.— A
From words like قَفًا, هَوًى, the form هَوَىَّ, قَفَىَّ, is used dialectically instead of قَفَاىَ, هَوَاىَ.—On أَبْ, أَخْ, حَمْ, هَنْ, فَمْ, and فُو, see § 316, rem.—[بُنَيِّى *a little son* has both بُنَىِّ and بُنَىَّ.]

Rem. *b.* Just as the verbal suffix نِى is sometimes shortened into نِ (§ 185, rem. *c*), so the nominal suffix ـِى occasionally becomes ـِ, particularly when the noun to which it is attached is in the vocative; as رَبِّ *my Lord!* يَا قَوْمِ *O my people!* [Comp. vol. ii. § 38*a*, rem. *b*.] B

Rem. *c.* What has been said in § 185, rem. *b*, of the change of the damma in هُ, هُمَا, هُمْ, هُنَّ, into kèsra after ـِ, ـِى, or ـَىْ, applies to the nominal as well as the verbal suffixes. E.g. كِتَابِهِ *of his book,* جَارِيَتَيْهِ *his two female slaves,* قَاتِلِيهِ *his murderers,* كِتَابِهِمَا, كِتَابِهِمْ ([before wasl and] in verse كِتَابِهِمُ, [which is the older form] or كِتَابِهِمِ), etc.

[Rem. *d.* If no ambiguity of meaning can arise, the dual before C a suffix in the dual is not unfrequently replaced by the singular or the plural, as قَلْبُهُمَا and قُلُوبُهُمَا *the heart of them both.*]

B. The Numerals.

1. *The Cardinal Numbers.*

318. The cardinal numbers from *one* to *ten* are :—

	Masc.	Fem.		Masc.	Fem.
1.	أَحَدٌ	إِحْدَى	5.	خَمْسٌ	خَمْسَةٌ
	وَاحِدٌ	وَاحِدَةٌ	6.	سِتٌّ	سِتَّةٌ
2.	اِثْنَانِ	اِثْنَتَانِ	7.	سَبْعٌ	سَبْعَةٌ
		ثِنْتَانِ	8.	ثَمَانٍ	ثَمَانِيَةٌ
3.	ثَلَاثٌ	ثَلَاثَةٌ	9.	تِسْعٌ	تِسْعَةٌ
4.	أَرْبَعٌ	أَرْبَعَةٌ	10.	عَشْرٌ	عَشَرَةٌ

D

A REM. *a.* For ثَلَاثٌ, ثَلَاثَةٌ, we may also write ثَلٰثٌ, ثَلٰثَةٌ, and for ثَمَانِيَةٌ, ثَمٰنِيَةٌ (§ 6, rem. *a*).—سِتٌّ stands, according to the Arab lexicographers, for سِدْتٌ (compare § 14, *c*), and that for سِدْسٌ. The correctness of this view is proved [as they say] by the diminutive سُدَيْسَةٌ, the fraction سُدُسٌ, *a sixth*, and the ordinal adj. سَادِسٌ, *sixth*.

REM. *b.* If we compare the above numerals with those of the cognate languages, it is easy to perceive their perfect identity; and,
B therefore, only one or two forms deserve notice here.—The Assyrian for *one* in the sing. masc. is *istin* (עִשְׁתֵּן), apparently identical with the Heb. עַשְׁתֵּי in עַשְׁתֵּי עָשָׂר; but the fem. is *iḥit* (אחת) = אַחַת (for אַחֶדֶת).—The Aram. תְּרֵין, f. תַּרְתֵּין, is a contraction for תְּנַיִן, which may be either the equivalent of the Heb. שְׁנַיִם (ת becoming שׁ, as in תַּלְגָּא, *snow*, = שֶׁלֶג, and נ exchanging with ר, as in דְּנַח, *to rise*, = זָרַח); or, as others think, derived from the
C rad. ܬܪ, as it were the dual of وِتْرٌ *single, sole.* The daghesh in the Heb. fem. שְׁתַּיִם (also pronounced אֶשְׁתַּיִם) indicates the loss of the *n* in ثِنْتَانِ.—The Heb. שֵׁשׁ, שִׁשָּׁה, stand for שֶׁדְשׁ, שִׁדְשָׁה (see rem. *a*, and compare the Æth. *sĕdĕstū* and *sĕssu*, for *sĕdsū*). The Jewish Aram. form שִׁת (שֵׁת), שִׁתָּה, is identical with the Arabic; whilst in the Syriac ܫܶܬ݁ or ܐܶܫܬ݁ the original doubling has left its trace in the hard sound of the *t* (compare שְׁתַּיִם).

D **319.** The cardinal numbers from 3 to 10 take the *fem.* form, when the objects numbered are of the *masc.* gender; and conversely, the *masc.* form, when the objects numbered are *fem.* E.g. رِجَالٌ عَشَرَةٌ, or عَشَرَةُ رِجَالٍ, *ten men* (lit., *men, a decade,* and *a decade of men*); نِسَآءٌ عَشْرٌ, or عَشْرُ نِسَآءٍ, *ten women.*

REM. *a.* The cause of this phenomenon, which also occurs in the other Semitic languages, seems to lie in the effort to give prominence to the independent substantive nature (§ 321) of the

cardinal numbers, in virtue of which they differ from the dependent A
adjectives, which follow the gender of their substantives.—That ثَلٰثٌ, أَرْبَعٌ, etc., are really *masc.*,—and consequently ثَلٰثَةٌ, أَرْبَعَةٌ, etc., *fem.*,—is evident from the construction of عَشْرٌ, in the sense of *ten days*, either as a singular masc. or as a broken plur. (viz. the implied أَيَّامٌ). We may say, for example, either ٱلْعَشْرُ ٱلْأَوْسَطُ مِنْ رَمَضَانَ *the middle ten days of Ramaḍān*, ٱلْعَشْرُ ٱلْأَخِيرُ مِنْ رَمَضَانَ *the last ten days of R.*, or ٱلْعَشْرُ ٱلْأَوَاخِرُ, ٱلْعَشْرُ ٱلْأَوَاسِطُ, etc. See also § 322, rem. *b*. B

Rem. *b*. An undefined number from 3 to 10 is expressed by بِضْعٌ ([or بَضْعٌ], literally, *a part* or *portion*); as بِضْعُ رِجَالٍ *some men*, بِضْعُ نِسْوَةٍ *some women*, فِى بِضْعِ سِنِينَ *in a few years*. The use of بِضْعَةٌ belongs to post-classical times; as بِضْعَةُ أَشْهُرٍ *some months*. [Comp. vol. ii. § 99, rem.]

320. The cardinal numbers from 1 to 10 are triptote, with the exception of the duals اِثْنَانِ, and اِثْنَتَانِ or ثِنْتَانِ.—ثَمَانٍ stands for C
ثَمَانِىٌ, and has in the genit. ثَمَانٍ, acc. ثَمَانِيًا (according to § 311).

321. The cardinal numbers from 3 to 10 are always *substantives*. They either follow the objects numbered, and are put in apposition with them, as رِجَالٍ ثَلَاثَةٍ, *of three men* (lit., *of men, a triad*); or they precede them, in which case the numeral governs the other substantive in the genitive of the plural, as ثَلَاثَةُ رِجَالٍ, *three men* (lit., *a triad of* D
men), except in the single instance of مِائَةٌ *a hundred* (see § 325).

Rem. *a*. ثَمَانٍ has, in the construct state, nom. and gen. ثَمَانِى, acc. ثَمَانِىَ (see § 320).

Rem. *b*. If the numerals from 3 to 10 take the article, they of course lose the tènwīn (§ 314, *a*).

Rem. *c*. اِثْنَانِ and اِثْنَتَانِ are very rarely construed with the

A genit. sing. of the objects numbered, and then of course drop their final ن (§ 315, *b*); as ثِنْتَا حَنْظَلٍ *two colocynths*, instead of اِثْنَتَانِ مِنَ ٱلْحَنْظَلِ, or simply حَنْظَلَتَانِ.

REM. *d.* بِضْعٌ and بِضْعَةٌ always precede the objects numbered, which are in the genitive of the plur. fractus (see § 319, rem. *b*).

322. The cardinal numbers from 11 to 19 are:—

B

	Masc.	Fem.		Masc.	Fem.
11.	أَحَدَ عَشَرَ	إِحْدَى عَشْرَةَ	15.	خَمْسَةَ عَشَرَ	خَمْسَ عَشْرَةَ
12.	اِثْنَا عَشَرَ	اِثْنَتَا عَشْرَةَ / ثِنْتَا عَشْرَةَ	16.	سِتَّةَ عَشَرَ	سِتَّ عَشْرَةَ
			17.	سَبْعَةَ عَشَرَ	سَبْعَ عَشْرَةَ
13.	ثَلَاثَةَ عَشَرَ	ثَلَاثَ عَشْرَةَ	18.	ثَمَانِيَةَ عَشَرَ	ثَمَانِيَ عَشْرَةَ
14.	أَرْبَعَةَ عَشَرَ	أَرْبَعَ عَشْرَةَ	19.	تِسْعَةَ عَشَرَ	تِسْعَ عَشْرَةَ

C REM. *a.* Instead of عَشْرَةَ some of the Arabs pronounce عَشِرَةَ, and the form عَشَرَةَ is said to occur.—For ثَمَانِيَ عَشْرَةَ we also find ثَمَانِي عَشْرَةَ, [and incorrectly] ثَمَانِ عَشْرَةَ and ثَمَانَ عَشْرَةَ. [In manuscripts we often find ثمان عشرة, which may be either of the two preceding forms, or the vulgar ثمانْ عشرة.]

REM. *b.* The cardinal numbers which indicate the *units* in these compounds, from 3 to 9, vary in gender according to the rule laid down in § 319; but the *ten* does not follow that rule, for it has
D here the form عَشَرَ with masculine nouns, and عَشْرَةَ with feminine. The same holds with regard to the undefined number, which is in this case masc. بِضْعَةَ عَشَرَ, fem. بِضْعَ عَشْرَةَ, *some, a few* (from 11 to 19). The objects numbered are placed after them in the *acc. sing.*

REM. *c.* These numerals are usually indeclinable, even when they take the article, with the exception of اِثْنَا عَشَرَ and اِثْنَتَا (ثِنْتَا) عَشْرَةَ, which have in the oblique cases اِثْنَيْ عَشَرَ and اِثْنَتَيْ (ثِنْتَيْ) عَشْرَةَ.

REM. *d.* The contraction of these compound numerals into *one* word began at a very early period, as may be seen from the Aramaic dialects, and the Arab grammarians mention such forms as أَحَدَعْشَرَ. In modern times they are greatly corrupted, being pronounced, for example, in Algiers, إِحْدَاش, إِتْنَاش, تَلَاتَّاش, أَرْبَعْتَاش, خَمْسْتَاش, سِتَّاش, سَبْعَتَاش, تَمَانْتَاش, تِسْعَتَاش. A

323. The cardinal numbers from 20 to 90 are :— B

20.	عِشْرُونَ	50.	خَمْسُونَ	80.	ثَمَانُونَ
30.	ثَلَاثُونَ	60.	سِتُّونَ	90.	تِسْعُونَ
40.	أَرْبَعُونَ	70.	سَبْعُونَ		

REM. *a.* ثَلَاثُونَ and ثَمَانُونَ may also be written ثَلٰثُونَ, ثَمٰنُونَ.

REM. *b.* The cardinal numbers from 20 to 90 are both masc. and fem., and have, like the ordinary plur. sanus masc., ـُونَ in the C nom., and ـِينَ in the oblique cases. They are *substantives*, and take the objects numbered after them in the *acc. sing.*, so that they do not lose the final ن. Sometimes, however, they are construed with the genit. of the possessor, when, of course, the ن disappears, leaving in the nom. ـُو, in the genit. and acc. ـِي.

REM. *c.* The Hebrew and Aramaic dialects agree with the Arabic as to the form of the tens; עֶשְׂרִים, ܥܣܪܝܢ, etc. But the Assyrian and Æthiopic curiously coincide in employing a form in D *ā* (for *ān*); Assyr. *isrā, silasā, irbā, ḫansā*; Æth. *ʻesrā, salasā, ʼarbĕʻā, ḫamsā*, etc.

324. The numerals which indicate numbers compounded of the units and the tens, are formed by prefixing the unit to the ten, and uniting them by the conjunction وَ, *and*; as أَحَدٌ وَعِشْرُونَ *one and twenty, twenty-one.* Both are declined; as gen. أَحَدٍ وَعِشْرِينَ, acc. أَحَدًا وَعِشْرِينَ.

A REM. The undefined unit is in this case نَيِّفٌ (lit., *excess, surplus*), as نَيِّفٌ وَعِشْرُونَ *twenty and odd;* but بِضْعٌ and بِضْعَةٌ are also used.

325. The numerals from 100 to 900 are :—

B

100. مِائَةٌ	600. سِتُّ مِائَةٍ
200. مِائَتَانِ	700. سَبْعُ مِائَةٍ
300. ثَلَاثُ مِائَةٍ	800. ثَمَانِي مِائَةٍ / ثَمَانِ مِائَةٍ
400. أَرْبَعُ مِائَةٍ	
500. خَمْسُ مِائَةٍ	900. تِسْعُ مِائَةٍ

REM. *a.* For مِائَةٌ (Æth. ምእት: *me'et*, Heb. מֵאָה, Aram. מְאָה, ܡܐܐ, Assyr. *mī*) we also find مِئَةٌ [and sometimes مِأَةٌ. For مِئَةٌ we find often مِيَةٌ, and more recently مِيَّةٌ. The dual مِائَتَانِ is
C written occasionally مِأَتَانِ, and hence in poetry مِاتَانِ. D. G.] The plur. is مِئُونَ, مِئَاتٌ, or مِأًى; the forms مِئِينَ, مُؤُونَ (like سِنِينَ from سَنَةٌ *a year*), and مِئًى (with the article, اَلْمِئِي) are rare. The strange spelling of مِائَةٌ seems to be due merely to a piece of bungling on the part of the oldest writers of the Ḳor'ān. The ا was probably meant to indicate the vowel of the second syllable, but was inadvertently placed before, instead of after, the ئ (ء).

D REM. *b.* The numerals from 3 to 9 are often united with مِائَةٌ into one word, as ثَلْثُمِائَةٍ. [In this case we find often in manuscripts ثمانمائة i.e. ثَمَانِمِائَةٍ, though the correct form is ثَمَانِي مِائَةٍ.] The regular construction ثَلْثُ مِئِينَ, etc. (see § 321), is very rarely employed [in poetry].

REM. *c.* مِائَةٌ usually takes the objects numbered after it in the *genit. sing.*, as مِائَةُ سَنَةٍ, مِائَتَا سَنَةٍ, ثَلْثُمِائَةِ سَنَةٍ.

326. The numerals from 1000 upwards are :— A

1000.	أَلْفٌ	100,000.	مِائَةُ أَلْفٍ
2000.	أَلْفَانِ	200,000.	مِائَتَا أَلْفٍ
3000.	ثَلَاثَةُ آلَافٍ	300,000.	ثَلْثُمِائَةِ أَلْفٍ
4000.	أَرْبَعَةُ آلَافٍ	400,000.	أَرْبَعُمِائَةِ أَلْفٍ
	etc.		etc. B
11,000.	أَحَدَ عَشَرَ أَلْفًا	1,000,000.	أَلْفُ أَلْفٍ
12,000.	اِثْنَا عَشَرَ أَلْفًا	2,000,000.	أَلْفَا أَلْفٍ
13,000.	ثَلَاثَةَ عَشَرَ أَلْفًا	3,000,000.	ثَلَاثَةُ آلَافِ أَلْفٍ
	etc.		etc.

REM. The plur. of أَلْفٌ (Heb. אֶלֶף, Aram. אַלְפָּא, ܐܠܦܐ, C but Æth. *'elf*, 10,000) is أُلُوفٌ, آلَافٌ, and آلُفٌ. It takes the objects numbered after it in the *genit. sing.*, as أَلْفُ دِرْهَمٍ, أَلْفَا دِرْهَمٍ, ثَلٰثَةُ آلَافِ دِرْهَمٍ. [The plural آلُفٌ is only used in the combination ثَلَاثَةُ آلُفٍ, but آلَافٌ with all numerals from 3 to 10. In manuscripts it is often written defectively الف (أَلٰفٌ). The plurals أُلُوفٌ and مِئُونَ, are only employed of indefinite numbers, *thousands, hundreds*. D. G.]

327. The numerals which indicate numbers made up of thousands, D hundreds, tens, and units, may be compounded in two ways. Either (*a*) the thousands are put first, and followed successively by the hundreds, units, and tens, as ثَلَاثَةُ آلَافٍ وَسَبْعُ مِائَةٍ وَأَحَدٌ وَعِشْرُونَ, 3721 ; or (*b*) the order is reversed, and becomes units, tens, hundreds, thousands, as أَحَدٌ وَعِشْرُونَ وَسَبْعُمِائَةٍ وَثَلٰثَةُ آلَافٍ.

A *2. The Ordinal Numbers.*

328. The ordinal adjectives from *first* to *tenth* are :—

Masc.	Fem.		Masc.	Fem.	
الأَوَّلُ	الأُولَى	*the first.*	سَادِسٌ	سَادِسَةٌ	*sixth.*
ثَانٍ	ثَانِيَةٌ	*second.*	سَابِعٌ	سَابِعَةٌ	*seventh.*
ثَالِثٌ	ثَالِثَةٌ	*third.*	ثَامِنٌ	ثَامِنَةٌ	*eighth.*
رَابِعٌ	رَابِعَةٌ	*fourth.*	تَاسِعٌ	تَاسِعَةٌ	*ninth.*
خَامِسٌ	خَامِسَةٌ	*fifth.*	عَاشِرٌ	عَاشِرَةٌ	*tenth.*

B

REM. *a.* الأَوَّلُ stands for الأَأْوَلُ or الأَوْأَلُ, الأُولَى for الأُؤْلَى or الوُولَى, according to the superlative form أَفْعَلُ, f. فُعْلَى, from the rad. أول or وأل. Its plurals are: الأَوَّلُونَ, الأَوَائِلُ, الأَوَالِي, and
C الأُوَلُ for the masc.; الأُوَلُ (rarely الأُوَّلُ) for the fem.*

---

* [If أَوَّلٌ is used as a noun, it takes the tènwīn, as in the verse of the *Naḳāiḍ* (f. 182 *b*) quoted by Wright on the margin, لَهُمْ أَوَّلٌ يَعْلُو عَلَى كُلِّ أَوَّلِ *they have a past* (or *an ancestor*) *surpassing the past* (or *ancestor*) *of everybody else*, and another *apud* Wright, *Opusc.* 106, l. 7 (where it means *ancestor*), as also in the phrase مَا تَرَكَ لَهُ أَوَّلًا وَلَا
D آخِرًا *he left him neither past* (قَدِيمًا) *nor present* (حَدِيثًا). The fem. plur. occurs in the phrase هُنَّ الأَوَّلَاتُ دُخُولًا وَالآخِرَاتُ خُرُوجًا *they are the first to enter, the last to leave*, as plurals of أَوَّلَةٌ and آخِرَةٌ. In later times the fem. أَوَّلَةٌ is very common also as an adjective (comp. Fleischer, *Kl. Schr.* i. 336 *seq.*); likewise the adverb أَوَّلًا (as in أَوَّلًا وَآخِرًا) for the correct أَوَّلَ *formerly.* So it is interpreted in the phrase لَقِيتُهُ عَامًا أَوَّلًا *I met him in a year before*, as some say instead of عَامًا أَوَّلَ *last year* (comp. Lane s. v. عام). D. G.]

Rem. *b.* ثَانٍ makes, of course, in the construct state and with the art. ثَانِى, اَلثَّانِى; in the acc. ثَانِيًا, construct state and with the art. ثَانِىَ, اَلثَّانِىَ. And so with the rest; ثَالِثٌ, اَلثَّالِثُ, etc. A

Rem. *c.* Instead of سَادِسٌ the forms سَادٍ (acc. سَادِيًا) and سَاتٌّ (formed directly from سِتٌّ, سِتَّةٌ) are occasionally used.—ثَالٍ, acc. ثَالِيًا, also occurs for ثَالِثٌ [and خَامٍ for خَامِسٌ].

329. The ordinals from *eleventh* to *nineteenth* are:— B

Masc.	Fem.	
حَادِىَ عَشَرَ	حَادِيَةَ عَشْرَةَ	*eleventh.*
ثَانِىَ عَشَرَ	ثَانِيَةَ عَشْرَةَ	*twelfth.*
ثَالِثَ عَشَرَ	ثَالِثَةَ عَشْرَةَ	*thirteenth.*
رَابِعَ عَشَرَ	رَابِعَةَ عَشْرَةَ	*fourteenth.*
etc.	etc.	

Rem. These numerals are not declined, when they are undefined; and even if defined by the article, they remain unchanged, as اَلثَّالِثَ عَشَرَ, اَلثَّالِثَةَ عَشْرَةَ. For اَلْحَادِىَ عَشَرَ and اَلثَّانِىَ عَشَرَ we may say اَلْحَادِى عَشَرَ and اَلثَّانِى عَشَرَ. Some, however, admit the inflection of the unit, when defined, as اَلثَّالِثُ عَشَرَ, اَلثَّالِثَةُ عَشْرَةَ; in which case اَلْحَادِى (اَلثَّانِى) عَشَرَ is the nom. and genit., اَلْحَادِىَ (اَلثَّانِىَ) عَشَرَ the accus. C

330. The ordinals from *twentieth* to *ninetieth* are identical in form with the cardinals; as عِشْرُونَ *twentieth,* اَلْعِشْرُونَ *the twentieth.* If joined to the ordinals of the units, these latter precede, and the two are united by وَ; as حَادٍ وَعِشْرُونَ *one and twentieth, twenty-first* (gen. حَادٍ وَعِشْرِينَ, acc. حَادِيًا وَعِشْرِينَ), fem. حَادِيَةٌ وَعِشْرُونَ. If a compound of this sort be defined, both its parts take the article; as D

A اَلْحَادِى وَٱلْعِشْرُونَ (acc. اَلْحَادِىَ وَٱلْعِشْرِينَ) *the twenty-first*, اَلرَّابِعُ وَٱلْعِشْرُونَ *the twenty-fourth.*

[REM. Later writers use instead of these forms حَادِى عِشْرِينَ, رَابِعُ عِشْرِينَ and with the article, اَلْحَادِى عِشْرِينَ, اَلرَّابِعُ عِشْرِينَ, lit. *the first of the twenties, the fourth of the twenties.* Comp. vol. ii. § 108. D. G.]

B 3. *The remaining Classes of Numerals.*

331. The numeral adverbs, *once, twice, thrice*, etc., are capable of being expressed in two ways. (*a*) By the accusative of the nomen vicis (§ 219), or, if this should be wanting, of the nomen verbi; as قَامَ قَوْمَةً أَوْ قَوْمَتَيْنِ, *he rose up once or twice;* قَاتَلَ قِتَالًا وَاحِدًا أَوْ قِتَالَيْنِ, *he fought once or twice.* It is also permitted to use the simple cardinal numbers, the nomen verbi being understood; as أَمَتَّنَا ٱثْنَتَيْنِ
C وَأَحْيَيْتَنَا ٱثْنَتَيْنِ, *thou hast given us death twice, and thou hast given us life twice*, i.e. إِمَاتَتَيْنِ and إِحْيَاءَتَيْنِ. (*b*) By the noun مَرَّةٌ, and similar words, in the accus.; as مَرَّةً *once*, مَرَّتَيْنِ *twice*, ثَلٰثَ مَرَّاتٍ, or ثَلٰثَ مِرَارٍ, or ثَلٰثَ دَفَعَاتٍ, *thrice;* عِشْرِينَ كَرَّةً *twenty times;* تَارَةً وَأُخْرَى *once and again;* etc.

332. The numeral adverbs *a first, second, third time*, etc., are
D expressed either by adding the accus. of the ordinal adjective to a finite form of a verb (in which case the corresponding nomen verbi is understood); or by means of one of the words مَرَّةٌ, دَفْعَةٌ, etc., in the accus., accompanied by an ordinal adjective agreeing with it. E.g. جَآءَ ثَالِثًا (i.e. جَآءَ مَجِيئًا ثَالِثًا), or جَآءَ مَرَّةً ثَالِثَةً, *he came a third time;* جَآءَ ٱلثَّالِثَ (i.e. جَآءَ ٱلْمَجِىْءَ ٱلثَّالِثَ), or جَآءَ ٱلْمَرَّةَ ٱلثَّالِثَةَ, *he came the third time.*

333. The *distributive* adjectives are expressed by repeating the cardinal numbers once; or by words of the forms فُعَالُ and مَفْعَلُ,

either singly or repeated. E.g. جَآءَ ٱلْقَوْمُ ٱثْنَيْنِ ٱثْنَيْنِ, or جَآءَ ٱلْقَوْمُ A
مَثْنَى, *the people came two by two;* جَآءُوا ثُلَاثَ ثُلَاثَ, or جَآءُوا مَثْلَثَ
مَثْلَثَ, *they came three by three;* مَرَرْتُ بِقَوْمٍ مَثْنَى وَثُلَاثَ *I passed by a party of men, (walking) by twos and threes;* فَٱنْكِحُوا مَا طَابَ لَكُمْ مِنَ ٱلنِّسَآءِ مَثْنَى وَثُلَاثَ وَرُبَاعَ *then marry what pleaseth you of women, two and three and four at a time.* The most common words of the forms
فُعَالُ and مَفْعَلُ are أُحَادُ, وُحَادُ, مَوْحَدُ; ثُنَآءُ, مَثْنَى (for مَثْنَيُ); ثُلَاثُ, B
مَثْلَثُ; and رُبَاعُ, مَرْبَعُ; but the formation is admitted [by some] up to 10 [; the best authorities mentioning only عُشَارُ].

334. The *multiplicative* adjectives are expressed by nomina patientis of the second form, derived from the cardinal numbers; e.g. مُثَنًّى *twofold, double, dualized;* مُثَلَّثٌ *threefold, triple, triangular;* مُرَبَّعٌ *fourfold, square;* مُخَمَّسٌ *fivefold, pentagonal;* etc. *Single* or *simple* is مُفْرَدٌ (nom. patient. IV.). C

335. Numeral adjectives, expressing the number of parts of which a whole is made up, take the form فُعَالِيٌّ; as ثُنَائِيٌّ *biliteral;* ثُلَاثِيٌّ *triliteral, three cubits in length* or *height;* رُبَاعِيٌّ *quadriliteral, four spans* or *cubits in height, a tetrastich;* خُمَاسِيٌّ *quinqueliteral, five spans in height;* etc.

336. The *fractions,* from *a third* up to *a tenth,* are expressed by D
words of the forms فُعْلٌ, فُعُلٌ, and فَعِيلٌ, pl. أَفْعَالٌ; as ثُلْثٌ, ثُلُثٌ, or ثَلِيثٌ, pl. أَثْلَاثٌ, *a third;* سُدْسٌ, سُدُسٌ, or سَدِيسٌ, pl. أَسْدَاسٌ, *a sixth;* ثُمْنٌ, ثُمُنٌ, or ثَمِينٌ, pl. أَثْمَانٌ, *an eighth.*—[The form مِفْعَالٌ is exclusively employed for *a fourth* مِرْبَاعٌ and *a tenth,* مِعْشَارٌ, together with رُبْعٌ, رُبُعٌ and عُشْرٌ, عُشُرٌ or عَشِيرٌ. According to Zamaḫšarī, *Fāïḳ* ii. 659 the form رَبِيعٌ never occurs in this signification, nor, according

A to Abū Zèid (*Nawādir* 193) ثَلِيثٌ and خَمِيسٌ. D. G.] *A half* is نِصْفٌ, less frequently نَصْفٌ, نُصْفٌ (vulg. نُصّ), or نَصِيفٌ, pl. أَنْصَافٌ.— The fractions above *a tenth* are expressed by a circumlocution; e.g. ثَلٰثَةُ أَجْزَآءٍ مِنْ عِشْرِينَ جُزْءًا, *three parts out of twenty*, $\frac{3}{20}$; [نِصْفُ العُشْرِ $\frac{1}{20}$; عُشْرُ العُشْرِ $\frac{1}{100}$; نِصْفٌ وَرُبْعٌ $\frac{3}{4}$; نِصْفٌ وسُدْسٌ $\frac{2}{3}$; نِصْفٌ وثُلْثٌ عُشْرٍ $\frac{8}{15}$; نِصْفٌ وثُلْثٌ ونِصْفُ عُشْرٍ $\frac{53}{60}$; etc.*]

B REM. The form فُعْلٌ occurs in the same sense in Assyrian, Heb. and Aram.; e.g. ܬܘܠܬܐ *a third*, "rubu," רֹבַע, *a fourth*, חֹמֶשׁ *a fifth*.

337. The period, at the end of which an event usually recurs, is expressed by a noun of the form فِعْلٌ, in the accus., either with or without the article; as ثِلْثًا, or اَلثِّلْثَ, *every third* (day, month, year, etc.); رِبْعًا, or اَلرِّبْعَ, *every fourth*; etc. Synonymous with ثِلْثٌ is غِبٌّ, C as حُمَّى ٱلثِّلْثِ, or حُمَّى ٱلْغِبِّ, *the tertian fever*.

C. THE NOMINA DEMONSTRATIVA AND CONJUNCTIVA.

338. We treat of the nomina demonstrativa (including the article), and the nomina conjunctiva (including the nomina interrogativa), in one chapter, because they are both, according to our terminology, pronouns, the former being the demonstrative pronouns, D the latter the relative.

1. *The Demonstrative Pronouns and the Article.*

339. The demonstrative pronouns, أَسْمَآءُ ٱلْإِشَارَةِ, are either simple or compound.

---

* [On a similar expression of whole numbers by circumlocution see Goldziher in *Zeitschr. D. M. G.* xlix. 210 *seqq.*]

340. The simple demonstrative pronoun is ذَا, *this, that.* A

	Masc.	Fem.
Sing.	ذَا	ذِى (ذِهْ, ذِهِ, ذِهِى);
		تَا, تِى (تِهْ, تِهِ, تِهِى).
Dual. Nom.	ذَانِ (ذَانِّ)	تَانِ (تَانِّ).
Gen. Acc.	ذَيْنِ (ذَيْنِّ)	تَيْنِ (تَيْنِّ).

Plur. comm. gen. أُلَى, أُلَا, or أُولَى ; أُلَآءِ or أُولَآءِ. B

This simple form of the demonstrative pronoun is used to indicate a person or thing which is *near* to the speaker.

Rem. *a.* The *u* in أُولَى and أُولَآءِ is always *short*, و being merely scriptio plena. In this way أُولَى can be distinguished in verse from أُولَى, the fem. of أَوَّلُ, *first*, in which the *u* is long. The و may have been inserted in order the more easily to distinguish أُلَى and أُلَآءِ from إِلَى and آلَآءُ. C

Rem. *b.* The diminutive of ذَا is ذَيَّا, f. تَيَّا; du. ذَيَّانِ, f. تَيَّانِ; pl. أُولَيَّا, أُولَيَّآءِ.

Rem. *c.* Closely connected in its origin with ذَا is another monosyllable, viz. ذُو (= Heb. זֶה, Phœn. ז and אז, *this*) which is commonly used in the sense of *possessor*, *owner*. It is thus declined.

	Masc.	Fem.
Sing. Nom.	ذُو (זֶה)	ذَاتُ (זאת). D
Gen.	ذِى	ذَاتِ.
Acc.	ذَا	ذَاتَ.
Du. Nom.	ذَوَا	ذَوَاتَا (ذَاتَا).
Gen. Acc.	ذَوَىْ	ذَوَاتَىْ (ذَاتَىْ).
Plur. Nom.	ذَوُو, أُلُو or أُولُو (אֵלֶּה)	ذَوَاتُ, أُلَاتُ or أُولَاتُ.
Gen. Acc.	ذَوِى, أُلِى or أُولِى	ذَوَاتِ, أُلَاتِ or أُولَاتِ.

A The *u* in أُولُو and أُولَاتُ is always *short*, as in أُولَى and أُولَاءِ.—The form أَذْوَاءُ is used as a plural of ذُو, when this word forms part of the names or surnames of the kings or princes of ĕl-Yèmèn, as ذُو يَزَنَ, ذُو نُوَاسٍ, ذُو رُعَيْنٍ, ذُو ٱلْكَلَاعِ, etc. These are called أَذْوَاءُ ٱلْيَمَنِ, formed as if from a singular ذَوًى.

[REM. *d.* كَذَا (sometimes written كَذَى) *thus, so and so, so and so much* or *many*, is compounded of كَ *as, like* and the
B demonstrative pronoun ذَا. Comp. Vol. ii. § 44, *e*, rem. *d*.]

341. From the simple demonstrative pronoun are formed compounds :

(*a*) By adding the pronominal suffix of the second person (كَ, كِ ; كُمَا ; كُمْ, كُنَّ), either (α) alone, or (β) with the interposition of the demonstrative syllable لِ.

(*b*) By prefixing the particle هَا.

C **342.** The gender and number of the pronominal suffix, appended to the simple demonstrative pronoun, depend upon the sex and number of the persons addressed. In speaking to a *single man*, ذَاكَ is used; to a *single woman*, ذَاكِ ; to *two persons*, ذَاكُمَا ; to *several men*, ذَاكُمْ ; to *several women*, ذَاكُنَّ. But the form ذَاكَ may also be—and in fact usually is—employed, whatever be the sex and number of the persons spoken to; and so with the rest. In regard to their signification, these compound forms differ from the simple pronoun in indicating a *distant* object.

D

	Masc.	Fem.
Sing.	ذَاكَ (ذَآئِكَ*) *that*.	تَاكَ, تِيكَ (vulg. ذِيكَ).
Du. Nom.	ذَانِكَ	تَانِكَ.
Gen. Acc.	ذَيْنِكَ	تَيْنِكَ.

Plur. comm. gen. أُلَاكَ or أُولَاكَ, أُلَآئِكَ or أُولَآئِكَ.

---

* [Some say that ذَآئِكَ is a mispronunciation for ذٰلِكَ.]

Rem. *a.* The *u* is *short* in أُولَاكَ and أُولَآئِكَ, just as in أُولَى, A
أُولَآءِ, and أُولُو (§ 340, rem. *a*, *c*).

Rem. *b.* · The diminutive of ذَاكَ is ذَيَّاكَ, f. تَيَّاكَ, etc.

343. By inserting the demonstrative syllable لِ before the pronominal suffix, we get a longer form ذَالِكَ or ذٰلِكَ (often written ذَلِكَ, § 6, rem. *a*). B

	Masc.	Fem.
Sing.	ذٰلِكَ *that.*	تِلْكَ (تَالِكَ).
Du. Nom.	ذَانِّكَ	تَانِّكَ.
Gen. Acc.	ذَيْنِّكَ	تَيْنِّكَ.

Plur. comm. gen. أُلَالِكَ or أُولَالِكَ.

Rem. *a.* تِلْكَ is a contraction for تِيلِكَ. In the dual, ذَانِّكَ, C
تَانِّكَ, stand for ذَانِلِكَ, تَانِلِكَ; and ذَيْنِّكَ, تَيْنِّكَ, for ذَيْنِلِكَ, تَيْنِلِكَ. The plur. is rare, أُولَاكَ or أُولَآئِكَ (§ 342) being generally used instead. Some authorities regard ذَانِّكَ, تَانِّكَ, as the dual of ذَاكَ, the second *n* being in their opinion merely corroborative.

Rem. *b.* Some grammarians assert that there is a slight difference of meaning between ذَاكَ and ذٰلِكَ, the former referring in their opinion to the nearer of two distant objects, the latter to the more remote. D

Rem. *c.* The syllable لِ must not be mistaken for the preposition لِ (which, when united with the pronominal suffixes of the second and third persons, becomes لَ), but is to be viewed as a demonstrative syllable, which occurs also in the article and in the relative pronoun. See §§ 345 and 347.

Rem. *d.* The diminutive of ذٰلِكَ is ذَيَّالِكَ, f. تَيَّالِكَ. [A com-

A pound of كَ and ذٰلِكَ (comp. § 340, rem. *d*) is كَذٰلِكَ *so, in like manner**.]

344. The particle هَا (which has the same demonstrative force as the Latin *ce* in *hicce*) is called by the Arabs حَرْفُ ٱلتَّنْبِيهِ, *the particle that excites attention*. It is prefixed both to the simple demonstrative ذَا, and to the compound ذَاكَ (but not to ذٰلِكَ). Before ذَا it is usually written defectively, هٰذَا or هَذَا; before ذَاكَ in full, هَاذَاكَ.

B

	Masc.	Fem.
Sing.	هٰذَا *this.*	هٰذِهِ (هٰذِهْ), هٰذِى
		(هَاتِهِ, هَاتِى, هَاتَا, هٰذَاتِ).
Du. Nom.	هٰذَانِ	هَاتَانِ or هٰتَانِ.
Gen. Acc.	هٰذَيْنِ	هَاتَيْنِ or هٰتَيْنِ.

C Plur. comm. gen. هَاؤُلَا or هٰؤُلَا, هَاؤُلَآءِ or هٰؤُلَآءِ.

In like manner, هَاذَاكَ or هٰذَاكَ, fem. هَاتَاكَ, هَاتِيكَ, etc.

REM. *a*. هَا is identical with the Aram. הָא, ܗܳܐ, *this*, as an interjection, *lo!* Heb. הֵא.

REM. *b*. In the dual some say هٰذَانِّ, with double *n*.—The diminutive of هٰذَا is هٰذَيَّا, f. هَاتَيَّا, pl. هٰؤُلَيَّآءِ; of هٰذَاكَ, هٰذَيَّاكَ, pl.
D هٰؤُلَيَّائِكَ. [By prefixing ها to كذا is formed هٰكَذَا *thus*.]

[REM. *c*. To these demonstratives belong also ذَيْتَ وَذَيْتَ and كَيْتَ وَكَيْتَ, *thus and thus, so and so, such and such things*, for which we also find ذَيْتِ وَذَيْتِ, كَيْتِ وكَيْتِ (rarely ذَيْتُ وَذَيْتُ, كَيْتُ وَكَيْتُ) and for the former ذَيَّةَ وَذَيَّةَ, ذَيَّآءِ وَذَيَّآءِ, for the latter كَيَّةَ وَكَيَّةَ. According to some scholars there is originally a slight difference between these expressions, the former relating to what

* [A singular contraction (or modification) of كذلك is كاك used by the poet ĕš-Šanfarā, as quoted in the *Ḥamāsa*, p. 244, l. 21.]

has been said, the latter to what has been done, as كَذَا refers to A
quantity (comp. Ḥarīrī, *Durrat*, ed. Thorb. p. 99). D. G.]

345. The article أَلْ—called by the Arabs أَدَاةُ ٱلتَّعْرِيفِ *the instrument of definition*, ٱلْأَلِفُ وَٱللَّامُ *the ělif and lām*, لَامُ [or حَرْفُ] ٱلتَّعْرِيفِ *the lām of definition*, or simply اَللَّامُ *the lām*,—is composed of the demonstrative letter ل (see § 343, rem. *c*, and § 347) and the prosthetic اَ, which is prefixed only to lighten the pronunciation B
(هَمْزَةُ ٱلْوَصْلِ, § 19 *a*, and rem. *f*). [It is always written in conjunction with the following word.] Though it has become determinative, it was originally demonstrative, as still appears in such words as اَلْيَوْمَ *to-day*, اَلْآنَ *now*, etc.

[Rem. *a*. The article, if employed to indicate the genus, i.e. any individual (animate or inanimate) bearing the name, is called اَللَّامُ لِتَعْرِيفِ ٱلْجِنْسِ, or simply لَامُ ٱلْجِنْسِ, as أَهْلَكَ ٱلنَّاسَ ٱلدِّينَارُ وَٱلدِّرْهَمُ *dīnār and dirhem bring men to perdition*, اَلرَّجُلُ C
خَيْرٌ مِنَ ٱلْمَرْأَةِ *man is better than woman*; if indicating a particular individual it is called اَللَّامُ لِتَعْرِيفِ ٱلْعَهْدِ, or simply لَامُ ٱلْعَهْدِ.]

Rem. *b*. Some grammarians regard the ělif as an integral part of the article, and say that it was originally أَلْ (with أَلِفُ ٱلْقَطْعِ, of the same form as هَلْ, بَلْ), gradually weakened to اَلْ. But sometimes the Arabs suppress the ا, saying for instance لَحْمَرُ for اَلْأَحْمَرُ (comp. Vol. ii. § 242, footnote). D

Rem. *c*. It is sometimes, though very rarely, used as a relative pronoun (=اَلَّذِى, § 347); as مَنْ لَا يَزَالُ شَاكِرًا عَلَى ٱلْمَعَهْ *he who does not cease to be grateful for what is with him* (or *for what he has*), where ٱلْمَعَهْ = اَلَّذِى مَعَهُ; مِنَ ٱلْقَوْمِ ٱلرَّسُولُ ٱللهِ مِنْهُمْ *of the people of whom is the Apostle of God*, where ٱلرَّسُولُ ٱللهِ = اَلَّذِينَ رَسُولُ ٱللهِ; مَا أَنْتَ بِٱلْحَكَمِ ٱلتُّرْضَى حُكُومَتُهُ *thou art not the judge*

A *whose sentence is approved*, where اَلتُّرْضَى = اَلَّذِى تُرْضَى. Compare, for example, in German, *der* = *welcher*, and our *that* for *who* and *which*.

REM. *d.* اَلْ is [in all probability (see *Comp. Gr.* p. 114)] identical with the Hebrew art. .הַ, for הַל. In South Arabia اَمْ was (and even still is) used for اَلْ, but without assimilation; as لَيْسَ مِنَ آمْبِرِّ آمْصِيَامُ فِى آمْسَفَرِ *fasting in journeying is not (an act) of piety;* يَرْمِى وَرَآئِى بِآمْسَهْمِ وَآمْسَلِمَةْ *he casts (standing) behind me with arrow*
B *and stone;* for اَلْبِرِّ, اَلصِّيَامُ, اَلسَّفَرِ, بِٱلسَّهْمِ, and وَٱلسَّلِمَةِ.

2. *The Conjunctive (Relative) and Interrogative Pronouns.*

(a) *The Conjunctive Pronouns.*

346. The conjunctive pronouns are :—

(1) اَلَّذِى *who, which, that;* fem. اَلَّتِى.

(2) مَنْ *he who, she who, whoever;*

C مَا *that which, whatever.*

(3) أَىٌّ *he who, whoever;* fem. أَيَّةٌ *she who, whoever.*

(4) أَيُّمَنْ *every one who, whosoever;*

أَيُّمَا *everything which, whatsoever.*

REM. مَنْ, مَا, أَىٌّ, أَيَّةٌ, and their compounds, أَيُّمَنْ, أَيُّمَا, are also interrogatives, which indeed is their original signification (see
D § 351 and foll.). They ought therefore to be treated of first as interrogatives and then as conjunctives; but it is convenient to reverse this order, so as to connect the relatives with the demonstratives.

347. The conjunctive اَلَّذِى is compounded of the article اَلْ, the demonstrative letter لَ (see §§ 343 and 345), and the demonstrative pronoun ذَا, or ذُو (§ 340, rem. *c*). When used substantively, it has the same meaning as مَنْ, مَا, viz. *he who, that which, whoever, whatever;* when used adjectively, it signifies *who, which, that,* and refers necessarily to a definite substantive, with which it agrees in gender, number, *and case.* It is declined as follows:— A

	Masc.	Fem.	
Sing.	اَلَّذِى (اَلَّذِ ; اَلَّذْ ; اَلَّذِىُّ,	اَلَّتِى (اَلَّتِ ; اَلَّتْ :	
	اَلَّذِىِّ ; لَذِى).	اَللَّاتِى).	
Du. Nom.	اَللَّذَانِ (اَللَّذَانِّ ; اَللَّذَا).	اَللَّتَانِ (اَللَّتَانِّ ; اَللَّتَا).	B
Gen. Acc.	اَللَّذَيْنِ (اَللَّذَيْنِّ).	اَللَّتَيْنِ (اَللَّتَيْنِّ).	
Plur.	اَلَّذِينَ (اَلَّذِى ; [اَللَّآءِى] ;	اَللَّاتِى ; اَللَّاتِ (اَللَّآءَاتِ ;	
	اَللَّآءِ ; [اَللَّآؤُونَ Nom.,	اَللَّوَاتِى ; اَللَّوَاتِ (اَللَّوَا ;	
	اَللَّآئِينَ (Gen. Acc.]) ;	اَللَّآءِى ; اَللَّآءِ ;	
	اَلْأُلَى or اَلْأُولَى*.	اَلْأُلَى or اَلْأُولَى.	C

Rem. *a.* اَلَّذِى, اَلَّتِى, and اَلَّذِينَ, are written defectively, because of their frequent occurrence, instead of اَللَّذِى, اَللَّتِى, and اَللَّذِينَ. The other forms, which are not in such constant use, generally retain the double ل of the article and the demonstrative.—The modern, vulgar form, for all numbers and genders, is اَلِّي or اَللِّي.

Rem. *b.* The tribe of Hudèil (هُذَيْل), according to the Arab grammarians, used اَلَّذُونَ in the nom. plur. masc., اَلَّذِينَ in the gen. D and acc. This اَلَّذُونَ must, of course, at one time have been universally employed as the nom., اَلَّذِينَ being the form which belongs to the oblique cases; but gradually the latter supplanted the

* [According to aṣ-Ṣabbān, as quoted by Landberg (*Nylander's Specimenschrift*, p. 30) the relative pronoun is only اَلْأُلَى, the article sufficing to distinguish it from the prepos. إِلَى. Comp. § 340, rem. *a.* D. G.]

A former, just as in modern Arabic the oblique form of the plur. sanus, ـِينَ, has everywhere usurped the place of the direct form ـُونَ. Even the sing. اَلَّذِى is an oblique form, the nom. of which ought properly to be اَلَّذُو.—The forms اَلْلَّاؤُونَ, gen. and acc. اَلْلَّائِينَ, and اَللَّاؤُو are also said to occur.

REM. *c.* اَلَّذِى was originally, as its derivation shows, a demonstrative pron., and has its precise Hebrew equivalent in הַלָּזֶה,
B fem. הַלֵּזוּ, comm. הַלָּז (= اَلَّذْ). See *Comp. Gr.* p. 117.

REM. *d.* From اَلَّذِى are formed the diminutives اَللَّتَيَّا, اَللَّذَيَّا; du. اَللَّذَيَّانِ, اَللَّتَيَّانِ; pl. اَللَّذَيُّونَ, اَللَّتَيَّاتُ. The forms اَللُّذَيَّا, اَللُّتَيَّا, are vulgar and incorrect.

REM. *e.* Instead of اَلَّذِى, some of the Arabs, especially the tribe of *Ṭayyi'* (طَيِّءٌ), employ ذُو (Heb. זוּ, Aram. דִּי, דְּ, Æth. H: *za*).
C It is then either wholly *indeclinable*, which is more usual; as فَحَسْبِى مِنْ ذُو عِنْدَهُمْ مَا كَفَانِيَا *then enough for me of that which is with them* (of their property) *is what suffices me*, for مِنَ ٱلَّذِى (كَفَانِيَا in rhyme for كَفَانِى); لَأَنْتَحِيَنْ لِلْعَظْمِ ذُو أَنَا عَارِقُهْ *I will set to work in earnest on the bone which I am gnawing* (on the satire which I am meditating), for اَلَّذِى (عَارِقُهْ in rhyme for عَارِقُهُ); وَبِئْرِى ذُو حَفَرْتُ وَذُو طَوَيْتُ *and my well which I dug and which*
D *I lined* (or *cased*), for اَلَّتِى and وَٱلَّتِى; [فَلَا وَذُو بَيْتُهُ فِى ٱلسَّمَآءِ *no! by Him whose residence is in heaven*, *'Aġānī* xi. 25, l. 18. D. G.] or else declined as follows :—

		Masc.	Fem.
Sing.	Nom.	ذُو	ذَاتُ
	Gen.	ذِى	ذَاتُ (ذَاتِ)
	Acc.	ذَا	ذَاتُ (ذَاتِ)

	Masc.	Fem.
Du. Nom.	ذَوَا	ذَوَاتَا
Gen. Acc.	ذَوَىْ	ذَوَاتَىْ
Plur. Nom.	ذُوُو	ذَوَاتُ
Gen. Acc.	ذَوِى	ذَوَاتُ (ذَوَاتِ)

A

An example of this use is بِٱلْفَضْلِ ذُو فَضَّلَكُمُ ٱللّٰهُ بِهِ وَٱلْكَرَامَةِ ذَاتُ أَكْرَمَكُمُ ٱللّٰهُ بِهَا *by the excellence wherewith God hath made* B *you excel, and the honour wherewith God hath honoured you,* for ٱلَّذِى and ٱلَّتِى; [a woman in Yèmèn said ('Omāra, ed. Kay, p. 147, l. 9, 11) لا بد من ذى حكم الامير دو بُد من for لَا بُدَّ مِنَ ٱلَّذِى حَكَمَ ٱلْأَمِيرُ *you cannot but obey the decision of the Prince.* D. G.]

348. The conjunctive pronouns مَنْ and مَا are indeclinable, and differ from ٱلَّذِى in never being used adjectively, but always substantively, so that they correspond to the Latin *is qui, ea quæ, id quod,* C Gr. ὅστις, ἥτις, ὅ,τι. The former (مَنْ) is used of beings endowed with reason, the latter (مَا) of all other objects. [They are either definite (مَوْصُول) as ٱلَّذِى, or indefinite (مَوْصُوف), مَنْ signifying in the latter case *one who,* ما *something that,* and may also have a collective meaning *persons who, things that,* being nevertheless construed as singulars.]

Rem. For the corresponding forms in the other Semitic languages see *Comp. Gr.* pp. 123—127.

349. The conjunctive pronoun أَيٌّ, fem. أَيَّةٌ, *he who, she who,* D *whoever,* is regularly declined in the sing. according to the triptote declension, but has commonly neither dual nor plural.

Rem. The Æth. has the same word, አይ፡ (*'ay*) *who? of what sort?* The corresponding Heb. vocable is אִי, used as an adverb, *where?* in interrogative phrases אֵי, which appears in Æth. in አይቴ፡ (*'aytē*) *where?* እፎ፡ (*'ĕfō*) *how?* Syr. ܐܝܟܐ *where?* ܐܝܢܐ *who?* ܐܝܟܢܐ *how long?* etc.

A **350.** Of أَيٌّ and مَنْ, مَا, are compounded أَيُّمَنْ *he who, she who, whosoever,* أَيُّمَا *that which, whatsoever.* Only the first part of the compound admits of being declined; gen. أَيِّمَنْ, أَيِّمَا; acc. أَيَّمَنْ, أَيَّمَا.

(b) *The Interrogative Pronouns.*

351. It has been already stated (§ 346, rem.) that the conjunctive pronouns, with the exception of اَلَّذِى, are also interrogative, which is
B indeed their original signification. To them may be added كَمْ [and كَأَيٍّ or كَأَيِّنْ], *how much* [or *many*], which are (*a*) interrogative, (*b*) according to our ideas, exclamatory, according to the Arab grammarians, enuntiative (لِلْإِخْبَارِ); but never conjunctive.

REM. The interrogative مَا may be* shortened after prepositions into مَ, and is then united in writing both with those prepositions with which such a union is usual, and with those with
C which it is not, (though, in the latter case, it is better to keep them apart); e.g. بِمَ, لِمَ, فِيمَ, مِمَّ, عَمَّ (for مِنْ مَ, عَنْ مَ), إِلَامَ, عَلَامَ, حَتَّامَ (better حَتَّى مَ, عَلَى مَ, إِلَى مَ). In such cases, the accent is transferred from مَ to the preceding syllable (as *bíma, 'ilá ma,* etc.); whence it happens that بِمَ and لِمَ are sometimes shortened in poetry into بِمْ and لِمْ. This is also the origin of كَمْ, for كَمَ or كَمَا (lit., *the like of what? the worth of what?*), Heb. כַּמֶּה, כַּמָּה,
D Aram. כְּמָא, ܟܡܐ [see *Comp. Gr.* p. 125].—In pause these words are written بِمَهْ, عَمَّهْ, حَتَّامَهْ, etc. Similarly we find فَمَهْ for فَمَا *what then?* and كَيْمَهْ *that what? for what purpose?* as when one

---

* [Rather, "is usually shortened." Zamahšarī, *Fāiḳ*, ii. 159 calls it "the commoner" form (الْأَشْيَعُ). The grammarians of the school of Baṣra say that it must always be shortened in prose; in poetry the élif may be retained. Comp. Fleischer, *Kl. Schr.* i. 364. D. G.]

says قَصَدْتُ فُلَانًا *I went to (the house of) so and so*, to which you A
rejoin كَيْمَهْ, and the answer is كَيْ أُحْسِنَ إِلَيْهِ *that I might do him a kindness.* [The shortening of مَا takes place also in such sentences as مَجِىءَ مَ جِئْتَ *in what manner did you arrive?* and مِثْلَ مَ أَنْتَ *what are you like?*]

352. The interrogative pronoun مَنْ, *who?* has the distinctions of gender, number, and case, only when it stands alone; as if one should say *Some one is come*, or *I have seen some one*, and another B
should ask *Who? Whom?* In this case its declension is as follows:—

		Masc.	Fem.
Sing.	Nom.	مَنُو	
	Gen.	مَنِى	مَنَهْ (مَنْتْ).
	Acc.	مَنَا	
Du.	Nom.	مَنَانْ	مَنْتَانْ (مَنَتَانْ).
	Gen. Acc.	مَنَيْنْ	مَنْتَيْنْ (مَنَتَيْنْ). C
Plur.	Nom.	مَنُونْ	مَنَاتْ.
	Gen. Acc.	مَنِينْ	

Rem. *a.* Only a poet could venture to say أَتَوْا نَارِى فَقُلْتُ مَنُونَ أَنْتُمْ *they came to my fire, and I said, Who are ye?*

Rem. *b.* The interrogative pronoun مَا *what?* is never declined under any circumstances. D

[Rem. *c.* From مَنْ is formed the relative adjective مَنِّىٌّ, with the article الْمَنِّىُّ (comp. Vol. ii. § 170, rem. *b*). The dual is اَلْمَنِّيَّانِ, the plural اَلْمَنِّيُّونَ.]

353. The interrogative pronoun أَىٌّ, fem. أَيَّةٌ, *who?* is either construed with a following noun in the genitive, or with a suffix, or stands alone. In the first two cases, it loses the tènwīn (§§ 315, *a*, 316, *a*, *c*), and, if followed by a noun, is generally masc. sing.; as

A أَىُّ كِتَابٍ *which book* (lit. *quid libri*)? gen. أَىِّ كِتَابٍ, acc. أَىَّ كِتَابٍ; أَىُّ عَيْنٍ *which eye* or *fountain?* أَىُّ ٱلْمَرْأَتَيْنِ *which of the two women?* أَىُّ ٱلنِّسَآءِ *which of the women?* [The feminine form is of rare occurrence, as أَيَّةُ أُكْلَةٍ *whatever morsel* (ĕl-Mubarrad 86, l. 17) and أَيَّةُ أُنْثَى *which female?* (Dîw. Huḏêil, n. 201, vs. 2). D. G.] In the second case, when prefixed to a fem. pronoun, it may be masc. or fem. أَيُّهُنَّ or أَيَّتُهُنَّ *which of them?* meaning women, the latter being the
B more common. When standing alone, or used like مَنْ in § 352, it has all the numbers and cases, the pausal forms being:—

Sing. masc., nom. أَىْ or أَىّْ, gen. أَىِّ or أَىّْ, acc. أَيَّا; fem. أَيَّهْ.

Dual masc., nom. أَيَّانْ, gen. acc. أَيَّيْنْ; fem., nom. أَيَّتَانْ, gen. acc. أَيَّتَيْنْ.

Plur. masc., nom. أَيُّونْ, gen. acc. أَيِّينْ; fem. أَيَّاتْ.

C In أَىُّ and أَىِّ the final vowel is said to be obscurely sounded or slurred (اَلرَّوْمُ).

REM. *a.* With the suffixes أَىٌّ is sometimes shortened into أَىْ, as أَيْهُمَا, for أَيُّهُمَا, *which of the two?* and so in [the interrogative أَيْمَ *what?* for أَىُّ مَا, as أَيْمَ تَقُولُ *what dost thou say?* and] the vulga interrogative أَيْشْ *what?* for أَىُّ شَىْءٍ.

REM. *b.* Instead of أَىٌّ with [a following noun in the genitive or] a suffix, the more general and indefinite أَيُّمَا is sometimes used;
D as أَيُّمَا أَحَبُّ إِلَيْكَ هُوَ أَمْ أَنَا, *which is dearer to you, he or I?* in which example أَيُّمَا stands for أَيُّنَا, *which of us?*

REM. *c.* From أَىٌّ are formed the relative adjective أَيِّىٌّ *from what place?* (see Lane, art. اى, p. 134 *c*), and the compound كَأَىِّ or كَأَيِّنْ (also written كَآءٍ or كَائِنْ, كَىْءٍ, كَيْءٍ or كَيْئِنْ, كَأْيٍ and كَأْ (§ 351 and Vol. ii. § 34, *e*, rem. *d*).

REM. *d.* See *Comp. Gr.* pp. 120—122.

[3. *The Indefinite Pronouns.* A

353*. 1. The interrogative pronouns مَنْ and مَا have passed into indefinites (*Comp. Gr.* p. 125)*, with the sense of *somebody, something,* but are never thus employed unless with a qualificative complement (صِفَةٌ), and are therefore called مَوْصُوفَةٌ (§ 348). This complement is very rarely an adjective or participle, but usually a preposition with following genitive, as مَا لِى *something which I have,* B or an adverb as مَنْ هُنَاكَ *somebody here,* or a qualificative clause, as مَنْ قَالَ *one who says.* Comp. Vol. ii. § 172, rem. *a.*

2. The indefinite pronoun مَا is used to introduce a clause equivalent to the *maṣdar* or infinitive, and is in that case called مَا ٱلْمَصْدَرِيَّةُ (Vol. ii. § 88, § 114, § 127, rem *e*); hence its use in conditional clauses as مَا ٱلشَّرْطِيَّةُ (Vol. ii. § 6), or in reference to time as مَا ٱلزَّمَانِيَّةُ or مَا ٱلدَّيْمُومَةُ (Vol. ii. § 7); if added to certain adverbial C nouns, it gives them a conditional and general signification, as the Latin termination *cunque,* e.g. أَيْنَمَا *wherever,* حَيْثُمَا *wherever, whenever,* مَهْمَا *whatever;* if appended to إِنَّ, أَنَّ, كَأَنَّ and لٰكِنَّ it hinders their regimen and is therefore called مَا ٱلْكَافَّةُ (Vol. ii. § 36, rem. *d*); with the same effect it is added to لَيْتَ, عَلَّ and لَعَلَّ (*ibid.* rem. *f*) and to رُبَّ (Vol. ii. § 84, rem. *a* and *b*); in apposition to an indefinite noun, it has a vague intensifying force and is called مَا ٱلْإِبْهَامِيَّةُ D (Vol. ii. § 136 *a,* rem. *e*); added to the affirmative لَ it serves to strengthen the affirmation مَا مَزِيدَةٌ لِلتَّأْكِيدِ (see an example § 361 near the end, and Vol. ii. § 36, rem. *e*); it is often inserted after the

---

* [Prym, *Diss. de enuntiationibus relativis Semiticis,* p. 100 and Fleischer, *Kl. Schr.* i. 360 *seq.*, 706 *seq.* reject this theory, considering the indefinite meaning of مَنْ and مَا as the original, whence the interrogative has been derived.]

A prepositions مِنْ, عَنْ and بِ without affecting their regimen, and is then called مَا ٱلْمَزِيدَةُ or مَا ٱلزَّائِدَةُ (Vol. ii. § 70, rem. *f*). In like manner it is also put after رُبَّ (Vol. ii. § 84, rem. *a*) and in other cases (Vol. ii. § 90, rem.).]

3. فُلَانٌ, fem. فُلَانَةُ (§ 309, *b*, δ, rem. *b*), as كِنَايَاتٌ عَنْ أَسَامِى ٱلْأَنَاسِىِّ, stand for names of persons, like ὁ, ἡ δεῖνα, *so and so, M.* or *N.*;
B as فُلَانُ ٱبْنُ فُلَانٍ ὁ δεῖνα τοῦ δεῖνος, أَلَا قَاتَلَ ٱللّٰهُ ٱلْوُشَاةَ وَقَوْلَهُمْ فُلَانَةُ أَضْحَتْ خُلَّةً لِفُلَانِ, *O may God curse all talebearers and their saying "So and so has become a sweetheart of so and so."* Syr. ܦܠܢ, fem. ܦܠܢܝܬܐ, Heb. פְּלֹנִי. In speaking of animals, ٱلْفُلَانُ and ٱلْفُلَانَةُ are employed, as رَكِبْتُ ٱلْفُلَانَ *I rode on such and such a one.*—هَنٌ *a thing*, and its fem. هَنَةٌ, are similarly used for substantives of the class
C أَسْمَآءُ ٱلْجِنْسِ (§ 191, rem. *b*, 3, 4).—On the use of these words in the vocative, see the Syntax.

III. THE PARTICLES.

354. There are *four* sorts of particles (حَرْفٌ, pl. حُرُوفٌ, [or أَدَاةٌ, pl. أَدَوَاتٌ]); viz., Prepositions, Adverbs, Conjunctions, and Inter-
D jections.

A. THE PREPOSITIONS.

355. The prepositions are called by the Arabs حُرُوفُ ٱلْجَرِّ, *the particles of attraction*, or ٱلْجَوَارُّ (from the sing. ٱلْجَارُّ or ٱلْجَارَّةُ), *the attractives*, i.e. the particles which govern the genitive. They are also named حُرُوفُ ٱلْخَفْضِ, *the particles of depression*, and حُرُوفُ ٱلْإِضَافَةِ, *the particles of annexation* or *connection*, because the

distinctive vowel of the genitive (*i*), and consequently the genitive A
itself, is called اَلْخَفْضُ (see § 308, footnote), and because this case has its peculiar place in that connection which many prepositions with their genitives really represent (see § 358). They are divided into *separable* prepositions, i.e. those which are written as separate words, and *inseparable*, i.e. those which are always united in writing with the following noun.

356. The *inseparable* prepositions consist of *one* consonant with B
its vowel. They are:—

(*a*) بِ *in, at, near, by, with, through* (Heb. Aram. בְּ, Æth. በ: *ba*). [بِلَا, *without*, is a compound of بِ with the negative لَا. Comp. Vol. ii. § 56, rem. *c*.]

(*b*) تَ *by*, in swearing, as تَٱللّٰهِ *by God!**

(*c*) لِ *to* (sign of the Dative), *for, on account of* (Heb. Aram. לְ, Æth. ለ: *la*).

(*d*) وَ *by*, in swearing, as وَٱللّٰهِ *by God!* C

Rem. *a*. The damma of the suffixed pronouns of the 3d pers. هُ, هُمَا, هُمْ, هُنَّ, is changed after بِ into kèsra; as بِهِ, بِهِمْ. See § 185, rem. *b*, and § 317, rem. *c*. The ancient and poetic form هُمُ changes either both vowels, or the first only; بِهِمِ or بِهِمُ.

Rem. *b*. The kèsra of the prep. لِ passes before the pronominal suffixes into fètha; as لَهُ *to him*, لَكُمْ *to you*, لَنَا *to us*. Except the suffix of the 1st pers. sing., which absorbs the vowel of the preposition; لِى *to me*. D

---

* [تَ was especially in use at Mekka. It seems to be the remnant of some word, as it is (probably of another) in تَحِينَ (= لَاتَ حِينَ ?) and تَلَانَ (= اَلْآنَ). Comp. the abbreviation of أَيْمُنُ ٱللّٰهِ, Vol. ii. § 62, rem. *b*. I take the وَ in وَٱللّٰهِ and the وَاوُ رُبَّ (Vol. ii. § 235) to be also remnants of words. D. G.]

A REM. *c.* كَ *as, like* (Heb. Aram. כְּ), which is commonly reckoned a preposition, is really not so. It is a formally undeveloped noun, which occurs only as the governing word in the genitive connection, but runs in this position through all the relations of case (*similitudo, instar*).

357. The *separable* prepositions are of *two* sorts. Those of the first class, which are all biliteral or triliteral, have different terminations; those of the second class are simply nouns of different forms
B in the accus. sing., determined by the following genitive, and they consequently end in fĕtḥa without tènwīn (ـَ).

358. The separable prepositions of the first class are:—

(*a*) إِلَى *to* (Heb. אֱלֵי, אֶל־).

(*b*) حَتَّى *till, up to, as far as* (Heb. עַד, Æth. እስከ:). A dialectic variety is عَتَّى.

C (*c*) عَلَى *over, above, upon, against, to, on account of, notwithstanding* (Heb. עֲלֵי, עַל־, Aram. עַל, ܥܠ).

(*d*) عَنْ *from, away from, after, for.*

(*e*) فِي *in, into, among, about.*

(*f*) لَدُنْ, or لَدَى (لَدَا), *with* (penes, apud). Rarer forms are: لَدَنْ (لَدًا, لَدِنْ, لُدْنْ), لَدْنِ (لَدْنُ), لُدْنِ (لُدْنُ), لَدُ. لَدْ, لُدْ, لُدُ.

D (*g*) مَعَ *with* (Heb. עִם, Syr. ܥܡ); dialectically مَعْ, which becomes in the waṣl مَعِ.

(*h*) مِنْ *of, from, on account of* (Heb. Aram. מִן, ܡܢ, Æth. እምነ: *'ĕmna*, or እም: *ĕm*). See § 20, *d*.

(*i*) مُنْذُ, or مُذْ, *from* a certain time, *since* (compounded of مِنْ and ذُو, *ex quo*; see § 347. rem. *e* and comp. מִן־דִּי, Ezra v. 12). Rarer

forms are: مُنْذَ, مِنْذُ, مِذْ, and مُذُ. In the waṣl مُذْ usually becomes A
مُذُ (§ 20, *d*), rarely مُذِ or مُذَ.

Rem. *a.* إِلَى, عَلَى, and لَدَى, preserve before the suffixes their original pronunciation إِلَيْ, عَلَيْ, and لَدَيْ (compare אֱלֵי and עֲלֵי); as إِلَيْهِ, عَلَيْهِ, إِلَيْكُمْ, لَدَيْهَا. The ḍamma of the suffixes of the 3d pers. passes after the diphthong into kèsra, according to § 185, rem. *b*, and § 317, rem. *c*. The suffix of the 1st pers. sing., ـِى (orig. ـِىَ),
combines with إِلَى, عَلَى, and لَدَى into إِلَيَّ, عَلَيَّ, لَدَيَّ; with فِى B
into فِىَّ. See § 317, rem. *a*.

Rem. *b*. The ن of عَنْ, مِنْ, and لَدُنْ, is doubled in connection with the suffixes of the 1st pers.; عَنِّى, مِنِّى, لَدُنِّى, [عَنَّا, etc.]. If عَنْ and مِنْ are prefixed to مَنْ and مَا, the ن is assimilated to the م in pronunciation, and the two are usually written as one word; عَمَّنْ, عَمَّا, مِمَّنْ, مِمَّا, for عَنْمَّنْ or عَنْ مَّنْ, etc. (see § 14, *b*).

Rem. *c*. When followed by the article, the prepositions مِنْ and C
عَلَى are occasionally abbreviated in poetry, مِنَ ٱلْ being contracted into مِلْ, and عَلَى ٱلْ into عَلْ; as مِلْمَالِ, or مِلْ مَالِ, for مِنَ ٱلْمَالِ; عَلْمَآءِ for عَلَى ٱلْمَآءِ. [Comp. p. 24, note.]

359. Examples of prepositions of the second class are: أَمَامَ *before* (of place); بَيْنَ *between, among* (בֵּין); بَعْدَ *after* (בְּעַד), dimin.
بُعَيْدَ; تَحْتَ *under, beneath* (תַּחַת), dimin. تُحَيْتَ; تُجَاهَ or تِجَاهَ, D
تِلْقَآءَ, حِذَآءَ, *over against, opposite to;* حَوْلَ *round, about;* خَلْفَ *behind, after;* دُونَ *below, under, beneath, on this side of,* dimin. دُوَيْنَ; عِنْدَ (also عَنْدَ, which is the modern and vulgar form, rarely عُنْدَ) *with, in possession of* (*apud, penes,* Fr. *chez;* [עִמָּד(י)]; [قِبَلَ *do.*]; عِوَضَ *instead of, for;* فَوْقَ *above,* dimin. فُوَيْقَ; قَبْلَ *before* (of time, קֳבֵל),

A dimin. قُبَيْلَ ; قُدَّامَ *before* (of place, קֳדָם) ; وَرَآءَ *behind, after, beyond ;* وَسْطَ *in the middle, among.* These are all, as before said, the construct accusatives of nouns ; such as بَيْنٌ *interval,* حَوْلٌ *circumference,* etc.

B. THE ADVERBS.

360. There are *three* sorts of adverbs. The first class consists of
B *particles* of various origin, partly inseparable, partly separable ; the second class of *indeclinable nouns* ending in *u* ; the third class of *nouns* in the *accusative.*

361. The inseparable adverbial particles are :—

(*a*) أ, interrogative, حَرْفُ ٱلِٱسْتِفْهَامِ, *the particle of questioning* (*num? utrum? an?* Heb. הֲ) ; [comp. § 21, *d*]. The form هَ occurs
C dialectically, for example in هَمَا *nonne?* for أَمَا (see § 362, *h*), هَذَا ٱلَّذِى for أَذَا ٱلَّذِى, *is this he who—?* [In alternative questions it is followed by أَمْ or أَوْ.]

[REM. When أ is followed by another èlif with hèmza, an ا is inserted between the two hèmzas, as ءَاأَنْتَ, also written آأَنْتَ, but some do not do this. If the following èlif is pronounced with kèsra, it is converted into ى with hèmza, as أَئِذَا, أَئِنَّكَ.]

D (*b*) سَ, prefixed to the Imperfect of the verb to express real futurity, as سَيَكْفِيكَهُمُ ٱللّٰهُ, *God will suffice thee against them.* It is an abbreviation of سَوْفَ, *in the end* (Heb. Aram. סוֹף, ܣܘܦܐ, *end*), [and is called حَرْفُ ٱلتَّنْفِيسِ *the particle of amplification*].

(*c*) لَ, affirmative, *certainly, surely.* This may be (α) لَامُ جَوَابِ ٱلْقَسَمِ, *the* la *that corresponds to,* or *is the complement of, an oath,* as وَٱللّٰهِ لَأَفْعَلَنَّ *by God, I will certainly do (it)* ; وَٱللّٰهِ لَقَدْ خَرَجَ *by God,*

he has certainly gone out; (β) اَللَّامُ ٱلْمُوَطِّئَةُ لِلْقَسَمِ *the* la *that smooths* A
the way for the oath, as the first *la* in وَٱللّٰهِ لَئِنْ أَكْرَمْتَنِى لَأُكْرِمَنَّكَ
by God, if indeed you show me honour, I will certainly show you honour; (γ) لَامُ جَوَابِ لَوْ وَلَوْلَا *the* la *that corresponds to*, or *is the complement of* lau (*if*) *and* lau-lā (*if not*), as لَوْلَا فَضْلُ ٱللّٰهِ عَلَيْكُمْ وَرَحْمَتُهُ لَاتَّبَعْتُمُ ٱلشَّيْطَانَ *if it had not been for the goodness of God towards you and His mercy, verily ye would have followed Satan*;
(δ) [لَامُ ٱلتَّوْكِيدِ (ٱلتَّأْكِيدِ) *the affirmative* la, or] لَامُ ٱلِٱبْتِدَآءِ *the* B
inchoative or *inceptive* la, prefixed to a noun or a verb in the imperfect, as لَأَنْتُمْ أَشَدُّ رَهْبَةً فِى صُدُورِهِمْ مِنَ ٱللّٰهِ *verily ye are more feared in their breasts than God*; إِنَّ رَبَّكَ لَيَحْكُمُ بَيْنَهُمْ يَوْمَ ٱلْقِيٰمَةِ *verily thy Lord will judge between them on the day of the resurrection*; (ε) اَللَّامُ ٱلْفَارِقَةُ [or اَللَّامُ ٱلْفَاصِلَةُ] *the distinguishing* la, which is prefixed to the predicate of إِنْ, standing for إِنَّ (إِنِ ٱلْمُخَفَّفَةُ مِنَ ٱلثَّقِيلَةِ), [in order to
distinguish it from the negative إِنْ], as إِنْ كُلُّ نَفْسٍ لَمَا عَلَيْهَا حَافِظٌ C
verily over every soul there is a guardian; وَإِنْ كُنَّا عَنْ دِرَاسَتِهِمْ لَغَافِلِينَ *but verily we were careless of their studies.* [Comp. Vol. ii. § 36.]

362. The most common separable adverbial particles are the following.

(*a*) أَجَلْ *yes, certainly*; confirming a previous statement, as
قَدْ أَتَاكَ زَيْدٌ *Zèid has come to thee*, أَجَلْ *yes*, (*he has*); مَا قَامَ زَيْدٌ D
Zèid did not stand up, أَجَلْ *yes*, (*he did not*); سَوْفَ تَذْهَبُ *thou wilt go away*, أَجَلْ *yes*, (*I will*). But in reply to an interrogation, it is better to use نَعَمْ.

(*b*) إِذْ and إِذَا in the sense of *lo! see! behold!* إِذْ is used after بَيْنَا and بَيْنَمَا, *while*, and is followed by a verb stating a fact, as بَيْنَا زَيْدٌ قَائِمٌ إِذْ رَأَى عَمْرًا *while Zèid was standing, behold, he saw 'Amr*;

A فَبَيْنَمَا ٱلْعُسْرُ إِذْ دَارَتْ مَيَاسِيرُ *for while (there has been) adversity, lo, prosperity has come round.* إِذَا, called by the grammarians إِذَا ٱلْمُفَاجَأَةِ, or إِذَا ٱلْفُجَائِيَّةِ, that is to say *'iḏā indicating something unexpected,* is followed only by a nominal proposition, and refers to the same time as the preceding statement; as خَرَجْتُ فَإِذَا زَيْدٌ بِٱلْبَابِ *I went out, and lo, Zèid was at the door;* بَيْنَمَا نَحْنُ بِمَكَانِ كَذَا إِذَا زَيْدٌ قَدْ طَلَعَ عَلَيْنَا
B *while we were in such and such a place, lo, Zèid came upon us.*

[(*c*) إِذْ ذَاكَ or إِذَّاكَ *then.*]

(*d*) إِذَنْ, or إِذًا, *well then, in that case, if it be so.* See § 367, *b.* A rare dialectic form is ذَنْ.

(*e*) أَلَا *nonne?* Compounded of أَ (§ 361, *a*) and لَا *not* (Heb. הֲלֹא). [It is very often followed by إِنَّ or وَإِنَّ: أَلَا إِنَّ (وَإِنَّ) *now surely.*]

C [(*f*) أَلَّا *nonne?* syn. of هَلَّا.]

(*g*) أَمْ, interrogative, *an?* أَمْ . . . . أَ (Heb. אִם . . . . הֲ), *utrum . . . . an?*

(*h*) أَمَا *nonne?* Compounded of أَ and مَا *not.* Dialectic varieties are أَمَ, هَمَا, هَمَ, عَمَا, عَمَ, and حَمَا or حَمَى. [أَمَا إِنَّ *truly, now surely.*]

[(*i*) إِمَّالَا or إِمَّالِى *in that case, then at least.*]

[(*k*) إِنْ *not,* syn. of مَا, frequent in the Ḳor'ân and in old poems.
D In later times it is only used in combination with the negative مَا as a corroborative, مَا إِنْ *not indeed* (comp. Vol. ii. § 158 and Fleischer, *Kl. Schr.* i. 448).]

[(*l*) إِنْ *verily,* called *the lightened 'in* (إِنِ ٱلْمُخَفَّفَةُ مِنَ ٱلثَّقِيلَةِ, § 361, *c, ε*), usually without government.]

(*m*) إِنَّ *certainly, surely, truly;* literally *lo! see! en, ecce* (Heb. הֵן, הִנֵּה, Syr. ܐܶܢ). It is joined to the *accus.* of a following noun or

pronominal suffix, but in the 1st pers. sing. إِنِّى is used as well as إِنَّنِى A
(Heb. הִנְנִי), [and in the 1st pers. pl. إِنَّا as well as إِنَّنَا]. The suffix ـهُ
in this case often represents and anticipates a whole subsequent clause (ضَمِيرُ ٱلشَّأْنِ [or ضَمِيرُ القِصَّةِ] *the pronoun of the fact*).—إِنَّ introduces the subject, and is frequently followed by لَ with the predicate; as إِنَّ ٱللّٰهَ لَكَبِيرٌ, *verily God is great.* This the grammarians regard as an inceptive or inchoative *la* (§ 360, *c*, δ), the example given standing for لَإِنَّ ٱللّٰهَ كَبِيرٌ, whence it is sometimes called اَللَّامُ ٱلْمُزَحْلَقَةُ *the* la *that* B
is pushed away (*from its proper place*).—The form هِنَّ is said to occur in the compound لَهِنَّ for لَإِنَّ.

(*n*) إِنَّمَا, restrictive, *only* (*dumtaxat*). [*verily*] Compounded of إِنَّ and مَا.

(*o*) أَنَّى *whence?* [*where?*] *how?* [*when?* With the signification of *whencesoever*, *wherever*, *however*, *whenever* it is a conjunction.] C

(*p*) أَىْ, explicative, *that is*, frequently used by commentators.

(*q*) إِى *yes, yea;* always followed by an oath, as إِى وَٱللّٰهِ *yes, by God!* This formula is sometimes shortened into إِىَ ٱللّٰهِ, إِى ٱللّٰهِ, and إِ ٱللّٰهِ. The dialectic variety هِى is said to occur.—From إِى وَٱللّٰهِ comes the vulgar أَيْوَهْ [إِيوَهْ, أَيْوَا].

[(*r*) أَيَّانَ *when?* Dialectically also إِيَّانَ. It is a conjunction D
when it signifies *whenever*.]

(*s*) أَيْنَ *where?* مِنْ أَيْنَ *whence?* إِلَى أَيْنَ *whither?* أَيْنَمَا *wherever* (Heb. אַיִן in מֵאַיִן, אָן, אָנָה).

(*t*) بَلْ, *nay, nay rather, not so, on the contrary, but* (Heb. בַּל, אֲבָל, Phœn. בל). [When it is followed by a single word it is a conjunction.]

(*u*) بَلَى *yes*, used in giving an affirmative answer to a negative

A question, or in affirming a negative proposition; as أَلَسْتُ بِرَبِّكُمْ قَالُوا بَلَى *am I not your Lord? They said, Yes,* (*Thou art*); لَمْ يَقُمْ زَيْدٌ *Zèid did not stand up,* بَلَى *yes,* (*he did*).

(*v*) بَيْنَا [and بَيْنَمَا] *while, whilst* (connected with the prep. بَيْنَ *between, among*).

(*w*) ثَمَّ [or ثَمَّهْ], in pause ثَمَّهْ, *there* (Heb. שָׁם, שָׁמָּה, Syr. ܬܡܢ).

B (*x*) جَيْرِ, sometimes جَيْرَ, *yes.*

(*y*) فَقَطْ *only, solely, merely* (lit. *and enough*).

(*z*) قَدْ, with the *Perfect, now, already, really* (*jam*). It expresses that something uncertain has really taken place, that something expected has been realised, that something has happened in agreement with, or in opposition to, certain symptoms or circumstances; as كُنْتُ أَرْجُو مَجِيئَهُ فَقَدْ جَآءَ, *I was hoping that he would come, and he is*
C *really come;* كَانَ سَالِمًا صَحِيحًا فَقَدْ مَاتَ, *he was hale and well, and now he is dead.* It also serves to mark the position of a past act or event as prior to the present time or to another past act or event, and consequently expresses merely our *Perf.* or *Pluperf.* With the *Imperfect* it means *sometimes, perhaps,* as إِنَّ ٱلْكَذُوبَ قَدْ يَصْدُقُ *the* (*habitual*) *liar sometimes speaks the truth,* in which case it is said to be used لِلتَّقْلِيلِ *to express rarity* or *paucity;* [but also *frequency,* thus according with رُبَّمَا in its two acceptations*].

D (*aa*) قَطُّ *ever;* always with the *Perfect* or *Jussive* and a *negative,* as مَا رَأَيْتُهُ قَطُّ, or لَمْ أَرَهُ قَطُّ, *I have never seen him;* [or in an interrogative sentence هَلْ رَأَيْتَهُ قَطُّ *did you ever see him?*]†. Rarer forms are قَطَ, قُطُّ, قُطُ, قَطِّ, قَطُ and in pause قُطْ.

---

* [In poetry قَدْ أَرَى may be used for قَدْ كُنْتُ أَرَى *videbam;* see Nöldeke, *Delectus,* 32, l. 2; 98, l. 4. R. S.]

† [On the use of قَطُّ in affirmative sentences, and its vulgar use with the Future, see Fleischer, *Kl. Schr.* i. 434 *seq.*]

[(*bb*) كذا *thus* (§ 340, rem. *d*) and كَذٰلِكَ *likewise* (§ 343, rem. *d*).] A

(*cc*) كَلَّا *not at all, by no means,* حَرْفُ ٱلرَّدْعِ *the particle of repelling* or *averting*; as رَبِّى أَهَانَنِى كَلَّا *my Lord hath humbled* or *despised me; by no means.*

(*dd*) لَا, used (α) as negative of the future and indefinite present, and as representative of the other negatives after وَ (*and*), *not*; (β) as a prohibitive particle (*ne*), joined to the *Jussive.* It thus combines (like the Aram. לָא, לָו) the significations of the Heb. לֹא and אַל. B

(*ee*) لٰكِنَّ, لٰكِنْ, often with وَ prefixed, *but, yet.* لٰكِنَّ is placed only before nouns and pronominal suffixes in the *accusative*, but in the 1st pers. لٰكِنِى, لٰكِنَّا are used as well as لٰكِنَّنِى, لٰكِنَّنَا. [When لٰكِنْ is followed by a single word, it is a conjunction.]

(*ff*) لَمْ [in poetry also لَمَّا], negative of the *Perfect*, but always joined to the *Jussive* in the sense of the perfect, *not.*

(*gg*) لَمَّا *not yet*, joined to the *Jussive.* C

(*hh*) لَنْ, a contraction for لَا أَنْ (i.e. لَا يَكُونُ أَنْ *it will not be that—*), *not*, joined to the *Subjunctive.*

[(*ii*) لَوْلَا and لَوْمَا *why not?* syn. of أَلَّا and هَلَّا (Vol. ii. § 169).]

(*kk*) مَا, negative of the definite or absolute present and of the perfect, *not.*

(*ll*) مَتَى *when?* Heb. מָתַי. [It is also used as a conjunction, § 367, *q*.] D

(*mm*) نَعَمْ *yes* (abbreviated for نَعِمَ, *it is agreeable*), affirming any preceding statement or question; as أَقَامَ زَيْدٌ *has Zèid stood up?* نَعَمْ *yes*, (*he has*); لَمْ يَقُمْ *he has not stood up*, نَعَمْ *yes*, (*he has not*). Other forms are نَعِمْ, and more rarely نِعِمْ, نَعَامْ, and نَحَمْ.

[(*nn*) هٰكَذَا *thus* (§ 344, rem. *b*).]

A (*oo*) هَلْ, interrogative, *num? utrum?* The form أَلْ also occurs.

(*pp*) هَلَّا (أَلَّا) *nonne?* Compounded of هَلْ and لَا.

(*qq*) هُنَا, demonstrative, *here;* whence are derived هَاهُنَا or هٰهُنَا, هُنَاكَ, and هُنَالِكَ (see §§ 342—344).

(*rr*) هَنَّا (also هِنَّا and هُنَّا), demonstrative, *there* (compare Heb. הֵנָּה); whence are derived هَهُنَّا, هَاهَنَّا or هٰهَنَّا, هَنَّاكَ, and هٰهَنَّاكَ.

B **363.** The same substantives of which the accusatives serve as prepositions (§ 359), can in general be used as adverbs, in which case they take the termination *u*, and are indeclinable. E.g. بَعْدُ [*yet,* mostly in negative phrases; بَعْدُ], مِنْ بَعْدُ, *afterwards;* تَحْتُ, مِنْ تَحْتُ, *beneath;* مِنْ عَلُ *above*;* فَوْقُ, مِنْ فَوْقُ, *above;* قَبْلُ, مِنْ قَبْلُ, *before;* حَيْثُ *where,* مِنْ حَيْثُ *whence,* إِلَى حَيْثُ *whither,* حَيْثُمَا *wherever;* عَوْضُ (also عَوْضَ and عَوْضِ) *ever,* joined to the *Imperf. Indic.*, but always preceded by a *negative,* as لَا أُفَارِقُكَ عَوْضُ,
C *I will never leave you;* غَيْرُ, in لَا غَيْرُ or لَيْسَ غَيْرُ, *nothing else, only this;* [حَسْبُ *enough, only;* also فَحَسْبُ]

364. The *accusative* is the adverbial case κατ' ἐξοχήν in Arabic. A few of the most common examples of it are the following: أَبَدًا, referring to future time, *ever,* with a negative, *never;* [آنِفًا *just now, a little while ago;* أَلْبَتَّةَ *decidedly,* usually with a negative لَا أَفْعَلُهُ أَلْبَتَّةَ *I will not do it, decidedly*]; جِدًّا *very, very much, extremely,* placed
D after an adjective; جَمِيعًا *together,* of two or more; خَارِجًا *outside, without;* دَاخِلًا *inside, within;* [رُوَيْدًا *gently*]; شِمَالًا *to the left,* يَمِينًا *to the right;* كَثِيرًا *much,* قَلِيلًا *little;* لَيْلًا *by night,* نَهَارًا *by day;*

* [On the various forms of this phrase see ên-Naḥḥâs on 'Imrulḳais *Mo'all.* p. 41. R. S.]

يَوْمًا *one day, once;* اَلْآنَ *now, at present;* اَلْيَوْمَ *today* (Æth. ዮም: A
yōm), غَدًا *tomorrow;* مَجَّانًا *gratis* (Aram. מַגָּן); مَعًا *together;* etc.
To the same class belong the following adverbs:

[(*a*) بَيْدَ *except, but.*]

(*b*) حِينَ *when* (lit., *at the time of—*).

(*c*) رُبَّمَا [*often,* but more usually] *sometimes; perhaps;* lit., *O the quantity of that which—* (رُبَّ = Heb. רֹב); [comp. Vol. ii. § 84, rem. *c*]. B

(*d*) رَيْثَ, رَيْثَمَا, *whilst, during.*

(*e*) سَوْفَ, prefixed to the *Imperf.* to indicate real futurity (see § 361, *b*); lit., *in the end.*

(*f*) لَا سِيَّمَا, and, with the omission of the negative, سِيَّمَا, *above all, especially, particularly;* lit., *there is not the equal* or *like of—.* Rarer forms are لَا سِيَمَا and لَا سَيَّمَا.

(*g*) كَيْفَ *how?** C

[(*h*) لَا مَحَالَةَ *most certainly;* lit., *there is no avoiding of it,* and therefore also construed with مِنْ like its synonym لَا بُدَّ.]†

(*i*) وَحْدَ, used only in connection with pronominal suffixes, as وَحْدَهُ *he alone,* وَحْدَهُمْ *they alone.* It is etymologically = יַחַד, but in sense = בַּד in לְבַדּוֹ, לְבַדָּם.

[Here too may be mentioned the adverbial expressions بَيْتَ بَيْتَ lit., *tent to tent* or *house to house* in هُوَ جَارِي بَيْتَ بَيْتَ *he is my next-door neighbour;* صَبَاحَ مَسَاءَ *every morning and evening;* شَتَاتَ شَتَاتَ *in* D

* [On the derivation of كيف see a conjecture of Fleischer's, *Kl. Schr.* i. 381, footnote.]

† [لَا جَرَمَ (also لَا ذَا جَرَمَ and لَا ذَا جَرَ), *verily, truly,* seems to be compounded of لَا *nay* and the verb جُرِمَ *it is decided* (comp. Fleischer, *Kl. Schr.* i. 449 *seq.*) D. G.]

A *sundry parties.* The rule is that when two nouns are made one, they lose their tènwīn and become indeclinable, ending in fètḥa, as خَمْسَةَ عَشَرَ. In like manner are to be explained بَيْنَ بَيْنَ *between good and bad*, حَيْصَ بَيْصَ *straitness.* D. G.]

REM. *a.* In أَمْسِ, *yesterday*, Heb. אֶמֶשׁ, the kèsra is not the mark of the genitive, but merely a light vowel, added to render the pronunciation more easy. We may also say بِٱلْأَمْسِ and ٱلْأَمْسَ.

B Some of the Arabs used مُذْ أَمْسَ instead of مُذْ أَمْسِ, *since yesterday.*

REM. *b.* لَيْتَ, *utinam, would that—!* and عَلَّ or لَعَلَّ, *perhaps*, seem to be, not nouns in the accusative, but *verbs.* They are construed with the accusative, and take pronominal suffixes; as لَيْتَنِي *would that I—!* (rarely لَيْتِي), لَيْتَكَ, etc.; لَعَلِّي *perhaps I—* (rarely لَعَلَّنِي), لَعَلَّكَ, etc.—Dialectically, however, لَعَلَّ governs the genitive. The word has several rarer forms, viz. عَنَّ, غَنَّ, أَنَّ, لَعَنَّ,
C لَغَنَّ, لَأَنَّ, لَوَنَّ, رَعَلَّ, and رَغَنَّ.

C. THE CONJUNCTIONS.

365. The conjunctions (which the Arab grammarians call, according to their different significations, حُرُوفُ ٱلْعَطْفِ [or ٱلْعَوَاطِفُ] *connective particles*, or حُرُوفُ ٱلشَّرْطِ *conditional particles*, etc.) are,
D like the prepositions and adverbs, either separable or inseparable.

366. The inseparable conjunctions are :—

(*a*) وَ (حَرْفُ عَطْفٍ), which connects words and clauses as a simple co-ordinative, *and* (Æth. ወ: *wa*, Heb. Aram. וְ, וּ).

(*b*) فَ (حَرْفُ عَطْفٍ, or more exactly حَرْفُ تَرْتِيبٍ, *particle of classification* or *gradation*), which sometimes unites single words, indicating that the objects enumerated immediately succeed or are

closely behind one another; but more usually connects two clauses, A
showing either that the latter is immediately subsequent to the former in time, or that it is connected with it by some internal link, such as that of cause and effect. It may be rendered *and so, and thereupon, and consequently, for*, although in this last sense فَإِنَّ is more usually employed. In conditional sentences, فَ is used to separate the apodosis from the protasis, like the German *so*; and it also invariably introduces the apodosis after the disjunctive particle أَمَّا*.

[Rem. The conjunctions وَ and فَ may be preceded by the B
interrogative particle أَ; thus أَوَلَا means *nonne?* أَفَلَا *nonne igitur?*]

(*c*) لِ. This may be (*α*) لَامُ ٱلْأَمْرِ *the* li *of command*, which is usually prefixed to the 3d pers. sing. of the Jussive, to give it an imperative sense, as لِيَطِبْ قَلْبُكَ *let thy heart be at ease.* When preceded by وَ or فَ, the kèsr is usually dropped, as فَلْيَسْتَجِيبُوا لِى وَلْيُؤْمِنُوا بِى, *therefore let them hearken unto me, and believe in me.*
Or it may be (*β*) اَللَّامُ ٱلنَّاصِبَةُ *the* li *which governs the verb in the* C
Subjunctive of the Imperfect, signifying *that, so that, in order that*, as تُبْ لِيَغْفِرَ لَكَ ٱللّٰهُ *repent, that God may forgive thee.* This latter لِ is identical with the preposition لِ (§ 356, *c*), used لِلتَّعْلِيلِ to indicate the purpose for which, or the reason why, a thing is done; and hence the Arab grammarians take it to stand in all cases for the fuller لِأَنْ or لِكَىْ.

367. The most common separable conjunctions are :— D

(*a*) إِذْ *when, since*, of past time, and prefixed either to a nominal or a verbal proposition. [Compound إِذْ مَا *whenever.*]

---

* [Sometimes in old poetry, e.g. *Ḥamāsa* 74, l. 9, Ṭabarī i. 852, l. 10, and very often in later prose, the apodosis is also introduced by فَ after لَمَّا *when.* D. G.]

A (*b*) إِذَا *when*, usually denoting future time and implying a condition, in which case it is always prefixed to a verbal proposition. Both of these conjunctions, as well as إِذًا (§ 362, *d*), are connected with the obsolete noun إِذْ, *time*, the genitive of which occurs, for example, in حِينَئِذٍ *at that time*, يَوْمَئِذٍ *on that day*. Compare Heb. אָז and אֱזַי, Bibl. Aram. אֱדַיִן, Æth. ይእዜ: *now*, መዓዜ: *when?* [Compound إِذَامَا *whenever*.]

B [(*c*) أَمْ *or*, as syn. of أَوْ in alternative questions.]

(*d*) أَمَّا, followed by فَ, *as for, as regards*; e.g. أَمَّا ٱلسَّفِينَةُ فَكَانَتْ لِمَسَاكِينَ يَعْمَلُونَ فِي ٱلْبَحْرِ *as for the ship, it belonged to poor men who worked on the sea*. The form أَيْمَا also occurs. Used twice or oftener, it corresponds to the Greek μὲν—δὲ.

(*e*) أَنْ *that, so that, in order that* (*ut*), *that* (*quod*). A dialectic C variety is عَنْ. Compounds: كَأَنْ *as it were, as if*; لِأَنْ *that, in order that, because*; see *g*. Further: أَلَّا *that not* (*ut non, ne, quod non*), comp. of أَنْ and لَا (see § 14, *b*); لِئَلَّا *in order that not* (*ideo ne*).—Like כִּי in Heb. and ὅτι in Gr., أَنْ also serves to introduce direct quotations (أَنِ ٱلْمُفَسِّرَةُ *the explicative 'an*), as وَنُودُوا أَنْ تِلْكُمُ ٱلْجَنَّةُ *and it shall be proclaimed to them, That is Paradise*; even an D Imperative, as أَشَارَتْ إِلَيَّ أَنْ خُذْهَا *she made a sign to me meaning Take her*.

(*f*) إِنْ [and إِمَّا, conditional particle] (حَرْفُ شَرْطٍ) *if*, dialectically هِنْ; وَإِنْ *although* (*etsi*), sometimes written وَلَئِنْ or وَلِنْ to distinguish it from وَإِنْ *and if*, and hence called إِنِ ٱلْوَصْلِيَّةُ; compounded with لَ (§ 361, *c*), لَئِنْ *verily if, if indeed*; Aram. ܐܶܢ, إِنْ; Æth. እመ: *'ema*; Heb. אִם.—إِلَّا, compounded of إِنْ and لَا, (*α*) *if not*, in which case it stands for a whole clause; (*β*) حَرْفُ ٱسْتِثْنَاءٍ (exceptive particle), *unless*,

*saving, except, but**, with a preceding negative, *only*. Heb. אִם־לֹא, A
Aram. אֶלָּא, ܐܠܐ; Æth. አላ: (*'allā*) *but*.—إِمَّا, rarely إِيمَا [or أَيْمَا], compounded of إِنْ and مَا; .... وَإِمَّا .... إِمَّا, or .... أَوْ .... إِمَّا, *either* —— *or* ——

(*g*) أَنَّ *that* (*quod*). It is followed by a noun or pronominal suffix in the *accus.*, but in the 1st pers. أَنِّى, أَنَّا are used as well as أَنَّنِى, أَنَّنَا. The suffix هُ in this case often represents and anticipates a whole subsequent clause (ضَمِيرُ ٱلْقِصَّةِ, or ضَمِيرُ ٱلشَّأْنِ, *the pronoun of the story* B
or *fact*). See § 362, *m*.—Compounds: كَأَنَّ *as it were, as if;* لِأَنَّ *because.* See *e*.

(*h*) أَوْ *or* (*vel, sive*). Heb. אוֹ, Syr. ܐܘ.

(*i*) ثُمَّ, ثُمَّتَ (ثُمَّتْ, فُمَّ, فُمَّتَ), *then, thereupon, next;* a حَرْفُ تَرْتِيبٍ (§ 366, *b*), connecting words and clauses, but implying succession at an interval. [In genealogical statements ثُمَّ is often used (like the German *und zwar*) to indicate a transition from the general to the C
more special. e.g. حُذَيْفَةُ ٱلذُّبْيَانِىُّ ثُمَّ ٱلْفَزَارِىُّ, *Ḥuḏeifa of the tribe of Dubyān and of the subdivision Fazāra.*] Connected with it is the adverb ثَمَّ (§ 362, *w*).

(*k*) حَتَّى *till, until, until that, so that;* identical with the preposition, § 358, *b*. [On its sense of *even*, see Vol. ii. § 52, rem. *c*.]

[(*l*) عِنْدَمَا *when* (syn. of لَمَّا).]

(*m*) كَىْ (حَرْفُ تَعْلِيلٍ, *a particle assigning the motive* or *reason*) D
in order that, with the *Subjunctive*.—Compounds: لِكَىْ *in order that,* كَيْلَا *in order that not.*

---

* [إِلَّا أَنْ and غَيْرَ أَنْ are very often used in the sense of *but* = لٰكِنْ. D. G.]

A (*n*) لَمَّا (also لَمَّا أَنْ) *after, when (postquam),* [*as, since (quoniam),*] with the *Perfect.* [لَمَّا is also syn. with إِلَّا *unless*, especially after the verbs that signify *to beseech.* D. G.]

(*o*) لَوْ hypothetical particle, *if* (Heb. לוּ).—Compounds: لَوْلَا, لَوْلَمْ, لَوْمَا, *if not,* [وَلَوْ *even though*].

(*p*) مَا (مَا ٱلدَّيْمُومَةِ, *mā denoting duration*), *as long as,* with the *Perfect.*

B [(*q*) مَتَى and مَتَى مَا (§ 362, *ll*) *when, whenever.*]

D. THE INTERJECTIONS.

368. The interjections are called by the Arabs أَصْوَاتٌ, *sounds* or *tones.* Some of those most commonly in use are: أَ or آ (أَلِفُ ٱلنِّدَآءِ), أَىْ, أَيَا (هَيَا), *O! ho!* يَا *O!* before nouns in the nomin. or accus.
C *without* the article; أَيُّهَا, or يَا أَيُّهَا, *O!* before nouns in the nomin. *with* the article; هَا *lo! see! there!* (see § 344); أَهْ, أَهٍ, أَهِ, or آهْ, آهٍ, آهِ, آوِ, آوٍ, أَوِّ; (آوَّتَاهْ) أَوَّتَاهْ, (أَوَّاهٍ) أَوَّاهْ, (أَوَّهْ), أَوِّهِ, آوِّهْ, أَوَّهْ, (أَوَّهْ) أَوْهْ; آهًا, هَاهْ (هَاهُ); وَا, وَاهًا, *Oh! ah! alas!* وَىْ *woe!* (Aram. וַי, ܘܝ, Æth. ወይ: *wæ*); وَيْهَا, وَيْهِ, *come on!* أَلَا, هَلَا, *O! up! come!* [Heb. הַלְאָה, Aram. הָלְךְ]; حَيَّ *come!* followed by عَلَى, as حَيَّ عَلَى ٱلصَّلَاةِ
D *come to prayer!* in composition, حَيَّهَلْ or حَيَّهَلْ, حَيَّهَلَا or حَيَّهَلَا (حَيَّهْلًا or حَيَّهَلًا), حَيَّهَلَكَ, with إِلَى or عَلَى, and also with بِ (in the sense of أَسْرِعْ *make haste,* or اِلْزَمْ *keep to,* or أُدْعُ *call*); هَيْتَ (هِيتُ) *come here!* هَلُمَّ *come here, bring here!* (Heb. הֲלֹם) as هَلُمَّ إِلَيْنَا *come here to us,* هَلُمَّ شُهَدَآءَكُمْ *bring here your witnesses;* [هَيْهَاتَ *far from it!*]; هَيَّ, هَيَّا, and هَيَّا هَيَّا *make haste;* وَاهِ, وَاهًا, وَاهًا, *O!*

excellent! bravo! بَخْ, بَخٍ, بَخِ, بَخٍّ, بَخْ بَخْ, etc., *well done! bravo!* A
capital! أَخّ, إِخّ; أُفْ, أُفٌّ, أُفِّ, أُفُّ, أُفَّ, أُفٍّ, أُفًّا, أُفَّةً, *ugh! faugh! fie!* صَهْ, صَهٍ, *hush! silence!* إِيهًا *be silent! give up!* مَهْ, مَهٍ, *stop! give up! let alone!* إِيهِ, إِيهٍ, *go on! proceed! say on!*—Here too may be mentioned: (α) calls to domestic animals; e.g. in driving horses, هَلَا; mules, عَدَسْ; camels, حَآءِ, حَوْبُ, هِيدَ or هَيْدَ; in making camels B
kneel, نَخّ, هِيخِ or إِيخِ; in calling camels to water, جَوْتُ; in driving sheep or goats, هُسْ; in calling a dog, قُوس; in driving a dog away, هَجَا, هَجٍ, هَجْ; (β) words imitative of cries and sounds; e.g. مَآءِ (the bleat of an antelope), غَاقِ (the croak of a raven), شِيبِ (the sound made by the lips of a camel in drinking), طِيخِ طِيخِ (laughter), أُعْ أُعْ C
or هُعْ هُعْ (vomiting), طَاقِ (a blow), قَبْ (the stroke of a sword), طَقْ (the sound of a falling stone), طِقْ (the splash of a frog), etc.

Rem. *a.* يَا is often written defectively; as يٰرَسُولَ ٱللّٰهِ *O Apostle of God!* يٰأَخِى *O my brother!* يٰٱبْنَ عَمِّى *O son of my uncle!*—أَيُّهَا has a feminine أَيَّتُهَا, but the masc. form is often used even with feminine nouns.

Rem. *b.* The noun that follows وَا [and يَا *oh!*] not unfrequently D
takes, instead of the usual terminations, the ending ـَا, in pause ـَاهْ [called أَلِفُ ٱلنُّدْبَةِ]; as وَا زَيْدَا, or وَا زَيْدَاهْ, *Oh Zèid!* وَا أَمِيرَ ٱلْمُؤْمِنِينَاهْ *alas for the Commander of the Believers!* If the noun ends in ĕlif maḳṣûra (ـَى), the ى is changed into ا, and a simple ه added, as وَا مُوسَاهْ, *Oh Moses!* though وَا مُوسَيَا or وَا مُوسَيَاهْ may also be used. Instead of ـَا we sometimes find ـَى, as وَا أَسَفَى, or وَا حَرَبَى, *Oh my grief!*

A REM. *c.* From وَىْ (to which suffixes may be appended, as وَيْكَ *woe to thee!*) are formed the interjectional nouns وَيْحٌ and وَيْلٌ, whence we can say, for example, وَيْحٌ لِزَيْدٍ, وَيْحًا لِزَيْدٍ, وَيْحَ زَيْدٍ, وَيْحَكَ, وَيْحَهُ, وَيْلٌ لَهُ, وَيْلًا لَهُ, اَلْوَيْلُ لَهُ, وَيْلِى, وَيْلَكَ, etc. The expression وَىْ لِأُمِّهِ or وَيْلٌ لِأُمِّهِ is contracted into وَيْلُمِّهِ, usually written thus in one word.—Rarer interjectional nouns are وَيْبٌ, وَيْسٌ, and وَيْخٌ.

B REM. *d.* [Many interjections have, by origin or use, a certain verbal force and are called therefore أَسْمَآءُ ٱلْأَفْعَالِ, that is, they are either originally Imperatives, as هَاتِ *give here* (§ 45, rem. *d*), or equivalent to Imperatives (comp. Vol. ii. § 35, *b*, δ, rem. *b*), and, in some cases, admitting its construction and inflection. Accordingly] some of the Arabs decline هَلُمَّ like an Imperative; e.g. sing. fem. هَلُمِّى, dual هَلُمَّا, plur. masc. هَلُمُّوا, fem. هَلْمُمْنَ (compare the Gothic *hiri*, du. *hirjats*, pl. *hirjith*).—هَيَّ takes the suffix of the
C 2nd pers., هَيَّكَ, or هَيْكَ, and is said to form a dual and plur., هَيَّا, هَيُّوا.—هَا may be joined with the pronominal suffixes of the second person, in which case it is equivalent to the Imperative of أَخَذَ; as هَاكَهَا *take her!* Or a hèmza may be substituted for the ك, and the word declined as follows: sing. m. هَآءَ, f. هَآءِ; dual هَآؤُمَا, pl. m. هَآؤُمْ, f. هَآؤُنَّ; as هَآؤُمُ ٱقْرَؤُوا كِتَابِيَهْ, *take, read my book.* Other varieties are: هَأْ (like هَبْ), f. هَائِى, etc.; هَاءِ (like رَامِ), f. هَاءِى, etc.; and هَآءَكَ, f. هَآءِكِ, etc.

PARADIGMS

OF THE

VERBS.

A

FIRST OR SIMPLE FORM

TABLE I. ACTIVE.

	Perfect.	*Imperfect.* *Indic.*	*Subj.*	*Jussive.*	*Energ.* I.	*Energ.* II.
Sing. 3. m.	قَتَلَ	يَقْتُلُ	يَقْتُلَ	يَقْتُلْ	يَقْتُلَنَّ	يَقْتُلَنْ
B f.	قَتَلَتْ	تَقْتُلُ	تَقْتُلَ	تَقْتُلْ	تَقْتُلَنَّ	تَقْتُلَنْ
2. m.	قَتَلْتَ	تَقْتُلُ	تَقْتُلَ	تَقْتُلْ	تَقْتُلَنَّ	تَقْتُلَنْ
f.	قَتَلْتِ	تَقْتُلِينَ	تَقْتُلِى	تَقْتُلِى	تَقْتُلِنَّ	تَقْتُلِنْ
1. c.	قَتَلْتُ	أَقْتُلُ	أَقْتُلَ	أَقْتُلْ	أَقْتُلَنَّ	أَقْتُلَنْ
Dual. 3. m.	قَتَلَا	يَقْتُلَانِ	يَقْتُلَا	يَقْتُلَا	يَقْتُلَانِّ	. . .
f.	قَتَلَتَا	تَقْتُلَانِ	تَقْتُلَا	تَقْتُلَا	تَقْتُلَانِّ	. . .
C 2. c.	قَتَلْتُمَا	تَقْتُلَانِ	تَقْتُلَا	تَقْتُلَا	تَقْتُلَانِّ	. . .
Plur. 3. m.	قَتَلُوا	يَقْتُلُونَ	يَقْتُلُوا	يَقْتُلُوا	يَقْتُلُنَّ	يَقْتُلُنْ
f.	قَتَلْنَ	يَقْتُلْنَ	يَقْتُلْنَ	يَقْتُلْنَ	يَقْتُلْنَانِّ	. . .
2. m.	قَتَلْتُمْ	تَقْتُلُونَ	تَقْتُلُوا	تَقْتُلُوا	تَقْتُلُنَّ	تَقْتُلُنْ
f.	قَتَلْتُنَّ	تَقْتُلْنَ	تَقْتُلْنَ	تَقْتُلْنَ	تَقْتُلْنَانِّ	. . .
1. c.	قَتَلْنَا	نَقْتُلُ	نَقْتُلَ	نَقْتُلْ	نَقْتُلَنَّ	نَقْتُلَنْ

	N. Ag.	*N. Verbi.*
D Sing. m.	قَاتِلٌ	قَتْلٌ
f.	قَاتِلَةٌ	

Imperative.	*Simple.*	*En.* I.	*En.* II.
Sing. 2. m.	اُقْتُلْ	اُقْتُلَنَّ	اُقْتُلَنْ
f.	اُقْتُلِى	اُقْتُلِنَّ	اُقْتُلِنْ
Dual. 2. c.	اُقْتُلَا	اُقْتُلَانِّ	. . .
Plur. 2. m.	اُقْتُلُوا	اُقْتُلُنَّ	اُقْتُلُنْ
f.	اُقْتُلْنَ	اُقْتُلْنَانِّ	

OF THE STRONG VERB. A

TABLE II. PASSIVE.

	Perfect.	*Imperfect.* *Indic.*	*Subj.*	*Jussive.*	*Energ.* I.	*Energ.* II.	
Sing. 3. m.	قُتِلَ	يُقْتَلُ	يُقْتَلَ	يُقْتَلْ	يُقْتَلَنَّ	يُقْتَلَنْ	
f.	قُتِلَتْ	تُقْتَلُ	تُقْتَلَ	تُقْتَلْ	تُقْتَلَنَّ	تُقْتَلَنْ	
2. m.	قُتِلْتَ	تُقْتَلُ	تُقْتَلَ	تُقْتَلْ	تُقْتَلَنَّ	تُقْتَلَنْ	B
f.	قُتِلْتِ	تُقْتَلِينَ	تُقْتَلِى	تُقْتَلِى	تُقْتَلِنَّ	تُقْتَلِنْ	
1. c.	قُتِلْتُ	أُقْتَلُ	أُقْتَلَ	أُقْتَلْ	أُقْتَلَنَّ	أُقْتَلَنْ	
Dual. 3. m.	قُتِلَا	يُقْتَلَانِ	يُقْتَلَا	يُقْتَلَا	يُقْتَلَانِّ	. . .	
f.	قُتِلَتَا	تُقْتَلَانِ	تُقْتَلَا	تُقْتَلَا	تُقْتَلَانِّ	. . .	
2. c.	قُتِلْتُمَا	تُقْتَلَانِ	تُقْتَلَا	تُقْتَلَا	تُقْتَلَانِّ	. . .	
Plur. 3. m.	قُتِلُوا	يُقْتَلُونَ	يُقْتَلُوا	يُقْتَلُوا	يُقْتَلُنَّ	يُقْتَلُنْ	C
f.	قُتِلْنَ	يُقْتَلْنَ	يُقْتَلْنَ	يُقْتَلْنَ	يُقْتَلْنَانِّ	. . .	
2. m.	قُتِلْتُمْ	تُقْتَلُونَ	تُقْتَلُوا	تُقْتَلُوا	تُقْتَلُنَّ	تُقْتَلُنْ	
f.	قُتِلْتُنَّ	تُقْتَلْنَ	تُقْتَلْنَ	تُقْتَلْنَ	تُقْتَلْنَانِّ	. . .	
1. c.	قُتِلْنَا	نُقْتَلُ	نُقْتَلَ	نُقْتَلْ	نُقْتَلَنَّ	نُقْتَلَنْ	

Nom. Pat. Sing. m. مَقْتُولٌ f. مَقْتُولَةٌ

Other Forms of the Perf., Impf., and Imper. Act., and the N. Verbi.

	Perf.	*Imperf.*	*Imperat.*	*N. Verbi.*	
Sing. 3. m.	جَلَسَ	يَجْلِسُ	اِجْلِسْ	جُلُوسٌ	D
	رَفَعَ	يَرْفَعُ	اِرْفَعْ	رَفْعٌ	
	فَرِقَ (2. m. فَرِقْتَ)	يَفْرَقُ	اِفْرَقْ	فَرَقٌ	
	خَشُنَ (2. m. خَشُنْتَ)	يَخْشُنُ	اُخْشُنْ	خُشُونَةٌ خَشَانَةٌ	

A

TABLE III. DERIVED FORMS

		II.	III.	IV.	V.	VI.
	Active Perf.	قَتَّلَ	قَاتَلَ	أَقْتَلَ	تَقَتَّلَ	تَقَاتَلَ
	Imperf.	يُقَتِّلُ	يُقَاتِلُ	يُقْتِلُ	يَتَقَتَّلُ	يَتَقَاتَلُ
	Imperat.	قَتِّلْ	قَاتِلْ	أَقْتِلْ	تَقَتَّلْ	تَقَاتَلْ
B	N. Ag.	مُقَتِّلٌ	مُقَاتِلٌ	مُقْتِلٌ	مُتَقَتِّلٌ	مُتَقَاتِلٌ
	N. Verbi.	تَقْتِيلٌ	قِتَالٌ	إِقْتَالٌ	تَقَتُّلٌ	تَقَاتُلٌ
		تَقْتِلَةٌ	مُقَاتَلَةٌ			
	Passive Perf.	قُتِّلَ	قُوتِلَ	أُقْتِلَ	تُقُتِّلَ	تُقُوتِلَ
	Imperf.	يُقَتَّلُ	يُقَاتَلُ	يُقْتَلُ	يُتَقَتَّلُ	يُتَقَاتَلُ
C	Nom. Pat.	مُقَتَّلٌ	مُقَاتَلٌ	مُقْتَلٌ	مُتَقَتَّلٌ	مُتَقَاتَلٌ

TABLE IV. THE QUADRI-

ACTIVE.

		I.	II.	III.	IV.
	Perf.	قَمْطَرَ	تَقَمْطَرَ	اِقْمَنْطَرَ	اِقْمَطَرَّ
D	Imperf.	يُقَمْطِرُ	يَتَقَمْطَرُ	يَقْمَنْطِرُ	يَقْمَطِرُّ
	Imperat.	قَمْطِرْ	تَقَمْطَرْ	اِقْمَنْطِرْ	اِقْمَطْرِرْ
	N. Ag.	مُقَمْطِرٌ	مُتَقَمْطِرٌ	مُقْمَنْطِرٌ	مُقْمَطِرٌّ
	N. Verbi.	قَمْطَرَةٌ	تَقَمْطُرٌ	اِقْمِنْطَارٌ	اِقْمِطْرَارٌ
		قِمْطَارٌ			

OF THE STRONG VERB.

A

VII.	VIII.	IX.	X.	• XI.	
اِنْقَتَلَ	اِقْتَتَلَ	اِقْتَلَّ	اِسْتَقْتَلَ	اِقْتَالَّ	
يَنْقَتِلُ	يَقْتَتِلُ	يَقْتَلُّ	يَسْتَقْتِلُ	يَقْتَالُّ	
اِنْقَتِلْ	اِقْتَتِلْ	اِقْتَلِلْ	اِسْتَقْتِلْ	اِقْتَالِلْ	B
مُنْقَتِلٌ	مُقْتَتِلٌ	مُقْتَلٌّ	مُسْتَقْتِلٌ	مُقْتَالٌّ	
اِنْقِتَالٌ	اِقْتِتَالٌ	اِقْتِلَالٌ	اِسْتِقْتَالٌ	اِقْتِيلَالٌ	
اُنْقُتِلَ	اُقْتُتِلَ		اُسْتُقْتِلَ		C
يُنْقَتَلُ	يُقْتَتَلُ		يُسْتَقْتَلُ		
مُنْقَتَلٌ	مُقْتَتَلٌ		مُسْتَقْتَلٌ		

LITERAL VERB.

PASSIVE.

	I.	II.	III.	IV.	D
Perf.	قُمْطِرَ	تُقُمْطِرَ	اُقْمُنْطِرَ	اُقْمُطِرَّ	
Imperf.	يُقَمْطَرُ	يُتَقَمْطَرُ	يُقْمَنْطَرُ	يُقْمَطَرُّ	
N. Pat.	مُقَمْطَرٌ	مُتَقَمْطَرٌ	مُقْمَنْطَرٌ	مُقْمَطَرٌّ	

A

TABLE V. *a*. FIRST FORM OF THE

Active.

	Perfect.	*Imperfect.* Indic.	Subj.	Jussive.	Energ. I.	Energ. II.
Sing. 3. m.	مَدَّ	يَمُدُّ	يَمُدَّ	يَمْدُدْ	يَمُدَّنَّ	يَمُدَّنْ
f.	مَدَّتْ	تَمُدُّ	تَمُدَّ	تَمْدُدْ	تَمُدَّنَّ	تَمُدَّنْ
B 2. m.	مَدَدْتَ	تَمُدُّ	تَمُدَّ	تَمْدُدْ	تَمُدَّنَّ	تَمُدَّنْ
f.	مَدَدْتِ	تَمُدِّينَ	تَمُدِّى	تَمُدِّى	تَمُدِّنَّ	تَمُدِّنْ
1. c.	مَدَدْتُ	أَمُدُّ	أَمُدَّ	أَمْدُدْ	أَمُدَّنَّ	أَمُدَّنْ
Dual. 3. m.	مَدَّا	يَمُدَّانِ	يَمُدَّا	يَمُدَّا	يَمُدَّانِّ	. . .
f.	مَدَّتَا	تَمُدَّانِ	تَمُدَّا	تَمُدَّا	تَمُدَّانِّ	. . .
2. c.	مَدَدْتُمَا	تَمُدَّانِ	تَمُدَّا	تَمُدَّا	تَمُدَّانِّ	. . .
C Plur. 3. m.	مَدُّوا	يَمُدُّونَ	يَمُدُّوا	يَمُدُّوا	يَمُدُّنَّ	يَمُدُّنْ
f.	مَدَدْنَ	يَمْدُدْنَ	يَمْدُدْنَ	يَمْدُدْنَ	يَمْدُدْنَانِّ	. . .
2. m.	مَدَدْتُمْ	تَمُدُّونَ	تَمُدُّوا	تَمُدُّوا	تَمُدُّنَّ	تَمُدُّنْ
f.	مَدَدْتُنَّ	تَمْدُدْنَ	تَمْدُدْنَ	تَمْدُدْنَ	تَمْدُدْنَانِّ	. . .
1. c.	مَدَدْنَا	نَمُدُّ	نَمُدَّ	نَمْدُدْ	نَمُدَّنَّ	نَمُدَّنْ

D

	N. Ag.	*N. Verbi.*
Sing. m.	مَادٌّ	مَدٌّ
f.	مَادَّةٌ	

Imperative.	Simple.	En. I.	En. II.
Sing. 2. m.	اُمْدُدْ	اُمْدُدَنَّ	اُمْدُدَنْ
f.	[اُمْدُدِى]	اُمْدُدِنَّ	اُمْدُدِنْ
Dual. 2. c.	[اُمْدُدَا]	اُمْدُدَانِّ	. . .
Plur. 2. m.	[اُمْدُدُوا]	اُمْدُدُنَّ	اُمْدُدُنْ
f.	اُمْدُدْنَ	اُمْدُدْنَانِّ	. . .

VERBUM MEDIÆ RAD GEMINATÆ. A

PASSIVE.

Perfect.		*Imperfect.*				
		Indic.	*Subj.*	*Jussive.*	*En.* I.	*En.* II.
Sing. 3. m.	مُدَّ	يُمَدُّ	يُمَدَّ	يُمْدَدْ	يُمَدَّنَّ	يُمَدَّنْ
f.	مُدَّتْ	تُمَدُّ	تُمَدَّ	تُمْدَدْ	تُمَدَّنَّ	تُمَدَّنْ B
2. m.	مُدِدْتَ	تُمَدُّ	تُمَدَّ	تُمْدَدْ	تُمَدَّنَّ	تُمَدَّنْ
f.	مُدِدْتِ	تُمَدِّينَ	تُمَدِّى	تُمَدِّى	تُمَدِّنَّ	تُمَدِّنْ
1. c.	مُدِدْتُ	أُمَدُّ	أُمَدَّ	أُمْدَدْ	أُمَدَّنَّ	أُمَدَّنْ
Dual. 3. m.	مُدَّا	يُمَدَّانِ	يُمَدَّا	يُمَدَّا	يُمَدَّانِّ	. . .
f.	مُدَّتَا	تُمَدَّانِ	تُمَدَّا	تُمَدَّا	تُمَدَّانِّ	. . .
2. c.	مُدِدْتُمَا	تُمَدَّانِ	تُمَدَّا	تُمَدَّا	تُمَدَّانِّ	. . . C
Plur. 3. m.	مُدُّوا	يُمَدُّونَ	يُمَدُّوا	يُمَدُّوا	يُمَدُّنَّ	يُمَدُّنْ
f.	مُدِدْنَ	يُمْدَدْنَ	يُمْدَدْنَ	يُمْدَدْنَ	يُمْدَدْنَانِّ	. . .
2. m.	مُدِدْتُمْ	تُمَدُّونَ	تُمَدُّوا	تُمَدُّوا	تُمَدُّنَّ	تُمَدُّنْ
f.	مُدِدْتُنَّ	تُمْدَدْنَ	تُمْدَدْنَ	تُمْدَدْنَ	تُمْدَدْنَانِّ	. . .
1. c.	مُدِدْنَا	نُمَدُّ	نُمَدَّ	نُمْدَدْ	نُمَدَّنَّ	نُمَدَّنْ

Nom. Pat. Sing. m. مَمْدُودٌ, f. مَمْدُودَةٌ. D

Other forms of the Perf., Imperf., Jussive, and Imperat. Act.

Perf.	*Imperf.*	*Jussive.*	*Imperat.*
Sing. 3. m. . . .	. . .	يَمُدَّ or يَمُدُّ	مُدَّ or مُدُّ
فَرَّ	يَفِرُّ	يَفْرِرْ, يَفِرَّ, or يَفِرِّ	اِفْرِرْ, فِرَّ, or فِرِّ
مَلَّ {(2. m.) (مَلِلْتَ)}	يَمَلُّ	يَمْلَلْ, يَمَلَّ, or يَمَلِّ	اِمْلَلْ, مَلَّ, or مَلِّ

A ## TABLE V. *b*. DERIVED FORMS OF THE VERBUM MEDIÆ RAD. GEMINATÆ.

	III.	IV.	VI.	VII.	VIII.	X.
Active Perf.	مَادَدَ	أَمَدَّ	تَمَادَدَ	اِنْفَلَّ	اِمْتَدَّ	اِسْتَمَدَّ
	or مَادَّ		or تَمَادَّ			
Imperf.	يُمَادِدُ	يُمِدُّ	يَتَمَادَدُ	يَنْفَلُّ	يَمْتَدُّ	يَسْتَمِدُّ
B	or يُمَادُّ		or يَتَمَادُّ			
Imperat.	مَادِدْ	أَمْدِدْ	تَمَادَدْ	اِنْفَلِلْ	اِمْتَدِدْ	اِسْتَمْدِدْ
		or أَمِدَّ			or اِمْتَدَّ	or اِسْتَمِدَّ
N. Ag.	مُمَادِدٌ	مُمِدٌّ	مُتَمَادِدٌ	مُنْفَلٌّ	مُمْتَدٌّ	مُسْتَمِدٌّ
	or مُمَادٌّ		or مُتَمَادٌّ			
N. Verbi.	مِدَادٌ	إِمْدَادٌ	تَمَادُدٌ	اِنْفِلَالٌ	اِمْتِدَادٌ	اِسْتِمْدَادٌ
C	مُمَادَّةٌ or مُمَادَدَةٌ		or تَمَادٌّ			
Passive Perf.	مُودِدَ	أُمِدَّ	تُمُودِدَ	اُنْفُلَّ	اُمْتُدَّ	اُسْتُمِدَّ
Imperf.	يُمَادَدُ	يُمَدُّ	يُتَمَادَدُ	يُنْفَلُّ	يُمْتَدُّ	يُسْتَمَدُّ
	or يُمَادُّ		or يُتَمَادُّ			
N. Pat.	مُمَادَدٌ	مُمَدٌّ	مُتَمَادَدٌ	مُنْفَلٌّ	مُمْتَدٌّ	مُسْتَمَدٌّ
	or مُمَادٌّ		or مُتَمَادٌّ			

D The remaining forms present no irregularity; e.g.

	Perf.	*Imperf.*	*Imperat.*	*N. Ag. et Pat.*	*N. Verbi.*
II. Act.	مَدَّدَ	يُمَدِّدُ	مَدِّدْ	مُمَدِّدٌ	تَمْدِيدٌ
Pass.	مُدِّدَ	يُمَدَّدُ		مُمَدَّدٌ	
V. Act.	تَمَدَّدَ	يَتَمَدَّدُ	تَمَدَّدْ	مُتَمَدِّدٌ	تَمَدُّدٌ
Pass.	تُمُدِّدَ	يُتَمَدَّدُ		مُتَمَدَّدٌ	

TABLE VI. VERBUM PRIMÆ RAD. HEMZATÆ. A

	I.		II.	III.	IV.	V.	VI.	
Active Perf.	أَسَرَ	أَثَرَ	أَثَّرَ	آثَرَ	آثَرَ	تَأَثَّرَ	تَآثَرَ or تَوَاثَرَ	
Imperf.	يَأْسِرُ	يَأْثُرُ	يُؤَثِّرُ	يُؤَاثِرُ	يُؤْثِرُ	يَتَأَثَّرُ	يَتَآثَرُ or يَتَوَاثَرُ	
Imperat.	اِيسِرْ	أُوثُرْ	أَثِّرْ	آثِرْ	آثِرْ	تَأَثَّرْ	تَآثَرْ or تَوَاثَرْ	B
N. Ag.	آسِرٌ		مُؤَثِّرٌ	مُؤَاثِرٌ	مُؤْثِرٌ	مُتَأَثِّرٌ	مُتَآثِرٌ or مُتَوَاثِرٌ	
N. Verbi.	أَسْرٌ		تَأْثِيرٌ	إِثَارٌ	إِيثَارٌ	تَأَثُّرٌ	تَآثُرٌ or تَوَاثُرٌ	
				مُؤَاثَرَةٌ				
Passive Perf.	أُسِرَ		أُثِّرَ	أُوثِرَ	أُوثِرَ	تُؤُثِّرَ	تُوثِرَ or تُوُوثِرَ	C
Imperf.	يُؤْسَرُ		يُؤَثَّرُ	يُؤَاثَرُ	يُؤْثَرُ	يُتَأَثَّرُ	يُتَآثَرُ or يُتَوَاثَرُ	
N. Pat.	مَأْسُورٌ		مُؤَثَّرٌ	مُؤَاثَرٌ	مُؤْثَرٌ	مُتَأَثَّرٌ	مُتَآثَرٌ or مُتَوَاثَرٌ	

	Perf.	*Imperf.*	*Imperat.*	*N. Ag. et Pat.*	*N. Verbi.*	
VIII. Act.	اِيتَثَرَ	يَأْتَثِرُ	اِيتَثِرْ	مُؤْتَثِرٌ	اِيتِثَارٌ	D
Pass.	أُوتُثِرَ	يُؤْتَثَرُ		مُؤْتَثَرٌ		
X. Act.	اِسْتَأْثَرَ	يَسْتَأْثِرُ	اِسْتَأْثِرْ	مُسْتَأْثِرٌ	اِسْتِئْثَارٌ	
Pass.	أُسْتُؤْثِرَ	يُسْتَأْثَرُ		مُسْتَأْثَرٌ		

The seventh form is wanting in verbs of this class, according to § 113.

A TABLE VII. VERBUM MEDIÆ RAD. HÈMZATÆ.

		I.			II.	III.	IV.
	Active Perf.	سَأَلَ	سَئِرَ	بَؤُسَ	لَأَّمَ	لَاءَمَ	أَلْأَمَ
	Imperf.	يَسْأَلُ	يَسْأَرُ	يَبْؤُسُ	يُلَئِّمُ	يُلَائِمُ	يُلْئِمُ
		يَسَلُ	يَسَرُ				
	Imperat.	اِسْأَلْ	اِسْأَرْ	اُبْؤُسْ	لَئِّمْ	لَائِمْ	أَلْئِمْ
B		اِسَلْ	اِسَرْ				
	N. Ag.	سَائِلٌ	سَائِرٌ	بَائِسٌ	مُلَئِّمٌ	مُلَائِمٌ	مُلْئِمٌ
	N. Verbi.	سُؤَالٌ	سُؤْرٌ	بَأْسٌ	تَلْئِيمٌ	مُلَاءَمَةٌ	إِلْآمٌ
	Passive Perf.	سُئِلَ			لُئِّمَ	لُوئِمَ	أُلْئِمَ
	Imperf.	يُسْأَلُ			يُلَأَّمُ	يُلَاءَمُ	يُلْأَمُ
C		يُسَلُ					
	N. Pat.	مَسْؤُولٌ			مُلَأَّمٌ	مُلَاءَمٌ	مُلْأَمٌ

		V.	VI.	VII.	VIII.	X.
	Active Perf.	تَلَأَّمَ	تَلَاءَمَ	اِنْجَأَثَ	اِلْتَأَمَ	اِسْتَلْأَمَ
	Imperf.	يَتَلَأَّمُ	يَتَلَاءَمُ	يَنْجَئِثُ	يَلْتَئِمُ	يَسْتَلْئِمُ
D	Imperat.	تَلَأَّمْ	تَلَاءَمْ	اِنْجَئِثْ	اِلْتَئِمْ	اِسْتَلْئِمْ
	N. Ag.	مُتَلَئِّمٌ	مُتَلَائِمٌ	مُنْجَئِثٌ	مُلْتَئِمٌ	مُسْتَلْئِمٌ
	N. Verbi.	تَلَؤُّمٌ	تَلَاؤُمٌ	اِنْجِئَاثٌ	اِلْتِئَامٌ	اِسْتِلْآمٌ
	Passive Perf.	تُلُئِّمَ	تُلُوئِمَ	اُنْجُئِثَ	اُلْتُئِمَ	اُسْتُلْئِمَ
	Imperf.	يُتَلَأَّمُ	يُتَلَاءَمُ	يُنْجَأُثُ	يُلْتَأَمُ	يُسْتَلْأَمُ
	Pat.	مُتَلَأَّمٌ	مُتَلَاءَمٌ	مُنْجَأَثٌ	مُلْتَأَمٌ	مُسْتَلْأَمٌ

TABLE VIII. VERBUM TERTIÆ RAD. HEMZATÆ. A

	I.				II.	III.	
Active Perf. 3. s. m.	بَرَأَ	هَنَأَ	خَطِئَ	دَنُؤَ	بَرَّأَ	بَارَأَ	
f.	بَرَأَتْ	هَنَأَتْ	خَطِئَتْ	دَنُؤَتْ	بَرَّأَتْ	بَارَأَتْ	
2. s. m.	بَرَأْتَ	هَنَأْتَ	خَطِئْتَ	دَنُؤْتَ	بَرَّأْتَ	بَارَأْتَ	
Imperf.	يَبْرَأُ	يَهْنِئُ	يَخْطَأُ	يَدْنُؤُ	يُبَرِّئُ	يُبَارِئُ	
Imperat.	اِبْرَأْ	اِهْنِئْ	اِخْطَأْ	اُدْنُؤْ	بَرِّئْ	بَارِئْ	B
N. Ag.	بَارِئٌ	هَانِئٌ	خَاطِئٌ	دَانِئٌ	مُبَرِّئٌ	مُبَارِئٌ	
N. Verbi.	بَرْءٌ	هَنْءٌ	خِطْأٌ	دَنَاءَةٌ	تَبْرِئَةٌ	مُبَارَأَةٌ	
				دُنُوءَةٌ	تَجْرِيءٌ		
Passive Perf.	بُرِئَ	هُنِئَ	خُطِئَ		بُرِّئَ	بُورِئَ	
Imperf.	يُبْرَأُ	يُهْنَأُ	يُخْطَأُ		يُبَرَّأُ	يُبَارَأُ	C
N. Pat.	مَبْرُوءٌ	مَهْنُوءٌ	مَخْطُوءٌ		مُبَرَّأٌ	مُبَارَأٌ	

	IV.	V.	VI.	VII.	VIII.	X.	
Active Perf.	أَبْرَأَ	تَبَرَّأَ	تَبَارَأَ	اِنْسَبَأَ	اِهْتَنَأَ	اِسْتَبْرَأَ	
Imperf.	يُبْرِئُ	يَتَبَرَّأُ	يَتَبَارَأُ	يَنْسَبِئُ	يَهْتَنِئُ	يَسْتَبْرِئُ	
Imperat.	أَبْرِئْ	تَبَرَّأْ	تَبَارَأْ	اِنْسَبِئْ	اِهْتَنِئْ	اِسْتَبْرِئْ	D
N. Ag.	مُبْرِئٌ	مُتَبَرِّئٌ	مُتَبَارِئٌ	مُنْسَبِئٌ	مُهْتَنِئٌ	مُسْتَبْرِئٌ	
N. Verbi.	إِبْرَاءٌ	تَبَرُّؤٌ	تَبَارُؤٌ	اِنْسِبَاءٌ	اِهْتِنَاءٌ	اِسْتِبْرَاءٌ	
Passive Perf.	أُبْرِئَ	تُبُرِّئَ	تُبُورِئَ	اُنْسُبِئَ	اُهْتُنِئَ	اُسْتُبْرِئَ	
Imperf.	يُبْرَأُ	يُتَبَرَّأُ	يُتَبَارَأُ	يُنْسَبَأُ	يُهْتَنَأُ	يُسْتَبْرَأُ	
N. Pat.	مُبْرَأٌ	مُتَبَرَّأٌ	مُتَبَارَأٌ	مُنْسَبَأٌ	مُهْتَنَأٌ	مُسْتَبْرَأٌ	

A — TABLE IX. VERBA PRIMÆ RAD. و ET ى.

		I.					
	Active Perf.	وَعَدَ	وَرِثَ	وَضَعَ	وَجِلَ	وَدَّ	يَسَرَ
	Imperf.	يَعِدُ	يَرِثُ	يَضَعُ	يَوْجَلُ	يَوَدُّ	يَيْسِرُ
	Imperat.	عِدْ	رِثْ	ضَعْ	اِيجَلْ	اِيدَدْ	اِيسِرْ
B	N. Verbi.	وَعْدٌ	وِرْثٌ	وَضْعٌ	وَجَلٌ	وُدٌّ	يَسْرٌ
		عِدَةٌ	رِثَةٌ	ضَعَةٌ			
	Passive Perf.	وُعِدَ	وُرِثَ	وُضِعَ		وُدَّ	يُسِرَ
	Imperf.	يُوعَدُ	يُورَثُ	يُوضَعُ		يُوَدُّ	يُوسَرُ
	N. Pat.	مَوْعُودٌ	مَوْرُوثٌ	مَوْضُوعٌ		مَوْدُودٌ	مَيْسُورٌ

C		IV.		VIII.		X.	
	Active Perf.	أَوْجَبَ	أَيْسَرَ	اِتَّعَدَ	اِتَّسَرَ	اِسْتَوْعَدَ	اِسْتَيْسَرَ
	Imperf.	يُوجِبُ	يُوسِرُ	يَتَّعِدُ	يَتَّسِرُ	يَسْتَوْعِدُ	يَسْتَيْسِرُ
	Imperat.	أَوْجِبْ	أَيْسِرْ	اِتَّعِدْ	اِتَّسِرْ	اِسْتَوْعِدْ	اِسْتَيْسِرْ
	N. Ag.	مُوجِبٌ	مُوسِرٌ	مُتَّعِدٌ	مُتَّسِرٌ	مُسْتَوْعِدٌ	مُسْتَيْسِرٌ
D	N. Verbi.	إِيجَابٌ	إِيسَارٌ	اِتِّعَادٌ	اِتِّسَارٌ	اِسْتِيعَادٌ	اِسْتِيسَارٌ
	Passive Perf.	أُوجِبَ	أُوسِرَ	اُتُّعِدَ	اُتُّسِرَ	اُسْتُوعِدَ	اُسْتُوسِرَ
	Imperf.	يُوجَبُ	يُوسَرُ	يُتَّعَدُ	يُتَّسَرُ	يُسْتَوْعَدُ	يُسْتَيْسَرُ
	N. Pat.	مُوجَبٌ	مُوسَرٌ	مُتَّعَدٌ	مُتَّسَرٌ	مُسْتَوْعَدٌ	مُسْتَيْسَرٌ

TABLE X. VERBUM MEDIÆ RAD. A

Active Voice of the First Form.

	Perfect.	*Imperfect.* Indic.	Subj.	Jussive.	En. I.	En. II.	
Sing. 3. m.	قَالَ	يَقُولُ	يَقُولَ	يَقُلْ	يَقُولَنَّ	يَقُولَنْ	
f.	قَالَتْ	تَقُولُ	تَقُولَ	تَقُلْ	تَقُولَنَّ	تَقُولَنْ	
2. m.	قُلْتَ	تَقُولُ	تَقُولَ	تَقُلْ	تَقُولَنَّ	تَقُولَنْ	B
f.	قُلْتِ	تَقُولِينَ	تَقُولِى	تَقُولِى	تَقُولِنَّ	تَقُولِنْ	
1. c.	قُلْتُ	أَقُولُ	أَقُولَ	أَقُلْ	أَقُولَنَّ	أَقُولَنْ	
Dual. 3. m.	قَالَا	يَقُولَانِ	يَقُولَا	يَقُولَا	يَقُولَانِّ	. . .	
f.	قَالَتَا	تَقُولَانِ	تَقُولَا	تَقُولَا	تَقُولَانِّ	. . .	
2. c.	قُلْتُمَا	تَقُولَانِ	تَقُولَا	تَقُولَا	تَقُولَانِّ	. . .	
Plur. 3. m.	قَالُوا	يَقُولُونَ	يَقُولُوا	يَقُولُوا	يَقُولُنَّ	يَقُولُنْ	C
f.	قُلْنَ	يَقُلْنَ	يَقُلْنَ	يَقُلْنَ	يَقُلْنَانِّ	. . .	
2. m.	قُلْتُمْ	تَقُولُونَ	تَقُولُوا	تَقُولُوا	تَقُولُنَّ	تَقُولُنْ	
f.	قُلْتُنَّ	تَقُلْنَ	تَقُلْنَ	تَقُلْنَ	تَقُلْنَانِّ	. . .	
1. c.	قُلْنَا	نَقُولُ	نَقُولَ	نَقُلْ	نَقُولَنَّ	نَقُولَنْ	

	N. Ag.	*N. Verbi.*	*Imperative.*	*Simple.*	*En.* I.	*En.* II.	D
Sing. m.	قَائِلٌ	قَوْلٌ	Sing. 2. m.	قُلْ	قُولَنَّ	قُولَنْ	
f.	قَائِلَةٌ		f.	قُولِى	قُولِنَّ	قُولِنْ	
			Dual. 2. c.	قُولَا	قُولَانِّ	. . .	
			Plur. 2. m.	قُولُوا	قُولُنَّ	قُولُنْ	
			f.	قُلْنَ	قُلْنَانِّ	. . .	

A

TABLE XI. VERBUM MEDIÆ RAD. ى.

Active Voice of the First Form.

		Perfect.	*Imperfect.* *Indic.*	*Subj.*	*Jussive.*	*En.* I.	*En.* II.
	Sing. 3. m.	سَارَ	يَسِيرُ	يَسِيرَ	يَسِرْ	يَسِيرَنَّ	يَسِيرَنْ
	f.	سَارَتْ	تَسِيرُ	تَسِيرَ	تَسِرْ	تَسِيرَنَّ	تَسِيرَنْ
B	2. m.	سِرْتَ	تَسِيرُ	تَسِيرَ	تَسِرْ	تَسِيرَنَّ	تَسِيرَنْ
	f.	سِرْتِ	تَسِيرِينَ	تَسِيرِى	تَسِيرِى	تَسِيرِنَّ	تَسِيرِنْ
	1. c.	سِرْتُ	أَسِيرُ	أَسِيرَ	أَسِرْ	أَسِيرَنَّ	أَسِيرَنْ
	Dual. 3. m.	سَارَا	يَسِيرَانِ	يَسِيرَا	يَسِيرَا	يَسِيرَانِّ	. . .
	f.	سَارَتَا	تَسِيرَانِ	تَسِيرَا	تَسِيرَا	تَسِيرَانِّ	. . .
	2. c.	سِرْتُمَا	تَسِيرَانِ	تَسِيرَا	تَسِيرَا	تَسِيرَانِّ	. . .
C	Plur. 3. m.	سَارُوا	يَسِيرُونَ	يَسِيرُوا	يَسِيرُوا	يَسِيرُنَّ	يَسِيرُنْ
	f.	سِرْنَ	يَسِرْنَ	يَسِرْنَ	يَسِرْنَ	يَسِرْنَانِّ	. . .
	2. m.	سِرْتُمْ	تَسِيرُونَ	تَسِيرُوا	تَسِيرُوا	تَسِيرُنَّ	تَسِيرُنْ
	f.	سِرْتُنَّ	تَسِرْنَ	تَسِرْنَ	تَسِرْنَ	تَسِرْنَانِّ	. . .
	1. c.	سِرْنَا	نَسِيرُ	نَسِيرَ	نَسِرْ	نَسِيرَنَّ	نَسِيرَنْ

D

	N. Ag.	*N. Verbi.*
Sing. m.	سَائِرٌ	سَيْرٌ
f.	سَائِرَةٌ	

Imperative.

	Simple.	*En.* I.	*En.* II.
Sing. 2. m.	سِرْ	سِيرَنَّ	سِيرَنْ
f.	سِيرِى	سِيرِنَّ	سِيرِنْ
Dual. ~~2~~. c.	سِيرَا	سِيرَانِّ	. . .
Plur. 2. m.	سِيرُوا	سِيرُنَّ	سِيرُنْ
f.	سِرْنَ	سِرْنَانِّ	. . .

TABLE XII. VERBA MEDIÆ RAD. و ET ى. A

Passive Voice of the First Form.

	Perfect.	Imperfect. Indic.	Subj.	Jussive.	Energ. I.	Energ. II.	
Sing. 3. m.	قِيلَ	يُقَالُ	يُقَالَ	يُقَلْ	يُقَالَنَّ	يُقَالَنْ	
f.	قِيلَتْ	تُقَالُ	تُقَالَ	تُقَلْ	تُقَالَنَّ	تُقَالَنْ	B
2. m.	قِلْتَ	تُقَالُ	تُقَالَ	تُقَلْ	تُقَالَنَّ	تُقَالَنْ	
f.	قِلْتِ	تُقَالِينَ	تُقَالِى	تُقَالِى	تُقَالِنَّ	تُقَالِنْ	
1. c.	قِلْتُ	أُقَالُ	أُقَالَ	أُقَلْ	أُقَالَنَّ	أُقَالَنْ	
Dual. 3. m.	قِيلَا	يُقَالَانِ	يُقَالَا	يُقَالَا	يُقَالَانِّ	. . .	
f.	قِيلَتَا	تُقَالَانِ	تُقَالَا	تُقَالَا	تُقَالَانِّ	. . .	C
2. c.	قِلْتُمَا	تُقَالَانِ	تُقَالَا	تُقَالَا	تُقَالَانِّ	. . .	
Plur. 3. m.	قِيلُوا	يُقَالُونَ	يُقَالُوا	يُقَالُوا	يُقَالُنَّ	يُقَالُنْ	
f.	قِلْنَ	يُقَلْنَ	يُقَلْنَ	يُقَلْنَ	يُقَلْنَانِّ	. . .	
2. m.	قِلْتُمْ	تُقَالُونَ	تُقَالُوا	تُقَالُوا	تُقَالُنَّ	تُقَالُنْ	
f.	قِلْتُنَّ	تُقَلْنَ	تُقَلْنَ	تُقَلْنَ	تُقَلْنَانِّ	. . .	D
1. c.	قِلْنَا	نُقَالُ	نُقَالَ	نُقَلْ	نُقَالَنَّ	نُقَالَنْ	

Nom. Pat. Sing. m. مَقُولٌ, f. مَقُولَةٌ

مَبِيعٌ, مَبِيعَةٌ

A TABLE XIII. VERBA MEDIÆ RAD. و ET ى.

THE DERIVED FORMS.

		IV.	VII.	VIII.	X.
A	Active Perf. 3. s. m.	أَقَالَ	اِنْشَالَ	اِقْتَالَ	اِسْتَقَامَ
	2. s. m.	أَقَلْتَ	اِنْشَلْتَ	اِقْتَلْتَ	اِسْتَقَمْتَ
B	Imperf.	يُقِيلُ	يَنْشَالُ	يَقْتَالُ	يَسْتَقِيمُ
	Imperat.	أَقِلْ	اِنْشَلْ	اِقْتَلْ	اِسْتَقِمْ
	N. Ag.	مُقِيلٌ	مُنْشَالٌ	مُقْتَالٌ	مُسْتَقِيمٌ
	N. Verbi.	إِقَالَةٌ	اِنْشِيَالٌ	اِقْتِيَالٌ	اِسْتِقَامَةٌ
	Passive Perf.	أُقِيلَ	اُنْشِيلَ	اُقْتِيلَ	اُسْتُقِيمَ
C	Imperf.	يُقَالُ	يُنْشَالُ	يُقْتَالُ	يُسْتَقَامُ
	N. Pat.	مُقَالٌ	مُنْشَالٌ	مُقْتَالٌ	مُسْتَقَامٌ

		II.	III.	V.	VI.
	Active Perf.	سَيَّرَ قَوَّلَ	سَايَرَ قَاوَلَ	تَسَيَّرَ تَقَوَّلَ	تَسَايَرَ تَقَاوَلَ
	Imperf.	يُسَيِّرُ يُقَوِّلُ	يُسَايِرُ يُقَاوِلُ	يَتَسَيَّرُ يَتَقَوَّلُ	يَتَسَايَرُ يَتَقَاوَلُ
D	N. Verbi.	تَسْيِيرٌ تَقْوِيلٌ	مُسَايَرَةٌ مُقَاوَلَةٌ	تَسَيُّرٌ تَقَوُّلٌ	تَسَايُرٌ تَقَاوُلٌ
	Passive Perf.	سُيِّرَ قُوِّلَ	سُويِرَ قُووِلَ	تُسُيِّرَ تُقُوِّلَ	تُسُويِرَ تُقُووِلَ

	Perf.	Imperf.	N. Verbi.
IX.	إِسْوَدَّ	يَسْوَدُّ	اِسْوِدَادٌ
XI.	اِسْوَادَّ	يَسْوَادُّ	اِسْوِيدَادٌ

TABLE XIV. VERBUM TERTIÆ RAD. و, MEDIÆ RAD. FÈTḤATÆ. A

Active Voice of the First Form.

	Perfect.	*Imperfect.* Indic.	Subj.	Jussive.	En. I.	En. II.	
Sing. 3. m.	نَدَا	يَنْدُو	يَنْدُوَ	يَنْدُ	يَنْدُوَنَّ	يَنْدُوَنْ	
f.	نَدَتْ	تَنْدُو	تَنْدُوَ	تَنْدُ	تَنْدُوَنَّ	تَنْدُوَنْ	
2. m.	نَدَوْتَ	تَنْدُو	تَنْدُوَ	تَنْدُ	تَنْدُوَنَّ	تَنْدُوَنْ	B
f.	نَدَوْتِ	تَنْدِينَ	تَنْدِي	تَنْدِي	تَنْدِنَّ	تَنْدِنْ	
1. c.	نَدَوْتُ	أَنْدُو	أَنْدُوَ	أَنْدُ	أَنْدُوَنَّ	أَنْدُوَنْ	
Dual. 3. m.	نَدَوَا	يَنْدُوَانِ	يَنْدُوَا	يَنْدُوَا	يَنْدُوَانِّ	. . .	
f.	نَدَتَا	تَنْدُوَانِ	تَنْدُوَا	تَنْدُوَا	تَنْدُوَانِّ	. . .	
2. c.	نَدَوْتُمَا	تَنْدُوَانِ	تَنْدُوَا	تَنْدُوَا	تَنْدُوَانِّ	. . .	C
Plur. 3. m.	نَدَوْا	يَنْدُونَ	يَنْدُوا	يَنْدُوا	يَنْدُنَّ	يَنْدُنْ	
f.	نَدَوْنَ	يَنْدُونَ	يَنْدُونَ	يَنْدُونَ	يَنْدُونَانِّ	. . .	
2. m.	نَدَوْتُمْ	تَنْدُونَ	تَنْدُوا	تَنْدُوا	تَنْدُنَّ	تَنْدُنْ	
f.	نَدَوْتُنَّ	تَنْدُونَ	تَنْدُونَ	تَنْدُونَ	تَنْدُونَانِّ	. . .	
1. c.	نَدَوْنَا	نَنْدُو	نَنْدُوَ	نَنْدُ	نَنْدُوَنَّ	نَنْدُوَنْ	

	N. Ag.	*N. Verbi.*		*Imperative.* Simple.	En. I.	En. II.	D
Sing. m.	نَادٍ	نَدْوٌ	Sing. 2. m.	أُنْدُ	أُنْدُوَنَّ	أُنْدُوَنْ	
f.	نَادِيَةٌ		f.	أُنْدِي	أُنْدِنَّ	أُنْدِنْ	
			Dual. 2. c.	أُنْدُوَا	أُنْدُوَانِّ	. . .	
			Plur. 2. m.	أُنْدُوا	أُنْدُنَّ	أُنْدُنْ	
			f.	أُنْدُونَ	أُنْدُونَانِّ	. . .	

A

TABLE XV. VERBUM TERTIÆ RAD. ى, MEDIÆ RAD. FÈTḤATÆ.

Active Voice of the First Form.

		Perfect.	*Imperfect.* Indic.	Subj.	Jussive.	En. I.	En. II.
	Sing. 3. m.	رَمَى	يَرْمِي	يَرْمِيَ	يَرْمِ	يَرْمِيَنَّ	يَرْمِيَنْ
	f.	رَمَتْ	تَرْمِي	تَرْمِيَ	تَرْمِ	تَرْمِيَنَّ	تَرْمِيَنْ
B	2. m.	رَمَيْتَ	تَرْمِي	تَرْمِيَ	تَرْمِ	تَرْمِيَنَّ	تَرْمِيَنْ
	f.	رَمَيْتِ	تَرْمِينَ	تَرْمِي	تَرْمِي	تَرْمِنَّ	تَرْمِنْ
	1. c.	رَمَيْتُ	أَرْمِي	أَرْمِيَ	أَرْمِ	أَرْمِيَنَّ	أَرْمِيَنْ
	Dual. 3. m.	رَمَيَا	يَرْمِيَانِ	يَرْمِيَا	يَرْمِيَا	يَرْمِيَانِّ	. . .
	f.	رَمَتَا	تَرْمِيَانِ	تَرْمِيَا	تَرْمِيَا	تَرْمِيَانِّ	. . .
	2. c.	رَمَيْتُمَا	تَرْمِيَانِ	تَرْمِيَا	تَرْمِيَا	تَرْمِيَانِّ	. . .
C	Plur. 3. m.	رَمَوْا	يَرْمُونَ	يَرْمُوا	يَرْمُوا	يَرْمُنَّ	يَرْمُنْ
	f.	رَمَيْنَ	يَرْمِينَ	يَرْمِينَ	يَرْمِينَ	يَرْمِينَانِّ	. . .
	2. m.	رَمَيْتُمْ	تَرْمُونَ	تَرْمُوا	تَرْمُوا	تَرْمُنَّ	تَرْمُنْ
	f.	رَمَيْتُنَّ	تَرْمِينَ	تَرْمِينَ	تَرْمِينَ	تَرْمِينَانِّ	. . .
	1. c.	رَمَيْنَا	نَرْمِي	نَرْمِيَ	نَرْمِ	نَرْمِيَنَّ	نَرْمِيَنْ

		N. Ag.	*N. Verbi.*
D	Sing. m.	رَامٍ	رَمْيٌ
	f.	رَامِيَةٌ	

Imperative.	Simple.	En. I.	En. II.
Sing. 2. m.	اِرْمِ	اِرْمِيَنَّ	اِرْمِيَنْ
f.	اِرْمِي	اِرْمِنَّ	اِرْمِنْ
Dual. 2. c.	اِرْمِيَا	اِرْمِيَانِّ	. . .
Plur. 2. m.	اِرْمُوا	اِرْمُنَّ	اِرْمُنْ
f.	اِرْمِينَ	اِرْمِينَانِّ	. . .

TABLE XVI. VERBA TERTIÆ RAD. و ET ى, MEDIÆ RAD. KÈSRATÆ. A

Active Voice of the First Form.

	Perfect.	*Imperfect.* *Indic.*	*Subj.*	*Jussive.*	*En.* I.	*En.* II.	
Sing. 3. m.	رَضِىَ	يَرْضَى	يَرْضَى	يَرْضَ	يَرْضَيَنَّ	يَرْضَيَنْ	
f.	رَضِيَتْ	تَرْضَى	تَرْضَى	تَرْضَ	تَرْضَيَنَّ	تَرْضَيَنْ	
2. m.	رَضِيتَ	تَرْضَى	تَرْضَى	تَرْضَ	تَرْضَيَنَّ	تَرْضَيَنْ	B
f.	رَضِيتِ	تَرْضَيْنَ	تَرْضَىْ	تَرْضَىْ	تَرْضَيِنَّ	تَرْضَيِنْ	
1. c.	رَضِيتُ	أَرْضَى	أَرْضَى	أَرْضَ	أَرْضَيَنَّ	أَرْضَيَنْ	
Dual. 3. m.	رَضِيَا	يَرْضَيَانِ	يَرْضَيَا	يَرْضَيَا	يَرْضَيَانِّ	. . .	
f.	رَضِيَتَا	تَرْضَيَانِ	تَرْضَيَا	تَرْضَيَا	تَرْضَيَانِّ	. . .	
2. c.	رَضِيتُمَا	تَرْضَيَانِ	تَرْضَيَا	تَرْضَيَا	تَرْضَيَانِّ	. . .	
Plur. 3. m.	رَضُوا	يَرْضَوْنَ	يَرْضَوْا	يَرْضَوْا	يَرْضَوُنَّ	يَرْضَوُنْ	C
f.	رَضِينَ	يَرْضَيْنَ	يَرْضَيْنَ	يَرْضَيْنَ	يَرْضَيْنَانِّ	. . .	
2. m.	رَضِيتُمْ	تَرْضَوْنَ	تَرْضَوْا	تَرْضَوْا	تَرْضَوُنَّ	تَرْضَوُنْ	
f.	رَضِيتُنَّ	تَرْضَيْنَ	تَرْضَيْنَ	تَرْضَيْنَ	تَرْضَيْنَانِّ	. . .	
1. c.	رَضِينَا	نَرْضَى	نَرْضَى	نَرْضَ	نَرْضَيَنَّ	نَرْضَيَنْ	

	N. Ag.	*N. Verbi.*
Sing. m.	رَاضٍ	رِضًا
f.	رَاضِيَةٌ	رِضْوَانٌ

Imperative. D

	Simple.	*En.* I.	*En.* II.
Sing. 2. m.	اِرْضَ	اِرْضَيَنَّ	اِرْضَيَنْ
f.	اِرْضَىْ	اِرْضَيِنَّ	اِرْضَيِنْ
Dual. 2. c.	اِرْضَيَا	اِرْضَيَانِّ	. . .
Plur. 2. m.	اِرْضَوْا	اِرْضَوُنَّ	اِرْضَوُنْ
f.	اِرْضَيْنَ	اِرْضَيْنَانِّ	. . .

A

TABLE XVII. VERBA TERTIÆ RAD. و ET ى.

Passive Voice of the First Form.

	Perfect.	Imperfect. Indic.	Subj.	Jussive.	En. I.	En. II.
Sing. 3. m.	نُدِيَ	يُنْدَى	يُنْدَى	يُنْدَ	يُنْدَيَنَّ	يُنْدَيَنْ
B f.	نُدِيَتْ	تُنْدَى	تُنْدَى	تُنْدَ	تُنْدَيَنَّ	تُنْدَيَنْ
2. m.	نُدِيتَ	تُنْدَى	تُنْدَى	تُنْدَ	تُنْدَيَنَّ	تُنْدَيَنْ
f.	نُدِيتِ	تُنْدَيْنَ	تُنْدَيْ	تُنْدَيْ	تُنْدَيِنَّ	تُنْدَيِنْ
1. c.	نُدِيتُ	أُنْدَى	أُنْدَى	أُنْدَ	أُنْدَيَنَّ	أُنْدَيَنْ
C Dual. 3. m.	نُدِيَا	يُنْدَيَانِ	يُنْدَيَا	يُنْدَيَا	يُنْدَيَانِّ	. . .
f.	نُدِيَتَا	تُنْدَيَانِ	تُنْدَيَا	تُنْدَيَا	تُنْدَيَانِّ	. . .
2. c.	نُدِيتُمَا	تُنْدَيَانِ	تُنْدَيَا	تُنْدَيَا	تُنْدَيَانِّ	. . .
Plur. 3. m.	نُدُوا	يُنْدَوْنَ	يُنْدَوْا	يُنْدَوْا	يُنْدَوُنَّ	يُنْدَوُنْ
f.	نُدِينَ	يُنْدَيْنَ	يُنْدَيْنَ	يُنْدَيْنَ	يُنْدَيْنَانِّ	. . .
D 2. m.	نُدِيتُمْ	تُنْدَوْنَ	تُنْدَوْا	تُنْدَوْا	تُنْدَوُنَّ	تُنْدَوُنْ
f.	نُدِيتُنَّ	تُنْدَيْنَ	تُنْدَيْنَ	تُنْدَيْنَ	تُنْدَيْنَانِّ	. . .
1. c.	نُدِينَا	نُنْدَى	نُنْدَى	نُنْدَ	نُنْدَيَنَّ	نُنْدَيَنْ

Nom. Pat. Sing. m. مَنْدُوٌّ f. مَنْدُوَّةٌ

مَرْمِيٌّ مَرْمِيَّةٌ

TABLE XVIII. VERBA TERTIÆ RAD. و ET ى. A

The Derived Forms.

	II.	III.	IV.	V.	VI.	
Active Perf.	قَضَّى	قَاضَى	أَقْضَى	تَقَضَّى	تَقَاضَى	
Imperf.	يُقَضِّى	يُقَاضِى	يُقْضِى	يَتَقَضَّى	يَتَقَاضَى	
Imperat.	قَضِّ	قَاضِ	أَقْضِ	تَقَضَّ	تَقَاضَ	B
N. Ag. m.	مُقَضٍّ	مُقَاضٍ	مُقْضٍ	مُتَقَضٍّ	مُتَقَاضٍ	
f.	مُقَضِّيَةٌ	مُقَاضِيَةٌ	مُقْضِيَةٌ	مُتَقَضِّيَةٌ	مُتَقَاضِيَةٌ	
N. Verbi.	تَقْضِيَةٌ	مُقَاضَاةٌ قِضَآءٌ	إِقْضَآءٌ	تَقَضٍّ	تَقَاضٍ	
Passive Perf.	قُضِّىَ	قُوضِىَ	أُقْضِىَ	تُقُضِّىَ	تُقُوضِىَ	
Imperf.	يُقَضَّى	يُقَاضَى	يُقْضَى	يُتَقَضَّى	يُتَقَاضَى	C
N. Pat. m.	مُقَضًّى	مُقَاضًى	مُقْضًى	مُتَقَضًّى	مُتَقَاضًى	
f.	مُقَضَّاةٌ	مُقَاضَاةٌ	مُقْضَاةٌ	مُتَقَضَّاةٌ	مُتَقَاضَاةٌ	

	Perf.	*Imperf.*	*Imperat.*	*N. Ag. et Pat.*	*N. Verbi.*	
VII. Act.	اِنْقَضَى	يَنْقَضِى	اِنْقَضِ	مُنْقَضٍ	اِنْقِضَآءٌ	
Pass.	اُنْقُضِىَ	يُنْقَضَى		مُنْقَضًى		D
VIII. Act.	اِقْتَضَى	يَقْتَضِى	اِقْتَضِ	مُقْتَضٍ	اِقْتِضَآءٌ	
Pass.	اُقْتُضِىَ	يُقْتَضَى		مُقْتَضًى		
X. Act.	اِسْتَقْضَى	يَسْتَقْضِى	اِسْتَقْضِ	مُسْتَقْضٍ	اِسْتِقْضَآءٌ	
Pass.	اُسْتُقْضِىَ	يُسْتَقْضَى		مُسْتَقْضًى		